THE HINDU CASTES THEIR LAW RELIGION AND CUSTOMS

THE HINDU CASTES THEIR LAW RELIGION AND CUSTOMS

By

ARTHUR STEELE

GYAN

Published by

Gyan Publishing House
5, Ansari Road
Daryaganj, New Delhi-110002
Phone: 011-47034999, 9811692060
E-mail: books@gyanbooks.com

Distribution Network
gyanbooks.com
India, USA, Canada, UK, Australia, France

ISBN: 978-81-212-6847-9 (PB)
First Published, 1826

2nd Impression 2023

Printed at: Gyan Press, Delhi.

THE HINDU CASTES THEIR LAW RELIGION AND CUSTOMS
Author: Arthur Steele

THE HINDU CASTES THEIR LAW RELIGION AND CUSTOMS

ARTHUR STEELE

PREFACE.

The following compilation was directed to be undertaken with the view of affording information on points of Hindoo Law and Custom hitherto referred to Shastrees of courts or special witnesses pending judicial decisions.

An obvious inconvenience resulting from this mode of investigation is the probability that the parties giving their opinion or evidence may be biassed by sinister influence. This consideration led Sir William Jones, so early as the year 1788, to propose the compilation of a Digest, on the model of the Pandects of Justinian, the execution of which, from the number of Sunskrit books to be consulted, and the discordant interpretations of different commentators, has hitherto been, for most practical purposes, a desideratum.* Other arguments are not wanting to show the great utility of elucidation on points, whether of written law or unwritten custom reverenced by numerous castes as law, on which, from the want of publications on the subject, little has hitherto been known, except by those gentlemen whose official practice may have enabled them to obtain local information.

"The Dhurm Shaster, it is understood, is a collection of ancient treatises neither clear nor consistent in themselves, and now buried under a heap of more modern commentaries; the whole beyond the knowledge of perhaps the most learned Pundits, and every part wholly unknown to

Minute of the Hon. the Governor, July. 22, 1823.

* See the following pages.

the people who live under it. Its place is supplied in many cases by known customs, founded indeed on the Dhurm Shaster, but modified by the convenience of different castes or communities, and no longer deriving authority from any written text. The uncertainty of all decisions obtained from such sources must be obvious, especially when required for the guidance of a foreign judge, himself a stranger both to the written law and to the usage which in some cases supplies its place. The usual resource when the Shaster is to be consulted is to refer to the Pundit of the court, on whose integrity the justice of the decision must in the first instance depend: supposing, however, that he is honest and learned (which last quality is not now common and must daily become more rare), he has the choice of a variety of books to quote from, and in many instances the same book has a variety of decisions on the same question." "When the question depends on custom, the evil is at least as great: the law is then to be collected from the examinations of private individuals, the looseness of tradition must lead to contrary opinions, and even when any rule is established, it is likely to be too vague to be easily applied to the case in point. Add to this the chance of corruption, faction, favour, and other sources of partiality among the witnesses." "There are but two courses by which a remedy can be applied: the first is, to make a new code, founded entirely on general principles, applicable to all ages and nations; the second is, to endeavour to compile a complete and consistent code from the mass of written law and the fragments of tradition, determining on general principles of jurisprudence those points where the Hindoo books and traditions present only conflicting authorities, and perhaps supplying on similar principles any glaring deficiencies that may remain when the matter for compilation has been exhausted. The first of these courses, if otherwise expedient, is rendered entirely impracticable here by the attachment of the natives to their own institutions, and by the degree to which their laws are interwoven with their religion and manners. The second plan* is, therefore, the only one which it is in our power to pursue. The first step towards the accomplishment of its objects appears to be to ascertain in each district whether there is any book of acknowledged authority either for the whole or any branch of the law; the next is to ascertain what exceptions there are to the written authorities, and what customs and traditions exist independent of them. The best modes of conducting these inquiries are, first, to examine the Shastrees, heads of castes, and other persons likely to be acquainted either with the law, the custom of castes, or the public opinion regarding the authority attached to each; and second, to extract from the records of the courts of justice the information already obtained on these subjects in the course of judicial investigation."

The period during which regular courts have been established in Guzerat naturally suggested those Zillahs as the field for inquiry of the second kind. The result of Mr. Borradaile's exertions in selecting cases decided by the Sudur Udalut has been lately printed, and that mode of investigation is about to be combined by that gentleman with a more extended system of local inquiry.

---

* On this point Sir W. Jones observes, in his letter to the Supreme Council of Bengal, March 19, 1788: "Nothing could be more obviously just than to determine private contests according to those laws which the parties themselves had ever considered as the rules of their conduct and engagements in civil life: nor could anything be wiser than by a legislative act to assure the Hindoo and Mahometan subjects of Great Britain that the private laws which they severally hold sacred, and a violation of which they would have thought the most grievous oppression, should not be superseded by a new system, of which they could have no knowledge, and which they must have considered as imposed on them by a spirit of rigour and intolerance."

In the Dekhun, on the contrary, the British rule had been much later introduced, and care had been taken to avoid the sudden adoption of strict judicial forms, in many cases alien to the habits of the people. The native Government had been altogether Hindoo; the Peshwa and many others in subordinate authority were Brahmins; in the city of Poona are many resident Shastrees, including those receiving stipends from Government in the College, besides casual visitors at the Hindoo festivals; lastly, its position seems adapted to display varieties in castes and professions, which in a large inland town in the midst of an agricultural country are less affected by the influence of commerce and immigration. Here, therefore, the inquiry of the first kind was ordered to be conducted.

The Regulation Committee having accordingly prepared queries as the foundation of others to be introduced in progress of the investigation, they were transmitted to Mr. Chaplin, late Commissioner, and to Colonel Briggs, Resident at Sattara, with a request that they would adopt the measures most expedient to obtain the information required throughout the territories under their superintendence. The collection of judicial awards, both of our own and the Peshwa's time, was suggested; and subsequently, in consequence of a proposal to the heads of castes at Surat having created some alarm among the people, the Commissioner was desired to confine the proposed experiment on that point to some one district under his control.

These were the objects in view by the Honourable the Governor in Council in undertaking the inquiry: it is in the next place proper to state the manner in which the instructions have been carried into effect, and the ulterior measures still necessary in order to perfect the original design.

The inquiry naturally resolved itself into three general heads: 1st, To ascertain the particular text-books and commentaries referred to by Shastrees as authorities; 2nd, To investigate the number and relations of existing castes, and their mode of preserving old or establishing new customs; 3rd, To compare the written law with the unwritten customs, and note their conformity with or opposition to each other.

1. *Law.*—Partly from the difficulty of the language, and partly also from the nature of the subject, our knowledge of the Hindoo law has hitherto been far from precise or extensive. Sir W. Jones observed on the code of Mr. Halhed (compiled by desire of Mr. Hastings), that however complete in appearance, it is in fact a translation of an injudicious Persian epitome, by no means faithfully rendering the original Sunskrit. The Institutes of Munoo, translated by Sir William himself, is an elementary work, treating, as most text-books and commentaries forming part of the Dhurmsastru would appear to do, of many topics foreign to what we term jurisprudence. The Digest of Jugunath, translated by Mr. Colebrooke, although other subjects are occasionally adverted to, is nominally confined to the law of contracts and successions, and the frequent occurrence of jarring texts and obscure commentaries forms a great objection to it as a work of practical reference. To supply the deficiency, we have Mr. Colebrooke's valuable translation of the treatise of Jimootavuhunu and of the chapter in the Mitakshura on Inheritance, the reports of cases decided by the Sudur Deewanee Udaluts at Calcutta and Surat, and the published works of Sir. F. Macnaghten and Sir T. Strange. The latter publication would appear in a great measure to have attained the object, so far as respects the law in force at Madras.

It has been ascertained, in the course of time, that different interpretations are given of original text-books by different commentators, and that among these, writers of particular tenets are held as authorities in different provinces of India. Many apparent contradictions have originated from taking as collateral authorities the glosses or interpretations of writers of different schools, whereof the leading divisions appear to be those of Bengal and Benares.

The books chiefly referred to in Wywusthas in the Dekhun are the text-books of Munoo and Yadnywulkyu; the Mitakshura or Vidyaneswuree, a commentary on the latter; the Myookh; Nirunesindhoo; Hemadree; Koustoobh; and Purasurmadhoo—all apparently of the Benares school. The Mitakshura is preferred on account of its comparative clearness and decision, and is the work most usually quoted by the *S*astrees of Poona.

It is to be understood that besides the foregoing all other books composing the Dhurmsastru, as well as the Veds, and in some instances the Poorans, are held of authority, though less generally known and less frequently referred to. In the pages following this introduction will be found a list of text-books and commentaries more or less imperfectly known to the *S*astrees consulted at Poona. It was furnished by Wamun *S*astree Satyu, and corrected by reference to the Hindoo College and other Brahmuns who attended the distribution of the Dukshuna in 1825.* Although in this list an approximation to correctness has been attained, it is not to be supposed that the exact number of *S*loks has been assigned to each work, nor that the particulars as to date and subject-matter are in all cases accurate; its errors and defects may form the subject of future investigation, and the catalogue, on further inquiry, be completed. All information respecting the *S*astrus has been, however, elicited with difficulty, partly

* Among these were Ragwacharee, Principal of the College; Sukharam *S*astree, Gooroo of the Dhurmsastru; Ragwendracharee, of Sattara; Siddheswur *S*astree, Moonsif of Joonur; Babacharee Adye, Jageerdar of Kher; Balacharee Toupe, Pundit of Dharwar; *S*emupacharee and Nursupacharee, of Holjee, near Bellary.

from the backwardness of the natives to give precise information on any subject, but chiefly from superstitious prejudices.

On comparing the one now published with the lists given by Mr. Colebrooke, some important variations are observable, apparently arising from the latter having chiefly included the writers of the Gouryu or Bengal school. Of the text-books, the work called Katyayun appears as a Sootr in the Poona list, and the latter includes Wamun,smrootee, Wridhsatatup, and the *S*lok, not found in the former. Of the twenty-one Oopusmrootees noticed by Mr. C. there are only two (Boudhyayun and Aswulayun) found in the Poona list. Ten commentaries and minor authorities only appear in both. Twenty-five mentioned by Mr. C. are omitted in the present, and upwards of 110 are found in the Poona Catalogue exclusively. Of their legal, as of their political, history the Brahmuns seem entirely ignorant, nor could the causes of the difference subsisting between commentators of different schools be at all traced in Poona.

The Abstract of Hindoo Law, as affecting Civil disputes, now published, has been prepared to answer purposes of reference, until the greater diffusion of original works* sanctioned as law shall have established the knowledge of it in a more perfect manner. It has been drawn up from answers to queries submitted to Bhalchundr *S*astree of Poona, and afterwards corrected by the Dhurmsastrees of the College. It had been preferable to have obtained all the replies from the College in the first instance, but those received directly from them were so very meagre as to afford little information.

It is satisfactory to observe, that on comparing this Abstract with the translation of the chapter on Inheritance

* The Mitakshura and others have been already published in Bengal. The Myookh has been printed by order of the Bombay Government.

in the Mitakshura, there has been found an exact conformity on all but two immaterial points. These have been since corrected, and some additional references introduced, from Mr. Borradaile's Reports of Selected Cases. Although nominally limited to Inheritance, the translation of Mr. Colebrooke refers to several points relative to Marriage and Adoption, so that the correctness of so large a portion gives a fair criterion of that of the whole.

Some points of law appearing to have been decided by the Supreme Court of Calcutta have been subjoined as notes, from Sir T. Macnaghten's work, and some quotations have been made from the Digest of Jugunath, in order to facilitate comparison between the opposing authorities of the different schools. The most important points on which a discrepancy exists are—on the power of widows to adopt and inherit, the limitation as to age in adoption, the power of fathers over ancestral property, and the tenure of inherited property by females generally.

II. *Castes.*—It is well known that the ancient Hindoo law-books recognize four castes only, and prescribe the duties to be followed by each with minute accuracy. The whole system is founded on the supremacy of the Brahmun caste, and the ignorance and dependence of the others. It confines to the former the duties of the priesthood and an acquaintance with the national law and literature; it enjoins that Brahmuns should receive from others gifts to any extent as alms, without prohibiting them from amassing wealth; and by assigning expulsion from caste as a punishment to offenders against their ordinances (especially intermarriage and even contact, if the parties are of different castes), a provision is made for constant degradation, while no possibility exists that a man of a lower should by any degree of merit whatever obtain admission into a higher caste.

Under the operation of this system, the Brahmuns themselves are, owing to irregular intermarriages and other local causes, divided into numerous sects, the majority of individuals in which neglect the duties of study and abstracted devotion prescribed by the *S*astru; the Kshutriy and Wys castes are thought no longer to exist, although several pretend to those titles; and besides the pure *S*oodrus (which the Mahratta Koonbees or cultivators are allowed to be) are a host of mixed castes, in various degrees of repute among the Hindoos of the present day.

In assigning the relative rank of the castes of Hindoos, there are two criteria chiefly to be borne in mind as influencing their estimation among themselves, viz. descent and occupation. The particulars of the former are to be found in several of the *S*astrus written on the subject, laying down the genealogy of the castes and the pursuit each is to follow; but the variations which time and irregular marriages have introduced have occasioned other modes of estimating the respect paid to the higher by the lower castes: these are, 1, intermarriage; 2, eating together (the higher caste not accepting the invitation of the lower); 3, receiving water to drink at the hands of a lower caste; 4, touching the person (the touch or approximation of a low-caste man being considered pollution requiring purification by bathing—spursdosh). There is less strictness on the last two points, and the acquisition by any individual or caste of rank, wealth, or power, has of course a tendency to counteract the prejudices arising from their descent or supposed impure practices, but, as in the case of Europeans, by no means to overcome them altogether.

The enumeration found in the present summary has been prepared with regard to all these criteria, and may serve as the groundwork of a future more complete investigation. The books consulted by the *S*astrees on the occasion were the Jatiwiwek, the Brohud Jatiwiwek, Jatdurpun, Madhwu

Kulpuntu, and Purseram-Prutap; and the compared list of castes, according to books and present usage in and near Poona, was drawn up by Wamun *S*astree Satyu, Abba Bhut (Pooranek of *S*am Row Pingule), Ramacharee Hoonhurleekur, Siddheswur *S*astree (Moonsif of Joonur). It was afterwards submitted to and approved by Neelkunt *S*astree Thute, Dadajee Chitwok, and Anaba Mendule of Poona. Many particulars have been since added from examination of the castes themselves.

The mythological origin of the four castes is generally known. Before the present Kulee-yoog a Brahmun was permitted to espouse a wife from each of the four castes; a Kshutriy was allowed to marry a Kshutriy, Wys, and *S*oodru; a Wys had two wives, one of his own and one of the *S*oodru caste; and a *S*oodru one only, of his own. Thence arose the distinction of the Unoolom and Pruteelom castes; the former consisting of the progeny of a higher-caste father with a lower caste mother; the latter *vice versâ;* all being in general the offspring of legal marriage. For example, the descendants of the Brahmun by his Brahmunee wife remained Brahmuns; those by his Kshutriy wife were termed Moordawusikt, &c. There are reckoned, besides the four original, six Unoolom and six Pruteelom castes.

The offspring by illegal marriage or adulterous connection between any of the foregoing sixteen castes, or of individuals among them expelled from the privileges of their caste, have gradually introduced the vast number of *S*unkurjat, Wurunsunkur, or mixed castes now prevailing. It is doubtful, indeed, whether some of the titles are not merely local or professional designations, the main ground of distinction being the practice of intermarriage and eating in company or otherwise. In all these, however, an adherence to hereditary custom is maintained by the authority of an assembly of the caste, who prescribe the penance to be performed by the offender, consisting of some sacrifice either in purse or person, and generally commutable into a fine or dinner given to the individuals of the caste.

From the above causes of intermixture, and the influence of immigration, the number of castes may be considered to be constantly augmenting, and the authority of the caste assemblies and of the Brahmuns over the rest to be decidedly on the decline since the introduction of the British Government.

From an examination of the lists, it appears that there are 133 castes mentioned in the books consulted, and about 150 castes and varieties said to exist in and round Poona. It will be seen that some of the *S*astru names are not appropriated by any existing caste in that part of the country; that some existing castes are not mentioned in the books consulted; and that the occupation and relative estimation of some castes are different at present from what they should be, according to the written standard. Some of the particulars relative to foreigners especially bear evident marks of ignorance and prejudice, but all have been retained as elucidatory of the opinions prevalent among the Brahmuns on such topics.

Compliance with ancestral custom forms, it appears, the standard of duty in the great majority of Hindoos. All are anxious to preserve their own caste from contamination by refusing to intermarry or eat in company with any individuals of a caste lower than their own; and the spirit of the written texts, by which the higher castes affect to be guided, is enforced in the lower by the authority of Brahminical priests and caste assemblies. The religious ceremonies practised on all occasions, ordinary and extraordinary, in private houses, in the temples, and by the roadside, and the periodical assemblies at festivals and pilgrimages, serve to strengthen the ties of obedience both to one and to the other; although it is difficult to recognize in the rude sculptures reverenced by the common people the Awutars and deities described in the books. As in other superstitious countries, there is a general belief in miraculous cures at particular shrines and tombs of saints (whether Hindoo or Moossulman) supposed to be invested with superhuman powers. Vows are made, and the condition performed, although attended with severe torture to the individual who inflicts it on himself. Departed spirits are believed to haunt particular places, or the bodies of particular persons, then said to be seized or possessed by a ghost or demon; and there is a generally supposed efficacy in astrology, spells, and sorcery, which is often not without real effect, acting through the imagination of the parties.

It would, however, be foreign to the objects of this Summary to enlarge further on the various ceremonies and opinions countenanced by the Hindoo religion or prevalent among the common people. It will be sufficient to annex the substance of replies received from different castes in Poona on the constitution of caste assemblies, the nature of the office of headman, and the mode in which their authority is exercised in taking cognizance of offences against caste discipline. Subjoined to these is a statement of the oaths said to be most binding in the different castes interrogated on that point.

III. *Existing Customs.*—The information compiled under the third title consists of the substance of replies from the castes and traders in Poona, together with details received by the late Commissioner in the Dekhun from the subordinate collectorates.

Under the letter P. is arranged—1. Replies from seventy-five of the resident castes to the inquiries prepared by the Regulation Committee, on the establishment of rules in castes, marriage, divorce, inheritance, wills and gifts, adoption, and funerals, transmitted by the Collector of Poona. 2. Replies from 101 castes resident in Poona (including the former) to supplementary queries suggested in the course of the inquiry on caste, marriage, parentage, adoption, service, and slavery, community of property and partition, contracts ; and on the customs of Sahookars and traders. The individuals consulted on this last branch were Siddheswur *S*astree, *S*am Row Perigule, Raghopunt Tuthe, Venkut Row Nana, Gopaul Row Despan*d*e, the Zumeendars of Joonur, Shesupa Naik Padshapoorkur, Bapoo Moonee, Bapoo Bhowanee Josee, Dada Lukree, Dyaram Atmaram, and other Sahookars. 3. As elucidatory of the rules in force among native tribunals, some cases have been selected from the Duftur of Ramsastree, Nyayudhish of Poona, in the time of the Peshwa Madhoo Row. The body of information is, however, chiefly compiled from direct replies.

By the letter S. are designated the extracts from a valuable report transmitted to the Commissioner by Colonel Briggs, resident at Sattara, containing replies to the queries prepared by the Regulation Committee, and a variety of additional information collected by that officer himself.

The abstract of inquiries conducted by Colonel Robertson in Khandesh (letter K.) consists of a few selected cases from the Register's file, of replies to the queries prepared by the Regulation Committee, and to others by the late Principal Collector and his assistants in the Southern Mahratta country. These replies appear to have been received from individuals of different castes and places of abode in the province assembled at Dhoolia, and selected on account of their experience and intelligence. It is matter of regret that the breaking out of the cholera before the completion of the inquiry rendered it less complete than it would otherwise have been ; enough has, however, been elicited to demonstrate the utility of the investigation in that province.

In consequence of the lamented death of Mr. Thackeray

pending the extended inquiries instituted by him, a detailed report of the investigations prosecuted in the Southern Mahratta country was never forwarded. To many queries, however, replies have been received; those especially on the subject of Marriage and Slavery, compiled by Mr. John Warden, will be found to contain much valuable information; all of which is designated in the Summary by the letter D.

A number of awards by Punchaets of native arbitrators were received from Ahmednuggur, translations of some of which have been selected and appended under the proper heads.

The Appendix will be found to consist of an account of the institutions of the Gosaens or Gosawees, a singular fraternity of self-styled devotees, whose customs in many respects are assimilated to those of the monastic rule. This account was drawn up by Mr. John Warden, from replies to queries prepared by that gentleman, and submitted to the Gosaen pilgrims who last year assembled at the source of the Gunga or Godavery, near Nasik.

By the marginal references to the preceding Summary of the Law, the points of agreement or of discrepancy between the Brahminical books and existing custom will be in most cases ascertained.

In Poona the castes were assembled successively, and each question was proposed in order. The answer was given after a consultation between the headman and the most intelligent individuals, or between the latter only, in the presence of the rest of the caste. The inquiry was tedious, but it was not difficult to procure the willing attendance of the people after the object was understood. It is to be regretted, however, that from the backwardness of some to elucidate, even remotely, their religious customs, and the want of intelligence exhibited by others, the information now submitted, however correct so far as it goes, is far from complete. Many of those consulted could of course speak only to points within their own limited observation; in other cases no definite rule appears to exist—at least the rule is liable to modification in a particular case from the prejudices or partialities of native arbitrators.

A general conformity is, however, observable with the leading principles of the Hindoo system, which (so far as they affect civil disputes) appear to be as follow:—

1. The supremacy, generally speaking, of the Brahmun caste. Some castes permit the agency of their own priests, but the ceremonies performed are imitations of the Brahminical rites.

2. Severe penalties annexed to intermarriage or association with a lower caste.

3. Adoption, even by widows, in order to secure the continued performance of funeral oblations.

4. Inheritance, generally speaking, in equal shares by males only in equal degree of relationship, the degree of consanguinity indicated by the customary performance of funeral oblations being the principle on which property is inherited.

5. Community of property among the members of one family; descended or ancestral property being considered as entailed.

On the other hand, the chief points on which the law and custom have been observed to be at variance are—1. The great variety of castes and sects; 2. The custom of a second and inferior marriage, allowed to wives and widows in many castes; 3. The small or irregular punishment in some cases enforced by caste assemblies; 4. The disregard to legal restrictions as to caste, in trading and taking interest; besides an infinity of local usages which have become established, unwarranted by *S*astru, if not in opposition to its rules.

Such being the original design of Government in instituting the inquiry, and the extent to which it has been hitherto

Letter from the Regulation Committee, July 13, 1826.

carried into partial effect, it has been considered expedient to circulate the whole in a printed form among the local authorities. In the first instance, by this means, the existence of usages may in some cases be established which are otherwise little known, or might be thought fabricated to answer a particular object, and in others misrepresentations will be more readily detected. But the great benefit proposed is, that by local investigations, gradually carried on on the same basis, the defects in the present compilation may be removed, and all peculiarities of partial extent and observance be recorded; so that after the applicability and correctness of the information successively acquired shall have stood the test of time and judicial examination, and the extent of innovation occasioned by the institution of positive enactments shall have been ascertained, the ultimate object originally proposed by Government may be attained of separating and classifying the rules binding on all Hindoos from those which are observed by particular castes only, or by local varieties of the latter. In the words of the minute previously quoted, "After the Digest shall have circulated for a certain time as a book of information, though not of authority, it may ultimately be improved by the decision of all doubtful questions, the removal of all glaring blemishes, and the filling up of all great deficiencies, until it forms a complete code of laws sanctioned by Government, and accessible in their vernacular language to all classes of its subjects."

August 3, 1826. ARTHUR STEELE.

NOTE.—In the orthography of such Sunskrit or Mahratta words as have not acquired by custom a particular English form, the plan of Dr. Gilchrist has been generally followed, as best adapted to express the sounds as well as to mark the letters of the original words. It may be remarked that Mahratta words are often spelt with slight variations by the natives; and some sounds, as those of व or य may be expressed indifferently in English by w, v, o; y, ee. An italic letter serves to distinguish the following characters: श, *s*; ड, *d*; ट, *t*. Uniform correctness on this point must not, however, be anticipated.

Abbreviations in the Summary of Law, as Authorities.

B. S.—Bhalchundr *S*astree.

P. C.—Poona College, agreeing with do.

Mit.—Reference to the Sunskrit Mitakshura.

Mit. Tr.—Do. to Mr. Colebrooke's translation of the Chapter of the Mitakshura on Inheritance.

C. Dig.—Do. to Mr. Colebrooke's translation of the Digest of Jugunath.

B.—Do. to Mr. Borradaile's Selected Cases from the File of the Sudur Udalut.

Sir F. M.—Do. to Sir Francis Macnaghten's work on Hindoo Law.

Sir T. St.—Do. to Sir Thomas Strange's Elements of Hindoo Law.

I.—LAW.

SUNSKRIT LAW BOOKS.

I.—LAW.

LIST OF SUNSKRIT BOOKS COMPOSING THE DHURM SASTRU.

MUNOO, SMROOTEE (No. of Grunth or *S*lok of 32 letters, 3,000).—Said to have been composed by the Rishee of that name in Benares, very anciently. It treats of Prayuschit (penance and expiation); Achar (religious ceremonies, purifications, and caste duties); Wyuwhar (worldly actions, including judicial questions, and generally with the latter signification); *S*raddh (ceremonies for deceased ancestors); and Karl (appointed days and times).

MEDHATITHEE (No. of Grunth, &c., 12,000).—The author is said to have been a Brahmun of that name, of Benares. It is a commentary on the text-book of Munoo, of very old date.

GOVINDARUNUVU (No. of Grunth, &c., 7,000).—The author is said to have been Govind Bhu*t*, of Benares. It is a commentary on Munoo, of very old date.

MADHWU (No. of Grunth, &c., 8,000).—The author is said to have been Sayunachary or Widyaruneswamee, a Sunyasee Brahmun of Anagoondy. It is a commentary on Munoo, of general authority, especially in the Carnatic; and supposed to have been composed 1,000 years ago.

NUNDURAJKRIT (No. of Grunth, &c., 14,000).—The

author is said to have been Nundraja of Anagoondy, of the Kshutryu caste. It is a commentary on Munoo, of old date.

KOOLOOBHUT (No. of Grunth, &c., 9,000).—The author is said to have been a Carnatic Brahmun of that name. It is a commentary on Munoo, of old date. The two last works are met within the Carnatic (Kurnatuk) and Mahratta (Maharashtr) countries; the two former and the original Smrootee throughout India.

UTREE,SMROOTEE (No. of Grunth, &c., 300).—By Utree, a Brahmun Rishee of Northern Hindoosthan. This work is very ancient, and universally known. It contains an abridgment of the subjects treated of in Munoo.

WISHNOO,SMROOTEE (No. of Grunth, &c., 600). — By Wishnoo, a Brahmun Rishee of Hindoosthan. This work is very ancient, and universally known. It treats of Achar, Wyuwhar, and Prayuschit.

WAMUN,SMROOTEE (No. of Grunth, &c., 400).—By Wamun, a Brahmun Rishee of Hindoosthan. Do. do.

SLOK (No. of Grunth, &c., 200).—By the same author. Do. on Prayuschit.

HUREETU,SMROOTEE (No. of Grunth, &c. — BRUHUD, Large, 1,500; LUGHOO, Small, 200).—By Hureetu, a Brahmun Rishee of Hindoosthan. Do. on Achar, Wyuwhar, and Prayuschit.

YADNYAWULKYU,SMROOTEE (No. of Grunth, &c., 1,200).—By a Brahmun Rishee of Hindoosthan of that name. Do. do.

WIDYANESWUREE or MITAKSHURA (No. of Grunth, &c., 12,000).—1. On Achar; 2. Wyuwhar; 3. Prayuschit. By Widyaneswureeswamee, a Brahmun of Hindoosthan. Its date is supposed by Mr. Colebrooke to be from 500 to 1,000 years ago: it is a commentary on the text-book of Yadnyawulkyu, and is of general authority in the Mahratta country.

OOSENA, SMROOTEE (No. of Grunth, &c., 500).—By a Brahmun Rishee of Hindoosthan. Do. do.

UNGIRA, SMROOTEE (No. of Grunth, &c., 400).—Do. do. do.

ASWULAYUN, SMROOTEE (No. of Grunth, &c., 1,000).—Do. do. do.

PURASUR, SMROOTEE, BRUHUD and LUGHOO (No. of Grunth, &c., 3,000).—Do. do. do.

VYAS, SMROOTEE (No. of Grunth, &c., 500.)—Do. do. do.

SUNK, SMROOTEE (No. of Grunth, &c., 100).—Do. do. do.

LIKHIT, SMROOTEE (No. of Grunth, &c., 150).—Do. do. do.

DUKSH, SMROOTEE (No. of Grunth, &c., 300).—Do. do. do.

GOUTUMU, SMROOTEE (No. of Grunth, &c.—LUGHOO, 1,000; SLOK, 500).—Do. do. do.

SATATUP, SMROOTEE (No. of Grunth, &c., 300).—Do. do. do.

WUSISHT, SMROOTEE (No. of Grunth, &c., 500).—Do. do. do.

UPUSTUMBH, SMROOTEE (No. of Grunth, &c., 1,500).—Do. do. do.

YUMU, SMROOTEE (No. of Grunth, &c., 500).—Do. do. do.

BRUHM, SMROOTEE (No. of Grunth, &c., 40).—By a Brahmun named Bruhusputee—On Gifts or Alms (Dan).

KOKILA, SMROOTEE.—A copy of this work is said to be a Solapoor; there is none in Poona.

SUMWURT, SMROOTEE (No. of Grunth, &c., 200).—Do.

WRIDHSATATUP, SMROOTEE.—This work is known in the Carnatic.

ASWULAYUN, SOOTR (No. of Grunth, &c., 4,000).—This is an ancient work, generally known. It treats of the Hom or Fire-sacrifice in Sraoot (worship of deities), and Smart (performance of Sunskars, or purifying ceremonies), both constituting Unooshtan.

*VRITEE, TEEKA (No. of Grunth, &c., 6,000).—By Widyaruneswamee, a Sunyasee Brahmun of Anagoondy. About 1,000 years old.

*BHASHY,TEEKA (No. of Grunth, &c., 8,000).—Of the same supposed date.

*ANOTHER (No. of Grunth, &c., 3,000).—Do.

*KARIKABHASHY (No. of Grunth, &c., 4,500).—By Sunkurachary, a Sunyasee Brahmun of the Drewir Carnatic country. Do.

*(*These four works are Commentaries on the Aswulay-un, sootr.*)

KATYAYUN,SOOTR (No. of Grunth, &c., 9,000).—By a Rishee of Hindoosthan. It is generally known, and of great antiquity. It treats of Sraoot-smart.

RENOOKARKARIKA (No. of Grunth, &c., 3,500).—By Renoo Dikshit, a Brahmun of Benares. Do. do. It was composed 550 years ago, and is a Commentary on the former.

BOUDHYAYUN,SOOTR (No. of Grunth, &c., 700).—By do. do. do.

BOUDHYAYUNTEEKA (No. of Grunth, &c., 1,000).—By Bhowswamee, a Sunyasee. Do. do. a Commentary on the former.

UPUSTUMBH,SOOTR (No. of Grunth, &c., 6,000).—By the Brahmun Rishee of that name. Do. do.

ATEEKA, or COMMENTARY (No. of Grunth, &c., 8,000). —By Doortswamee, a Drewir Brahmun of the Carnatic. Do. do.

HIRUNYUKESEE,SOOTR, or SUTYADHAR (No. of Grunth, &c., 6,000).—By Hirunye and Sutyachary, Rishees of Hindoosthan. Do. do.

OOJWULA, A COMMENTARY (No. of Grunth, &c., 5,000).—By Mahadeo Somyanee, a Drewir Brahmun of the Carnatic. Do. do.

MATRDUT, DO. (No. of Grunth, &c., 3,000).—By Matrdut Suruswutee-prusad-alubhd (protected by Suruswutee), a Drewir Brahmun. Do. do.

GOPEENAT,BHUTEE, DO. (No. of Grunth, &c., 10,000).—By Gopeenat Dikshit Wok Kaseekur, a Kokunust Brahmun of Poona. It was written fifty years ago, and is known in the Mahratta country.

GOBHILU,SOOTR (No. of Grunth, &c, 4,000).—By Gobhil, a Rishee of Hindoosthan.

SRAOOT,SOOTR (No. of Grunth, &c.,) 6,000; SMART,SOOTR, (No. of Grunth, &c., 1,000).—By Aswulayun Rishee.

KOUSTOOBH.—There are twelve divisions of this work, or separate works with this title affixed. All are to be met with in Benares, but two only are known in Poona, viz.:—

SUNSKAR-KOUSTOOBH (No. of Grunth, &c., 8,000).—By Anunt Deo Kaseekur, a Kokunust Chitpawunee Brahmun. On the several Sunskars.

SMROOTEE-KOUSTOOBH (No. of Grunth, &c., 10,000).—By do. On Achar, Wyuwhar, and Prayuschit.

SOODR-KUMULAKARUN (No. of Grunth, &c., 8,000).—By Kumulakar Bhut Kaseekur, a Desust Brahmun. It treats of the customs ordained for the *Soodr* castes; it is generally known, and was composed about 250 years ago.

SANTEE-KUMULAKARUN (No. of Grunth, &c., 3,000).—By do. On the ceremonies to be performed for arresting ill-omened positions of the stars at the maturity of women and other periods.

MYOOKH (No. of Grunth, &c., 36,000).—By Neelkunt Bhut Kaseekur, a Desust Brahmun. This work was composed about 300 years ago; it is of chief notoriety in the Carnatic, though attended to both in Poona and at Benares. (There are twelve divisions of this work, or separate works with the title affixed.)

SUNSKAR-MYOOKH.

SANTEE-MYOOKH.

Wyuwhar-Myookh.

Prayuschit-Myookh.

Sraddh-Myookh.

Sumye-Myookh (on Times and Seasons).

Neetee-Myookh (on Moral Duties).

Prutishta-Myookh.—On the Consecration of Idols in Temples, whereby the Kulla or Divine Influence is supposed to reside in them.

Ootsurga-Myookh.—On the taking Idols out of the Temples at the Dussera and other periods.

Achar-Myookh.

Dan-Myookh.

Soodhee-Myookh.—On Sin and Purification.

Dyot, containing twelve divisions (No. of Grunth, &c., 80,000).—By Gaga Bhut Kaseekur, a Desust Brahmun. It was written about a century ago, and treats of all subjects.

Kurmuwipakurk (No. of Grunth, &c., 3,000).—By Sunkur Bhut Kaseekur, a Desust Brahmun, father of the author of the Myookh. It treats of the pleasures and pains of the present life, resulting from the virtues and vices of the former, and is of general notoriety.

Wurtark (No. of Grunth, &c., 12,000).—By do. It treats of the essence of the 365 daily ceremonies prescribed by the god Krishn to Dhurmraja when in seclusion.

Pursuram-prutap (No. of Grunth, &c., 100,000).—By Pundits, at the order of Sabajee Prutap, Raja of the Eastern Tylung country, about 500 years ago. It treats of Achar, Wyuwhar, Prayuschit, &c., and is of general notoriety.

Soobodhinee.—The title only of this work is known at Poona.

Kalatutwuwivechun (No. of Grunth, &c., 10,000).—By Rugoonath Bhut Kaseekur, a Desust Brahmun. It treats of the time of seating idols (Wurtkarl), the means of realizing wishes (Ishtapoortee), the time of performing the Hom in

Sunskars (Smart-karl), and the ceremonies of mourning for the dead (Asouch).

NIRUNYAMOORT (No. of Grunth, &c., 4,000).—By Narayun Bhut Kaseekur, or Sidhsaruswut Bhut, a Desust Brahmun. It was composed about 300 years ago, and is of general notoriety. It treats of Ishtapoortee, Wurt, and of (Tithee) the monthly division of fortnights.

POOROOSHARTH-CHINTAMUN (No. of Grunth, &c., 11,000). —By Wishnoo Bhut Atwule, a Kokunust Brahmun of Nasik. It treats of Achar, Sunskars, and Prayuschit, not of Wyuwhar. It was written 250 years ago, and is of notoriety in the Mahratta country.

ACHAR-RUTN (No. of Grunth, &c., 6,000).—By Lukshmun Bhut Kaseekur, a Desust Brahmun. It treats of Achar only, and is 400 years old.

KARLNIRUNE-PRUKAS (No. of Grunth, &c., 4,000).—By Ramchundr Bhut Kaseekur, a Desust Brahmun. It treats of times and seasons, was written about 600 years ago, and is of general notoriety.

KULPTUROO (No. of Grunth, &c., 10,000).—By Anund Bhut Kaseekur, a Desust Brahmun.

KULP-RUTNAWULE (No. of Grunth, &c., 200).—By Ramchundr Bhut Kaseekur, a Desust Brahmun. It is 400 years old. It treats of morning devotions, and the Wurt ceremonies, and is generally known.

NIRUNESINDHOO (No. of Grunth, &c., 12,000).—By Kumulakur Bhut Kaseekur, a Desust Brahmun. It was written 214 years ago, and is of general authority. It treats of general subjects, as Tithee, Karl, Asouch, Sraddh, Sunskars, &c., but not of Wyuwhar.

PRAYUSCHITENDOO-SEKUR (No. of Grunth, &c., 2,200.)—By Nabojee Bhut Kaseekur, a Desust Brahmun. It treats of particular Prayuschit not described in other works on that subject.

Hemadree, containing twelve divisions (No. of Grunth, &c. 100,000).—By Hemadree Bhut Kaseekur. This is a very ancient work of notoriety, treating of all subjects.

Dhurmsindhoo, or Dhurmabdhisar (No. of Grunth, &c., 12,000). — By Bababadye Punderpoorker, a Kurare Brahmun. It was written half a century ago, treats of Sraddh, Sunskar, Asouch, Karl, Tithee, &c., exclusive of Wyuwhar.

Wrutraj (No. of Grunth, &c. 1,600).—By Wiswunath Bhut of Sungumeswur in the Southern Kokun. It was written ninety years ago, and is of notoriety in the Mahratta country. It treats of the Wurt ceremonies, &c.

Karlnirune (No. of Grunth, &c., 3,000).—By Ramchunder Achary. It treats of times and seasons, and is of general notoriety.

Karlnirune-prukas (No. of Grunth, &c., 4,000).—By Ramchundr Tukshut Kaseekur. This is a commentary on the former.

Wrut-Koumoodee (No. of Grunth, &c., 3,000).—By Balum Bhut Ghod, a Chitpawun Brahmun. It was composed 112 years ago, and is of notoriety in the Mahratta country, and in Benares.

Sooryu-aroone-sumwad (No. of Grunth, &c., 2,000).

Jysinh-prutap (No. of Grunth, &c., 25,000).

Sunskar-rutn (No. of Grunth, &c., 8,000).

Pryog-durpun (No. of Grunth, &c., 12,000).—By Pudmakur Dikshit Yijoorvedee of Nasik. It is of notoriety in the Dekhun.

Pryog-rutn (No. of Grunth, &c., 15,000).—By Kasee Dikshit Yijoorvedee of Benares. An ancient work, generally known. On Sraoot-smart.

Nursinh prutap (No. of Grunth, &c., 2,000).

Weermitrode.—By Mitrumisra, a Brahmun, composed about 600 years ago by order of Weersinh Raja, of the

Mithil country. It treats of Wyuwhar only, and is of general notoriety.

Ekadusee-nirune (No. of Grunth, &c., 300). — By Hureedut Achary, a Drewir Brahmun. A modern work, generally known, treating of the period of the Ekadusee (on which the Wishnoo and Siw Brahmuns differ.)

Gotr-pruwur-nirune (No. of Grunth, &c., 600). — By Kumulakur Bhut, a Brahmun of Benares. It is a modern work, generally known. It treats of the particulars of genealogy to be inquired into in marriages.

Supindu-nirune (No. of Grunth, &c., 300).—By Anunt Deo Brahmun Kaseekur. Treating of the offering of funeral cakes: generally known.

Asouch-nirune (No. of Grunth, &c., 800).—By Nagojee Bhut Kaseekur. It was composed 300 years ago, is generally known, and treats of the number of days for mourning (Sootuk).

Tithe-nirune (No. of Grunth, &c., 800).—By Bhutojee Dikshit Brahmun Kaseekur. On the days of the kalendar, lucky or otherwise, adapted for particular occasions. It is generally known.

Jat-wiwek (No. of Grunth, &c., Bruhud, 700; Lughoo, 400). — This work treats of the origin and genealogy of the various castes.

Gudadhr-bhashy (No. of Grunth, &c., 51,000).—By a Brahmun of that name. It treats of Smart, and is of general notoriety.

Kurk-bhashy (No. of Grunth, &c., 11,000).—Do. do. do.

Kaseenathkritbhashy.

Jyram-kritbhashy (No. of Grunth, &c., 1,250). — By Jyram Bhut. Do. do.

Poort-kumulakarun (No. of Grunth, &c., 3,000).—By Kumulakur Bhut, a Desust Brahmun. Its date is 250 years ago. It treats of the ceremonies on the building of tanks, wells, &c., and planting gardens,—also of the Deo-prutishta, or consecration of images.

ANHEEK (No. of Grunth, &c., 3,500).—By Bhu*t*ojee Dikshit-Kaseekur, a Desust Brahmun. This work is generally known; it was composed 700 years ago, on the daily morning and evening ceremonies of Brahmuns.

NAGDEO-KRITANHEK (No. of Grunth, &c., 1,600).—By Nagdeo Bhu*t*, Yejoorvedee of Nasik. Its date is 600 years ago. Do. do.

ANHEEK-KUMULAKARUN (No. of Grunth, &c., 1,800).—By Kumulakur Bhu*t* Kaseekur. Of partial notoriety. Date 500 years ago. Do. do.

PRITHWEE-CHUNDRODE (No. of Grunth, &c., 12,000).—This work treats of Achar, Wyuwhar, and Prayuschit.

ASOUCH-SEKUR (No. of Grunth, &c., 3,000).—By Nagojee Bhu*t* Kaseekur. This is an ancient work, of partial notoriety.

PURIKSHA-MITRODE (No. of Grunth, &c., 3,000).—By a Gour Brahmun of Bengal. It is not generally known. It treats of the qualities proper for the *S*aligram, a stone to which Brahmuns make Pooja in their houses, and in which divine energy is supposed to reside,—also of men and animals.

WYUWHAR-MITRODE (No. of Grunth, &c., 12,000).—By a Gour Brahmun of Bengal, composed 200 years ago. It is a work of notoriety.

NAGOJEE-BHU*T*-KRITANHEK (No. of Grunth, &c., 1,500).—By a Brahmun of Benares. It treats of the daily ceremonies. Do.

BHU*T*OJEE-KRITANHEK (No. of Grunth, &c., 3,000).—By Bhu*t*ojee Dikshit. It was composed 300 years ago, and is of notoriety. On the daily ceremonies.

WYUWHAR-SEKUR (No. of Grunth, &c., 8,000). — By Nagojee Bhu*t*, a Desust Brahmun of Benares. It is an ancient work, of general notoriety.

SARSUNGRUHA (No. of Grunth, &c., 3,000).—This work treats of Prayuschit, Smart, Wyuwhar, &c., but not fully.

KURUM-WIPAKURK (No. of Grunth, &c., 4,000).—This is a modern abridgment (Sunkshep) of a larger work, met with in the Mahratta countries. It treats of expiation of sins committed in a former life, the supposed cause of disease and misfortunes.

DAN-CHUNDRIKA (No. of Grunth, &c., 2,500.)—By Dewakur Bhut Karle, a Kokunust Brahmun of Poona. It is a modern work, well known in the Dekhun, treating of gifts and alms, and the Muntrus proper for each.

WRUT-CHUNDRIKA (No. of Grunth, &c., 3,000).

SMOORT-URTHSAR (No. of Grunth, &c., 3,000).—By Sumbhoo Bhut, a Drewir Brahmun of the Carnatic. It is an ancient work, treating of Achar, Wyuwhar, &c.

MUDDUN-RUTN (No. of Grunth, &c., 4,300).—By Muddun Sinh, a Brahmun of Hindoosthan. It treats of Achar, Wyuwhar, and Prayuschit, and is an ancient work of notoriety.

ESWUNT-BHASKUR (No. of Grunth, &c., 6,000).—By a Brahmun of that name. This work treats of the Sunskars.

NIRBUNDH-SIROMUNEE.

RAMWAJ-PEYE (No. of Grunth, &c., 1,000).—By Ramchundr Bhutwaj Peye, of Nymeesharun. It was composed 326 years ago, and is of general notoriety. It treats of Unooshtan (worship) and the Koond (a calculation of the dimensions proper for the spot where the Hom sacrifice is performed).

PRUWUR-MUNJURE (No. of Grunth, &c., 250).—This work treats of Gotrus affecting intermarriage.

PRYOG-PARAJAT.

MUDDUN-PARAJAT (No. of Grunth, &c., 12,000).—By Muddunpal, a Brahmun of Hindoosthan. It treats of Achar and Wyuwhar, and is well known in the Carnatic.

NIRUNE-DEEPIKA.

MUDDUN-MAHARUNUWU (No. of Grunth, &c., 8,000).—By Mundhuta, son of Muddunpal. It is an ancient work of general notoriety, treating of the Muntrus for obviating the consequences of sin committed in a former life (kurumuwipak).

KAKDURUSUN.

SUNSKARUSAR.

SMROOTEE-DURTPUN (No. of Grunth, &c., 500).—By Rugoonath Bhut Kaseekur. This is a modern work on Tithee.

DAYU-WIBHAG (No. of Grunth, &c., 3,000).—By a Gour Brahmun of Bengal; it is a modern work of notoriety, on Wyuwhar.

NARAYUN-BHUTEE (No. of Grunth, &c., 12,000).—By Narayun Bhut Kaseekur. It was composed on the basis of the Roog Ved, 400 years ago; it treats of the sixteen Sunskars, and is very generally known.

SUNKUR-BHUTEE (No. of Grunth, &c., 3,000).—By Sunkur Bhut, a Kokunust Brahmun of the Mahratta country. This was composed on the basis of the Hirunyukesee-sootr, treating of the Sunskars. It is an ancient work of notoriety.

MYHESBHUTEE (No. of Grunth, &c., 3,000).—By Myhesbhut, a Chitpawun Brahmun of the Mahratta country. It treats of the Sunskars according to Hirunyukesee; it is an ancient work of general notoriety.

URUWEEK (No. of Grunth, &c., 8,000).—By a Drewir Brahmun of the Carnatic. It treats of the Sunskars according to the Upustumbh-sootr. It is also ancient, and of general notoriety.

BHARGWARCHUNDEEPIKA (No. of Grunth, &c., 2,000).

RAMARCHUN CHUNDRIKA (No. of Grunth, &c., 4,000).

NURSINHARCHUN CHUNDRIKA.

NAK,POOSHP, MARLA (No. of Grunth, &c., 300).—By Kesoo Josee, a Chitpawun Brahmun of Benares. It treats of the Gotrus relative to marriage. It is a modern work of notoriety.

SUNYASPUDUTEE (No. of Grunth, &c., 300).—By —— Toro of Nasik, a Desust Brahmun of the Mahratta country. On the means of becoming a devotee. It is modern and generally known.

PUNGTEE-ARADHWU (No. of Grunth, &c., 1,000).—By Sayunachary Widnyaruneswamee, a Sunyasee of Anagoondy. It was composed about 1,000 years ago, and is generally known. It treats of Wurt, &c.

URCHA-SOODHEE (No. of Grunth, &c., 100).—This work treats of reconsecrating deities after being polluted by the touch of low-caste persons. It is an ancient work, the author unknown.

TRYEMBUKEE (No. of Grunth, &c., 300).—By Tryembuk Bhu*t*, a Chitpawun Brahmun of the Mahratta country. It treats of Asouch or mourning, and is a modern work of notoriety.

SUPINDE-PRUDEEP (No. of Grunth, &c., 300).—By Kesoo Dywugne Pytunkur, a Desust Brahmun of the Mahratta country. It is a modern work, generally known, and treats of the funeral cakes offered for connections by marriage.

CHURUN-WYOOH (No. of Grunth, &c., 400).—By Boodhayun Rishee, of Hindoosthan. It treats of the number of Grunth in the four Veds, and in the Poorans, and of the proper mode of reading those books.

OOPUWYOOH-BHASHY (No. of Grunth, &c., 600).—This is a commentary on the former, by Mydas Gour, a Brahmun of Bengal. Both are ancient, and of notoriety.

WASOODEVEE (No. of Grunth, &c., 1,500).—By Wasoodeo Bhu*t* Kaseekur. A modern work, on the Deoprutishta.

SMART-WYSHNOO-EKADUSEE-NIRUNE (No. of Grunth, &c., 100).—A modern work, on the day on which the Ekadusee ceremonies are to be performed.

Dan-khund (No. of Grunth, &c., 3,000).—A modern work of notoriety. On Wurt, and Gifts or Alms.

Chutoor-wiwshutee-smrootee-wakyu.—This is an ancient commentary, and abridgment of the twenty-four Smrootees.

Roodr-pudhutee (No. of Grunth, &c., 1,500).—This is an ancient work, on the worship of *S*iw as Roodru.

*S*iksha-bhashy (No. of Grunth, &c., 400).—By Widyaruneswamee, a Sunyasee of Anagoondy. It is an exposition of the Veds, and treats of the mode of reading them. It was composed 1,000 years ago.

Bhogun-kootoohul (No. of Grunth, &c., 6,000).—By Rugoonath Bhu*t* Deo, a Desust Brahmun of Benares. It is an ancient work of notoriety, treating of the mixture of different articles of food (as part of Achar).

Gotr-pruwur-nirune (No. of Grunth, &c., 400).—By Kesoo Josee, a Chitpawun Brahmun of Benares. It is modern, and generally known.

Supinde-nirune (2nd) (No. of Grunth, &c., 400).—By Narayun Bhu*t*, a Brahmun of Benares. A modern work.

Tithee-nirune (2nd) (No. of Grunth, &c., 600.)—By Gungaram Bhu*t*, a Gour Brahmun of Koomou. This is a modern work, partially known.

Dwyt-nirune (No. of Grunth, &c., 5,000).—By *S*unkur Bhu*t*, a Brahmun of Benares. It treats of the individuality of things as distinct from the divine spirit. It was written 300 years ago, and is generally known.

Karl-madhwu.—By Widyaruneswamee, Drewir Sunyasee of Anagoondy. Its date is 1,000 years ago. It treats of the time of performing Wurt.

Jeewunt-sraddh-pudhutee (No. of Grunth, &c., 1,000).—By Ramkrishn Bhu*t* Kaseekur, Desust. This work treats of the performing, or at least arranging, a man's own funeral ceremonies, previously to his death, and of the heirs' consequent duties.

JYSINH-KULPUDROOMA (No. of Grunth, &c., 1,400).—By Rutnakur Bhut, a Brahmun of Jysinh,nuggur. Of notoriety. It was written 112 years ago, and treats of the last ceremonies on the Wurt of Gunputtee.

SUNSKAR-RUTNUMARLA (No. of Grunth, &c., 20,000).—By Gopeenath Dikshit Wok, a Kokunust Brahmun of Poona, sixty years ago. Its subject is the Sunskars, and it is well known in the Mahratta country.

GRYHEE,UGNI,SAGUR (No. of Grunth, &c., 4,600).—By Narayun Bhut Urde, a Brahmun of Bhoganuggur or Hydrabad, 185 years ago. It is known in the Mahratta country, in the Nizam's dominions. It treats of Achar and Prayuschit.

KRITYARUTNAWULEE (No. of Grunth, &c., 2,200).—By Ramchundr Tukshit Kaseekur, treating of duties and ceremonies of particular days. It is of notoriety in the Mahratta country and Benares.

HUREEHUR-BHASHY (No. of Grunth, &c., 4,250).—By Hureehur Bhut Kaseekur. On Sraoot-smart; generally known.

ASWULAYUN-WRITY (No. of Grunth, &c., 11,000).—On the same. Do.

KASEE-DIKSHIT-UNHEEK (No. of Grunth, &c., 1,200).—By a Brahmun of that name. On Ablutions. Do. do.

DINKUR-UDYOT (No. of Grunth, &c., 36,000).—This work has twelve divisions. By Wisweswurop Ramuk Goga Bhut Kaseekur. On Achar and Wyuwhar. Do. do.

PRITHWEE-CHUNDRODE-SUMYEKHUND (No. of Grunth, &c., 6,000).

WIDHAN-PARAJAT (No. of Grunth, &c., 12,000).—By Mudhun Bhut Kanuwa, a Brahmun of Hindoosthan. The work treats of Sunskars, and is of notoriety in Benares and in the Dekhun.

SANTEESAR (No. of Grunth, &c., 5,000).—By Dinkur Bhut of Hindoosthan. On Purification. Do.

PRYWSUT-SLOKEE (No. of Grunth, &c., 800).

ACHARARK (No. of Grunth, &c., 4,000).—By Sunkur Bhut Kaseekur. On Achar and Wyuwhar. Of general notoriety.

DUT-MEEMANS.—This is a work well known in the Carnatic country.

DUT-KOUSTOOBH. Do.

SMOORT-URTHSAR. Do.

KARLANULA. Do.

SMOORT-URTH-SUNGRUHA. Do.

DHURM-PRUWURTEE. Do.

KULPA. Do.

UNHEEK-NIRUNE. Do.

CHULAREE. Do. This work was composed 100 years ago by *S*eshachary, Gooroo of Nursinh Achary, of the Carnatic.

The following books of the Dhurmsastru are mentioned both in the preceding Catalogue and by Mr. Colebrooke:—

All the SMROOTEES, except Wamun, Wridhsatatup, and a work called the *S*lok. The work called KATYAYUN appears as a Sootr in the Poona list.

Two OOPUSMROOTEES, Boudhyayun and Aswulayun.

MEDHATITHEE, GOVINDARUNUWU, Commentaries on Munoo.

VEERMITRODAYU, followed by the Benares school.

KUMULAKUR ?

MUDDUNPARAJAT.

WYUWHAR MYOOKHEE.

KULPTUROO.

SMROOTURTHSAR.

HEMADREE.

DAYUWIBHAG ?

The following Commentators and minor Authorities are mentioned by Mr. Colebrooke, and omitted in the Poona Catalogue:—

MUNAVURTEE MOOKTAVULEE, DHURMUDHUR, Commentaries on Munoo.

HURUDUTTEE, a Commentary on Goutuma.

NUNDUPUNDITU, Do. on Vishnoo.

DEEPUKULIKA, Do. on Yadnyawulkya, followed by the Gour or Bengal school.

DHURM,RUTN, by Jimootavuhunu, do. This includes the Dayu-bhagu.

WYUWHAREE-TUTWU, followed by the Bengal school.

DAYU-TUTWU, Do.

DAYU-RUMU-SUNGRUHU, Do.

THREE Commentaries on the Dayubhagu, Do.

ONE do. on the Dayu-tutwu, Do.

SMROOTEE-RUTNAWULEE, Do.

DAYU-NIRUNYU, Do.

WIWADU-RUTNUKARU, followed by the Mithil school.

WYUWHAR-RUTNUKARU, Do.

THREE Chintamunee of Wachusputee Misra, followed by the Mithil school.

WIWADU-CHUNDRU.

BALUMBHU*t*, a Commentary on the Mitakshura.

SMROOTEE-CHUNDRIKA.

NYAYU-SUWUSWU.

WYUWHAR-TILUKU.

The following list of books referred to as Authorities for explaining Law, was furnished by the persons assembled in Khandesh :—

The FOUR VEDS, called *S*rootee-Roog, Yejoor, *S*am, and Utharwun.

EIGHTEEN SMROOTEES, Vishnoo, Purasur, Duksh, Sumwurt, Hureetu, Wusisht, Satatup, Yumu, Upustumbh, Goutumu, Dewulu, Sunkh, Oosena, Bhurudwaj (?), Utree, Sonunku (?), and Yadnyawulkya.

ELEVEN OOPUSMROOTEES, Munoo, Narayun, Katyayun, Aswulayun, Kasup, Bruhusputee, Rujaputtee, Longakshee (?), Ungira, Jymeeyu, and Jaballee (?).

EIGHTEEN POORANS, Bhuwishy, Bhagwut, Mutsyu, Markundu, Brumhund, Brumhu, Wishnoo, Brumhuwiwur, Wura, Wamun, Wayoo, Ugni, Ling, Pudm, Nursinh, Koorum, Skund, and Gurood.

FOUR OOPUPOORANS, Moodgul, Gunes, Kalee, Sour.

TWO ITEEHAS, Bharut and Ramayun.

Compilations from the above authorities.

WYUWHAR WIDYANESWUREE.

,, MYOOKH.

,, DINKURODYOT.

,, MADHWU.

,, PRUTAPUST,KHUND.*

The following Catalogue of works said to be written in the Sunskrit, and held of authority in the Lingaet or Jungum castes, was furnished by Busaya, Gooroo of the Lingaets in Poona.

SIDDHANT-SIKAWUNEE (No. of Grunth, &c., 1,500).—An ancient work treating of Achar, well known in the Carnatic and Tylung countries, as well as among the Mahrattas. It was composed by Siwyogeswur Jungum, Tylung.

---

* The Smrootee are of superior authority to the Iteehas and Poorans; the Srootee are paramount. The signification of the former word is "recollected," of the latter "heard," from immediate divine revelation.

PURMESWUR-TUNTR (No. of Grunth, &c., 2,000). An ancient work on Prayuschit, claiming the god *S*iw for its author.

VEERSYWOKUR-DEEPIKA (No. of Grunth, &c., 500).—This work was written 100 years ago, by Chunveeraswamee, Jungum of the Carnatic. Its subject is Achar.

*S*UNKUR-SUMWITA (No. of Grunth, &c., 700).—Said to be written by Vyas, author of the Poorans. It treats of Achar and Prayuschit.

PURUM-RAHUSYU (No. of Grunth, &c., 125).—This is said to have been composed by *S*iw. It treats of Achar.

VEERSYWU-ACHAR-KOUSTOOBH (No. of Grunth, &c., 12,000).—This is a modern work met with in the Carnatic, but not at Poona. It treats of Achar, and was written by Mounupa, Jungum of Bidnoor, in the Carnatic.

UNOOBHOW-SOOTR (No. of Grunth, &c., 1,000).—By Mugle Mahadeo, Jungum of the Carnatic. It is a modern work on Achar and Prayuschit, of notoriety in the *S*olapoor country.

VEERSYWU-CHINTAMUNEE (No. of Grunth, &c., 25,000). —By Nyugoonuswamee, Jungum of the Carnatic. It is an ancient work on Achar.

WIWEK-CHINTAMUNEE (No. of Grunth, &c., 10,000).—Do. on Achar and Prayuschit.

VEERSYWUROHUDUDHEE (No. of Grunth, &c., 20,000). —Do. explanatory of the Mahadeo Dhurm; viz. the worship of *S*iw, and the customs of the caste.

KUTHA-DUMBUR (No. of Grunth, &c., 100,000).—This ancient work is met with in the Carnatic and Tylung countries.

PASOOPUTY-UGUMU (No. of Grunth, &c., 700).—Do. on Achar and Prayuschit. This work is met with in the Carnatic.

*S*YEWIDNYAKUR (No. of Grunth, &c., 8,000).—The author

of this work was a Brahmun of the Tylung country. It treats of Achar and Prayuschit.

SOOKSHMU-TUNTR (No. of Grunth, &c., 800).—This is said to have been composed by Mahadeo. It is found in the Drewir and Carnatic countries. Do.

BUSWUPOORAN (No. of Grunth, &c., 10,000).—By Achary Swamee, a Brahmun Sunyasee of *S*ringeree, in the Carnatic. It treats of the god *S*iw, and is known in the Carnatic and *S*olapoor countries.

VEERAGUMU (No. of Grunth, &c., 12,000).—This and the following are said to have been composed by Mahadeo. They are met with in the Carnatic. Both treat of Achar and Prayuschit.

WATOOLAGUMU (No. of Grunth, &c., 4,000).

The Jyns in Poona stated that books exist different from the Brahminical *S*astrus, which are occasionally consulted by their Gooroo on occasions of penance. They mentioned the Poonyuhawachun, Ubhishek, and others, but were ignorant of particulars, and would appear to consult Brahmuns on most disputed points. Nothing like a catalogue of their own books could be procured at Poona.

MARRIAGE.

I. Sixteen purifying ceremonies, called Sunskars, performed at different periods, are prescribed for all males of the three leading castes, Brahmun, Kshutriyu, and Wys:—1, Gurbhadhan, a ceremony performed after the future mother has attained maturity; 2, Pooswun, at the period of conception; 3, Unwulobhun, at three months' pregnancy; 4, Seemuntonyun, at five months'; 5, Wishnoobhutee, at seven months'; 6, Jatkurum, at birth; 7, Namkurum, on naming the child, at the twelfth day after birth; 8, Nishkrumun, on bringing the child outside the house, at three months old; 9, Sooryuwulokun, on his being presented to the Sun, at four months; 10, Unnuprasun, on his being fed by hand, at six months; 11, Choul, on his head being first shaved, at three years of age; 12, Oopunyun, the ceremony of Moonj, or investiture with the jenwa, or sacred thread, by which regeneration is supposed to be effected, at eight years of age; 13, Mahenamyu, the ceremony of the Gayutree, performed subsequently to the Moonj; 14, Sumawurtun, performed before marriage; 15, Wiwuha, marriage; 16, Swurgarohun, funeral ceremonies. Males of the *S*oodru caste are not entitled to the 12th, 13th, and 14th, B. S. (Narayun Bhutee, *S*oodrukumulakarun, &c.). According to the *S*oodru Kumulakarun, twelve Sunskars only are appropriated to *S*oodrus, P. C. Females of all castes are not entitled to the 12th, 13th, and 14th; their principal Sunskar being marriage, its early celebration, and fidelity on the woman's part, are strictly enjoined, B. S. The ceremonies previous to marriage, according to the Soobod- Of the Sunskars.

hinee, refer to males only, and not to females, Mit. Tr. note 288. A different enumeration of the Sunskars is given in C. Dig. 3, 104. *See* note in Mit. Tr. 285.

Marriage of eight kinds.

II. There are eight kinds of marriage recognized in the Sastrus:—1, Bruhm, where the charges are incurred solely by the girl's father; 2, Dyv, where the girl's father gives her in marriage to a Brahmun during the Hom sacrifice; 3, Ursh, where the girl is given in exchange for a cow and a bullock; 4, Prajaputyu, where she is given with the view of obtaining offspring; 5, Usoor, where she is taken in exchange for wealth, and married: this species is peculiar to the Wys and Soodru castes, B. S. (Mit.) The sale of a girl in marriage is forbidden, B.S. (Mit.) *See* Munoo, 3, 20, 34. It is considered as Usoorwiwuha, and Stree-soolk, and the money, if unpaid, is an unlawful debt, B. 2, 199—*see* paragraph 26. 6, Gandhurvu, where the marriage is agreed on by the parties without the parents' knowledge; 7, Rakshus, where the girl is seized and married with tumult and violence. The 6th and 7th species are peculiar to the Kshutriyu caste. 8, Pysach, where the girl is stolen by night from her place of sleep. This species is forbidden, B. S. (Mit.) C. Dig. 3, 604 (Yadn.)

Betrothment.

III. The agreement by Brahmun parents on both sides to marry their son and daughter is called Wagnischyuh. There is no prescribed limit as to time, but it is enjoined that betrothment should precede marriage by as short an interval as possible, lest a quarrel should interrupt the contract. The Magune, or asking in marriage, practised by Soodrus, is also at no fixed period. If, after the agreement to marry, a relation on either side die, or either party be discovered to be of lower caste, or to have some disease, as leprosy, &c., or if the intended husband be discovered to be impotent, or the girl to be unchaste, the marriage cannot take place. Neither can a marriage be solemnized between parties whose Nukshutr is

Time.

How broken off.

in the same Nadee,* B. S. (Nirunesindhoo Koustoobh.) If one party break off a marriage causelessly, he should pay the expenses with interest to the other party, being also liable to fine, P. C. C. Dig. 2, 492 (Yadn.) Mit. Tr. 373. At the Wagnischyuh, the boy's father is directed to give presents of clothes and jewels to the girl, which must be returned, should the marriage be broken off causelessly, B. S. (Mit.) If a betrothed damsel die, the betrother is to take back his presents to her, paying the expenses: her jewels and streedhun go to her uterine brothers, Mit. Tr. 374. The punishment of theft is awarded to the detention of a girl, C. Dig. 2, 489 (Yadn.)†

Age of marriage.

IV. A Brahmun is enjoined to remain with his Gooroo as a student until twenty years of age, or at least sixteen, and on leaving him to marry. Beyond that period there is no limit at which he may not marry, B. S. (Koustoobh.) A female should be married at eight years of age, but not under six (Nirunesindhoo and Mit.), nor can the marriage be delayed to her twelfth year except by reason of distress, B. S. (Koustoobh and Mit.) Should the signs of puberty appear before the marriage of a Brahmunee, she may be married after certain prescribed ceremonies of penance, P. C. B. S.

---

* Viz., subdivision of the twenty-seven lunar mansions. There are three Nadees, nine Nukshutrus in each. From the Nukshutr of the parties is known whether they are of the human, divine, or diabolical *Gun*. The first and last cannot intermarry; the second and third are supposed to produce discord between the parties. The parties may intermarry if of the same *Gun*, and the first and second are of course preferred. Marriage cannot take place if certain Goon or astrological conjunctions are unfavourable, known by inspecting the calculation made at the birth of the parties, and written in their Junum, putrika. Also if the boy's constellation is the sixth or eighth in order before that of the girl, they cannot intermarry, B. S. (Shudashruk.)

† According to Munoo, although giving a girl to a second suitor is forbidden, if the betrother die, she may with her own consent be given to his brother or other Supindu relation, C. Dig. 2, 485.

According to Katyayun, if a girl be betrothed to two persons, and the first return before her marriage, he is to take her; otherwise, the second; in the first case the second, in the second case the first, recovers his expenses. The girl is to wait three years, C. Dig. 2, 491.

(Nirunesindhoo); or married privately as one who has lost caste; or even abandoned altogether, B. S. (Skund Pooran.) The second marriage of a wife or widow (called Pat by the Mahrattas, and Natra in Goozerat) is forbidden in the present age at least, and to twice-born castes. *See* Munoo. C. Dig. 2, 473. But it is not forbidden to *S*oodrus, B. S.

Whose consent necessary.

V. The consent of both parents on both sides is necessary to a regular marriage, in which the gift and giver are both requisite. Should the father be dead, that of the mother and brother is sufficient, or of the other male relations by the father's side (Sukoolyu), B. S. (Myookh.) The order in the text of the Mitakshura is :—1, Father; 2, Parental grandfather; 3, Brother; 4, Sukoolyu relations; 5, Mother; the next of sound mind in default of the former. There is a text of Yadnyawulkya, that if there be no persons competent to give a girl in marriage, she may herself choose a suitable husband (C. Dig. 2, 387) (swyumwur.) But it is said in the Wyuwhar-Myookh that such swyumwur marriage is forbidden in the present Kuleeyoog, B. S. (Poorans.)

Restrictions in selection.

The law is considered in the present age to limit the choice of a wife to within the husband's caste. Her Gotr must be different from his own; that is, she must be descended from a different Rishee, B. S. (Mit.) Intermarriage within the *S*ugotr Supindu* is forbidden, and with a female of another

* That is, relationship within the degrees of which all are descended from the same ancient sage, and each performs for the benefit of the others deceased the funeral offerings of rice, called Pind. Of such relations, the common ancestor must be within seven generations. Supindu offerings are made both for relations and connections by marriage, but the spiritual benefit to the deceased is supposed to result from the nearness of the relationship. In an undivided family, the Ekadusee and Supindakurum ceremonies are to be performed on the eleventh and twelfth days after a father's death, by the eldest son only; the first ten days' ceremonies, and (in case of necessity) the annual *S*raddh, by each son separately. In a divided family, the Supindudan and twelfth days' ceremonies are to be performed by the eldest son only, or in default the youngest. In the former case, the whole expense is a charge on the estate; in the latter, each pays his own; and though there be no assets, sin is incurred by non-performance, B. S. B.

*S*raddh ceremonies are performed on the anniversary of a father's death. The caste, P. C. (Mit.); and besides the Wirood Sumbund, or prohibited degree of connection within seven degrees, marriage is forbidden with the following Usogotr supindu connections: a parent's sister's daughter, a mother's brother's daughter, and a sister's daughter. A former connection by marriage between the two families is not objected to, B. S. (Mit.)

Order of marriage in a family.

VII. In a family composed entirely of sons, or of daughters, each is to be married in order of birth; where there are both boys and girls, the preference may be given to the girls, on their arriving at the prescribed age, B. S. (Myookh).

Restrictions as to time of celebration.

VIII. The prescribed period for the marriage ceremonies are the months of Margsirsh, Magh, Phalgoon, Wysakh, Jesht. To the N. of the river Gunga or Godavery, marriage may also be celebrated during the month Ashad, provided it be previous to the conjunction of the sun with the zodiacal star or Nukshutr Ardra, the sixth of the twenty-seven lunar mansions in the constellation Gemini (*see* Sir W. Jones on the Antiquity of the Hindoo Zodiac). During the period of the planet Jupiter's remaining within the Lion constellation (one year in twelve), thence called the Sinhust year, it is forbidden to marry on the N. of the river Krishn or Kistna. There

---

Puksh ceremonies are performed subsequent to the first year after a father's death, at some time during the month Bahadrupud. There are also daily and monthly offerings for the benefit of a father and ancestors deceased.

In the Supindakurum, small heaps of rice are named according to the ancestors and relations of the deceased within certain degrees, as Sugotrus, or connections by marriage; and are mixed together with his. After marriage, a wife's Gotr becomes that of her husband.

Mrit-sootuk, or mourning ceremonial, consists in sitting apart and abstaining from worldly business for a certain period on the death of a relation. The sootuk on the death of a father is prolonged to the fourteenth day. On the death of a relation within the degree of Dushantil bhow, that is, if the common ancestor is within seven generations, to ten days; if within fourteen generations, to three and a half days; and if the common ancestor is beyond twenty-one degrees, ablution only is necessary.

Jat-sootuk, or Vridhee, is the ceremony of sitting apart on the birth of a relation's child, B. S. The period varies according to the degree of relationship.

are some sacred places (as *S*reevenkute*s*wur, in the Carnatic, near Gootee) at which marriage may be celebrated at all times and seasons, B. S. (Nirune*s*indhoo).

Ceremonies of marriage.

IX. The ceremonies enjoined to Brahmuns are the following:—1, Poonyuhawachun, recitation of Muntrus; 2, Nandeeh*s*raddh, offering of food to ancestors; 3, Deoprutishta, consecration of the marriage god on its being deposited in the house (suptumatrikstapun); 4, Munduppruti*s*h*t*a, consecration of the canopy, &c.; 5, Muddoopurk, gift of dhee and honey to the bridegroom by the father-in-law, with other presents; 6, Untuhput, in which a veil or curtain is interposed between the bride and her husband; 7, Kunyadan, gift of the daughter to her husband; 8, *S*oubhagyuwayundan, in which the husband and bride give a cocoanut, &c., to the wife of a Brahmun, to propitiate their future happiness; 9, Kunyapaneegruhun, in which the husband takes the wife's hand; 10, Kunkunbundun, in which each party ties turmeric to the other's wrist; 11, Ugneeprutish*t*a, bringing the sacred fire; 12, Wiwahahom, Lajahom, different parts of the fire sacrifice; 13, Suptapudu, in which the parties' garments are tied together; they pace seven steps over the floor, and the Sheshahom or concluding fire sacrifice is performed. This concludes the regular marriage, after which the contract is indissoluble, B. S. (Nirune*s*indhoo Narayunbhu*t*ee.) On the second or third day it is usual for the *S*oonmookh, or first interview between the boy's mother and the girl, to take place; this is not prescribed in the books. The Sare follows, in which the girl's relations commit her to her new family in the hope of obtaining progeny (wans-patrdan). In conclusion, the bride is conducted to her father-in-law's house, where the Lukshmee-pooja is performed: the marriage-god is dismissed by the ceremony of Deokstapun; and the Mundup is removed, (Mundupstapun) B. S.

Presents given at marriage.

X. The bridegroom receives from the bride's father the

Muddoopurk at the time of marriage (Mit. II. 48, 2, 5. Tr. 268), and what other presents may be then given him he is entitled to receive as separately acquired property. So presents to the bride at marriage constitute part of her Streedhun, B. S. P. C. On the death of a husband without sons, the wife takes the jewels and clothes; and on the death of a childless wife, the husband is entitled to them, P. C. (Mit.)

XI. On the wife attaining her maturity, before which period she is supposed to have lived chiefly with her parents, and occasionally in her father-in-law's house, she is to undergo the Sunskar ceremony of Gurbhadhan. After which the Poonyuhawachun and Hom sacrifice are to be performed; presents of flowers, &c., are to be given to the wife, who thereupon enters on her household and conjugal duties. This period is termed the Rootoo or Shanee; and should the parties have intercourse either before or after it, without the prescribed ceremonies, both must perform Prayuschit, B. S. (Nirunesindhoo and Koustoobh.) Period of cohabitation.

XII. The *S*astrus are not explicit on the question to whom the jewels belong in the event of the husband's refusing to receive his wife, or the parents to send her to him. A false accuser of a girl is finable, and penance is awarded in cases of irregular marriage, P. C. Should it be discovered after marriage that any Muntrus have not been properly recited, Prayuschit must be performed, and the words repronounced correctly. Should the husband prove of lower caste, provided the Gurbhadhan has not been performed, the girl is to perform Prayuschit [and be remarried, and this is the only case in which a woman can be married a second time, B. S. Nirunesindhoo]. She ought in such case to be repudiated with maintenance, P. S. The first case refers to the husband's proving of very low caste, B. S. But if the Gurbhadhan has been performed, the wife must remain with her low-caste Consequences of an irregular marriage.

husband. Should the wife prove of lower caste, the husband must perform Prayuschit, and she may be repudiated with maintenance, but her child is not legitimate, B. S. (Myookh.) Should the parties prove to be within the prohibited degrees of marriage (*see* paragraph 5), the wife must be repudiated with maintenance, and expiation performed, B. S. The children are illegitimate and lose caste. A discovery of irregularities in astrological calculations is of no consequence, B. S. A marriage concluded without consent of parents is not void, if the prescribed ceremonies have been performed, P. C. (Nirunesindhoo.) A marriage is not annulled by the discovery of leprosy or other like disease, or impotence, or barrenness, B. S. (Myookh).

Polygamy and second marriage of women.

XIII. A husband is legally permitted to marry a second wife, and supersede the first married or elder wife, in the event of the latter proving barren, bearing daughters only, or being incurably diseased. Also if she be of expensive, abusive, mischievous, or drunken habits, Yadn. C. Dig. 2, 418. Mit. I. 9, 2, 1. The last is expressly assigned as a sufficient cause of supercession to a *S*oodru. The consent of the elder wife is, however, essential, B. S. (Hureedut teeka), and is as it were purchased by giving her a present equal to half that assigned to the second wife on her marriage, or (should the former have received no Streedhun before) an equal present, Yadn. C. Dig. 3, 17. She must be maintained and kindly treated (Yadn); but may be confined or abandoned if she leave the house in consequence of such second marriage of her husband, Munoo. C. Dig. 2, 421. Anciently a Brahmun might marry a wife of each of the four castes; a Kshutriy three wives; a Wy*s* two; and a *S*oodru one, of course of his own caste, B. S. (Mit.) In the present age each is limited to his own caste. The second marriage of a wife or widow, though anciently allowed in case of a brother's dying childless, and some others, is considered prohibited to twice-born castes, at least in the present Kuleeyoog. *See* Munoo. C. Dig. 2, 473.

Precedence among wives.

XIV. Of several wives, being of the Brahmun caste, the one first married enjoys the precedence; if they are of different castes, the Brahmunee is considered the elder. The elder wife sits by her husband at marriages and other religious ceremonies (*see* Yadn. C. Dig. 2, 405), is head of the family, and entitled to adopt a son on her husband's death without sons.

Relations of husband and wife cohabiting.

XV. A husband is directed to punish his wife according to the magnitude of her offence: the degree varies from a blow, not with a metal instrument, to suspension of conjugal rites and repudiation. In case of aggravated adultery, she may be turned out of the house and abandoned, B. S. Mit. A female is declared to be in perpetual dependence on her legal protectors, whether father, husband, son, or brother-in-law; and in default of male relations from whom she may receive food, clothing, and ornaments, the Raja is to supply the place of guardian, Munoo. Yadn. C. Dig. 2, 381. She is enjoined to occupy her mind in domestic employments, in the preparation of food and the nurture of children. (Munoo, &c.) Mutual fidelity during life is enjoined to both parties. Munoo. C. Dig. 2, 497. A virtuous wife will remain with her husband, even should he abandon her society in favour of a low-caste female, and perform his expiation, B. S. For the incidents of Streedhun, or women's property, *see* paragraph 76. A wife living with her husband can contract no debts without his express order, P. C. A husband or wife is not liable to defray the debts of the other unless on account of Sunsar or necessary family expenses and alms, (B. 2, 203), except where a man's livelihood chiefly depends on the wife's labour, Yadn. C. Dig. 317.

Mutual evidence.

XVI. The husband and wife are discouraged from litigation, and on the general rules of evidence cannot be witnesses in each other's cause. If they persist on admonition, justice is to be done, B. S. (Mit). In a period of distress, for the maintenance of the family, or the family not opposing, the whole family property may be given away, except property from parting with which the destruction of the family will ensue, as especially a wife or son (or Vritee or immovable property, B. S.), Mit. II. 68, 2, 16.

Sale of wife or son.

Murder of either by the other.

XVII. A Brahmun murdering his own wife, or the wife of another man, is not liable to capital punishment, but, as in other cases of great crime, to a punishment similar to death, viz. confiscation of property, shaving the head, mutilation of the ears and nose, and banishment. A *S*oodr murdering a Brahmun is to be put to death. A woman of any caste is subject to the same punishment for murder as a Brahmun, B. S. (Mit.)

Separation between husband and wife.

XVIII. In the event of the husband's losing caste entirely, a wife is permitted to live separately, retaining her property, P. C. (Mit.) A husband repudiating his wife, without a crime on her part, being mother of a virtuous son, is enjoined to provide for her maintenance, to pay her debts incurred on that account, and, if rich, to assign to her one-third of his property, Yadn. C. Dig. 2, 420. P. (Mit.)

Repudiation with loss of caste and consequences of adultery.

XIX. A husband is allowed to repudiate his wife, without maintenance, only for such offences as may occasion her total loss of caste, viz. adultery with a man of caste lower than her own, attempting her husband's death, procuring abortion, eating or drinking forbidden things. Repudiation for such crime of the highest degree (Ootumpatuk) is considered equivalent to death; the woman is turned out of the house and abandoned, and a semblance of her funeral obsequies is performed by burning her effigy, composed of durubh grass, and performing the Sootuk usual on the death of a wife. This ceremony is called Ghu*t*usphot, B. S. Mit. The punishment for adultery (Wyubhichar) in other cases is regulated by the relative caste of the parties and the means used to effect the object—whether persuasion, mutual agreement, or force. 1st. If at the woman's invitation, both being Brahmuns, the woman is to perform Prayuschit, after which she may return to her husband's embraces; if a Soodr woman invite a Brahmun, the expiation is trifling; if a Brahmunee invite a Soodr, she is to undergo an excessive penance,* the man is to pay a fine, and to be admonished by the magistrate against repetition. 2nd. If the parties meet by mutual agreement, both being Brahmuns, both must perform penance: if the paramour be a Soodr, the Brahmunee is to lose caste, be exposed and banished, and the man is to pay a fine to the Raja. 3rd. If the crime be committed forcibly, the woman is to perform a slight penance, and a heavy fine is to be exacted from the man, both being Brahmuns. In case of a Soodr committing a rape on a Brahmunee, the penance to the latter is heavy, and the former is condemned to mutilation and banishment; and in case of a Brahmun committing a rape on a Soodr woman, he is to be sentenced to a small fine. The principle is the same as regards the other castes. In case of adultery with the wife of a Gooroo, pupil, friend, relative, Poojaree, or magistrate, each of whose wives are considered as a mother, both parties are liable to capital punishment, but commutable as above explained. The penance in such cases consists in branding or other corporal punishment, in the obligation of performing a certain pilgrimage, feeding Brahmuns, or paying a fine to the Gooroo or Dhurmadhikaree, or merely a public admonition. According to the Dhurmsindhoo, the paramour is to pay the

* According to Halhed, she is to be drowned, or eaten by dogs after mutilation. Some variations are observable in the other cases mentioned, but the principle is the same. "If two texts differ, reason must prevail." Yadn. C. Dig. 3, 25.

expenses of the wife's penance, and in case of her not choosing to return to her husband, he must pay the marriage expenses to the latter, and keep the woman. Otherwise it is presumed the husband would defray such charges, B. S.

Effect of loss of caste in children.

XX. In the event of either party losing caste, of children subsequently born, girls may be readmitted into the caste, and married; but boys remain excluded, B. S. Mit.

Case of absentees.

XXI. A man absenting himself, and as to whom no intelligence arrives of his existence during twenty-four years (in case he should be under fifty years of age), or twelve years (in case he should be above that age), is to be considered dead. His wife then becomes a widow, his property is inherited, and his *S*raddh performed. Certain prescribed ceremonies are enjoined in case of his subsequent reappearance, B. S. (Nirunesindhoo.)

Duties of a separated wife.

XXII. During his absence his wife, as in other cases of unavoidable separation from her husband, should, if maintained, perform religious duties and austerities. Otherwise she should live with her relations, Yadn. C. Dig. 2, 450. And she may, if necessary, provide for her own maintenance by spinning or other blameless arts, Munoo. C. D. 2, 404.

Duties of a widow.

XXIII. A widow is allowed to perform her husband's funeral rites, both Kreea and *S*raddh, provided he has left no son, grandson, brother, or brother's son, B. S.* (Nirunesindhoo.) She is enjoined to promote her own and husband's future happiness by becoming a Suttee; or otherwise, by avoiding all sensual pleasures, practising ceremonial worship, chastity, feeding Brahmuns, making charitable gifts to temples, &c., and performing pilgrimages to holy places. These

* The text of the Nirunesindhoo (Book 3) gives the following order of performers of the *S*raddh :—1, son; 2, grandson; 3, great-grandson; 4, adopted son; 5, widow; 6, brother or his son; 7, father; 8, mother; 9, sister or her son; 10, supindus; 11, family priest or preceptor (Mit. VI. 6, 23). But this appears to apply to the case of the late husband's death previous to a partition with his brothers. *See* B. 1, 70.

constitute the duties of a Bruhmacharyu and devotee, B. S. (Mitakshura. Nirunesindhoo.) No woman can enjoy property unless living a chaste life, or at least performing expiation for a breach of chastity. Failing to do so, she is entitled to food and clothing only, and in case of Ootumputuk, and consequent degradation from caste and Ghutusphot (*see* paragraph 19), she loses all title even to maintenance.

Suttees.

XXIV. The most virtuous mode of becoming a Suttee is to die of grief and affliction on the husband's death. The usual practice is self-immolation on the husband's funeral pile. The pile should be constructed of light grass and leaves surrounding, as is the present custom at Poona. A widow is excused from becoming a Suttee—1st, if pregnant; 2nd, if under puberty; 3rd, if she have a suckling infant; 4th, if she have a desire to attain Moksh (absorption into the divine spirit); for a woman sacrifices herself on the pile in view to another happy birth with her deceased husband, and the Sunskrit term (" Suhugumun ") applied to Suttees signifies "to accompany;" 5th, if the sacrifice is made merely with the view of escaping distress from harsh treatment of relations, or want of maintenance. It must be purely voluntary (Swusuntoshit). B. S. (Mitakshura. Nirunesindhoo.)

Rights of a widow as to property.

XXV. If no partition have taken place between the deceased husband and his brother, the widow is to remain under the guardianship of her son, or husband's brother, receiving her maintenance, B. S. Mit. Tr. 326, 331. She is at liberty to keep her jewels, and to expend the interest of the rest of her Streedhun deposited, or even the principal, for good and charitable purposes; the remainder, if any, descends to her heirs. *See* an opinion of Pundits in B. 1, 425. Gifts of movables by a husband to a wife may be alienated by her *ad libitum*, but not immovable property, Mit. Tr. 254, 273, 375. Ornaments worn by women during their husband's life must not be divided by his heirs, Mit.

If a partition have taken place previously to the husband's death, his widow, if she have no son of the age of sixteen, has a right to contract debts, and alienate the family movables for the family subsistence, or for charitable purposes; and if he have left no son or his representative to the fourth in descent, she succeeds by inheritance to the whole of his share of the family property and acquisitions. But no woman has a right to alienate immovable property, except her own Streedhun,* even for charitable purposes, without the consent of all the male heirs, B. S. Myookh, B. 1, 58. In all cases of females enjoying property, their living virtuously is presumed: a widow guilty of incontinency is to have maintenance only, Mit. Tr. 340. If a man die leaving two widows, it does not appear on whom the right of guardianship and management devolves; it may be inferred from the equal inheritance of widows, that the elder has no exclusive right,† B. S.

PARENTAGE.

Parental authority.

XXVI. Parents are enjoined to indulge their children until they attain the age of five; from five to sixteen they are to be instructed in the fourteen sciences (Widya) and sixty-four arts (Kulla), or some of them; after sixteen they are only to be verbally admonished, B. S. (Muddunparajat.)

The fourteen sciences are enumerated as follows, viz.—

* The Mitakshura, in an isolated text before referred to, denies the right of a woman to alienate immovable Streedhun given by her husband, Mit. Tr. 254. *A fortiori*, therefore, it would appear not to recognize this right as to immovables inherited by a widow.

In a case mentioned in B. 2, 175, it was held by the *Sastrees* that a widow could not alienate immovable property inherited from her own father, in discharge of her late husband's debts, without the consent of her son, after his majority (16).

† *See* Sir F. M. 25. He states that in case of four widows, two mothers of sons, one mother of daughters, and one childless, the two former would be managers till the majority of the eldest son.

The four Veds; Roog, *S*am, Yejoor, Utharvun; consisting of expositions of the leading Hindoo tenets, legends, and hymns to deities and others. The last of these is considered generally inexplicable. In the Poona College are Gooroos of three Veds, Roog, Yejoor, and Upustumbh. *See* Ward on the Hindoos and Colebrooke on the Veds, As. Res. Vol. 8.

The Oopuvedus, on medicine, music, military and mechanical sciences.

The six Ungus Jyotish (astronomy and astrology, with arithmetic), Wyakurun (grammar), Chundu (prosody and verse), Ukshyu (pronunciation), and Nirookt (explanatory of the Veds).

The four Oopungus :—1, Nyayusastru, comprising the inquiry into and classification of external objects, their source and annihilation; the investigation of truth by sensation, inference, comparison, and sensible signs; the nature of the divine and human soul, the former being exempt from pleasure and pain; and the avoidance of pain by attainment of union with the divine spirit (Moksh).

Mimansu,sastru, *see* Ward on the Hindoos. The writers on the Mimansu, Vedant, and other systems hold different metaphysical opinions on the eternity of matter, and of God as the animating soul of the world. Virtue and happiness are supposed the consequences of virtues performed in a former transmigration, and the forerunners of another, or in its highest degree causing the union of the soul with the divine spirit.

Dhurmsastru.—On customary civil and religious duties, expiation and punishment of crimes, origin of castes, &c. *See* the Catalogue.

The eighteen Poorans and eighteen Oopupoorans.—These contain legends of the Hindoo deities and of eminent individuals; also Cosmography, and the fabulous history of the four Yoogs or ages of the present world.

The sixty-four arts are enumerated as follows; viz.—

1, Gayunu (singing); 2, Wady (drum-beating); 3, Nrityu (dancing); 4, Natyu (masquerading); 5, Aleky (writing); 6, Sawee (tiluk, putting Sandal on the forehead); 7, (making artificial flowers); 8, (making a bed of flowers); 9, (colouring the teeth and garments); 10, Munibhoomikurun (adorning an earthen floor with seal-impressions); 11, Syuruchunum (making beds); 12, Ooduk,wady (musical sounds from water); 13, Chitryoguhu (drawing pictures); 14, (making necklaces and turban ornaments of flowers); 15, Sekrupeeruyojunum (putting on a turban); 16, Nyputyoguhu (artificial jewels); 17, Kurumuputr,bunguha (staining the face with colours); 18, Soogunduyooktuhee (extracting perfumed oils); 19, Bhooshunyojunum (proper disposition of jewels in dress); 20, Ayindrujalun (alchemy, conjuring earth into gold, &c.); 21, (making figures of clay); 22, Hustulaguwu (quickness of hand); 23, (Cookery); 24, Chitrsakapoopbukt, wikarukreea (mixing sherbet, lemonade, &c.); 25, Soochuwanukurum (tailoring); 26, Sooturukreeda (paper balloons); 27, (beating dumroos, tambourines); 28, Pruhelika (swinging); 29, Prutimala (?); 30, (?); 31, Poostuk,wachun (reading); 32, (explaining the Natuk books, tales in verse and prose); 33, (do. the Kawye books, on rhetoric and style); 34, (flourishing with a sword, bow and arrow, and spear); 35, Turkukurumu (drawing inferences); 36, Tukshun (carpentry); 37, Wastuwidy (building houses); 38, Roopupuriksha (assaying silver); 39, Duhootuwad (do. gold); 40, Muneeragudnayum (do. rings); 41, Akarudnayum (observant action); 42, Wirookshyuveduyoguhu (gardening); 43, (teaching rams, cocks, and quails to fight); 44, (teaching parrots); 45, Oochadunum (jocularly speaking); 46, (arranging the hair, plaited, &c.); 47, (talking by signs); 48, Mlechturukuwikulpuhu (?); 49, Desbhashadnayum (speaking the country dialects); 50, (making carriages of flowers) ; 51, Nimityudnayum (inferring causes) ; 52, Yuntru,matrika (connoisseurship in images) ; 53, Darun,-matrika (placing images) ; 54, Somwuchun (speaking well) ; 55, Manusekawekrika (guessing thoughts) ; 56, Ubhidan-koshu (understanding the vocabularies) ; 57, Chundudnayum (understanding different songs) ; 58, Kreeawikulpuha (understanding funeral rites) ; 59, Chultupryoguha (doing mischief) ; 60, Wustrugopunamee (changing garments) ; 61, Dyootwiseshy (playing at Songtee) ; 62, Ukurshunkreeda (playing with a bandalore) ; 63, Balukreedunkurun (arithmetical recreations) ; 64, Wynayukeenam, wyjeeyukeenam, wyasukeenam, widya (understanding Muntrus, conjuration of snakes and scorpions, &c., and the nature of evil spirits).

Age of majority.

XXVII. Every boy not a student is of age at the end of his sixteenth year. Munoo, 8, 27. A boy is entitled to sign papers and make oath as soon as he understands their nature, and is capable of conducting his worldly affairs. He may acquire and possess property at any age ; after sixteen his consent is necessary to alienations of descended or self-acquired property, until a partition take place between him and his father or brothers, B. S. (Mit.) P. C. A girl is considered of age at her marriage, B. S. (Muddunparajat.)

Sale of children.

XXVIII. Parents are enjoined not to sell their children. The consent of the child is at least necessary, if old enough to understand the nature of what is done respecting it ; the sale of children under such age being permitted only in case of distress,* and then not in case of an only son, B. S. (Mit. Myookh. Poorans.) A text in Mit. II. 68, 2, 16, excepts a wife and son, allowing all family property to be given

* According to Vusishta, both parents may give, sell, or desert their son for just reasons, C. Dig. 3, 242. The passage, however, refers to adoption.

away in time of distress, for the maintenance of the family, or the family not opposing.

Deprivation of inheritance.

XXIX. A father has a right to deprive a son of inheritance only as to property he himself may have acquired, not as to descended wealth, Mit. II. 16, 1, 5. The cases of persons incapable of inheriting altogether would appear to be exceptions to this general rule.

Liability to pay debts.

XXX. A son is bound to pay all debts incurred by his parents during his minority, and those incurred on account of Sunsar after that period. Sunsar includes the maintenance of the family, the charges of their several Sunskar ceremonies, especially marriage; also charitable gifts, feeding Brahmuns, building or repairing sacred places, houses, or wells, planting trees, and charges of pilgrimage, B. S. (Mit.) But a son is not bound to pay a father's debt, if contracted on account of liquor, sexual intercourse, or gambling, or a fine, or toll?* (Soolk), or a gift or money promised to swindlers, Mit. *See* C. Dig. 1, 311. With or without property, a son, after attaining twenty years of age, is bound to pay a father's debts with interest; a grandson, &c., may pay a grandfather's debts without interest, Mit. B. S. And a father is in like manner obliged, should his son die before partition, to defray all his debts incurred on account of Sunsar. And a mother in like manner. Parents and children are reciprocally to maintain each other if in want, B. S. (Mit.)

Precedence among sons.

XXXI. The son of the myheshee, or wife first married, is the elder, B. S. (Poorans.) But there is no text on this point in the Mitakshura. As to the case of twins, there is

---

* Money promised to be given annually until a marriage should be procured, was considered stree-soolk, and as such not binding on the son, being an illegal debt, B. 2, 200. *See* paragraph 61. The word soolk signifies—1, interest; 2, customs-duties; 3, price of sale; 4, money paid to a girl's father as the price of marriage, B. S.

a text of Munoo quoted in the Nirunesindhoo, that the son first seen by the father is the elder. In the Bhagwut, as quoted in the Nirunesindhoo, the last-born twin is the elder, B. S. The eldest son of a Raja succeeds to the sovereignty. (Munoo.) But, if incompetent, a younger would exercise the regal office, (Bharut. Ruowghoans) B. S. Vritee or hereditary office does not descend to the eldest son, but is partible, B. S. (Mit.)

Illegitimate children.

XXXII. The caste of children born of an adulteress is termed Koondugoluk, that of children born during widowhood, Goluk, in case the parents are Brahmuns. The Jatiwiwek details the titles of other castes of spurious origin, on account of the impurity of the paternal or maternal ancestor, or the illegality of their union. (These appellations of the Wurunsunkur or mixed castes will be found in the second part of this Summary.) B. S. Legitimate and illegitimate children are not entitled to share equally, P. C. Children of a kept woman born in the house, as of a slave, are of their mother's caste. The father is bound to maintain and give them in marriage, B. S. P. C. (Mit.) Sons of a *Soodru* by his slave-girl may even succeed to their father's property, in default of sons by legitimate marriage or daughter's son; they may receive a share by the father's gift, and on the father's death shall be allowed half a share of a legitimate son, Yadn. C. Dig. 3, 143. The term pootrprutee-nidhee, signifying the holder of a son's likeness, is applied to a favourite nephew, &c., not only to an illegitimate son or boy maintained from kindness.

Foundlings.

XXXIII. Should the caste of an exposed child be discovered to be Brahmun, the finder should nourish it as his child; should it be a *Soodr*, he may bring it up as a Das or slave, B. S. Mit.

ADOPTION.

Why adoption is permitted.

XXXIV. Adoption is permitted to ensure the following objects :—1. To preserve the adopting parent from Nuruku (the Hindoo place of torment), and to secure his happiness in the future state, by the adopted son's or his descendant's performance of funeral rites (Kreea), mourning (Sootuk), and annual oblations of rice (*S*raddh supindudan). 2. To preserve the adopting parent's good name in the present world by the practise of almsgiving, feeding Brahmuns, pilgrimages, and other Hindoo virtues, B. S. (Koustoobh.) Insanity of a begotten son is no legal cause of adoption. An adoption can take place only where no begotten son or grandson exists, or where the begotten son has lost caste, P. C. B. S.

Different kinds of sons.

XXXV. Twelve kinds of sons are enumerated in the *S*astrus, all qualified to offer funeral cakes :—1, Ourus, son begotten in legal marriage; 2, Pootrika soot, son of a daughter promised at her previous marriage to be transferred to his grandfather; 3, Kshytrij, of two kinds; son of a wife, by religious compact with a supindu relation; or son by a brother's widow, under the order of the Gooroo and relations. This refers to the obsolete forms of second marriage, or procreation by appointment. *See* C. Dig. 3, 196. 4, Gourhuja, son of a wife by an uncertain father, ten relations living together; 5, Kuneena, son by a girl under eight years of age, previously to marriage; 6, Poonurbhow-ukshut, son by a wife married a second time, the first marriage not having been consummated. P. Kshut, son by a wife who had previously to marriage connection with a paramour; 7, Dut, a son given in adoption, one of the ceremonies being that usual in gifts, viz. Julsunkulp, or pouring water on the hands; 8, Kritriha, a son purchased for adoption (*see* Sir T. Strange, App. 107 to 167); 9, Kritrimuha, an orphan conducted by the adopter to his house and named heir of his property by showing to him a house, field, &c., and saying "This is yours;" 10, Swyundutuha, a son who offers himself for adoption; 11, Suhordujuha, a son begotten by an uncertain father, but born after marriage, and brought up by the mother's husband; 12, Upuwidhuhu, a foundling, B. S. Mit. Tr. 301. Of these twelve kinds of sons, only two are recognized in the present age (in any caste)—the Ourus or begotten, and the Dut, given in adoption, Udityu Pooran. C. Dig. 3, 272. *See* Sir T. Strange, 2, 164. The Myookh, however, recognizes two species of the latter, the simply adopted, and the Dwyumooshayuna, over whom the natural father retains certain rights, Mit. Tr. 296.*

Disqualifications.

XXXVI. A man degraded from caste cannot adopt; no one would give a son in adoption to him. An impotent man could not adopt—at least, unless after marriage. There is no reason why a man become blind, deaf, dumb, diseased, or insane, should not adopt, either himself or through his wife, and the adoptee will succeed to all his property, descended or otherwise. There is no exception to the case of an adoptee; he may adopt after marriage, B. S.

Age of the parties.

XXXVII. Although there exists no legal restriction as to the adopter's age, it is inferred that he should not adopt until no hope remain of begetting a son, B. S. *See* Replies from the Poona Sastrees, quoted in B. 2, 92. If the Gotr of the adopter and of the adoptee be the same, the age of the latter also is not restricted; but if it be different, the adoptee should be under five years of age at the time of adoption, Myookh. Mit. Tr. 310. The latter, however, ought to be as

* The rights of obsolete species of sons to inherit to their own father only, and in what proportion, are variously stated in texts cited in C. Dig. 3, 145 and seq. The Pootreshtu ceremony, and the distinction of Nity and Unity adoptions, are not recognized in Poona. *See* Sir T. Strange, 2, 187. The ninth son is called by Mr. Borradaile a son chosen from fancy; and by Mr. Colebrooke, a son made or adopted by the man himself, Mit. Tr. 302.

young as possible, both on account of the supervision of the Sunskars (including the Moonj), as well as the filial and parental relation of the parties. The Poona Sastrees do not, however, recognize the necessity that adoption should precede moonj and marriage;* the passage so interpreting the law is said, by the author of the Myookh, to be an interpolation, Mit. Tr. 310. B. S.

Preference in selection.

XXXVIII. Any brother's son should be the first selected for adoption; should there be none, or should the boy's parents, &c., refuse consent, his place is to be supplied by, 2nd, Any boy of the same Gotr, and descended from a common ancestor within three generations (Sunghit, Sugotr, Supindu); 3rd, Any boy connected with the family by the female line of connections, for whom funeral cakes are offered (Usugotr supindu); such are the mother's brother's son, or the father's sister's son; 4th, Any boy of the same Gotr, descended from a common ancestor within seven generations, within which degree marriage is prohibited (wirood sumbund); these relations are called the Sugotr dushantil; 5th, Any boy of the same Gotr, the genealogy of whose relationship is otherwise unknown (Sugotr-matr); 6th, A boy of a different Gotr, but of the same caste (Purgotr). Such are the sister's son and daughter's son, who are adoptible in default of the preceding, P. C. (Koustoobh and Nirunesindhoo.) A paternal uncle cannot be adopted, being in place of his father. Nor a maternal uncle, for "an elder relation" (without regard to the relative age of the parties) "cannot be adopted." It is inferred that a younger brother may be adopted by an elder brother, because the latter is "in place of a father" (Ramayun), though he is nowhere enjoined to do so, B. S.†

---

* As appears to be the case in Bengal, *see* Sir F. M. 139 and 141 to 146. The adoptee from a different Gotr, after having received the Moonj in his natural Gotr, is called Unity and temporary, Sir T. Strange, 2, 98.

† The order of selection is otherwise stated :—1, Bundhoopootr; 2, Sugotr

XXXIX. An only son, a youngest, or an eldest son, ought not to be given in adoption, Mit. Tr. 310. Except to his uncle or to the widow of the latter, the children of a brother being considered as one family, Munoo, 9, 182. B. S. (Mahabharut, &c.) *See* Sir F. M. 147. **Who are not adoptible.**

XL. It is necessary to obtain the consent to an adoption of the adoptee's father; and of his mother, provided she be resident with her husband, and not insane or otherwise incapable of consenting, Mit. Tr. 309. It is enjoined that notice of an adoption should be given to the relations within the Sugotr Supindu,* and to the Raja, though no provision appears in case of their disapprobation, even in adoptions by widows, B. S. (Myookh. Mit.) **Consent of whom necessary.**

XLI. In the case of the death of an adopted son (and total loss of caste is considered equivalent to death), another may be selected and given in the same manner; but a man, after adopting one boy, cannot adopt another at the desire of a second wife, &c. Only one adopted son can subsist at one time, B. S. (Mit.)† **Successive adoptions.**

XLII. Of the numerous ceremonies enjoined in the *Sastrus*, the following are the most essential:—1. Prutigruhu, the formal giving away of the boy by his parents, and acceptance by the other party, with the form of Julsunkulp, or pouring water on the hands. Presents may or may not be given. 2. Mustukawugrun, the placing the boy in the adopter's lap, **Forms in adoption.**

Supindu ; 3, Usugotr supindu ; 4, Sugotr-matr ; 5, Purgotr, B. S. The passage, it appears from Mit. Tr. 311, is very obscure, and variously read and interpreted.

One opinion of the Poona *Sastrees* quoted in B. 2, 99, agreeably to the Koustoobh, excludes the son of a sister, or of a daughter, or of a mother within the wirood sumbund. (This does not affect *Soodrus*). *See* note on Marriage, para. 6. *See* Sir Fr. M. 149, 154, and Sir T. Strange, 71 and 2, 77.

* The word Nyatee is translated by Colebrooke "Gentile relations." This is in a restricted sense. It is sometimes held to mean "caste." *See* note in B. 2, 450. An ambiguity which is very important.

† This is contrary to the rule in Bengal, Sir T. Strange, 66. But the passages referred to apply to begotten sons only, B. S.

the latter breathing on his head. 3. Hom, fire sacrifice performed by the Poorohit or others. This is said to be unnecessary in adoptions of a brother's or daughter's son (or younger brother, B. S.) which are performed by Wakyudan, or verbal gift, B. 2, 85. Soodrus cannot perform any ceremonies requiring Muntrus from the Veds (Vedokt-kurum). 4. Deepwarna, the revolution of a lamp, a ceremony at Pooja, or worship of the idol. 5. Brahmunbhojun, alms of food, &c., to Brahmuns, B. S. (Koustoobh.) Myookh, ch. on Adoption, B. 2, 85. Such of these ceremonies as require the repetition of Muntrus, as the Mustukawugrun, &c., cannot be performed by a female adopter, personally; she must go through the essential form of taking the adoptee in her lap, and supply funds for Brahmun agency in other respects,* B. S. Mit. Tr. 308. After these ceremonies (Widhan) have been fully performed, an adoption cannot be annulled, B. 1, 78. Pending their performance, another may be chosen, Do. 80. On account of the previous inquiry, few cases can occur of the discovery subsequent to adoption that the boy has not been adopted in the prescribed order, or that his age exceeds the limit, or that he was an only son, or that the consent of the prescribed persons has not been obtained; should such discovery be made, the adoption cannot be annulled after the above ceremonies have been performed, and they are not essential where the adoptee is of the same Gotr. But in case of discovery that the boy, being of another Gotr, was not adopted with those ceremonies, or that he was of another caste, the adoption is null, and the boy is to receive maintenance as a Das or slave. This is, however, an inference only, for nothing has been met with in the Mitakshura respecting nullity of an adoption. Previous inquiry is enjoined as a duty, B. S.

---

* Wachusputee Misra and the Mythil school therefore restrict a woman's power of adopting to during her husband's life.

XLIII. An adopted son is to be considered in all respects as a begotten son. As he is heir to his adoptive father, so he inherits property descended to the latter from his father or brothers. P. C. Mit. *See* Sir F. M. 132, &c. He cannot after being adopted claim the family and estate of his natural father, which follow the funeral oblations; nor is he liable to pay his natural father's debts. *See* Mit. Tr. 318. Only in case of being adopted by his father's brother, the adoptee is enjoined to perform the *Shradd* both for his natural and adoptive fathers, inheriting the property of the former, however, only in default of heirs in order of succession before brothers' sons.* An adopted son is restricted from intermarrying with any girl of either his natural or adoptive families within the prohibited degrees (*See* Marriage, para. 6), and his descendants are under a similar restriction with regard to the former family to the third generation, viz. so long as remembrance may continue of the adoption, B. S. (Koustoobh.) *See* in B. No. 133, a singular case of an adopted son returning into his own family by regeneration a second time performed.

Consequences of a son afterwards born.

XLIV. If, after the adoption of a boy, a son be legally begotten and born in marriage, the latter will inherit three-fourths of the father's property, the former one-fourth, B. S. Mit. Tr. 316. The Koustoobh gives the adoptee one-third or even one-half.† The share should vary according to the personal quality of the individual (Mahabharut), B. S. No exception occurs of Soodrus, B. S.

Adoption by females.

XLV. It is preferable that a wife or widow should adopt

---

* Yadn. C. Dig. 3, 203, restricts this to the case of the Dwyamooshyayun, or son begotten by appointment on a brother's betrothed, called the son to two fathers. This, though not illegal, as the appointment of a wife or widow, is not practised in the present age, Sir T. Strange, 2, 94.

† According to the Dayubhagu, the adoptee takes in this case one-third, being excluded from inheriting property of Supindus, Colebrooke's Tr. 155. Sir F. M. 137, 151.

5 *

a son by the order or sanction of her husband, and if the latter has not been obtained, the sanction of her husband's Supindu relations, or caste (Nyatee) is necessary, B. S. Myookh, B. 2, 451. For a woman, according to Munoo and Yadnyawulkya, is under perpetual guardianship. So a boy may be given in adoption by his mother if her husband be absent, or though present incapable of assenting. *See* Mit. Tr. 307.* If there be two widows, they ought to adopt by mutual consent; otherwise the elder should have the preference in point of right, P. C. B. S. It is inferred that the younger may adopt by order of the elder, not without it, B. S. Although no text has been observed in the Mitakshura declaring the order of the elder widow essential to the validity of an adoption by the younger, P. C. But, as in other cases, the younger widow cannot after the death of the elder, having adopted a son, adopt another to supersede him during his life, B. S. Neither can a widow adopt while under puberty, B. S. In a case mentioned in B. 2, 452, the consent of an adoptive mother-in-law to an adoption by her adopted son's widow was inferred, from her not having expressly prohibited it; here the relation of the parties was similar to that of an elder and younger widow. The eldest son, as in place of his father, should concur with his mother in giving a younger brother in adoption,† B. S. With these limitations, including that mentioned in para. 42, the provisions regarding adoption are the same as regards males or females adopting. In respect to property, a widow after an adoption has only a life interest in it, with the exception of her Streedhun, the adopted son being both manager and

* According to the Gour on Bengal school, the husband's order is absolutely necessary, Mit. Tr. 308. Sir F. M. 155.

† Sir F. M. 223, highly disapproves of an elder brother's right to give a younger in adoption. And even of the right of a mother being a widow, though he states this to be allowed by a commentary on the Mit. 155.

heir. And should they separate, the widow and adoptee take equal shares, Mit. Tr. 285. *See* the case in B. 2, 452, where the adopted son of an adoptive daughter-in-law obtained from his adoptive grandmother one-half the inheritance, the whole having previously been in the possession of the grandmother.

GUARDIANSHIP.

XLVI. In case of a partition not having taken place between the father of a young child and his brothers previously to his decease, the father's brother (Mit. B. S. or by custom P. C., called Pitruwyu) is to take charge of the maintenance and education of the child, and assume the management of the property. Should there have been a partition, the mother or the eldest son, being of age, or, in default, friends or nearest relations, will be guardians; the latter giving notice to the Raja or magistrate, to whom, in the event of the child's having no relations, the charge in the last resort devolves. The same order should be observed in appointing guardians of lunatics, B. S. The charges of the Sunskar ceremonies of minors are to be paid out of the whole estate, where one of a family has died pending community of property, Mit. Tr. 286. In the event of abuse of trust, the Raja would inquire and punish, as he is the ultimate guardian; nothing precise has been found in the Mit. on this point, B. S.

Of children.

Of lunatics, charges of maintenance.

Abuse of trust.

XLVII. The Gooroo and Sishy are bound by the respective ties of teaching and obedience. In the event of either dying without other heirs, the survivor is entitled to his property. No express mention is made in the *Sastrus* of dying gifts or testamentary bequests, in this or other cases, B. S. A pupil is to remain in the house of an artificer for the purpose of

Spiritual guide and pupil.

learning his art for as long a period as may be agreed on, during which he is to receive food and clothing from his master, and deliver to him the produce of his labour, Yadn. C. Dig. 2, 215. Mit. B. S.

SERVICE AND SLAVERY.

Relation of master and servant.

XLVIII. The relation of master and servant, independent of pupils and apprentices, results from their mutual contract, the latter performing specified work in consideration of the master's giving him wages of labour either in money or maintenance, and sometimes a share of the profits accruing from his labour. Servants comprise soldiers, husbandmen, and porters or domestic hired servants. The master is enjoined to maintain and treat his servant kindly according to the performance of the service, and to maintain him during temporary sickness; he is authorized to beat or otherwise punish him in proportion to his fault. A master and servant cannot be witnesses in each other's cause; a master has a right to interfere with another injuring his servant, or attempting to punish him, but he is not answerable for theft or other heinous crime committed by the servant. Neither is the servant responsible for losses of property committed to him, if by internal commotion, robbery, fire, or flood, without his wilful negligence, for which, and for refusing to perform stipulated work, fines are specified, B. S. (Mit.)

Slaves of different kinds.

XLIX. Slaves are of fifteen kinds:—1, Children of a female slave born in the master's house by any father; 2, Purchased with money; 3, Given by another; 4, Hereditary in the family; 5, Maintained originally in the house to preserve their lives from death by famine; 6, Mortgaged by another; 7, Self-mortgaged, the new master being answerable for the debt; 8, Taken in war, the prisoner begging his life from the conqueror; 9, When the party has staked himself as a slave on the issue of a game of chance; 10, Where the party offers himself as a slave; 11, A Sunyasee who has lost caste; 12, Temporary slavery on condition of some act to be performed by the master; 13, Maintained with food and clothing and kreea performed only (Buktdas); 14, On agreement with the master of a female slave on condition of connection with her;* 15, Self-sold, B. S. Mit.

Conditions of servitude and emancipation.

L. Of these the master should maintain and pay the marriage expenses of the 1st, 2nd, 3rd, 4th, and 13th descriptions, being permanent and hereditary slaves, B. S. (Mit.) The conditions of servitude are easy, but such slaves cannot emancipate themselves without the master's consent. Other kinds of slaves may emancipate themselves, or "take leave of their master," on presenting him with the value of what he has expended in food and clothing on their account. The 6th and 7th are emancipated on payment of the debt and interest. The 12th, at the expiration of the period. The 8th, 9th, and 10th may enfranchise themselves by offering substitutes. One enslaved by force and sold by robbers is to be released from slavery, as is a slave who saves his master's life from a tiger or robbers; and in case of the master having a son by his female slave, having no other son at the time, the boy and his mother are to be emancipated, † B. S. (Mit.) Slaves are transferable property on the same tenure, and time is allowed for their examination and trial, as of grain, cattle, &c., Yadn. C. Dig. 2, 3, 10.

* A female slave, married to a male slave, becomes the slave of his master; so a free woman marrying a slave, and a man marrying a female slave, becomes the slave of her owner, B. S.

† The form of emancipation is stated in C. Dig. 2, 248, to be breaking a pitcher, sprinkling on the slave's head water, rice, and flowers, and pronouncing him free three times.

It is inferred they class as movables, but no text has been found on the point, B. S. Slaves are not partible, but after a partition their labour is claimable in turn, and female slaves remain with the party who has hitherto appropriated them, if living, B. S.

Rights of slaves as to property.

LI. A slave is incapable of acquiring property, except by his master's permission; being in this respect on the footing of a son during minority, B. S. (Mit.) But the slave of a *S*oodr succeeds to his property, if he die without relations, (Mit.) The son of a *S*oodr by his slave is to be allotted half a son's share on the father's death, and if there be no daughter's son, he takes the whole, Yadn. C. Dig. 3, 143. The estate of a Brahmun dying in such circumstances, though taken by the Raja, is to be committed to the slave for his maintenance and for charitable expenditure, B. S. (Mit.) A slave is not excluded from giving evidence as such, provided he possess intelligence and is trustworthy, but he cannot be a witness in his master's cause. This is on the general rule of incompetency, B. S.

Rights over the slave's person.

LII. A slave may be punished with greater severity than a son, not extending to capital punishment, and in proportion to the offence committed, B. S. (Mit.) A man of a higher cannot become slave to a lower caste man, (Mit.) Occupations the most revolting are spoken of as performed by a slave, but considered (U*s*oobh) impure even as respects him, (Mit.) The inference is that a slave must perform, at least, all other commands of his master, B. S.

Children of slaves.

LIII. The ownership of slaves is not affected by their marriage; the child of a man's female slave remains his property. The child of a free-woman by a slave-father is lower than a slave, B. S. (Jatiwiwek.) The master may, it is presumed, retain the children of permanent and hereditary slaves on the emancipation of their parents, but the *S*astrus are not explicit on this point, B. S.

LIV. In case of foundlings brought up as slaves, the parents may recover their child at any time on recognizing it, and paying for its maintenance in the meantime, if able and willing to do so, B. S. (Mit.) **Foundling slaves.**

COMMUNITY OF PROPERTY.

LV. There are distinctions in the books between property descended, reacquired, or acquired *de novo*. The first species may have been acquisitions by the father or grandfather, and descended to the possessor by inheritance. This is called Pitrarjit-dhun. The second signifies property possessed by an ancestor, since unjustly seized by another, and afterwards reacquired by the rightful owner. The third comprehends all property acquired by a man, whether by his own unaided exertions, or with the aid of his father, or relations, or of inherited property. Acquisitions by unaided exertions comprehend wealth acquired by knowledge, through friendship, marriage, hospitality (Munoo, 9, 206), or by arms, service, trade, agriculture, or gaming, B. S. **Different kinds of property.**

Property is also distinguished as immovable (Sthir-Drewy) and movable (Chur-Drewy). In the first chapter of the translation of the Mitakshura is considered the abstract question whether property is of a temporal or spiritual nature.

LVI. While a family retains its property in common, the father, son, elder brother, or younger brother (the former being dead, or unoomutees uyogyu, viz. incapable of managing affairs), or other male relation capable, is to be recognized as the manager, such manager (kurta, karbaree) is to be obeyed as a father and consulted on all occasions, enjoying precedence; he is entitled to an equal share of the **Rights of the manager, and alienation of common property.**

descended family property, B. S. (Mit.)* The elder, as manager, is not at liberty to sell, give, or mortgage the family property without the consent of the others, provided they are of age and discretion to give it; and the latter may claim such alienated property on good cause shown after attaining majority. But in a period of distress, any one of the family, the rest being from nonage or absence, &c., incapable of consenting, may dispose of even inherited immovable property, for the sake of the family, and especially for pious purposes, feeding Brahmuns, and almsgiving,† P. C. Mit. Tr. 257. *See* paragraph 77 as to gifts while in community to a son-in-law on his marriage.

Property acquired by one of a family during community.

LVII. Property acquired by one of an undivided family, through his personal unaided exertions, without the aid of, and without detriment to, his family, or the patrimony, may be reserved wholly by the acquirer.‡ Such as what has been gained by science, given by a friend, or at marriage, or hereditary property recovered by the exertions of one, with the acquiescence of the rest (with the exception, that of land recovered, the recoverer, on the authority of a text of Sunkhu, quoted below, is entitled to one-fourth), besides an equal share with the rest after that deduction, Mit. Tr. 286, 268. Wealth acquired by learning, presented to a guest, given by a friend, or received at or on account of marriage, is reserved by the acquirer (Munoo, 9, 206), and is not partible except by the owner's consent, Munoo, C. Dig. p. 339. Immovable ancestral property, recovered by the exertions of one, is to

* The Poona College are doubtful whether the manager is not entitled to a larger share of acquisitions made by the family during his management. Naredu (C. Dig. 3, 69) states, that a son performing the business of the family should be supplied by the rest with food and clothing.

† Sir F. M. states that the purchaser of joint property from one of an undivided family must look to the necessity of selling, and to the proper application of the purchase-money, 8, 26.

‡ Sir F. M. 48.

be shared equally, the acquirer first receiving a fourth, Sunkhu, C. Dig. 3, 365. *See* Dayubhagu. Tr. 118. If any one of the family assisted in the acquisition, by exertions or with money, he is entitled to a (proportionate) share in the acquisition, B. S. (Mit.) An ignorant brother, maintaining the family of a student, shall share the wealth he may acquire by his learning, Mit. Tr. 270. Naredu. C. Dig. 3, 361.* The P. C. state that although a son may reserve a double share of his acquisitions, the rules for unequal distribution in this or other cases are not now recognized, *See* Mit. Tr. 264.

PARTITION.

LVIII. During the father's life, partition between himself and sons is at his option, B. S. But his becoming a devotee, or incurring the loss of caste,† is considered a civil death; and on a father's natural or civil death, the elder son may take his place, or brother in order of guardianship, if the family be undivided, or widow, and the family may continue to enjoy their property and perform their religious rites in common, B. S. (Mit.) A father may make partition when the mother is past child-bearing, when all the daughters have been married, and when he himself desires to withdraw from worldly concerns, Naredu, C. Dig. 3, 48. Mit. Tr. 260. Should his family not agree to live in common, they may separate in a friendly manner, after which the benefit of sacrifices and religious acts will accrue to the

Period of partition.

* On this point of sole right to personal acquisitions numerous texts are cited in C. Dig. 3, 336 to 356. Nusisthu assigns a double share to the acquirer, Do. 109. Katyayun assigns of acquisitions by the son one-half to the father, unless acquired through the patrimony, Dig. 3, 53.

† But a relation losing caste is to receive his share after expiation, although a partition between the others may have taken place in the interval, (Mit.) B. S.

separate performers, Mit. Tr. 377. The sons have a right to demand partition of ancestral property, (Myookh. Mit.) B. S.

Proof of partition.

LIX. A partition is proved to have taken place by written documents, by the evidence of relations, and by the separate performance of religious ceremonies (including the Punchbhag or Punch Muhayudu, viz. the putting aside at meals five morsels for the Wiswudeo or spirits of departed relations, in atonement for unwitting himsa or destruction of life in the five daily operations, B. 1, 213). The worship of the household or family god (Kooldeo), the offerings of food to the gods (Nywedy), and the daily fire sacrifice to the Wiswudeo (Wyswu), are performed separately after partition. The parties also cook their food separately, make separate contracts, and keep separate accounts of income and expenses, P. C. *See* Mit. Tr. 376.*

Separation of one and reunion.

LX. One of several heirs may separate, leaving the rest in community, and a reunion with a father, brother, or paternal uncle may at any time take place, at the option of the parties, P. C. Mit. Tr. 357.†

Reservations on partition.

LXI. The shares of minors and absentees are to be reserved for their benefit, and a posthumous son is to receive his share, partition having been deferred during the widow's pregnancy, Mit. Tr. 283. Previously to a partition between a father and his sons, provision is to be made for aged and diseased persons of the family, infants, pregnant females, guests, and servants, B. S. Also for wives of the father and grandfather, who may not have had male issue, Yadn., C. Dig. 3, 5, 11, 19, and 20. Wives are to have their Streedhun made up to equal a son's share, Mit. Tr.

---

* According to Sir F. M., united families may separate as to board, property, and religious ceremonies, *or* any two of them, 55.

† No case of reunion has been noticed by Sir F. M. *See* p. 108. He considers that a widow, taking property as heiress, has a similar right of separation, and that a mother of one son may take her share on separating from the rest, as in case of partition among the sons generally, 46.

261, 262, and unmarried daughters are to receive in the proportion of one-fourth a son's share, B. S. B. Previously to partition between brothers, provision is to be made for the father's funeral and funeral oblations, for the Sunskar ceremonies of the younger brothers and sisters hitherto unperformed, for bequests of movables, and of immovable property to the alienation of which the brothers have consented, and for the father's debts, at least for those incurred in necessary expenses of the family, P. C. Mit. Tr. 286. The mother and father's wife are entitled each to a son's share, a grandmother to food and clothing, B. S. (Mit.); and, as in other cases (*see* para. 25), they may alienate movables, for subsistence or charitable purposes, without the consent of the male relations. *See* texts cited in C. Dig. 3, 13, 17, 31, 82.*

See paragraph 30.

The share of a sister is to be in proportion to the property and to the brother's shares, viz. one-fourth of the latter, to provide for her marriage expenses, Mit. Tr. 217. Hence she is not entitled to receive it if her marriage have been previously performed.†

---

* Whether the mother takes this property on a life interest, or absolutely (viz. with full power to alienate it without the consent of the next heirs), and whether there is any distinction between immovable, movable, ancestral, and acquired property, are points on which contradictory texts have been cited in Bengal. Sir F. M. seems to recognize no distinction in the two latter cases, and thinks that females generally taking a life interest only, cannot without consent of the next heirs alienate any but a *moderate* part of their property, and that for necessary subsistence, or religious and charitable purposes, 11 to 25, 32. Of course this does not prevent the gift by a widow to her husband's next heir, even of ancestral immovable property, 308. But she cannot settle property on one heir while another may be subsequently born, 318. Sir F. M. thinks that mothers of daughters and childless wives are entitled to maintenance only, 59. Mothers of sons are entitled to share only on a partition between their own sons, or their descendants, not on that between their own sons and other relations, 42. A mother of one son cannot share with him, but she may with his sons as grandmother, 54. Even if a woman's great-grandsons are among the partitioners, she may share provided some one or more of her more immediate descendants are parties to the partition, 31. The Dayubhagu infers that partition among brothers can only take place after the mother's death, or by her consent, Tr. 57.

† Sir F. M. considers the sister to possess a claim rather than a right, 56, 98 to 106.

Between father and sons.

LXII. Of property to be partitioned between a father and his sons, that which is immovable and inherited from the grandfather, as well as that gained by its means, cannot be alienated by the father to one son, or (*à fortiori*) to a stranger by (will, or) deed of gift, without the consent of all the sons,* Mit. Tr. 279. P. C. Nor are the sons justified in consuming ancestral immovable property, although with their father's permission, Mit. Tr. 254. B. S. On a partition the father and sons take equal shares (Sumu,wibhag) of all descended property. The father is at liberty to give to his sons (Wishum,wibhag) unequal shares of movables and acquired property, B. S. The father may reserve to himself one extra share of all property acquired by his own exertions, Mit. Tr. 259; and as respects that property, he may even deprive his son of succession to it, but the son has an indefeasible right to inherit descended property,† P. C. Mit. Tr. 257, 277. A son having a competence from his own occupation may debar himself and descendants from his share, receiving a trifle to prevent future discussion, Munoo,

---

* *See* texts cited in C. Dig. 3, 15, and to 36. The question, according to the law books current in Bengal, seems an exceedingly perplexed one, Sir F. M. 242, 266, 291. It had been decided by the Sudur Deewanee Udalut that a father has the power of unequally distributing among his sons ancestral immovable property, if formally given and possessed, though the act was considered immoral. A contrary decision is quoted in p. 277, but it depended on the construction of a local law. Another in p. 285, unless it turned on the point of no possession having been allowed, is also contrary. And an opinion of Pundits quoted in p. 300 denies the validity of the gift of the whole of such property by a father to a younger son during the life of the elder. The power of a father to distribute ancestral immovable property unequally among his sons, by will, has been recognized in the Calcutta Supreme Court, and its alienation to a stranger would on the same way be held valid, though immoral, 274.

So also the Dayubhagu, which limits to cases of extreme family distress the alienation of immovables, Tr. 30.

Sir F. M. observes, that if possession at the time is essential to the validity of a gift, the right to bequeath property is denied, and the decisions of the two courts in Calcutta are at variance, 296.

† According to the Dayubhagu, the father and sons take equal shares, or the former a double share, of ancestral immovable property, the father being at liberty to distribute all movables and immovable acquired property *ad libitum*,

C. Dig. 3, 67. Mit. Tr. 262, B. No. 133. A son born after partition is entitled to the father's reserved share (sharing it with his reunited brothers, if any), becoming responsible for the father's debts contracted since the partition, Mit. Tr. 281. B. S. Sir F. M. 109. A mother and son may make partition in equal shares, but the former should remain in the usual dependence, residing with her son, Mit. B. S.

LXIII. After the specified reservations, the property of the father is to be divided in equal shares among the sons, or their lineal male representatives to the fourth in descent; or in default of the latter, according to the prescribed order of succession hereafter stated, P. C. Although rules for unequal partition* are to be found in the sacred ordinances, they are not to be followed, because the practice is abhorred by the world, Mit. Tr. 264. But property acquired by one brother, through his personal exertion, without the aid of, and without detriment to, his family or the patrimony, may be wholly reserved by the acquirer. Any one who assisted him ought to receive his proportion, B. S. (Mit.) *See* paragraph 30 on the liability of sons to pay their father's debts. Generally, sharers of property are bound to defray the debts of the late possessor, according to their ability (Mit.

Tr. 27, 29. *See* texts in the third vol. of C. Dig., where rules are given for the father's unequal distribution of his wealth among his sons; he is directed to give a larger share to the eldest son, to a son of great virtue, to one who has a large family, and a less share to a disobedient and vicious son, being guided by a just judgment and not by partiality for a particular wife or child.

The commentators differ as to whether the sons have by birth a vested right in their shares, and consequently whether a father is fineable for a capricious exclusion, Sir F. M. 243. An opinion of Pundits quoted in p. 266 extends the father's optional disposal even to ancestral immovable property. The Hindoo Law in Bengal recognizes a distinction between legal and moral wrong. In the former case the act is null, in the latter (as in a majority of mere injunctions), though incurring a taint of sin, it is valid, and cannot be set aside, Dayubhagu, Tr. 32.

* These rules may be seen in C. Dig. 3; they refer to inequality of shares on account of the caste of the mothers, of the different descriptions of filiation, of the different qualifications of the sons, as primogeniture, prodigality, &c., Mit. Tr. 291. Dayubhagu, Tr. 30.

Myookh), and the payment is demandable from the manager. If a debt remain unpaid from the poverty of a debtor, the creditor ought to believe that he had in a former life unjustly detained property from the debtor, or that it will be repaid in a future transmigration. So treasure-trove is to be considered the payment of a debt due to the finder's ancestor in a former stage of existence, B. S. But the non-payment of debts contracted on account of Sunskar ceremonies entails impurity not expiable by the heir's performance of funeral rites, and the deceased is supposed to remain in Nuruku, B. S. (Mahabharut. Summut-Koomar-Sunhita Pooran.)*

Discovery of concealed effects.

LXIV. Effects concealed at the time of partition and afterwards discovered (as by ordeal of drinking the water with which the ablution of an idol has been performed) are to be divided equally, on the foregoing principles, Mit. Tr. 293. C. Dig. 3, 396. A partition, a marriage, and a gift, are by good men done once for all and irrevocably, Munoo, 9, 47. Punishment is assigned to the agents in a fraudulent partition.

Impartible property.

LXV. Primogeniture confers a customary title to succeed, exclusively of other heirs, to the territories of Rajas and chieftains of particular countries, Munoo, 9, 323 (Bharut, Rughoowans) B. S.

The following species of property are also declared impartible: houses, gardens, water in wells, tanks, &c., pastures, paths, idols, and consecrated places.

Family priests; concubines and slaves; food, water utensils, prepared grain, horses for riding, clothes and ornaments usually worn, professional books or tools the means of livelihood.

---

* In the Calcutta Supreme Court, a representative has been held liable for debts of the predecessor to the amount only of assets which have come into his hand, Sir F. M. 399. Parceners were considered liable before partition for necessary debts jointly and severally contracted; after partition, for the proportion of such debts to the amount of their respective shares.

Such articles are not to be divided, but kept by those who have hitherto appropriated them; or they may be used in turn according to the nature of the thing.* The partition must, on the whole, be equal.

Separate titl by partition.

LXVI. After partition, every separate acquirer of property retains his own acquisitions; and this applies to the case of separation between father and son, as to every other, B. S. But a co-heir should ask the consent of his relations before alienating his partitioned share; for the sake of publicity, not from any deficiency in the power of alienation, P. C. *See* Mit. Tr. 257.

INHERITANCE.

Exclusion from inheritance.

LXVII. The following persons are excluded from inheritance, unless the defect can be removed by medicaments or penance: any one, whether male or female, who is blind, deaf, dumb, unable to walk, leprous, impotent, insane or idiotic, totally out-caste, or (which is equivalent) guilty of Oottumpatuk,† P. C. Mit. Tr. 360. C. Dig. 3, 298 to 332, B. 1, 412. They, with their unmarried daughters and virtuous wives, are entitled to the usual maintenance, Munoo, C. Dig. 3, 318. Yadn., Do. 324, B. 1, 412. Their share is to be given to their sons, if any, except to those of an outcaste born after inexpiable degradation. Yadn., C. Dig. 3, 321, 2. *See* Do. 304, 316. Bodily infirmities are considered as punishments for sin commited in a former life, B. S. C.

* *See* Mit. Tr. 272, Sir F. M. 210, C. Dig. 3, 372 to 385.

† The five greatest offences constituting Oottumpatuk, Mahapatuk, or Utupatuk, are:—1, intention of killing a father or mother; 2, theft of land; 3, theft of gold; 4, incest with the wife of a Gooroo; 5, associating with such offenders, and, to a female, adultery with the aggravations mentioned in paragraph 19, attempting her husband's death, procuring abortion, eating or drinking forbidden things, B. S.

Dig. 3, 314. B. 1, 78; and the Poorans direct that persons with bodily, mental, or moral deficiencies as above described should be deprived of all funeral rites and oblations. *See* C. Dig. 3, 300, 309 to 313. A father has a right to disinherit a son as to property acquired by himself, Mit. II. 16, 1, 5.*

Performance of the deceased's funeral rites.

LXVIII. According to the Nirunesindhoo, in default of sons, the following persons are successively entitled to perform the *S*raddh of a man dying before partition: grandson, great-grandson, adopted son, widow, brother, brother's son, father, mother, sister, sister's son, supindu relations, family priest or preceptor (Mit. VI. 6, 2, 3). *See* B. 1, 17. In an undivided family, the Ekadusee and Supindu ceremonies are to be performed by the eldest son, or in default, by the youngest, on the eleventh and twelfth days after a father's death. The first ten days' ceremonies and the annual *S*raddh, in case of necessity, may be performed by each son separately. The whole expense is a charge on the estate. But in a divided family, each performs ceremonies at his own charge. *See* note on paragraph 6. The right to succeed to the enjoyment of the property is not dependent on the performance of *S*raddh; a stranger deputed to perform them is to receive bhrit-roop, or a reward analogous to wages, P. C. (Mit.) Sin is, however, supposed to be incurred by the heir's non-performance.

Case of absentee.

LXIX. Should no intelligence arrive of the existence of an absentee during twenty-four years (in case he should be under fifty years of age), or twelve years (in case he should be above that age), his relations may consider him dead,

---

* According to some texts quoted in the Digest, a son entering a devotional order, a son the issue of an irregular marriage, a son averse to performing his father's obsequies, or an enemy to his father, or illegally acquiring wealth, is excluded from inheritance; and a prodigal is to receive his share after deducting the amount he has dissipated on other than necessary Sunskars of the family.

perform his funeral rites in effigy, and the periodical oblations, inheriting his property, B. S. (Nirunesindhoo.)

Representation.

LXX. On partition and succession, in case of the death of one son, his sons are entitled to receive his share among them; and this principle of representation applies to lineal male descendants, as far as the great-grandsons, B. S. Mit. C. Dig. Sir F. M. 3.

Inheritance to property of a separate brother.

LXXI. The supreme dignity of Raja is to be held by the eldest son. Other species of property are subject to the rules mentioned in paragraph 65 as impartible, and a separate acquirer of property is entitled to the whole of it, with these exceptions: in case the sons on the father's death choose to separate, and provided the father died subsequent to partition with his father or brothers, his property is to be shared by the sons in equal shares, or by their lineal male representatives to the fourth in descent* (B. S. P. C. Mit. Tr. 331, 2), subject to the provisions of reservation on partition noticed in paragraph 61.

In default. 2. Widow or widows.

LXXII. In default of sons or their lineal male representatives to the fourth in descent, the divided property of the deceased is taken by his widow, or shared by his widows, if more than one, Mit. Tr. 324. Females, however, possess a life-interest only in immovable inherited property, and cannot therefore alienate it without consent of the next male heirs, B. S. Myookh. A text of Munoo referred to in the Mitakshura (Tr. 365) enumerates inherited property among Streedhun, and it might therefore be inferred that although a widow remain under her male relation's guardianship, he or they cannot control her absolutely as to disposing of her property, as if the immovable wealth were entailed to the male heirs; but this interpretation is not recognized, and

* Sir F. M. states that an estate cannot descend to a great-grandson unless there be an intermediate heir living at the period of the death of the last possessor, 3.

6 *

property inherited by females after their death is held to follow the order of succession to property of a separated brother,* and not that of succession to Streedhun.

In default. 3. Daughters.

LXXIII. In default of a widow, the daughter of the deceased takes his property, but for life only. An unmarried daughter is preferred to a married child-bearing daughter, Mit. Tr. 391; the estate therefore devolves on the latter after the former has held it for life (*see* case, B. 1, 91); a widowed daughter is last in order. All the daughters being single, or child-bearing, or widowed, they inherit in equal shares, and on the death of each, such property being held to be Streedhun, would descend to the daughters of the deceased,† and, in default of issue, to her husband, B. S. Mit. II. 11, 31. But it is inferred from the Myookh (held of superior authority on this point) that such property would go to the next heirs as property of a separated brother, viz. on the death of each daughter to her sons, &c., but not to

* The Myookh, which is also followed in Goozerat on this point of law, admits varieties of Streedhun besides those quoted from Munoo in Mit. Tr. 365, but restricts a woman from alienating such property without the next heir's consent. The *Sastrees* in Goozerat do not include property inherited by women among Streedhun, B. S. The Dayubhagu expressly states that a widow's inherited property is shared on her death by her husband's heirs, Tr. 181. The widow may mortgage or sell it, under her relation's guardianship, for subsistence or religious purposes (as her husband's obsequies), 184. Sir F. M., however, states that one widow's share is to go on her death to her daughters, not to other widows, and that a widow inherits whether her husband were of a divided or undivided family, 5, 6. It was decided in the S. C. at Calcutta, amid a variety of opinions, that a widow has a life-interest in all property to which she is heiress, but that she may alienate it to a *moderate* extent without consent of the next heirs, even for other than religious or charitable purposes. It is enjoined, however, that she should in preference give it to her husband's relations, or for the good of his soul, 11 to 25. Sir F. M. is of opinion that the courts should secure the principal of a widow's property for the next heir, giving her for life its annual produce, 74.

The ambiguous answers seem partly to arise from a desire on the part of Brahmun *Sastrees* to relax the strict rules of entail in cases of gifts to their own caste, for the endowment of temples, &c. (Dan-Dhurm).

† The Bengal authorities favour the title of those who would have succeeded had it never vested in such daughter, viz. first of the surviving daughters, and after their death of the daughters' sons equally, C. Dig. 494.

her husband (*see* paragraphs 74, 76); and if immovable, the daughters cannot without their conesnt alienate it.

LXXIV. If the deceased left no daughters, the son or sons, in equal shares, of his daughters are entitled to his property, Mit. Tr. 342. 4. Daughters' sons.

In default of daughters' sons, the mother, or in default of the mother, the father inherits, Mit. Tr. 345. The Myookh and Dayubhagu postpone the mother to the father. So also the P. C. and Sir F. M. 5. Mother. 6. Father.

In default of parents, the brothers of the deceased inherit in equal shares, Mit. Tr. 346. The whole blood is preferred, P. C. Mit. 7. Brothers.

In default of brothers, brothers' sons,. in equal shares, inherit the property of the deceased, P. C. Mit. Tr. 8. Brothers' sons.

The succession next devolves on the Gotruj relations, being Sukoolyus or connected by supindu funeral oblations, whose common ancestor is within seven generations; viz. in succession— 9. Sugotr Supindu relations.

Paternal grandmother: if none,
Paternal grandfather: do.,
Uncles and their sons in succession: do.,
Paternal great-grandmother: do.,
Paternal great-grandfather: do.,
Great-uncles and their issue.

In default of Sukoolyus, the succession devolves on those Gotruj or Gentile relations who are Samonadukas, viz. connected by oblations of water within the fourteenth degree. 10. Sugotr Samonadukas.

In default of these, the Bundhoo, or cognate kindred enumerated in Mit. Tr. 352, inherit. 11. Bundhoo.

In default of all the above, the pupil and fellow-student are heirs; should there be none, the property of a deceased Brahmun should be given to Brahmuns, and that of any other caste to the Raja.* 12. Pupil and fellow-student. 13. Brahmuns; or Raja.

* The above is the order prescribed in the Mitakshura. That in the Myookh

All connected in an equal degree by funeral ceremonies take equally.

Sunyasees. To the property of a Wanuprust or jungle-devotee succeeds his fellow-student. To that of a Sunyasee his virtuous disciple, and to that of a Bruhmachary, his Gooroo, Mit. Tr. 354.

Inheritance to property of an unseparated brother. LXXV. If no partition have taken place between the deceased and his collateral relations, the above order of succession will apply to his acquired property (they not having aided in the acquisition), and ancestral property, &c., will be shared by the collaterals in the same order, but reckoning from the ancestor receiving his share on the last family partition, or the separate acquirer of hitherto unpartitioned property, instead of from the deceased, Mit. Tr. 276.

Streedhun. LXXVI. Streedhun is of six kinds:—1, 2, Gifts to a woman by her father and mother at her marriage; 3, Do. by her brother on her first going to reside with her husband; 4, Do. by her husband on his marrying a second wife; 5, Do. by her maternal uncle after her marriage; 6, Do. by any other person at any period, B. S. (Mit.) According to Munoo, it consists of, 1, What was given before the nuptial fire; 2, In the bridal procession; 3, Out of affection; 4, By a brother; 5, By the mother; 6, By the father, Munoo, 9, 194. Other enumerations are given in Mit. Tr. 365, &c.

---

is in some points different; it interposes the sister between the paternal grandfather and grandmother. In a case mentioned in B. 1, 71, of property inherited by a man from his maternal grandfather, claimed by his paternal uncle's widow, his sister was declared heiress. The principle, however, in this case avowed by the *Sastrees*, seems rather to have been the acquisition of the property through the female or maternal line.

After parents, Sir F. M. gives the following order of succession:—uterine brothers, brothers of the half-blood, sons of uterine brothers, sons of brothers by the half-blood, grandsons of uterine brothers, grandsons of brothers by the half-blood, sisters' sons and their heirs, paternal grandfather, his widow, sons and heirs, &c., 1, 2.

See C. Dig. 3, 459 to 489. Some texts prefer the brothers to the widow, but these refer (as explained in 477) to an undivi led estate.

Property acquired by inheritance, purchase, partition, seizure, or finding, is classed among Streedhun in a text of Munoo, but the interpretation is not recognized. *See* note on paragraph 72. The Myookh excepts from Streedhun property acquired by a woman by Oopadhu (in war, &c.); or given by way of deposit, &c., at any other time than above specified by her husband, father, or brother; or gained by virtuous accomplishments, as drawing, &c. A woman may recover by judicial complaint the value of her Streedhun taken by her husband for any purpose except in time of famine, for necessary purposes of religion, in sickness or in imprisonment, Mit. II. 16, 1, 5. B. 1, 371. But the husband possesses the right of alienating the wife's Streedhun in those cases,* Mit. Tr. 374, although the husband's creditor has no right to seize it, and the wife's power of unlimited alienation is held to extend to movables only, viz. her wearing apparel and ornaments.

Succession to Streedhun.

The succession to Streedhun is different from that to ordinary property. An unmarried girl's Streedhun descends, 1, to her Sodur, *i.e.* her uterine brothers and sisters; 2, to her mother; 3, to her father. And if betrothed, the betrother may on her death retake his presents, paying charges incurred on both sides, Mit. Tr. 374. Sir F. M. 239. A married woman may give away her Streedhun during her life, to her daughters, for religious, charitable, or other purposes; and on her death, after payment of her debts, it descends to her—

1. Daughters, the preference being given to single over married, and to unendowed over endowed, Mit. Tr. 267, 369. In default of daughters, to her

---

* Sir F. M. states that the husband retains for life a controlling power over immovable property given by him to his wife, while movables are absolutely at the wife's disposal from the time of the gift, 4. Other distinctions are mentioned, 9.

2. Grand-daughters, B. S., viz. daughters of daughters, through the mothers. In default, to

3. Daughters' sons, do.

4. Sons, preference being given to the whole blood, do.

5. Grandsons, viz. sons of sons, do.

6. Husband, do.

7. Male relations of the husband, the common ancestor being within seven generations, B. S. Mit. Tr. 368. Streedhun given in the bridal procession goes to the brothers in the first instance, Mit.

A separated wife's or widow's Streedhun is subject to the same order, as far as the fifth in succession, P. C. Mit.*

Limitations on alienating property.

LXXVII. It has been seen that a father, son, or brother in community may without the consent of his next heirs alienate property acquired by himself, if wholly unassisted in the acquisition; and that females have the power of so alienating their Streedhun and inherited property, to the extent of movables. In distress, for the maintenance of the family, or the family not opposing, the whole family property may be given away except a wife or son. But not to the extent of the whole of a man's estate if he have issue living, nor what he has promised to another, Mit. II. 68, 2, 16. In ordinary cases, descended property cannot be alienated by brothers in community without the consent of the next heirs, being capable of contracting; nor can such property, if immovable, be alienated by a father without the consent of his sons or next heirs. The heirs are not bound to surrender such property to a claimant under a bequest, unless their signatures were affixed to the deed (Danputr †), P. C. On

---

* Some commentators assign a different order according to the various kinds of marriage now obsolete, and according to the different species of Streedhun. A more minute specification may be seen in the Mit. Tr. Int. VI., or Sir F. M. 239.

† The Sastrees of Goozerat appear to favour gifts for religious or charitable purposes, *i.e.* to Brahmuns (called Krishnarpun or gifts by Dhurumputr), so far as not to insist on the attestation of heirs, even in case of real property, B.

the alienation of Vritee Sthirdrowy, and members of the family, *see* paragraph 16. In gifts, a movable should be received by the donee with the ceremony of Julsunkulp, or pouring water on the hands. A house should be shown to the donee, and pronounced to be his before witnesses. Enjoyment (Oopubhag) by the donee exclusive of acceptance (Prutigruhu) is not essential, Mit. The latter implies enjoyment of a part of the thing given, though temporary. Gifts to a son-in-law on a daughter's marriage, during community of property, not immovable, are valid, and the movables so given descend to the children by the marriage. But if no Dan-putr has been signed by the relations, their claim on immovable property ceases on the expiration of the Smartkarl or Smurun-wishae, viz. the period to which recollection extends, interpreted to mean three generations, or one hundred years, Mit.

No distinction is recognized in the books between gifts and bequests. Mr. Colebrooke has interpreted the law of gifts in Jimootavuhuna to extend to wills, but the latter is not a Hindoo institution.*

CONTRACTS.

LXXVIII. A person is incapacitated from signing contracts, or witnessing documents, or giving evidence, by old age, by the passions of anger and lust, intoxication, idiotcy, insanity, or minority. Loss of caste and devoteeship are a civil death. Slaves can only contract by their master's per- Capacity to contract.

* The Calcutta Supreme Court recognize the validity of bequests as to property that might be given during the testator's life, viz. all acquired property, and movables descended. A will bequeathing the whole of a man's property to an idol was set aside, and a partition ordered, Sir F. M. 322. More limited bequests, for similar superstitious purposes, and to a large amount, have been frequently allowed, 347, 376. The abstract right to bequeath even ancestral

mission, B. S. The mind of the party must be in a sound and intelligent state, Mit. Sales by a drunken insane man or idiot, or for a base price, or by a dependant, are to be annulled (Myookh), B. 2, 118. In such cases the intent of the party cannot be presumed in favour of the transfer.

Documents. LXXIX. On the same principle, a document, the signature to which has been obtained by force or fraud, or in any way contrary to the intent of the party signing, as by mistake, or for an illegal object, may be annulled on positive proof of the fact. Witnesses to the signature of a party giving a bond, if friends of his or otherwise incompetent, would not be admissible to prove it. So a bribe may be returned although the unlawful act have been performed; otherwise the contract would be void.

Deposits. LXXX. The degree of responsibility of the bailee depends on the degree of benefit resulting to him from the bailment. *See* Sir W. Jones's Treatise. A deposit with a person for safe custody need not be restored in value to the depositor if lost or destroyed during war or internal commotion (Rajkrant), by fire, by robbers, or by the flood of rivers; but should it be proved that the person with whom the property was entrusted took greater care of his own property, he is adjudged to pay the value of the deposit to the owner, without further punishment; interest is only payable on special agreement to that effect. A deposit with hired workmen, or for carriage, will depend on the same principles, interpreted with more strictness in favour of the owner, and generally depending on special agreement. Rules are prescribed for

immovable property was recognized in a decree, 341. A will bequeathing the whole of a man's property to brothers, excluding a childless widow, and another similar will excluding a widow and two daughters, were held valid by the Supreme Court, 360, 361. A widow becoming a suttee was held to have died simultaneously with her husband, and her legacies, therefore, lapsed as part of the testator's estate, 374. A father would not be allowed to prevent his descendants partitioning property unequally bequeathed to them, at their option, 327. *See* also cases in Sir T. Strange's chapter on the Testamentary Power.

contracts affecting the rearing of cattle, the nature of which is partly that of service, and partly of hire.

A person with whom goods are deposited for safe custody may not use or consume them without asking the owner's consent, unless they are from their nature liable to decay (as grain, ghee, &c.) The same permission is held to extend to land given to hold in deposit, as without cultivation it would be injured. A friend receiving property as a deposit for a certain time, with liberty of using it or enjoying its proceeds, is not bound to restore its value if destroyed by internal commotion, fire, flood, or robbers, unless he took greater care of his own property, and unless he has suffered the limited period to expire without giving notice to the owner and obtaining his permission to retain it. He must replace it, if lost by other means than Rajkrant, and if damaged by his fault the amount of the damage will lessen the interest. But if it perish naturally in course of time, another pledge must be given by the debtor. The owner may obtain his property on demand, even before the period fixed on has elapsed.

LXXXI. Pledge is of two kinds; 1, Gopyu, of gold, silver, or other movables for custody; 2, Bhagyu, of land and houses for use. The party receiving the property in pledge is supposed to keep it in his custody, and to enjoy its proceeds or revenues, if susceptible thereof, in discharge of the debt and interest for which it has been pledged. As to loss or damage of a pledge, *vide suprà* on friendly deposits for use. It does not appear that if the borrower be robbed of his money the pawnee should lose the debt, though the contract of pledge is reciprocally advantageous. *See* Macnaghten on Moohumudan Law, p. lxviii. A pledge for custody may be used after the period fixed for its redemption has passed by default of the other party; and a pledge for use may in the same case be sold and the proceeds applied Pledges.

in discharge of the debt. The party enjoying the pledged property is directed to give notice to the owner if it receive injury, and it is to continue in his custody only in the event of the owner then giving permission to that effect. A pledge is alienable strictly on the same tenure. In the event of a house, &c., being mortgaged to two or more persons, the right is with the prior party who entered into possession, not with the prior contractor. It is the fault of the first mortgagee if he have not taken possession implied in all Hindoo pledges. In all civil cases, except mortgage, gift, and sale, the posterior act is of the greater validity; but in pledges, if priority be not ascertained, he has a right (in case of a house) to enjoy its possession who first entered and fastened the door: if several thus entered on possession at once, all must enjoy the property equally. The case is not altered by a deed of sale given by the owner to a new party, prior possession under the tenure agreed on being held to prevail. There is no limit to the right of ownership of property pledged by lapse of time; heirs of the original pledger may always claim it on repayment of the debt and interest. It is not allowed to use a pledge after twice the principal has been realized from its enjoyment, nor, according to Munoo, to receive at the same time a sum for interest greater than the amount of the principal.

Interest on loans.

LXXXII. On loans for consumption, as money, it is prohibited to take from Brahmuns interest on interest, *i.e.* compound interest (Chukr,vriddhee). Twenty per cent. per mensem is the highest limit of interest; and that to be taken from a sea-trader. Four per cent. per mensem may be taken from a *S*oodr. Three per cent. is the maximum to be exacted from a Wy*s*; $1\frac{3}{4}$ per cent. from a Kshutriyu. From a Brahmun 8 annas (wasthwik, just); 12 annas (Sumany, moderate); to $1\frac{1}{4}$ per cent. (Nidan, immoderate). Higher interest is allowed if no pledge or security have been given, if in a period of distress, or if there be any extraordinary risk. Grain and some other articles may be doubled, tripled, &c., on repayment. There are also particular injunctions relative to different countries and seasons, to the nature of the loan, and the thing lent. It is prohibited to take interest from a Gooroo or a friend; or on articles given with the donor's free will. Property lent and refused to be retaken on tender, may be deposited with a third person, and bears no interest afterwards.

LXXXIII. The sons of a security for payment are bound to pay the debt without interest if required, and if the debt be first proved against the principal. The sons of a security for appearance are not bound to produce the person for whom their father was security. Joint securities for payment are answerable severally for the whole sum, unless there have been an agreement to make each answerable for a share. **Sureties.**

LXXXIV. A purchaser is bound to pay interest from a day specified, on taking away the article bought without paying its purchase-money, but paying the seller earnest-money (wisar), on special agreement to that effect. A person agreeing to purchase and afterwards refusing to take the property, is bound to defray the owner's loss on a resale, provided his agreement be proved by his having given earnest, by a written document, or by witnesses; not on the owner's simple word only. A person agreeing to sell afterwards refusing to give the property is in like manner, on similar proof only, bound to make up the other's loss. The earnest is forfeited by the buyer if the fault be on his side (Mit. II. 25, 1, 12), and if on that of the seller, the buyer receives from him double the value of the earnest. It is prohibited to purchase goods of a thief; purchases must be made after giving information to the sirkar, or to three or four traders in the bazaar: goods stolen, and purchased subsequently without such precaution in the street or bazaar **Purchase, barter, or exchange.**

privately, must be restored to the owner on his recognizing them. If within a certain number of days after sale, the period varying for different articles, the seller discover the thing sold to have been of greater value, or the buyer discover a defect in it, the sale may be annulled. Fines are also specified for various frauds.

Debtor and creditor, partnership.

LXXXV. It is at the pleasure of the person who has to repay debts either to give the priority of payment to a mortgagee, or to a prior debtor in point of time, or to pay all his creditors in equal proportions. It is allowed to a creditor to prevent his debtor from eating (Unusun), and from following his accustomed occupation (Karyerodh), but not if the debtor be a Brahmun. On the obligation of heirs to pay debts, *see* paragraphs 30 and 61. Profit and loss among partners are directed to be in proportion to the stock of each, according to agreement, Yadn., C. Dig. 2, 5. One partner is to make good losses incurred by his negligence or in disobedience to the orders of others, and to receive one-tenth of all recovered by him when endangered by Rajkrant, Yadn., C. Dig. 2, 12. A nominee may act for an incapable partner, and in case of the heir being incapable, will succeed.

PRESCRIPTION, &c.

Prescriptior.

LXXXVI. A man, after failing to demand for twenty years (having the power to do so), cannot claim the value of the proceeds of an immovable deposit for custody or gift, from the bailee (B. 2, 373), donor, or their representative, and after Smart-karl (the period beyond which recollection does not extend, viz. 100 years), he loses his ownership in the property. So after ten years he cannot claim the proceeds of a movable, and after twenty years he loses his ownership; in both cases, by neglect to prosecute his own right, the other party obtains prescriptive possession. If the heir of the last proprietor cannot prove his title by documents or witnesses, he cannot displace one who has actually enjoyed the property. But where default of the legal owner has been unavoidable, prescriptive possession will not avail against proof of ownership after any period.

LXXXVII. Should a superior Brahmun find property in a jungle, the Raja is directed to give him the whole; if a Brahmun of mean capacity, he is to receive one-third; any one finding property in his own field has a right to the whole; brothers before partition taking the whole, and the finder being entitled to an extra share on partition. The rightful owner may receive his property on claiming it within three years. There are many other distinctions. *See* Sir F. M. 435. **Treasure trove.**

LXXXVIII. A boundary dispute is to be settled by examination of, 1, Land-marks, as stones, trees, charcoal or rice husks buried in the fields; 2, Witnesses from the neighbourhood; 3, Enjoyment by either party; 4, Kreea or Ordeal. **Boundary disputes.**

EVIDENCE.

LXXXIX. Evidence is of two kinds; 1, Manooshyu, of men, whether written or oral; 2, Dyw, by divine demonstration, viz. the injury accruing to a false speaker after his undergoing the Kreea or ordeal. Of these the oath or ordeal is only to be administered in the absence of proof of the first kind. There are many kinds of oath and ordeal mentioned in the books. *See* Sir F. M. p. 461, &c., Asiatic Res. vol. 1. **Evidence.**

XC. The following persons are held incapable of giving evidence:—one under sixteen years of age; one who has become a devotee, &c.; one whose word is not believed by **Incompetent witnesses.**

any one; one who from extreme old age, as eighty years, has become imbecile in mind, or who has lost his memory; one who gives evidence for money; one who is a friend of the party for whom he gives evidence; an unseparated brother (Mit. Tr. 377), or a relation or dependant of the party; one who from enmity gives his evidence; one who has lost his energies of mind by dissipation and drunkenness, insanity, or disease, &c., &c., the Hindoo law carrying to the extreme the principle of incompetency. *See* Sir F. M. p. 446.

Written and oral evidence.

XCI. There is not a minimum to the number of witnesses. One man of character on one side is to be preferred to many false witnesses on the other. Written documents are to be proved by examination as to the time and place of their alleged execution, and by comparison of the handwriting of witnesses.

Female witnesses.

XCII. Women not dependent on their relations, but on whom their families are dependent, and those of dissolute character, may be summoned as evidence, Mit. In default of other evidence, that of an old man, woman, child, &c., is admissible (Munoo, 8, 70).

For a more detailed exposition of the Hindoo law on these subjects, may be consulted Halhed and Colebrooke, or the concluding chapter of Sir F. Macnaghten's work. They are merely curious as affording evidence of the similarity of law and custom in civil judicial procedure, and the simplicity with which such investigations have immemorially been conducted in this country.

On the subject of contracts, prescription, and evidence, the incidents of which are settled by custom on principles of natural equity, and on which little variation exists in the law of different countries, it has been in general thought sufficient to transcribe the quotations from the Mitakshura examined by the Poona College, without other reference.

II.—CASTES.

II.—CASTES.

The following enumeration has been prepared, partly from the Brahminical books consulted on the subject, and partly from local inquiries. It is to be observed that those castes only which are known to exist in or near Poona come under the latter denomination. The relative order of the whole is settled agreeably to the criteria mentioned in the Preface, to which the reader is referred for further general information.

The Brahmun caste ranks higher than the others in general estimation. It contains, however, a variety of subdivisions, among the individuals of which restrictions exist as to marriage and eating in company, chiefly arising from their relative strictness in diet or other religious observances.

Rank according to the Books.	Do. according to common estimation.
1.	1.

The Punchdrewir sects of Brahmuns consist of the Drewir (with six varieties), Maharashtr,* Undurtylung (eight varieties), Kurnatuk (seven varieties), and Goorjur (eighty-four varieties). The Punchgour sects of the Saruswut, Kankoobj, Gour, Ootkul, and Mythil are chiefly residents in Hindoosthan. The *S*enwee Brahmuns, being confined to three Kurum, or religious duties, and being less strict as to diet, are not invited to the houses of these ten subdivisions.

Individuals of these subdivisions bear the name of some

* The varieties of the Maharashtr Brahmuns are Desust, Kokunust, or Chitpawun, Deorookhee, Madyandin, Kunaw, or Prutumsakhee, Kurare, Ubheer, Mytraynnee, *S*enwee, Tirgool. The Desust consider themselves superior to others. The Kurare are accused of human sacrifices, but are invited by the other sects.

one of the numerous Rishis or ancient saints of the caste, according to their descent. Except among the Kokunust Brahmuns (containing fourteen of these Gotrus or family names), there is no limit, nor are particular Gotrus confined to particular subdivisions. It is prohibited by law to intermarry within the same Gotr.

The *S*astrus distinguish four titles of Brahmuns, according to the different periods of life; 1, the Pupil; 2, the Gruhust or householder; 3, the Wanuprust; and 4, the Sunyasee. The two last, professing religious austerities, are still found in the character of heads of Mu*t*hs. Bhikshook or professional beggars may be Gruhust, and may marry and have children, which the Sunyasees may not. The various ceremonies enjoined to the former in the *S*astrus are more or less observed among the Brahmuns of the present day who engage in worldly occupation. Those prescribed to all Brahmuns are:—

1, 2. Yudn,yejun, or Hom Sacrifice. This is now usually performed at marriages and other occasions by an Ugneehotree Brahmun who has no other occupation.

3, 4. Udhyyun, reading the Veds. The few who read are merely acquainted with the meaning of the original (if at all) through a Teeka or commentary. All Brahmuns, however, reckon themselves as readers of one of the four Veds, and there are priests at places of pilgrimage who by custom are attended by Brahmuns of one Ved only. This distinction, however, appears merely to occasion a difference of ceremonies, and does not affect their intermarriage or eating in company.

5. Dan, giving presents of food, &c., to other Brahmuns; a duty constantly inculcated, especially on occasion of pilgrimage.

6. Prutigruhu, the right to receive alms from all castes.

Ceremonies of general observance are the Pooja to

the household or other god, consisting of ablution, offering of food, and recitation of prayers before the idol, the various ceremonies on account of deceased relations, marriage, and other Sunskars. Almsgiving, receiving guests, building temples, tanks, wells, &c., are duties less extensively performed, depending mainly on the means of the individual.

The son of any Brahmun may choose his profession, whether Sunyasee, Acharyu, Gruhust,* or Bhikshook (Wydik or Loukik), and in general there is no refusal on this account either as to marriage or eating in company.

According to the deities held in peculiar estimation by individuals, Brahmuns are classed as Vishnoobukt or *S*iwbukt, &c. There are various minor ceremonial distinctions between them, and occasionally enmity, and in some parts of the country violent quarrels. Men of learning hold also different opinions as to the nature of the deity, and the human soul—some maintaining the doctrine of Maya or illusion—but in general agreeing in the efficacy of religious abstraction from worldly pleasure to procure after death a spiritual union with the Deity.

In this part of the country there are, besides the *S*enwee, other varieties (Tirgool, Sopare, Sowase, Kast, Ubheer, Deorookhee, Pulsee), with whom the pure Brahmuns of the Maharastr, Kurnatuk, and other subdivisions do not eat publicly, nor with the Goorjur and Hindoosthanees. Gour Brahmuns do not invite the inhabitants of Gya to eat with them, except on the day of *S*raddh, during their pilgrimage to that place.

According to the *S*astrus, the Wanuprust, and still more strictly, Sunyasee, devotes himself to religious abstraction, professing carelessness of pleasure or pain, living on alms of

* Brahmuns engage in every occupation except those of very low castes, as selling spirits, &c.

food, wandering from place to place, bathing often, &c. The practice of such devotion being in high esteem among Brahmuns as well as other castes, there are often to be found wandering mendicants who travel to different places of pilgrimage in the real or pretended hope of obtaining after death freedom from future transmigration and union with the divine spirit. They are attended by Sishy or disciples, the most eminent of whom, either by his Gooroo's bequest or election, succeed to his rank and honours after death.

Brahmun devotees are distinguished by different names; according to the Veds they profess to read, there are, 1, Kooteechuk; 2, Hans; 3, Bhowduk; 4, Purumhans. According to their affected mode of life they are termed Urunyupad (inhabiting the jungle), Purwutupad (do. hill), Asyumpad (do. Mu*t*h), Teerth,pad (do. place of pilgrimage), Bharuteepad, &c.

Of Sunyasees the holders of Mu*t*hs are the most important, as the head Sunyasee, Yutee, or Swamee, exercises jurisdiction over all Brahmuns of particular descriptions throughout large tracts of India, levying, either during personal circuits, or by deputation of disciples and agents, fines often to a large amount on the infringers of caste discipline. These Mu*t*hs are endowed with Jageer villages, Enam lands and other revenues, besides enjoying the oblations of their votaries, part of which are expended in sacrifices to the idol worshipped and in jewels to adorn him, part in alms of food to stranger Brahmuns, and part appropriated by the Swamee and his disciples. The service of the temple is conducted by numerous priests, besides attendants of both sexes on extraordinary festivals.

There are four great Mu*t*hs or Su*n*sthans of Brahmun Swamees called by their names; 1, *S*unkurachary,* whose

---

* This saint is said to have been an Awutar of *S*iw living 1,400 years ago; the intent of the god's incorporation being to preserve the world from the errors

jurisdiction extends particularly over the Smart, Arhattee or Siwbhukt Brahmuns. These wear the longitudinal mark on the forehead. 2, Mudwachary, supreme among the Kurhattee or Wishnoobhukt Brahmuns. These wear the perpendicular mark on the forehead. 3, Ramanoojachary, the disciples of whom call themselves brethren of Rama; 4, Wulubhachary, supreme among the Goojrathee Brahmuns.

Subordinate to these, but exercising jurisdiction over Brahmuns of particular sects or places, are the Dhurm,adhikarees. The Brahmun of this name is a Wuttundar; he has authority to inquire into alleged infractions of caste discipline and custom, prescribe penance, levy fines, and ordain exclusion from caste. When unfit for the office, a hereditary successor is sometimes put aside in favour of one more competent; or Goomashtas may be appointed to perform the duties.

The office of Wywharee Josee is held in some places by a Wuttundar, in others by a Sirkar Goomashta. This Brahmun exercises the priestly office in his own and other castes (where his authority has not been superseded by the caste priests as in the Lingaet, Purbhoo, and Sonar). His duties are thus enumerated: Huwe, worship of deities; Kuwe, Sraddh, and Puksh, ceremonies in honour of ancestors; Wanumuntrun, attendance on invitations to entertainments; Sunskar (especially marriage); Punchung, keeping the calendar and forming astrological calculations of birth, fortune, and propitious times; Dan,dhurm, almsgiving. The Wywharee Josee is entitled to fees of office, and may prescribe fine and penance. In Poona, among the Yejoorved Brahmuns, the Wywharee Josee officiates at funerals; among the Kokunust, Desust, and others, the payment of huks is not

of the Jyns or Materialists. He was afterwards cursed by Suruswutee, and one of his numerous Muths was in consequence established at Neermul, north of Bassein, where he died; another Muth is at Kolapoor, another at Sringaree in the Kurnatuk.

limited to one person—they are generally given to the Koolgooroo.

In Poona, the Wuttun of Dhurmadhikaree is farmed out by the Wywharee Josee, he being professor of both Wuttuns, which are alienable on general rules.

A Bhut exercises duties similar to those of a Wywharee Josee. The term, though strictly applicable to readers of the Veds, is also applied to Bhikshook or mendicant Brahmuns, Pooranecks, or reciters of Poorans, and is often prefixed to the names of individual Wydyus (physicians), Punchungees (professional astrologers), Poojarees in different temples, Gosaens, and others. If a hereditary Wuttundar, he may receive huks in certain villages, or in parts of them; and from all castes, or particular castes or subdivisions of castes, according to local tenure; and may appoint a Goomashta to act for himself. In some places, as on occasion of a resumed Wuttun, the late Government appointed a salaried Goomashta to perform the duties.

Dhurmoopadhyik is a title applied to receivers of huks or fees on account of Dhurm; viz. on occasions of building temples or other charitable appropriations. In a general sense, the term signifies the performance of religious and moral duties according to caste rule. Brahmuns with this title usually live at Kshetrus (or places of pilgrimage), and are Wuttundars. These are termed Teerth,oopadhyik: they also exercise in villages the duties of Wywharee Josee or Dhurmadhikaree.

Oopadhyuha signifies a reader or domestic tutor. A teacher of reading entertained in a family is termed Udyapuk. Brahmuns of this title are occasionally Wuttundars; they are also salaried teachers to their patrons' children, or subsist by begging. When also performing the religious ceremonies of the family, and the worship of the household deity, they are termed Koolgooroo. Oopadhyu and Poorohet Brahmuns, when Wuttundars, appoint Gomashtas who act for them, receiving specified huks, or a fixed salary, and performing selected duties. Their children by marriage succeed to the enjoyment of the Wuttun, sometimes taking the huks in turn, year by year. Some are entitled to huks from particular families, others from particular villages (Gram-oopadhya), others from all castes, &c. Some hold Wurshasuns or Nemnooks from Government.

Kshetr-oopadhyu and Teerth-oopadhyu are temporary and local spiritual guides to visitors at places of pilgrimage, all ceremonies on account of the pilgrim being performed there by him. Individuals of particular caste, Gotr, or name, coming as pilgrims, attach themselves to a particular Teerth,-oopadhya; their names are kept in a book as a memorial, which may be transferred by gift or sale to another Oopadyu possessing the same claims. Occasionally several relations divide the leaves of the book, taking their chance of visitors; or the total proceeds are divided among the relations. Women becoming entitled to such Wuttuns by inheritance may adopt or appoint a Goomashta, as in other cases; and on the commission of a great crime by the holder (as murder of a Brahmun, &c.), the Wuttun may be resumed by Government and a successor appointed.

The title of Ugneehotree is properly applied to a possessor of materials of the Hom sacrifice. All Brahmuns are directed to perform this ceremony, but it is usual to employ an Ugneehotree, who lives on alms and receives fees and presents. He may also be a Wuttundar.

Acharyu is a term implying superiority applied to the Wyshnoo priests or Bhuts; to the south of the Krishn it is used to distinguish Brahmuns performing religious duties from those who follow worldly occupation. Acharee, in the Sunskrit, signifies a domestic Brahmun, entertained as cook.

In a Nuggur Punchaet case (No. 25) a claim was preferred

before a Punch of four Brahmuns to eight Roosums payable to the holder of the office of Oopadhyik Josee of Kopergaon: —1, Juladhikar, on the pilgrim's performing worship and ablution in the river Gunga, and giving alms to Brahmuns; 2, Seladhikar, do. at his place of residence; 3, Gram,adhikar, do. in the village; 4, Koolulekun, dues on calculating nativities of children; 5, Bruhmasunum, do. on performing the Hom sacrifice at marriages; 6, Dund, fines from Brahmuns for infractions of caste discipline; 7, Poorohet, dues on pronouncing prayers during Pooja of the river; 8, Jyotish, on telling lucky and unlucky days for agriculture and all other occupations. Also to the Somwuttee (the right to all rupees, pearls, &c., left by women in their making circuit round the peepul tree on occasion of the new moon falling on a Monday).

It appeared that the villagers had originally determined that every pilgrim should pay his own Josee, disputes to be settled by ordeal of the river. The plaintiff's ancestor subsequently passed ordeal before *S*unkurachary, by laying hands on that holy man's wooden shoes; whereupon defendant's ancestor, who had been supported by a relation (Dewan of the Powar family), and had put his opponent out of caste, lost his cause.

This decision of *S*unkurachary is in the form of a written mandate, and runs thus:—" To my dear disciples in Kopurgaon. After obeisance to Narayun—Radha Ram Bhut Josee having, through ignorance of the *S*astrus, omitted to perform the ceremonies of *S*raddh and Sootuk, on the absconding of his brother's wife (whether she have lost caste or no), and having thereby fallen into disrepute, had supplicated Choudree Widwa*n*s to allow him to perform penance and obtain purification,—who, through avarice, proposed a written grant to himself to Roosums on the Gunga Pooja, thereby acknowledging the superior title of Radha Ram to those roosums.

The said Radha Ram having, in consequence, besought purification at this Muth, I have decided that no penance is necessary for the alleged fault. But as he has, on account of the disrepute into which he fell, omitted his prescribed purifications for three months, let him perform the Kritsur Prayuschit, and feed Brahmuns.

"To the above effect the disciple Barlsastree was sent with a letter to Kopurgaon, Nasik, and Trimbuk; but the said Choudree still refused to eat with the complainant, and used improper language to Barlsastree through covetousness of the Roosums. Wherefore, should the said Choudree come among you, you are to deprive him of his office of Josee. —Dated Margsirsh *S*ood 9, 1185 Fuslee."

The following order was produced by the plaintiff, issued by the Peshwa's Government. "To the Patells of six villages, Kopurgaon, &c.—Madhoo Row Pundit Prudhan. In the year ( ) 1190 Fuslee, &c. In the case of the dispute relative to the office of *Teerth Oopadhy*, in Kopurgaon, between Gunes Bhut Tobre and Govind Bhut Josee, and Janum Bhut Widwans and Bapoo Bhut Choudree, the office was resumed by Government pending inquiry—Suntojee Naik and Ragoo Puthar Khidmutgar are now sent to enforce an order to the Moamlutdar to allow the Punha to be again enjoyed by the first-named parties, and give them no reason to come with complaints in future."

In this cause the defendant's documents were declared by the Punchaet "to have no life in them."

List of Roosums claimed by a Dhurmadhikaree before a Nuggur Punchaet composed of Brahmuns, one being a Government Karkoon (No. 5), one a Sahookar, and three Koolkurnees.

1.—The right of giving cocoanuts and sharing out Dukshuna on the arrival of worshippers at Unkole.

2.—Ashwulan Roogvedeer, the right of serving as Oopadya (including the Pooja of Gunputtee, of Lukshmee at the Deepowlee, of Suruswutee at the Dussera, and the Hootashenee Pooja at the Holee) to any Moamlutdar arriving, being a Roogvedee Brahmun.

3.—The right to receive half the roosums on penance enjoined in the houses of *Soodrus* and Brahmuns.

4.—The right of Vyaspooja in Kartik Magh and Wysak when the Brahmuns parade their Dhurmadhikaree or Josee through the village on horseback.

5.—The right to roosums on placing Gunputtee, and to dues of cocoanuts, &c., on marriages.

6.—Urkeewiwaha, do. on second marriages.

7.—Ushwutwoodyapun, on feeding Brahmuns and distributing Dukshuna at the time of throwing the wood of the peepul tree.

8.—Prasadwastoo, on feeding Brahmuns at the time of building a temple.

9.—Wapeevoodyapun, do. do. a step-well.

10.—The right of being Oopadya to his superiors (Dhunee) among the blacks and whites (Ryuts and Mohturifu), and of taking all roosums on ceremonies in their houses except that of Gruhaputr or casting nativities.

11.—The right to make the Sreemuntpooja at marriages.

12.—Do. the Sumeepooja at the Dussera (worship of the Sumee tree).

13.—Do. the Ushtadhikar from *Soodrus*.

Poonayawachun, ceremony of pouring cold water on Mango leaves at marriage, Moonj, &c.

Seewapusuntoo, do. of libation in the god's name—Ubhishek, ablution of the god.

Nundesraddh, presentation of the household god after marriage.

Hom, sacrifice to fire.

Bhojun, feeding Brahmuns.

Ritwij, pronouncing Muntrus during the Hom.

Sumbhawun, precedence in receiving Dukshuna.

14.—Do. to roosums on digging a draw-well.

15.—Do. at Oodyapun (Gunputteepooja) and feeding Brahmuns on building a well.

16.—Do. to roosums as Oopadya to all sects of Brahmuns.

17.—Do. do. on building a Dhurmsala.

18.—Do. do. on building a Sumadhee or tomb on the decease of a Sunyasee.

CASTES WHO IN ESTIMATION RANK BETWEEN BRAHMUNS AND KOONBEES.

(Rank according to the Books. | Rank according to general estimation.)

The following castes are mentioned in the Books, but are not known to exist in this country :—

Moordawusikt, descended from a Brahmun father and a Kshutriy mother. To be estimated higher than Kshutriyus. Duties: to read the Uthurwun Ved, and conduct the Senaputtee (military department) of the Raja, and to rear elephants and horses. 2 —

Kshutriy, allowed the three Kurumus of Yejun, Udyyun, Dan. Duties (Dhun-oowidya): archery or the art of war, and (Prujapalun) the art of beneficent government. 3 —

The Brahmuns assert that Purseram destroyed the whole of the Kshutriyus.

The Purbhoos having claim to descent from Chundrusene Raja, maintain their right to the name and Kurum of the caste through a son born of his widow after Purseram destroyed him and the other Kshutriyus.

The Rajpoots, Maratha chiefs of the Sattara or Bhonsle and Kolapoor families, also the Patunkur, Ghorpure, Gharge, Sirke, and other houses lay claim to the title of Kshutriy,

Rank according to the Books. | Rank according to general estimation.

and wear the Jenwa. But they are considered *Soodrus* by the Brahmuns.

Wy*s*, called in the Books Umbu*s*t; superior to the Wy*s*,
4 — but their religious customs the same. Duties: archery, holding the flag, surgery, and medicine.

All castes now follow the profession of Wydy or physician.

5 — Wy*s*: rather inferior to the Kshutriy,—allowed their three Kurumus. Duties: cultivation of the land, rearing of cows, and trading in general.

There are no pure Wy*s* in this country. Beyond the Toongbuddra there are some castes professing the name, who perform the Moonj, &c.

6 — Josee or Mahishy, descended from a Kshutriy father and Wy*s* mother. Kurum the same as the Wy*s*. Duties: to read the Jyotish and Musical *S*astrus, and gain a livelihood by the sixty-four Kuluha (*see* Parentage).

The Brahmuns now appropriate the knowledge of the Jyotish *S*astru.

7 — Upurambu*s*t, descended from a Brahmun father and Kshutriy mother, by adulterous intercourse. Estimated lower than the Wy*s*. To read a small part of the Uturwun Ved, to learn the duties of a Josee, and serve the Raja.

10 — Sarthee or Soost, from Kshutriy father and Brahmun mother (Pruteelom): lower than the Wy*s*. Duties: to drive chariots drawn by elephants and horses.

This occupation is now followed by all castes except Brahmun.

19 — Sooryaoopa*s*uk (*S.*) Magadh, from a Brahmun father and Pooshp,sekur mother. Duties: to perform Pooja to the sun, &c.

A caste of this name is said to be in Hindoosthan, sellers of embroidered cloth.

The following castes are known to exist at present:—

— 2 Kast.—Their genealogy is not found in the Books; they

	Rank according to the Books.	Rank according to general estimation.
assume the name of Brahmuns, but are not received into their Pungut, nor received any Dukshuna under the Peshwa's Government; nor do they perform in their houses the Ugneehotr ceremonies. Their customs are not different from *S*oodrus, and their touch to Brahmuns equal Spur*s*-dosh.		
Koondugoluk.—Descended from a Brahmun father and mother by adulterous intercourse. Estimated rather above *S*oodrus; in one or two books their Kurum being that of Moordawusikt, in others that of *S*oodrus.	7	—
Of the Goluk caste now existing in Poona the descent is not known, whether from the Brahmun or other caste; some profess astrology, others are Karkoons, Suraffs, &c. Brahmuns consider their Spur*s*-dosh equal to that of a *S*oodr.	—	3
Rundugoluk.—Brahmun father and mother (being a widow). Estimated below Kundugoluk.	8	—
Sonar.—The following genealogy of this caste was given by the Brahmuns in Poona:—(*S.*) Parsuwu—Brahmun father and *S*oodru mother. Estimated superior to *S*oodru: allowed to perform ablution, to wear the Dotee, and manufacture gold and articles of jewellery.	11	—

Of the Sonars now existing, the Kanure, Punchal, and Kokunust Sonars wear the Jenwa, bathe and redress after going abroad, and wear sola or silk Dotee in religious ceremonies; they shave the heads of their widows, who do not remarry by Pat. They trade in gold and jewellery, &c., &c., and many are brokers.	— — —	4 5 6

It appears from a statement communicated by Mr. Wilson that the Sonars, Kayusths, and Vyds of Bengal, and even some Kolees of Orissa, wear the Poita (differing from the Jenwa applied with the ceremony of Moonj in some particulars), and are invested with it by Ved Muntrus. But Brahmuns, receiving the Huks, perform the ceremony.

Rank according to the Books. Rank according to the general estimation.

In Nuggur and Poona the Kanuree, Punchal, and Kokunust Sonars perform the Ved Kurum through Bhuts of their own caste, whereby the prescriptive dues of the Wywharee Josee have fallen off.

The following statement, asserting the descent of the Ruthkar Sonar caste, and their right to the Vedokt Kurum, was communicated by Jugunath *S*unkurset of Bombay. These Ruthkar Sonars deny that they are the Parsuwu of the books above mentioned.

Five different origins are attributed in the several Hindoo law books and the Veds to the Ruthkar Sonars or goldsmiths, from which the Kokunust Dywudnyee Ruthkars are descended.

1.

The *S*iwagum states that from the five mouths of *S*iw were produced five Oop Brahmuns called Panchal, viz. Munoo, Muya, Twasta, Shelpee, and Dywudnyu.

2.

According to the Rudriumul and Skundpooran, Brumaha was the father of Petamaha Munoo, who was the father of Prujaputee. The latter had eight sons, known by the designation of Wusoo. One of these, named Prubhas, had a son with five mouths and ten hands, called Wishwakurma, to whom were born five sons having the same names, occupations, and rights as those above mentioned, viz. Munoo, Muya, Twasta, Shelpee, and Dywudnyu.

3.

Agreeably to the order of Wishwakurma, Brumaha assumed the form of Virat, and from his mouth was produced Swayembhoo Munoo, from whom six Brahmuns and four Oop Brahmuns had their origin. The eldest of the latter, Silpayen, had five sons, the first Munoo, the second Muya, the third Twasta, the fourth Shelpee, and fifth Dywudnyu. These five learned the five Veds from the five who were produced from *S*iw's mouth, and their names, profession, rights, and qualities were the same as those of their teachers. Rank according to the Books. Rank according to the general estimation.

4.

From the deity Fire were produced a man and woman, who were termed Dywudny goldsmiths.

The above four had a pure origin, and were authorized to perform the Vedokt Kurums, and also the six rites called Shudkurm, viz. Yejun, Yajun, Dhuyen, Adhayen, Dan, and Prutigruhu.

5.

The Mahishi or Sunker Ruthkars are of Unoolom origin; and although this origin be not equally pure with the four above stated, still they are entitled to the performance of the Vedokt Kurmu. Their title to these rights is proved in many Hindoo law books; and the Rushi Brahmuns always required their assistance in the solemnization of Yudnyus, or sacrifices.

Rujpoot.—Kshutriy and *S*oodru. Duties: to fight bravely 12 7
in battle, inspire dread, acquire glory, and perform the Kurum of *S*oodrus. At the order of the Raja, to punish criminals and receive maintenance from him.

Many Hindoosthanees are of this caste, and residents in the Nizam's districts in Poona and Indapoor, chiefly soldiers by profession. They refuse to eat with every caste but their own. Some few are traders.

The caste of Yejoorvedee Wajusnee Brahmuns, resident in Bombay, referred to in page 81 as the Pulsee Brahmuns, claim the prescriptive possession of the Ushtadhikaree Wuttun there.

Rank according to the Books. | Rank according to general estimation.

Kayust, or Purbhoo.—Wydychu and Mahishy. To the northward they are termed Kayust, in the Dekhun Purbhoo; allowed the performance of Sunskars, to wear the Sendee, the Jenwa and red-coloured clothes, and to maintain them-
34 8 selves by writing or in the military profession. Three kinds are specified, the Kayust or Purbhoo, Upurkayust, and Purbha, the Kurum of all being the same.

35 — Upurkayust.—Kayust Purbhoo and widow of the same.

Purbha (Dalbhi).—Incestuous intercourse of Kshutriy, twin brother and sister. Estimated below *S*oodrus.

These distinctions are not now known; there are in Poona the Chundruseenee Kayusth Purbhoos, who claim descent from a posthumous son of Chundruseenee Raja, and thence the right of performing the Kshutriy Kurum of Yejún, Udyyun, and Dan. Many practise in consequence among themselves the Vedokt Kurum (ceremonies enjoined by the Veds) as Brahmuns; others eat fish. There are two other sects of the caste, not in Poona, the Putanee* Purbhoo and the Downee Purbhoo: the latter are found in Goa.

The Brahmuns do not allow of the alleged descent of the Chundruseenees from the Kshutriy Raja of that name, and consider the caste below *S*oodrus. Koonbees have been known not to eat with them.

There are in the city of Poona numerous traders known by the names of *Marwarree* and *Goojrathee* Wanee, whose religious tenets vary, some being of the Jyn Dhurm, according to the rules of the Parusnat Muths; others are worshippers of Vishnoo. These are termed Wysnoo Marwarree, Wysnoo Goojrathee, or Kurtewale. The latter worship Krishn according to the rules of Walubhachary, do not re-

* These are the Purbhoos resident in Bombay, Surat, and Cheool, so called from their ancient residence in Puttun, where they are said to have received a *S*rap from Bhroogoo Rishi. They practise the three Kurumu, or Kshutriy Kurum, through claim of descent from the Solar Kings.

marry widows by *Pat*, and in other respects their customs are similar to Brahmuns, and of purity superior to the *Soodru* castes.

The Jyn and Srawuk Wanees have lately built two temples in Poona, which they were not allowed to do under the late Government. Besides Marwarree and Goojrathees, there are some Mahrattas and Kanurese of the Jyn persuasion.

The Jyns, as such, do not rank so high in the list of castes as the Marwarrees and Goojrathees.

The Jyns in Poona possess forty or fifty houses; they stated that their number is small in the Mahratta country compared with that existing in Hindoosthan, Goojrat, or even the Kurnatuk. Besides Marwarrees, other castes, as Ugurwale, Bugurwale, Oswal, &c., consider the Jyns in a light similar to that in which other Hindoos view Brahmuns. The Jyns themselves said they have eighty-four varieties, of which five only are known in Poona, and they refuse to intermarry or eat together. Their names are the Setwal Jyn, Punchun, Dhawul, Chutoor, and Lar Jyn. No other caste is included in theirs, but any Hindoo professing the Jyn Dhurm may become a member of their caste.

The Jyns of the present day have, however, lost much of their authority from omitting their prescribed Dhurm, and betaking themselves to worldly occupation; still, however, obedience is paid to their Gooroo, resident at Latoor in the Nizam's country (Balaghat), named Visalkirtee Swamee, and his mandates. He makes circuits like Brahmun and Lingaet Swamees, levying contributions from his caste, coming to Poona every five or ten years in person, or otherwise sending a Pundit, Wydik, or Oopadya as a legate to collect the money and punish infractions of caste discipline. These fees vary from two or four rupees from every Jyn, &c., according to the ability of the donor.

The titles of rank in caste among the Jyns, also of the Sunskars, are the same as among Brahmuns; they have Gotrus also. They stated that Brahmuns here receive the Huks on Sunskars, which elsewhere they pay to their own priests. The Jyns in Poona generally consult Brahmuns in all disputed questions of law, but they stated that books exist of their own, different from those of the Brahmuns on the Dhurmsastr. Such are the Poonyawachun, Ubhishek, and others, sometimes consulted on occasions of penance enjoined by the Jyn Oopadya.

The Jyns affect to be descended from the sun, and to worship that luminary. They worship also a deity named Parusnat, whose names are twenty-four in number, and whose image is without clothes or ornaments. Hence their Dhurm is styled Digumburee, viz. clothed with the Ushtdik, or points of the compass, *i.e.* naked. They also worship a boy-god, said to have reigned during his youth, whence his image is decorated with ornaments. His name they call Situmburee. All these, they stated, are different names for the same deity. Jutees, or devotees, dress in white, carry a black stick (Krishndund), use earthen pots, do not shave the head, reply Dhurmlabh as a blessing, keep the mouth covered with a cloth to prevent incurring the sin of swallowing minute insects (Ahiwsa), and consider a Mhar's touch pollution.

Jyns are enjoined to fast on the 2nd, 5th, 8th, 11th, and 14th days of every fortnight. Except children and invalids, they neither eat nor drink when the sun is below the horizon. They have a great abhorrence of killing animals; hence they strain water several times through a cloth before drinking it. This they carry to so absurd a length as to pay poor wretches money to lie in a room exposed to the bites of vermin; they also establish a kind of hospital, by general Puttee or subscription among themselves, for blind and maimed men and animals outside a village. Individuals among them are bound not to eat or drink particular things, nor to go in the direction of a particular point of the compass (disa); an obligation which it is said no bribe could tempt them to swerve from.*

Rank according to the Books.	Rank according to the general estimation.

The Jyns in the southern Mahratta country stated that they came originally from near Delhi; they only knew they were of ancient origin, and that seven or eight of the eighty-four varieties of their caste were to be found in the Kurnatuk.

They stated that their supreme Muth is now at Delhi; three subordinate to it being at Mulkher, Bijnuggur, and Hombus. They described the stages of probation necessary to become a Sunyasee, viz. 1, Unoovrut, like the Brahmacharee, professing celibacy; 2, Mahavrut, who never feeds himself; 3, Neervandeeksh, who, if Digumburee, wears no clothes, and begs for subsistence. Swamees called Situmburee wear white clothes; both descriptions are prohibited from marriage, and succession in Muths is continued by disciples, as in Brahmun Sunyasee Muths, among Lingaet Jungums, Gosaees, and Byragees.

They stated that the name of their god is Ahuruntu or Nirakar; and that they profess a Dhurm dusalekshun (ten varieties of duty), among which is the Suptamon, or prohibition from speaking during worship, bathing, eating, and other occupations.

Ugurwale.—This title is assumed by Hindoosthanee traders of the Wysnoo persuasion. Their customs are equally pure with those of the Marwarrees and Goojrathees. — 10

* These answers were obtained from the Jyns in Poona, and bear marks of ignorance of the tenets of their religion. It appears from an account of the Jyns published in the ninth volume of the Asiatic Researches, that they have the distinction of four castes, and of Gurhust and Sunyasee, like the Brahminical Hindoos. Like the Budhists, they reject the Veds and Poorans, reverencing a number (twenty-four) of deified saints, and confess the belief of the eternity of the world. The Jyns also bury their dead.

Rank according to the Books. | Rank according to general estimation.

Johuree.—These are also Hindoosthanees, trading in jewellery. There are about fifty houses of this caste in Poona.

Komtee.—This caste resemble the *S*oodrus in their cus-
— 19 toms: they trade, make necklaces of toolsee, and manu-
— 12 facture snuff.

Bruhmukshutriy.—This caste are chiefly residents in the Nizam's country and Kurnatuk. They take water at a *S*oodru's hands; some of them form Pa*t*, others not; some eat flesh, others not. They wear daily clothes damped and dried (Sola). They practise trade in cotton cloth, as Suraffs, &c.

Note.—The Goojrathee and Marwarree Wanees, Ugurwale, Johuree, Komtee, and Bruhmukshutriy have not been found in the Books.

13 13 Kasar (*S*.) Kansikar.—Workers in the metal kan*s* (compounded of just, zinc; tamba, copper; kuthil, tin; and other metals). Descended from Senapee Kshutriy, of the Kartiwaree family, and a Kshutriy wife. Estimated higher than *S*oodrus in consequence. They worship the goddess Kalee; are manufacturers of copper, brass, and other metal utensils.

Their customs are of superior purity to the *S*oodrus: they wear Sola, &c., but it is not quite certain whether the Kokunee Kasars of Poona are the genuine descendants of the Kasikars of the Books.

20 — Lingaet.—Descended from a Wraty Wy*s* (a Wy*s* who had lost caste from not wearing the Jenwa) and a Wy*s* woman by adulterous intercourse. Their sons were—

Soodunhachary,

Bharoosh,

Wyjimma,

Mytre,

Satwut.

Considered rather superior to *S*oodrus. Directed to sell Chourees, salt, asafœtida, Kumlees, &c., to wear the Ling bound round the neck. One sect only, the Jungum, allowed to perform Pooja; the rest directed to perform Pooja to their Ling, and to officiate as spies and intelligencers in an enemy's country.

There are at present five subdivisions of this caste: Jungum, Punchum Wanee, Bungur-Wance, Tilelee Wanee, and Goolwee Wanee.

Rank according to the Books.	Rank according to the general estimation.
—	14
—	15
—	16
—	17
—	18

Of these the Jungums are the priests and devotees of the order. Like Sunyasees, they profess religious abstraction, worship the God *S*iw, accompanied by the Buswu or bull Nunda, and fasten a Ling round their necks, abandon the *S*indee fashion of their hair, wear reddish-coloured clothes (Bhugwee), and usually reside in Mu*th*s, abstaining from marriage, and keeping up the succession of superiors by electing a disciple to supply his place after death. The successor is in some places appointed by the Swamee previously to his death; in others the appointment of the disciples and caste is subject to the confirmation of the neighbouring Zumeendars and of the Sirkar. Such superior Jungums have authority to levy fines on irregularly binding the Ling, adultery, or other infractions of caste discipline. They also receive fees on second marriages of women. Superior Jungums (Virukt,-swamees) in the Kurnatuk country often possess great property, and make pilgrimages or circuits round the country, receiving alms and exacting fines; their disciples also are employed in collecting huks and writing answers to references in caste disputes. A punchaet of Jungum Swamees (of several Mu*th*s) is not unusual on such occasions.

There are in the Kurnatuk some Mu*th*s of married Jungums. In these the wives and families may reside in the Mu*th*; a son may, during his father's life, be appointed Puttadya, with his consent: if not his son, the consent of the disciples, and sometimes of the *S*ethees, Zumeendars, and Sirkar is necessary to appoint to, or in all cases to deprive of,

Rank according to the Books. | Rank according to the general estimation.

office. In general, however, they remain unmarried, having liberty to visit a selected Kulawantin (dancing girl) named Pyateebuswee. The Aya of a Muth has permission to eat in her house.

The Lingaets in Poona being comparatively few in number, follow, in many respects, the customs of other Hindoo castes. Many of them, however, do not sit apart on occasion of a birth, a death occurring, or oblige their women to do so, pending their monthly purification.

Exclusive of Jungums, the four varieties of the Lingaet caste are chiefly traders and shopkeepers.

It is not uncommon south of the Krishna for Lingaets and others of low caste to devote their sons to serve in the Ayas' Muth, on the success of a vow for the birth of a son, recovery from disease, &c. Occasionally a clever boy is adopted by a Churuntya, and succeeds to his office on his death. Others are married by the Muths, who retain some authority over their families, *D.* Individuals of other castes are also sometimes purified, and adopted as servants or disciples, *D.*

All property of individuals is the property of the Muth of which the Aya is manager, *D. K.*

21 — Koonbee.—Descended from the pure Soodrus of the Books. Directed to serve the three superior castes, and employ themselves in husbandry; allowed to bathe, to wear the dotee, and gold rings; to pronounce the name of Bhugwan in ablution, &c. (Nam,muntru). The other two Muntrus are Ved and Pooran, both appropriated by Brahmuns.

The following Koonbees are distinguished here—

— 19 Marathe Koonbee,

— 20 Koonbee Wanee,

— 21 Kanaree Kamatee,

— 22 Tylung Kamatee,

— 23 Hindoosthanee, { Lodhee Purdesee, Chuppurbund.

Koonbees are chiefly employed in agriculture; some trade (Koonbee Wanee); others serve as sepoys; others as servants to other castes.

Rank according to the Books.	Rank according to general estimation.

Such of them as are High Maratha (as the families of the Sattara Raja, and other houses of pure Maratha descent) do not allow their widows to form Pat. Their children by slave-girls are termed Kum-usul and *S*inda.

The Kamatees of Poona are rice-cleaners and grinders of corn and cutters of sticks; they also sell snuff, and some serve as tent or gun-lascars.

Lodhee Purdesees keep carriage-bullocks, selling *S*ya leaves and grass for Chuppurs, &c. The name of the Chuppurbund bespeaks their occupation.

CASTES EQUAL IN ESTIMATION TO KOONBEES.

Kasar bongar.—Brahmun and Ambust. Estimated in the book equal to *S*oodrus: to worship the goddess Kalee, and manufacture utensils of the metal kans. 30 25

This caste at present sell bangrees, and manufacture pots and utensils of various metals.

Tambut.—Parsuwu and Kshutriy. Equal to *S*oodrus: to make and sell copper utensils. 31 26

The caste still exercise this occupation.

Acharee.—Soot and Wydehu. Equal to *S*oodrus: to cook food for the four castes. 29 —

At present each caste keeps men of its own caste to cook their food; Brahmuns' cooks are called Acharee; *S*oodrus, Randhuna; and Moossulmans, &c., Yewun Baburchee.

Chutrdhur.—Brahmun and Wydehu: to hold the umbrella of the Raja, and fetch water for the four castes. 23 —

This caste is not now known here—Koonbees and other

Rank according to the Books. Rank according to general estimation.

castes carry umbrellas and aftabgeers; and generally each caste has its own water-carriers.

37 27 Burbhoonja and Hulwaee.—Wydehuk and *S*oodru: make
— 28 and sell sweetmeats and confectionary.

These castes are to be found chiefly in the country between the Jumna and Ganges, and at Ayoodya (Oude). The occupation of the first is preparing rice, grain, &c., for confectionary (pohe or chewre). Hulwaees prepare various articles of food and confectionary, with sugar, grain, cocoanuts, milk, spices, &c.

23 29 Bhat Rujpoot or Kuvee, Bhat Koonbee, } Wy*s* and Kshutriy: to recite the praises of Brahmuns and Rajas, and compose songs, to speak various languages, and contrive the amusement of their patrons.

The former name still exists in Hindoosthan, where the caste attend the presence of chieftains, and at marriages and festivals, to tell stories.

Bhat Koonbees are found in the Mahratta country, as attendants of Brahmuns and Mahratta Sirdars, De*s*mookhs and De*s*pan*d*es; some also are cultivators.

33 30 Dharee or Jangur—(*S.*) Wytalik Charun.—Occupation, to sing early in the morning, awaken the raja, the god, and the Brahmuns.

The caste is very numerous in Hindoosthan, where they sing in processions of chiefs, and act as bards.

14 8 Byragee.—These are described in the Books as of five kinds:—

1.—Wraty Brahmun (moonj not performed) and Brahmunee—(*S.*) Bhrijkunt.

15 — 2.—Bhrijkunt and Brahmunee—(*S.*) Awurtuk.

16 — 3.—Awurtuk and Brahmunee—(*S.*) Kuthudan.

17 — 4.—Kuthudan and Brahmunee—(*S.*) Pooshpu*s*chur.

18 — 5.—Brahmun and Magudh—(*S.*) Saswuteek Dewuluk.
Byragees of the four first kinds are directed to sing various

kinds of songs (Purbund, Doha, Uslok, &c.), in honour of Wishnoo and *S*iw; the fifth to perform the gods' pooja and apply gopeechundun, &c., to their foreheads.

At present Byragees under one general appellation perform the Saligram pooja and sing songs in honour of Wishnoo. Some apply teeluk,moodia,tripoond to their foreheads.

They do not exist as a caste by descent. Ramanund and Nimbadity are mentioned as the founders of Byragees, as they now exist, receiving disciples from any of the four principal castes. They do not marry, disciples succeeding to their teacher's station and property, and performing *S*raddh and Sootuk for him as for a father. A successor is chosen by the disciples and Byragees of neighbouring Mu*th*s, by putting on him the necklace of his predecessor, either on the latter dying, or departing on a distant pilgrimage.

Byragees, on being excluded from the privileges of their sect, marry,* and are called *Bhat Byragees.* Some of these trade, others sing songs; their wives exchange earthen pots for old embroidery and gold or silver fringes.

Occasionally Kanojee Brahmuns, Koonbees, and other castes, either from choice, loss of caste, or difficulty of procuring subsistence, take the profession of Byragee. They abandon their families and subsist by begging, especially near sacred rivers; or trade, making profitable pilgrimages round the country.

Brahmuns becoming Byragee do not wear the *S*indee nor jenwa. Byragees put the Gopeechundun mark on their foreheads, or wear a necklace of toolsee wood: they profess the worship of Vishnoo, give as a blessing the word Jysreeram, and consider the touch of a Mhar pollution.

The Ryuts of a village sometimes built a Mu*th* and en-

* It appears, however, there are some female Byragees. *See* Appendix B. on Gosaeens.

Rank according to the Books. | Rank according to the general estimation.

dowed it, with the approbation of the late Government. No instance is known of the sale of a headship of a Muth.

For an account of the Gosaeens, *see* the Appendix.

26 32 Rajgooroo.—They are directed to teach the Rajas' sons the use of weapons.

This caste is very little known: the title is found as an adnam (affix name) among some Koonbees, but not connected with the profession. Such teachers to chieftains may receive this name, or the general one of Wustad.

58 33 Gooruwu.—*S*iw-oopasuk Brahmun and *S*oodr Kulawantin. To be estimated below *S*oodrus. Directed to perform the Pooja of *S*iw, to apply bhusm (ashes of cowdung) and Roodrakshurdhan to their bodies, and to receive offerings of food, grain, &c., brought to the god *S*iw by his worshippers.

On this last account the caste is to be held lower than *S*oodrus.

At present this caste act as Poojarees, receiving the offerings brought to temples of *S*iw, Marotee, or Hunooman, as food for the god. Such offerings are termed Nywedy. The Poojaree or Urchuk is not everywhere a Wuttundar or Goomashta. The ceremony of Ubhishek (ablution) four times a month is usually performed by an Oopadya Brahmun, receiving Wurshasuns, &c., for the duty; others beat drums, &c., in the Ootsaa when Brahmuns are invited and fed, and tales in honour of the god recited; others sell prepared leaves for Brahmuns' dinners.

The Poojarees of Bhyroba are generally Koonbees or Gosaeens. Those of Venkoba, Vitoba (Vishnoo), and Gunputtee, usually Brahmuns only.

34 — Brahmunjaee.—Brahmun and *S*oodru—(*S.*) Daseepootr. To be estimated below *S*oodrus. To serve the other four castes and cultivate the land.

Some of these at present are in service; others trade; others cultivate.

	Rank according to the Books.	Rank according to general estimation.
Neech Sonar—Brahmun and *S*oodru—(*S.*) Nishad parswa. Estimated below *S*oodrus. Directed to kill impure jungle animals and eat them as food; also to make articles of jewellery.		
Dewagun, } These varieties of Sonars eat flesh and manufacture metals, trade, or act as Suraffs.	55	35
Ahir,	—	36
Lar,	—	37
Wys,	—	38

CASTES IN ESTIMATION LOWER THAN KOONBEES.

Goulee.—Brahmun and Maheshy—(*S.*) Ubheer. To subsist by keeping cows and selling the milk, butter, Ghee, &c.

	Rank according to the Books.	Rank according to general estimation.
Ahir Goulee, } Castes of these names exist in this country following the above occupation.	—	40
Kokune Do.	—	41
Lingaet Do.	—	42
Nhawee Kusbekur.—Brahmun and *S*oodru, unmarried—(*S.*) Napit. Equal to *S*oodrus: occupation, to shave the hair from the head to the middle.	24	43
Nhawee Gungateerkur.—Magudh and Oogru—(*S.*) Napit Koontul. At eclipses, &c., of the sun, and on the death of parents, on account of penance or Ugneehotr sacrifice, to shave the hair, moustaches, &c., of pilgrims to sacred places, as Nasik and on the Gunga river.	25	44
Neech-Nhawee.—Napit and Marga—(*S.*) Sakiny and Sasilp. Estimated below *S*oodrus. Directed to shave the hair from all parts of the body and apply the toomree (cupping-horn) and leeches.	73	—

This caste of Nhawees is not found here: it exists in the Kurnatuk country.

The Nhawees of Khandes cut off the hair of camels and buffaloes; they and the Nhawees of Goojrat act as Musals.

Rank according to the Books. | Rank according to general estimation.

Malee.—Mahishy and Nishadparsuwa—(*S.*) Malakar. To subsist by raising vegetables from ground watered by wells.

Malee, } These varieties of the caste are gardeners
50 45 Pahar Malee, } by occupation and sellers of vegetables.

— 46 Jiree Malee, } These varieties exist in the Balaghat
Hulud Malee, } country.

— 47 Phool Malee.—These raise and sell various flowers and fruits.

Note.—This caste ranks lower than *S*oodrus by descent, but their occupation being pure, Koonbees eat with them.

40 48 Paturwut.—Descended from *S*oodru and Wy*s*. Directed to work as stonemasons and artificers in stone.

The caste now existing follow this occupation. There are two varieties, Salkur and Punkur.

32* 49 Sootar.—Mahishy and Kurinee—(*S.*) Rutukar. Directed to build houses and work as carpenters and artificers in wood.

— 50 The caste has here two varieties, Marathe and Purdesee; the latter come from Hindoosthan. Sootars in villages make ploughs for the Ryuts, and perform all other carpenters' work.

53 — Jasood (*S.*) Jadhik.—Directed in the Books to subsist by carrying letters from one place to another.

The occupation is at present followed by Koonbees and other castes, the caste of Jasood not being known here.

49 — Syrundhree.—Office to apply oil and perfumes to the Raja and Brahmuns: females of the caste to wait on ladies of rank.

This caste is not known here. Persons of rank are in general attended by their household slaves, or by servants.

43 — Goorakhee.—*S*oodru and Ka*n*sikar (*S.*) Wuchila. Office, to tend cows and buffaloes at pasture.

---

* According to the Books, the castes numbered from 32 to 66 are below *S*oodrus, but above Lohars, Telees, &c.

Rank according to the Books. | Rank according to the general estimation.

This caste is not known here. Koonbees, &c., are employed in pasturing cattle.

Furash (S.) Syapal.—Office, to prepare the Raja's sleeping couch. 54 —

The caste is not known here. The office in great men's houses is performed by Koonbees, Kamatees, Moossulmans, &c.

Simpee—Soodru and a slave-woman (S.) Sindoluk. Estimated lower than Soodrus; directed to sew clothes and dye cloth, preparing the colours, whether permanent or otherwise. 46 —

Marathe Simpee, } These castes principally get their 51 —
Tylung do. } living as tailors. 52 —

Rungaree do.—These are dyers by occupation. 53 —

Simpee Kapre-wikunare.—Soodru and Patruwut (S.) Wustewikraee. Office, to sew and sell cloth.

These castes at present chiefly sell cloth; others are tailors, dyers, or engage in other trades. 47 54

Soogundhee.—Office, to extract perfumes. 42 —

The caste does not exist here. Perfumers are found of this name among the Goojrathee Wanees and other Hindoos. Moossulman perfumers are called Utars.

Kantaree.—Malakar and Kayust—(S.) Salikh and Garik. Office, to make beads of ivory, crystal, wood, &c. 30 55

Many of this caste are found in Marwar; those in Poona call themselves Brumuk-hutriy, but their customs are not conformable. They make wooden measures, bedsteads, chairs, and also beads, or other articles constructed with the lathe and bow.

Windharee and Muneekar. — Kshutriy and Wys, by adulterous connection—(S.) Muneekar. Estimated below Soodrus. To make beads, to drill pearls, &c., and to polish shells. 38 —

These castes do not exist here. Lar Sonars and Moossulmans use the drill, and polish gems for rings, &c.

Rank according to the Books.	Rank according to general estimation.	
—	56	Douree Gosawee,
—	57	Men Jogee,
—	58	Raoul,

These castes are not mentioned in the Books. They are said to have been originally disciples of three Kanphuttee Gosawees, named Goruksh, Muchindra, and Kaneepha.

Douree Gosawee and Men Jogee castes sing songs in honour of Bhyruwunat, the Kotwal of the gods, and beg alms, beating the Dour. The Raoul caste are manufacturers of Purum (strips of coarse cloth) and Naree (tape).

41 — Koombhar.—Brahmun and Oogra—(*S.*) Koombukar and Awurtuk. Estimated below *Soodrus*; occupation, making earthen utensils.

—	59	Marathe Koombhar,
—	60	Buldee Koombhar,
—	61	Purdesee Koombhar,

These varieties of the Koombhar castes make tiles, pots, bricks, and all kinds of utensils constructed of baked earth.

61 62 *Sekwutee Rajwutee Koombhar.*—Awurtuk and Dhikban (*S.*) Chitikar. Estimated below Koombhars; making earthen images of men and animals.

Some of this caste in Poona follow this occupation; others are potters, plasterers, and builders. (Goundee.)

62 — Goundee (*S.*) Prusadik.—Building temples, houses, &c.

This caste does not exist here. Their occupation is followed by the S. R. Koombhars and others.

45 — *Selka* (*S.*) Chagulik.—Directed to subsist by pasturing sheep.

This caste does not exist here. Some Koonbees have the adnam of *Selka*, but they are cultivators and not shepherds. The latter are of the Dhungur Kartik caste.

63	63	Dhungur Kootekur,
—	64	Dhungur Kartik,

Brijkunt and Chagulik (*S.*) Awrubhur.

To be estimated lower than *Soodrus*. Occupation, to sell sheep's and goats' milk, butter, ghee, and wool; and to make and sell Kumlees.

This occupation is followed by the Dhungurkootekurs.

The latter variety of the caste tend sheep and goats, and sell them.

	Rank according to the Books.	Rank according to general estimation.
Sungur.—*S*oodru and Ubheer. Occupation, to shear sheep, and manufacture Kumlees.	64	65

This caste now follows the above occupation.

Rubaree and Ku*r*hekur.—Chobdar and Awurtuk Byragee—(*S.*) Mahagooroo Ooshtrupal. To sell camels and their milk.	56	66

Wuttundars of this caste exist in several villages in the Gungturee, but are cultivators. In Marwar, the caste are camel-sellers. In this part of the country Marathas, or Moossulmans, called Sarwan, trade in camels.

Gondhulee.—(*S.*) Sooseel and Koo*s*eel. Occupation, to sing and dance, living a wandering life.	59	67

The caste here sing and dance at Gondhul festivals in the houses of Brahmuns, Koonbees, &c. Half of the fees on the festivals have in Poona been for many years held in mortgage by a Sahookar on account of his advancing a sum of money to the Sirkar on the settlement of a dispute between this caste and the Douree Gosawees on their relative right of precedence. Some wander about the country as dancers, tumblers, &c.; some subsist by begging.

Wasoodeo,	Descended from Wydehu and Patruwut (*S.*) Mytreya. To be estimated below Koonbees. Occupation, to wander about the streets early in the morning, to awaken the inhabitants.	60	68
Dhukot,		—	69
Surwudee Josee and Balsuntoshee,		—	70
Dakotee Josee,		—	71

The Wasoodeo caste are known here by wearing a peacock's feather cap. They go round begging early in the morning, striking the tal (two metal cups) and munjeree. These beggars are called Dhukot in Hindoosthan.

The Surwude Josee, Balsuntoshee, and Dakotee Josee study a Maratha *S*astru, or treatise on seasons and fortune-telling, composed by Suhudeo Mut. The Balsuntoshee are

Rank according to the Books. | Rank according to general estimation.

beggars; the others get their living by foretelling the weather, telling fortunes, &c.

Koontun.—Wys and Brahmunee—(*S.*) Wydehuk. To be
65 — estimated below *S*oodrus. Occupation, to have charge of the Raja's female apartments, superintending the maintenance of the ladies; also to call dancing girls to the Raja's presence, and attend them with music.

This caste is not found here. The occupation of Sajinda is followed by Gooruwus, *S*oodrus, Moossulmans, and others. Among Moossulmans of rank the practice of keeping eunuchs as guards of the women's apartments prevails.

83 — Utuk, Kuthum, } (*S.*) Bhrookans.—To be estimated far below *S*oodrus. Occupation, to instruct dancing girls.

The occupation is followed by the former caste in the Dekhun, and by the latter in Hindoosthan. In Poona, however, the Utuk caste is not known. Gooruwus, Moossulmans, and others instruct dancing girls in their accomplishments.

82 — Bhaud,
— 72 Bhouroopee, } (*S.*) Wunewu-hureemokul.—To be estimated far below *S*oodrus. Occupation, to sing and dance, to wear disguises of other castes and ranks, also to imitate the voice of animals for the Raja's amusement. A few of the former are in Hindoosthan, but the occupation is chiefly followed by Moossulmans. The Bhouroopees in the Dekhun also tell stories.

84 73 Kulawunt, Kowaltupe, Ganeharo, } Nut and Mahishy—(*S.*) Kalawunt.—Occupation, to sing and dance before the Raja for his amusement.

These castes occasionally come here from Hindoosthan. Some Hindoos of all kinds follow the occupation, but chiefly Moossulmans; and the name is no longer that of a caste but of a profession. The Kulawunt of Poona have five varieties—Patra, Ramjunee, Gheckuree, Rungunlee, Kunchun. They intermarry and eat in company,

(Rank according to the Books. — Rank according to general estimation.)

and follow the same profession of dancing, singing, and prostitution.

Ungamurdunee.—Mul and Kshutriy (*S.*) Selinda. Occupation, to rub the limbs and anoint the person with oil. 44 74

This caste is little known. Some persons of rank keep servants for the purpose.

Kachee Boondele, } *S*oodru and Oogruhe (*S.*) Mungulik. 52 75
Kachee Nurwure, } —Below *S*oodrus. Occupation, to sell — 76
vegetables and fruits. The caste here follow the same occupation.

Mewafurosh.—Brahmun and Kulawunt—(*S.*) Phul-wikraee. 51 77
Sellers of fruits.

This caste is found chiefly in large towns, where fruits are in demand. In smaller places Moossulman Baghwans supply their place.

Khutree.—Not found in the Books. Their occupation is — 78
cleaning and dyeing silk, manufacturing Pitumbur and other varieties of silks.

Sarlee.—Awurtuk and Wen *S*ambur. To be estimated 74 —
below *S*oodrus. Occupation, to weave white cloth.

Marathe Sarlee, } These two varieties of weavers exist here; they chiefly manufacture cloth without any dye. — 79
Tylung do. } — 80

Koshtee.—Awurtuk and Kookoot (*S.*) Kooruwind. Occupation, to manufacture silk and silk threads for necklaces and jewellery (Putwegar) and horse and Palkee furniture. 75 81

This caste manufacture undyed cloths and silks, *S*arees, &c. The occupation (as well as that of Putwegar) is also followed by Jungums, and especially by Moossulmans; the latter are termed Momin.

(*S.*) Salmul.—Brahmun and slave-girl. Occupation, to 48 —
prepare and sell Pan-Sooparee.

This occupation is now followed by the *Trigool* caste, said — 82
to have been descended from a Brahmun who brought up his children by wives of lower castes as Brahmuns, contrary to

Rank according to the Books.	Rank according to the general estimation.	
		the *S*astru. They call themselves Brahmuns, but the latter do not invite them to eat in company.
57	—	Chor-rukshuk.—Brahmun and slave-girl—(*S.*) Mungootawuree. Occupation, thief-taking.
		This caste does not exist at present.
27	—	Jethee and Gopal.—Jul and Kshutriy—(*S.*) Mul. Occupation, wrestling in the Raja's presence.
		Many of these are found in the Kurnatuk. Marathas following the occupation are called *Pyhilwan.*
—	83	Tambolee—(*S.*) Nagwulee Wikraee.—To be estimated far below *S*oodrus: to sell pan.
		The caste does not exist here. Moossulmans and Marathas follow the occupation.
—	84	TeleeMarathee,
—	85	Jeshwur,
—	86	Rathor,
—	87	Batree, — Parsuwn and Oogra—(*S.*) Moushkulik. —Occupation, to extract oil and sell it.
		The three latter varieties are natives of Hindoosthan. All follow the same occupation of extracting oil from cocoanut and seeds, and selling oil and oil-cake.
67	88	Lohar-Marathe,
—	89	Do. Boondele, — Kshutriy and Magudh—(*S.*) Oolmookh.—Occupation, to make various utensils and weapons of iron.
		The latter variety of the caste comes from Hindoosthan. They make ploughshares, and iron tools of every kind.
66*	90	Kungur Chobdar—(*S.*) Kohumek.—Occupation, to wait at the Raja's door.
		A few of the caste are found here, following the occupation of Chobdar. They also manufacture chobs.
80	91	Pangool—(*S.*) Putol.—Occupation, begging by wandering about the streets early in the morning, shouting the name of some deity; and by climbing trees and vociferating to the passenger.

* Beyond this No. to No. 119 the castes are considered in the Books below *S*oodrus, but above Chandals.

	Rank according to the Books.	Rank according to the general estimation.
They follow still the same mode of procuring subsistence. They say their customs are the same as those of Koonbees.		
Teergur and Soonat—(*S.*) *S*ekur Nirnumdelik.—Occupation, to fix feathers in arrows, and point them.	68	—
The caste do not exist at present. Moossulmans and others follow the occupation.		
Teer-Kurunar—(*S.*) Ishooka*r*.—Occupation, to fix the steel point on arrows.	69	—
See the remark on the preceding.		
Meet Lonaree—(*S.*) Koumik.—Occupation, to drain salt-marshes and prepare salt.	78	92
This caste is very numerous in the Kurnatuk, where they are called Oopar.		
Choone-Lonaree—(*S.*) Ungoosht.—Occupation, to prepare chunam and sell it.	98	93
The caste at present exist; they are preparers and sellers of chunam and charcoal.		
Bhoee Marathe, Kahar, } Brahmun and Wishad—(*S.*) Poushtik.—Occupation, to carry palkees, dolees, water-skins, &c., and cut and sell wood.	85	94
The latter are Hindoosthanees. Both varieties follow the occupation of porters, palkee-bearers, &c. They do not cut or sell wood at present: they eat fish.		
Kolee, Dheewur, Mul, } (*S.*) Kywust.—Occupation, to live in boats on fords and rivers, and catch fish.	87	96 — —
The latter names of the caste are current in Hindoosthan. The Koolees in the Dekhun in some places bring water to persons of rank arriving in the village, and are sharers in the Bullootee. Those who manage boats are called Nawuree, in the Kurnatuk, Umbigar; they also fill pukals with water, and catch fish.		
Wunjara—(*S.*) Poonsool.—Occupation, to make suleetas for camels, and other articles of coarse hemp (tag.)	86	97

Rank according to the Books. Rank according to the general estimation. This caste in the Dekhun manufacture tag or cultivate. Hindoosthanee Wunjaras trade in grain with bullocks: they are called Lumban. *See* an article in the Bombay Literary Society's Transactions.

88 98 Jeengur—Brahmun and Ayoguwee (*S.*) Dhigban.—Occupation, to manufacture saddles and bridles, and furniture for camels, horses, and elephants.

This caste at present exist as manufacturers and sellers of saddles, Kogeer, Pakra, Surosuree, Genjoree, &c., also sheaths for swords. Some are blacksmiths, others coppersmiths, tinsmiths (Kulegar), &c. In Hindoosthan some also make shoes; others design paintings for walls.

81 99 Bamtya and Oochuke—(*S.*) Dusyoo.—Occupation, to steal privately from the dwelling-house.

Persons of this caste exercise their profession at Jattras, on the banks of rivers, in bazaars, &c.; but the caste, as such, is scarcely recognized. The name is appropriated to pickpockets and thieves in general.

79 100 Kirar—(*S.*) Yawasik.—Occupation, to sell grass and Kurbee, and exercise the Raja's horses.

They at present sell grass and Kurbee. Moossulmans and other castes exercise horses as Chabook-Suwars.

76 — Neech Koshtee (*S.*) Shoushir.—Occupation, to weave silks from the shreds, &c., of prepared silks. They are not now distinguished from Koshtee, Momin, &c.

77 101 Niralee—(*S.*) Nileekar.—Occupation, to dye cloth with indigo.

The caste at present prepare indigo and other dark dyes, and some weave dark-coloured cloths.

72 102 Kuncharee—(*S.*) Kachkar.—Occupation, to manufacture glass and ornaments of that material.

The caste follow this occupation in Sewapoor, also in Khandesh and the Kokun. They require a great quantity of fire-wood in the manufacture.

Rank according to the Books. — Rank according to general estimation.

Burhaee—(*S.*) Kasht patree.—Occupation, manufacturing wooden utensils. Their descent is extremely low.

Burhaees are carpenters who are paid by the job, and are not, like Sootars, kept on wages. 72 103

Beldar—Brahmun Sunyasee and an unshaven widow (*S.*) Dol,kurum—Chandal.—Occupation, digging wells, blasting rocks, working on roads. 97 104

Beldars or pioneers have still the same occupation.

Ghisaree—(*S.*) Dhoosmeer.—Occupation, manufacturing iron spoons and other utensils. 95 105

Ghisarees work in iron, and are a kind of low-caste blacksmiths.

(*S.*) Kurumar.—Occupation, sharpening and polishing weapons: they exercise the same occupation, and are called Sikulgurs. Some Sikulgurs are Moossulmans. 89 106

Gursee—(*S.*) *S*ood-Marguk.—Occupation, beating tom-toms, &c. 91 107

This caste occasionally come to Poona: they are numerous about Punderpoor. In Poona, Gooruwus and Nhawees chiefly follow the occupation.

Busphor—(*S.*) Wysa gayik.—Occupation, attending dancing girls as musicians. 111 108

This caste occasionally come from Hindoosthan, where they are numerous. They beat the Pukwaj in attendance on dancing girls, and play on the Saringee. They also prepare the skin for the Pukwaj (a species of drum).

Wotaree—(*S.*) Ootaruk.—Occupation, manufacturing and selling images of the gods, also pots and toe-rings, composed of the mixed metal called Kans. 90 109

They follow the same occupation.

Kunjaree—(*S.*) Rujookar.—Occupation, making cotton and hemp ropes. 102 110

The men follow this trade. The women tell stories, with the accompaniment of rude music.

Rank according to the Books. Rank according to the general estimation.

Kulal and Bundaree—(*S.*) Sonshkul.—Occupation, preparing spirituous liquors.

The Kulal caste here prepare and sell arrack, &c. The
114* 111 Bundarees reside in the Kokun, and prepare Taree, Maree, and Sindee (spirituous extracts). Moossulmans also follow the occupation.

113 112 Kartik—(*S.*) Soumik.—Occupation, killing sheep and other animals and selling the flesh. This is one of the lowest castes, equal to Mhars, &c. These low castes live outside of villages, and their touch is considered contamination.

The occupation of butcher is followed by Hindoos of this caste, and by Moossulman Kusaees (Qusab).

92 113 Tanksarlee.—*S*oodru and Kshuta-nishad—(*S.*) Krodhuk Kokoot. Occupation, coining metals.

This caste is not very generally known. Sonars melt the metals. All castes are employed in mints.

122 — The Moossulmans and other foreign castes (called Yewun) are inserted in this place by the Brahmun compilers. Their origin, as fabulously told in several books, was from four causes. From the Dyty wife of Kusyup Rishee. From the fifty sons of Wiswumit Rishee who were cursed by him. From the Cow Kamdhenoo given to Wusisht Rishee by Bruhm. From Parsee Moond and Ardh Moond, sons of Sagur Raja, to whom Wusisht Raja presented the Sagur country (including Persia) to the westward. From Kshutriyas and other Hindoos who have from time to time lost caste. [Wishnoo Pooran.]

"During the 4,000 years of the Kuleeyoog, the sects of Yewun have increased to a great number. They reckon several thousand prophets and saints, whose tombs are endowed with spiritual energy (Kuramut) at the present day. The Chinese are a low caste of Yewun, who do not refuse any

---

* Beyond this No. the touch confers Spurs-dosh (impurity requiring ablution).

kind of food," and "The Yewun of Bokhara are accused, like the Portuguese, of making proselytes by force." "They distinguish three kinds of Yewun in Hindoosthan, Parsee, Moossulman, and 'Iswee,' including English, French, Portuguese, &c. These castes refuse no kind of occupation." (Rank according to the Books. — Rank according to the general estimation.)

Nalbund—(*S.*) *S*elik.—Occupation, to shoe horses and bullocks. 96 —

These do not exist as a caste. Moossulmans, Lohars, &c., follow the occupation.

Kootewan—(*S.*) Ansook-Mundulik.—Occupation, to tend the Raja's hunting dogs. 107 —

These do not exist as a caste. Moossulmans, called Durwesee, and other castes, follow the occupation; showmen of tigers, bears, &c., bear the same name.

Wuraree—(*S.*) Golik.—Occupation, rat-killing. 109 114

This caste is found chiefly in the Kurnatuk; they load carts with building-stones, which they sell. They also kill and eat rats and other vermin.

Caste	(*S.*) Sootrudhar.—Occupation, to exhibit dancing dolls, and attend their women (dancers) with music.	Rank according to the Books	Rank according to the general estimation
Kulasootree,		101	115
Khamsootree,		—	116
Chitrguthe,		—	117
Banamuthee,		—	118

Kulasootrees at present exhibit baholees or dancing dolls. Khamsootrees perform evolutions on a rope attached to a wooden post. Chitrguthes draw figures on paper, dance, &c. Banamuthees are conjurers by profession.

These castes also maintain themselves by prostituting their women.

Kolatee, Dombaree, } (*S.*) Nut.—Occupation, tumbling and rope-dancing. 100 119

Kolatees in this part of the country get their living by tumbling, &c. Dombarees are chiefly found in the Kurnatuk.

Jharekuree—(*S.*) Bundooluk.—Occupation, to remelt the 93 120

Rank according to the Books.	Rank according to general estimation.	
		dross of metals left by Sonars, and extract and sell the produce.
		Moossulmans here chiefly exercise the occupation; they are said to possess valuable secrets in the art of extracting and combining metals.
99	121	Oonch-Pureet—(*S.*) Munjoosuk.—Occupation, washing and cleaning clothes of the higher castes of Hindoos.
		They follow the same occupation.
112	122	Neech-Pureet—(*S.*) Chouldha.—Occupation, washing the clothes of the lower castes of Hindoos.
		These washermen are not numerous. Their place is supplied by Moossulmans and others.
103	123	Phanse-Pardhee—*Soodru* and Kshutriy (*S.*) Kshutanishad.—Occupation, to catch birds and smaller wild animals by snares, to inveigle deer, &c., and gather honey.
		This caste follows the occupation. They sell the animals, &c., they procure in the jungles, and are considered of impure life and violent character. They do not live in villages.
104	124	Booroor (*S.*) Kiwsook.—Occupation, making cages and baskets of wicker-work.
		This caste follows the same occupation.
105	125	Kykaree (*S.*) Upurukiwsook.—Occupation, making baskets.
		They at present make various articles for holding grain, &c., of the Tooree tree.
108	126	Garooree (*S.*) Ahitoonduk.—Occupation, exhibiting snakes.
		Moossulmans chiefly exercise this occupation; some practise conjuring (Nuzzurbundee).
106	127	Katkare (*S.*) Kudrod-Paduk.—Occupation, extracting the essence of Delk (galls), excrescences chiefly found on Khyr trees, especially in the Kokun, and preparing Kath or Terra Japonica, which is mixed with chunam, betel, &c.
		They follow the same occupation.
119	128	Lukharee (*S.*) Tuthar.—Occupation, making bangrees of lakh, tin, zinc, or other metals.

	Rank according to the Books.	Rank according to general estimation.

These at present follow the same occupation, making women's ornaments, especially for female Lumbanees.

Donguree Kolee (*S.*) Poolkus.—Occupation, killing jungle animals, and feeding on wild fruits and roots. 121 129

These at present are found in the Western Mawuls and in the Kokun. Some are cultivators, others thieves, others live on the wild animals they kill.

Gond (*S.*) Mynd.—Occupation, the same as the foregoing. 116 130

This caste is very numerous in the Nagpour country, where there are Zumeendars and persons of rank of the caste. Their occupation is the same as that of the *Thakoors* of the Kokun and Western Mawuls, and their caste is probably the same.

(*S.*) Bhil or Bheel.—Occupation, the same as the foregoing, 117 131
but a fiercer race.

This caste inhabits the jungly country, especially about the Satpoora range in Khandesh and the hills of the Gungture; some act as village guards, others pretend to customary dues of black-mail, others plunder travellers going to Jattras, &c. They are expert bowmen.

Ramosee and Bedur (*S.*) Bharoor.—Occupation, to act as 118 132
watchmen in villages; vociferating in order to keep the in- — 133
habitants awake.

Ramosees at present act as village watchmen, and receive their huks of Ballootee. Towards Beejapoor the occupation is followed by Bedurs; in the Kurnatuk by Tulwars; in the Tylung country by Chincheewars.

Holar.—This caste at present are beaters of bagintre, and — 134
beggars by profession.

There are other varieties of wandering mendicants, who are often imperative in their demands. Such are the Nanukshan and Kanputtees. The latter wear large pieces of wood in their ears, and are supposed to possess magical knowledge. Some marry, others adopt disciples.

Rank according to the Books.	Rank according to general estimation.		
110	135	Chambhar, viz. Sultungur,	(S.) Karawar. — Occupation, to make shoes and dye skins, selling articles made of leather.
—	136	Marathe Chambhar,	
—	137	Paradosh Purdesee,	
—	138	Huralbhukt,	
—	139	Dubalee,	
—	140	Woje,	
—	141	Chour,	

The Sultungur caste at present dye sheep's skins and sell them. Paradosh work on tents, routees, &c. The higher Chambhars make shoes. The Huralbhukt dye skins red, and make shoes; they are lower than Sultungur. The three last castes are below the rest in estimation; they make shoes, bridles, pukals, &c., and eat the flesh of bullocks and other animals who have died a natural death. The higher Chambhars will not eat with them.

115	142	Dohor,	(S.) Dorbhur.—Occupation, to dye skins of cows and other animals, and make various articles of the leather.
—	143	Kutaee,	
—	144	Dup,hgar,	

The Dhor caste manufacture pukals, well-buckets (mot), and hand-buckets (dol), and dye leather. Kutaees are cobblers; they also work on tents, and eat animals who died naturally. Dup,hgars make oil bottles, &c., and eat flesh of animals who have died naturally: these are of the lowest caste.

120 145 Hulalkhor (*S.*) Chandal.—Occupation, to officiate in the capacity of nightmen. They also take the clothes of dead persons.

Hindoos and Moossulmans both follow this occupation. Mhars are occasionally called Chandal in Hindoosthan.

123 146 Mhar (*S.*) Swupak.—Occupation, to take outside the village and eat the flesh of dead animals.

124 — Another variety (*S.*) Untyu-wusydong.—Occupation, to receive dues from the family of a person dead, and to sell the wood of funeral piles.

(Rank according to the Books. | Rank according to the general estimation.)

Another (*S.*) Plubuwusteer-Sanee.—Occupation, to carry outside the village and eat the flesh of dead horses and asses. 125 —

Another (*S.*) Kouwyadee.—Occupation, to watch the ashes of funeral piles, and keep the boundaries of villages; also to act as village watchmen. 126 —

Another (*S.*) Hustuk.—Occupation, to catch birds with bird-lime, and sell them. 127 —

Another (*S.*) Kayuk.—Occupation, to clear away the sewers of a village. 128 —

Another (*S.*) Heshuk.—Occupation, to take away the clothes and wood from funeral piles. 129 —

In the houses of Somusee Mhars the goddess Bhadulee is worshipped at present. The Tilwun, Wun, and Aduwun Mhars are found in Hindoosthan near Benares, descendants of the Dong. — 147

Mhars or Dhors exercise all the above occupations, and are distinguished by various names in different places. In the smaller villages one caste of Mhars generally is found. Exclusive of the Dong and Heshuk Mhars, all the others above mentioned are met with. They also bury low-caste men who have no friends to perform the office, act as Begarees, receive huks at marriages, perform village service under the Patell's orders, such as assembling the ryuts, carrying letters, collecting rents, and receiving Bulloota. They also hold enam land (Hudola, Hurkee), officiating as guides and preservers of the village boundaries, besides following all the above occupations mentioned in the Books.

Neech Mhar—(*S.*) Chesh.—Occupation, to act as executioner by the Raja's order, cutting off the limbs of criminals, afterwards carrying about from house to house the severed limbs by way of example, and receiving huks on the occasion. 130 —

This variety is not at present distinguished. The occupation is followed by Mang (*S.*).

Rank according to the Books.	Rank according to general estimation.	
131	148	Mang—(*S.*) Swupuch.—Occupation, to make ropes, &c., of skins. There are at present four or five varieties of Mang, Boonde Oochle, Gaon, Dulalwar, and Kokulwar. They act as village servants, and are entitled to Huks and Bulloota; of the two first varieties some are village watchmen, and others thieves. They are found in the Balaghat country. The two last varieties are of lower estimation than the rest.
132	—	Neech-Mang—(*S.*) Matung.—Occupation, to conjure evil spirits from the bodies of possessed persons. Garooree Mang, in the Mahratta country. Potraj and Dankun, in the Tylung and Konkun. The women of the Dankun Mangs sing or beg; they place the Kookoon mark on their foreheads.
133	—	Adum-Khor—(*S.*) Teka and Much.—Occupation, eating human flesh, and trafficking in slaves. This caste is not known to exist here at present. They are said to be found in the countries of Pegoo, Bokhara, and Sumurkund.

I.

On Existing Law of Usage, and the Establishment of New Rules in the Different Castes.

1.—*Answers from the Castes resident in Poona.*

Fifty-six castes stated that they have no written documents or books to which they refer as authority in points of disputed custom. Ancient usage, as determined by the caste on creditable evidence,* is the general guide. In cases of extraordinary difficulty Brahmuns are called in, who decide according to the written law of the Dhurmsastru.

* Wuttundars of one or more places, Koolgooroos or domestic priests, householders and men of experience.

In disputes among Brahmuns, the assembled caste profess to be guided by the decision of Sastrees. The Konkune and Kanure Sonars, and the Kayusth Prubhoos, have latterly made the same assumption.

The Lingaet* castes obey the orders of their Gooroo, as laid down by an order of Balsastree Nyayudhish in the time of the late Peshwa, and since followed by our Government.

Occasionally† Sadhunputr, or written decisions heretofore made, are referred to as authority for written customs, as well as books.

The castes do not recognize the establishment of new customs.

2.—*Answers from the Zumeendars and Inhabitants of Khandesh assembled at Dhoolia.*

There are no written rules. The Jumayut is guided by the usage of each caste. Before any new rule can be established, the elders of the caste and learned Brahmuns must be consulted.

3.—*Answers from Sattara.*

There are no written rules but the Sastru. Cases unprovided for are determined by an assembly of the caste, whose decision becomes in future a precedent equal to law. Custom has sanctioned many things in opposition to the Sastru.

Of these, many were contemporary with the first establishment of the numerous castes and sects now existing, which probably originated in prohibited intermarriages, or

* Jungum, Lingaet Wanee, Tilelee Wanee, Bungur Wanee, Goolwee Wanee.
† Answers from the Konkune and Kanure Sonars, Koshtee, Sootar, Komtee.

in the refusal of an obstinate minority to submit to penance for infractions of custom. The introduction of new customs is much facilitated under our Government, by the mixture of foreigners with the natives, by the diminished authority of the Brahmuns over other castes, and by the non-interference of the magistrate in the punishment or penance assigned for infractions of caste custom.

Information from Wamun *Sastree Satya* of Poona.

Many customs not warranted by the written law refer to various articles of forbidden diet; others to sexual intercourse; others to religious ceremonies; others to prohibited degrees of relationship in marriage; others to morality, as lying without due cause, concealing from parents property acquired, disobedience to parents, &c.

The chief distinctions observable between the law and existing custom on points of civil jurisdiction, will be gathered from the following abstract.

II.

On the Constitution of Assemblies of Caste for the Decision of Disputed Points of Custom, Punishment of Offenders, Exclusion and Readmission.

1.—*Answers from the Castes of Poona.*

All persons capable of managing their own affairs, being entitled to caste privileges, and inhabitants of the place, or (in points of importance) of adjacent places, meet to decide on disputed points of customs.

The Mehitra, in castes where there is one, invites the assembly to meet.

[7.] **Malee, Mahrathe, Telee Nhawe, Booroor, Kolee, Chambhar Mhar, Mang, &c.**

The Swamee, in the Lingaet castes, is accustomed, in

cases of doubt, to associate with himself four residents in the neighbourhood as a Punchayet.

It is not the custom to appoint deputies or Wukeels. Occasionally a man sends his son or a Poorohet* to the assembly to speak for him—and the caste, if necessary, appoint a Wukeel to communicate with the Sirkar, or an absentee of great experience in matters of custom.†

Ten castes‡ stated that a large majority is sufficient to decide a question; two, that a seceding (tul) minority is not regarded; § several, that all difference of opinion is terminated by successive meetings of the whole caste.‖

Answers from 1. Wasoodeo Dadajee, Wywharee Josee Oopady Ushtadhikaree of Poona. 2. Ragwacharee, Principal of the College.

Under the Government of the Peshwas the judicial office was exercised by a Nyayudhish, and included Brahminical supremacy in disputes of caste custom. This office was held by Ramsastree, the justice of whose decisions is much respected even at the present day, and at a later period by Barlsastree, Sudaseo Mankeswur, Gokle, and others. The Nyayudhish used to assemble such other Brahmuns who were noted for their knowledge or integrity, and with their concurrence pass decisions; after which, any recusants were punishable by that officer with fine and the usual penance.

At present it is usual in Poona for the Brahmuns to assemble, on the requisition of any Brahmun of repute for his superior knowledge as a Sastree (frequently of late Neelkunt Sastree), at the Toolseebagh, where they pass orders of exclusion from caste privileges, enjoin penance, fine, &c. In a dispute among one sect of Brahmuns, all Brahmuns are admissible; but, to prevent confusion, several of the particular sect usually decide on points affecting their own

* Punchal Sonar do. † Tylung Sarlee.

‡ Gooruwu, Wys Sonar, Malee, M. Telee, Gondhulee, Koombhar, D. Gosavee, Nhawee, Kolee, Mhar, Mang.

§ Ahir Sonar, Kantaree.

‖ Wunjaree, do. many of the replies to these queries were vague and irrelevant.

10

customs, and large assemblies pass decrees affecting the whole caste.

It is not considered necessary that the decision should be exactly according to the letter of the *Sastru*; though a conformity of the written law with the custom of the caste is thought preferable. Under the Nyayudhish unanimity was of no practical consequence: at present those who assemble invite the absentees, whose countenance and support they consider advisable, and on their declining to attend, come to a decision without them. A Wukeel is occasionally sent, but a man of eminent authority is expected to attend himself, or send a written opinion. Should there (as often happens) be a difference of opinion, the majority endeavour, by prescribing penance to the recusants, to render their decision effective; but if the minority can, by persuasion or bribery, assemble another meeting, both parties will proclaim the justice of their own cause, and the dispute remains, in effect, undecided, B. S.

2.—*From Khandesh.*

The castes deliberate in a body, and all persons who have arrived at years of discretion are entitled to vote. Should a deputation be assembled, the deputies are chosen from the elders and men of experience in each caste. No particular majority is necessary.

Absentees are allowed to appoint a person to vote for them.

3.—*From Sattara.*

Women, children, and idiots are excluded. The most respectable persons are appointed as a deputation of the caste. A majority carries a question. Absentees are not considered, unless they are parties concerned.

III.

In whom is Vested the Duty of Assembling and Advising the Caste on such Occasions.

1. In our caste the supremacy is vested in a few men of the caste possessing superior intelligence.

[36.] **Goluk, Komtee, Khutree, Kantaree, Wys, A. Konk. L. D. Kan. Sonar, P. Sootar, Lohar, Kasar, Bh. Wikunar, and Kur. Nhawee G., P. Malee, Bhat Koonbee, Sarlee, Kanure Kamatee, Lodhee Purd., Chupperbund, Burbhonjee, Kirad, B. Koombhar, P. Koombhar, S. R. Koombhar, Dhungur Kootekur, Douree Gosavee, Simpee, A. Simpee, T. Wanee, Koonbee Wanee, Kahar Bhoee, Sungur, Kolee, Kolartee.**

2. In our caste the supremacy is vested in the Mehitra, with men of intelligence, age, and experience, and the caste.

[16.] **Koshtee, Gooruwu, Sootar, Nhawe Kusbekur, Malee, Ty. Sarlee, Konkune Goulee, Dhungur Kartik, Mahrate Telee, Lonaree, Purit, Booroor, Chambhar, Mhar, Dohor, Mang.**

3. Do. in the Choudree, &c., as in (2).

[12.] **Lohar B. Johuree, A. Goulee, Hulwaee Purd. Mewafurosh, Ling, Goulee, J. Telee, B. Telee, R. Telee, Rungaree, Sultungur, Purd. Chambhar.**

4. Do. in the Patell, with men of age and experience in the caste.

[4.] **Kamatee Ty. Surwude Josee, Kahar Bhoee, Kachee Nurwure.**

5. In our caste the supremacy is vested in the Desmookh, Patell, Oopadya, Chougola, with the caste.

[2.] **Patrawut** (2).

6. Do. in the Naik or Naikwaree, with the caste.

[2.] **Mahratte Bhoee, Ramosee.**

7. Do. in the Gooroo and Mutputtee.

[2.] **Jungum, Punchum Wanee.**

10 *

8. Do. in the *Sette*, with several men of intelligence in the caste.

[2.] Punchal Sonar, Bungur Wanee.

9. Do. in those of the caste eminent for learning and extensive knowledge of the *Sastrus*.

[1.] Wywharee Josee.

10. Do. in our Mookhy-Swamee and, subordinate to him, the Punt Oopadye.

[1.] Jyn.

11. Do. in the Patell, Chougola, Thulkuree or Meerasdars, and men of intelligence in the caste.

[1.] Koonbee.

12. In our caste the supremacy is vested in the Pudwulkur, Powar, Chowhan, and Salonka families subsisting in our caste, with the assembled caste.

[1.] Ghisaree.

13. Do. in the Chitnees and Potnees.

[1.] Purbhoo.

14. Do. in the men of intelligence in the caste, with the Patell, Koolkurnee, Chougola, Undil, Mahajun, and the assembled caste.

[1.] Wotaree.

15. Do. in the men of experience in the caste, with the Mehitra, Chougola, Thulkur, and the assembled caste.

[1.] Koombhar.

16. Do. in Gumbeer Row and Prutap Row.

[1.] Wunjaree.

17. Do. in the family of Titha and two managers (Karbarees) under them, and the Gunacharee with the assembled caste.

[1.] Gondhulee

18. In our caste the supremacy is vested in the men of experience, with the Choudree and Kotwal assembled.

[1.] Bhat Byragee.

19. Do. in men of experience in the caste, the Choudree, the Bhugut, and the Sukhee, with the assembled caste.

[1.] Burhaee.

20. Do. in men of experience in the caste, the Surmehitra, Patell, and under them two Peth Mehitre (viz. of the Bhowanee and Mungulwar Peths of Poona, in which the caste reside).

[1.] Hulalkhor.

21. The Patrawut caste never bring complaints about caste before the Sirkar.

[1.] Patrawut.

IV.

On the Rights and Privileges attached to Headships in Different Castes.

1.—*Hereditary Office.*

1. In our caste there is no Mehitra.

[50.] Wywharee Josee, Goluk, Purbhoo, Komtee, Khutree, Kantaree, Wys, A. Konk. L. D. Kan. Sonar, Purd. Sootar, Lohar T. Kasar Bh. W. and Kr. Jyn, Nhawee K., P. Malee, Bhat Koonbee, Sarlee, Kamatee Kan. Buldee, Koombhar, Purd. Koombhar, A. Simpee, Dhungur Kot. Douree Gosavee, Simpee, Jungum, T. Wanee, P. Wanee, Koonbee Wanee, Ghisaree, Kahar Bhoee, Sungur, Kolee, Wunjaree, Kolartee, Kast, Brahmu,kshutree, Ugurwale, Brahmunjaee, Goolwee Wanee, Kacharee, Kykaree, Holar.

2. The Mehitra's office and honours are hereditary, similar to the estate of a Wuttundar; on the occurrence of marriages or other caste business he has the precedence and Man-Pan.

[20.] Koshtee, Gooruwu, Sootar, (2) Patrawut, Nhawee K., Malee, Ty. Sarlee, Konk. Goulee, Koombhar, Dhungur Kartik, Mar, Telee, Lonaree, Purit, Booroor, Chambhar, Dohor, Mhar, Mang, Hulalkhor.

3. The Choudree succeeds as a Wuttundar to his hereditary office; he enjoys Man-Pan and precedence superior to a Wuttundar.

[15.] Lohar B. Johuree, Ahir Goulee, Hulwaee Purd. S. R. Koombhar, Mewafurosh, B. Telee, R. Telee, Rungaree, Purd. Chambhar, Sultungur, Lukheree, Moolamgar.

4. In our caste the Patell and Chougola receive superior Man-Pan to the Wuttundars. [Note. In large towns, the caste has a Patell of its own; in small villages, this answer applies to the village Patell and other village officers.]

[5.] Koonbee, Kamatee, T., Surwudee Josee, Kachee Nurwuree, Kachee Boondele.

5. In our caste the Sette enjoys Man-Pan superior to the Wuttundars: his office is hereditary. [Note. These castes have Settees of their own. The Settees of a village, or of different Peths in a large town, is a Wuttundar established at the period of its first population, enjoying Huks and privileges given or recognized by the Sirkar. Such Settee possesses no authority over particular castes, but is the agent of the traders with the Government Revenue Officers, and as such possesses much influence.]

[2.] Punchal Sonar, Bungur Wanee.

6. In our caste the Naik enjoys Man-Pan and hereditary precedence.

[2.] Marathe Bhoee, Ramosee.

7. In our caste the Patell, Chougola, Undil, Koolkurnee, Mahajun, enjoy a hereditary title to greater Man-Pan than the Wuttundars.

[1.] Wotaree.

8. In our caste the Titha family, the Gunnacharee, and two Karbarees, enjoy do.

[1.] Gondhulee.

9. Among us the Bughut, Sukhee, and Choudree, enjoy

do. [The Bughut are a kind of priests similar to an Oopadhya or Byragee. The Sukhee distribute food at caste assemblies.]

[1.] Burhaee.

10. Among us the Choudree enjoys hereditary Man-Pan superior to the Wuttundars, but his office is forfeitable for ill-conduct and disobedience to the caste, and a successor may be appointed. We have also the Kotwal.

[1.] Bhat Byragee.

Of these Headships, some have valuable Huks, others have trifling dues attached to them. The professors of the former have of course more influence, but whether the caste are advised by their head, or he is called to account by them, mainly depends on the character of the individual for cleverness and experience.

2.—*With whose Consent Alienable.*

1. The office of a Mehitra may be sold or pledged with the consent of relations and the concurrence of the caste.

[20.] Koshtee, Gooruwu, Sotar, 2 Patrawut, Nhawee K., Malee, Ty. Sarlee, Konk. Goulee, Koombhar, Dhungur Kartik, Telee, Lonaree, Purit, Booroor, Chambhar, Dohor, Mhar, Mang, Hulalkhor, Moolamgar (but very unusual).

2. As in (1), substituting Choudree.

[9.] Purd. Lohar, A. Goulee, Hulwaee, S. R. Koombhar, Ling. Goulee, B. Telee, R. Telee, Rungaree, Sultungur.

3. The office of Choudree is not sold or pledged.

[6.] Johuree, Mewafurosh, J. Telee, Purdesee Chambhar, Lukheree, Kykaree.

4. The Wuttun of a village Patell or Chougola cannot be sold or pledged without the consent of the relations interested. The office of Patell of a caste may be alienated by consent of the caste.

[5.] Koonbee, Kamatee Tylung, Surwude Josee, Kachee Nurwuree, Kachee Boondelee.

5. As in (1), substituting *Settee.*

[2.] B. Wanee, P. Sonar.

6. The Naik has no right to alienate his office.

[2.] Mar. Bhoee, Ramosee.

7. With us the Mehitra is not a Wuttundar, and consequently has not power to sell or pledge his office to another.

[2.] Simpee, Kahar Bhoee.

8. As in (1), substituting five Mankurees.

[1.] Wotaree.

9. As in (1), Gunacharee, and (2), Karbarees.

[1.] Gondhulee.

10. The Choudree may alienate his office with the consent of his relations.

[1.] Burhaee.

11. Our caste has in Poona a nominal *Settee*, who is not a Wuttundar; we possess in the Konkun Wuttuns of Desmookh *Settee*, &c.: the sharers cannot alienate a part or the whole without the concurrence of all.

[1.] Kasar bh. w.

12. Our Kotwal is a Wuttundar; not so the Choudree, who has no power to alienate his office.

[1.] Bhat Byragee.

13. The Singar and others having no profits annexed to their office, its pledge or sale is never heard of.

[1.] Dakote Josee.

3.—*Dues, Precedence, and Exemptions.*

1. The Mehitra holds no land in virtue of his office; he takes Huks at marriages and festivals, and Pan.

[17.] Koshtee, Gooruwu, Malee, Simpee, Koombhar, Dhungur Kartik, Lonaree, Booroor, Dohor, Hulalkhor, Sootar, Patrawut (2), Tylung Sarlee, Konkunee Goulee, Purit.

The Mehitra of the Mang and Chambhar castes receives Bullota.

The Mehitra of the Kahar Bhoee caste receives a larger share of sweetmeats distributed at festivals.

The Mehitra of the Mahratte Telee, besides receiving Huks, is entitled to exemption from the ghurputtee (house-tax), but-chupaee (stamp-tax on weights and measures), and bigar (serving as a begarree), and receives a turban from the Sirkar on the Dussera.

The Mehitra of the Mhar caste is not entitled to a larger share of the Enam land and Bullottee Huks possessed by others of his caste. He receives Man-Pan.

The Mehitra of the Nhawee Kusbekur does not enjoy land in Poona, though he does in some other places. His Huks from Nhawees have been resumed by the Sirkar. He takes Man-Pan at marriages, &c.

2. The Choudree enjoys no Enam or other land, but is entitled to Huks. In the Goulee Lingaet and Ahir castes he is exempted from paying Mhusee (buffalo-tax) and but-chupaee, and he enjoys a Huk of two rupees on a Pat or widow's marriage, and Pan.

[7.] **Lohar, Boondele, Johuree, S. R. Koombhar, Mewafurosh, Rathor Telee, Purd. Chambhar, Sultungur, Batree Telee, Rungaree, Burhaee.**

In the Hulwaee caste, the Mootee (*S*ew or Fuskee) and Zukat are not levied on the Choudree. He enjoys a Huk of two rupees and Pan.

In the Jeshwur Telee caste, the Choudree receives double Huks on marriages, &c.

3. The Patell of these castes enjoys Man-Pan only.

[5.] **Koonbee, Kamatee Tylung, Surwude Josee, Kachee Boondele, and Nurwuree.**

4. The *S*ettee of these castes enjoys no land. On marriages, &c., he receives sandal, Pan, &c.

[2.] **Punchal Sonar, Bungur Wanee.**

5. Do. substituting Naik. (The Ramoosee Naik is entitled to Bulloote from some villages.)

[2.] Mahratte Bhoee, Ramosee.

6. Do. Gunnacharee, &c.

[1.] Gondhulee.

7. Do. Choudree and Kotwal, who receives Pan at marriages, &c.

[1.] Bhat Byragee.

8. Do. Patell, Chougola, &c.

[1.] Wotaree.

9. In Poona the *S*ettee receives nothing: in some villages he is entitled to a cocoanut, sandal, and Pan on marriages, &c.

[1.] Kásar bhande Kurunar.

10. The Choudree enjoys no land; merely Tila and Gund (sandal), Pan Sooparee and La*r*oo, and precedence in receiving these marks of courtesy at festivals.

[2.] Moolamgar, Lukhoree.

11. There is no land enjoyed by Suntojee as head of the caste.

[1.] Rawul Jogee.

Particulars of the Huks and Privileges enjoyed by Head Men of some Castes in Poona.

Koshtee.—The Mehitra's wife is invited to the entertainments on marriages. He receives a piece of cocoanut, on occasion of a wife being sent home to her husband's house. His wife is invited at entertainments called Gondhul (when tales of the gods are recited, with music, &c.). He receives a turban on occasions of adopting a son, and of a Gotaee (entertainment given to the caste on readmitting an offender). On every occasion he receives a double allowance of Pan; the sandal (gund) is first put on his forehead, his signature is first written in all documents in which the caste are concerned; he enjoys exemption from the Government tax on houses and some other items; his signature is affixed to deeds of sale.

Gooruwu.—The Mehitra and his wife are invited to marriage entertainments, entertainments on adoption, on widow's marriage (Pat), &c., and receive Pan previously to the other guests. On a Gotaee, he receives a Sela and turban.

Sootar.—On marriages, &c., the Mehitra receives Pan. On adoptions and Gotaee a turban, &c., according to the parties' ability.

Nhawee Kusbekur.—The Mehitra is exempted from Mohturifa and house-tax. On the fourth day of marriages, when turmeric is applied to the persons of the boy and girl who are married, the Mehitra's wife is invited and receives turmeric, the mark on the forehead called Koonkoo, and Pan. On the day of marriage, the Mehitra receives water previously to eating, sandal on the forehead, and his wife Koonkoo and Pan. The bride and bridegroom being seated on the raised floor under a canopy, the Mehitra performs the lamp evolutions before them, as at Pooja, and throws a pice over them. On the application of the turmeric, the Mehitra receives some old clothes. At Gondhul entertainments, the Mehitra gives money to the Gondhulees (performers) previously to the rest of the guests giving their present. At a Gotaee, he receives Sandal (choo) water in the hand, Pan, and a turban, &c., according to the ability of the parties. At Pat, Sandal, choo, Pan, and a turban or a few pice. At funerals, the Mehitra, on the thirteenth day, ties on the turban of the deceased's eldest son. At adoptions, he receives a Sela, turban, &c.

There may be one Mehitra over the caste in one village; or a Sur-Mehitra over the caste resident in five or ten villages. The Sur-Mehitra receives from the village Nhawee one rupee and two pylees of grain. In the Poona district, there are 360 villages over which this right (whether resumed or still enforced is not clear) is claimed by the Sur-Mehitra of Poona.

The Sur-Mehitra receives the orders of the Sirkar, and transmits them to other Nhawees. On the sale of a Mehitra Wuttun, or on the new appointment of a Mehitra by the caste, the last possessor dying heirless, the Sur-Mehitra attends and receives a *S*ela and turban from the new Wuttundar. In all assemblies of the caste, the Mehitra is first invited.

The Mehitra attends the circumcision (Soonta) of Moossulmans, performing the ceremony and receiving a *S*ela and turban. He shaves Brahmuns on their investiture with the thread (Moonj), and receives a similar present. On the festival of the Nag Punchmee, in the month Srawun, the Mehitra performs Pooja at the Warool or Cobra-capel's hole. (This Man is at present discontinued, pending a dispute between the relations, sharers in the Mehitra Wuttun.)

Malee.—The Mehitra puts rice (sej or seth) on the forehead of the bride and bridegroom, receiving previously to other guests sandal (Gund or tila) and Pan, &c.

Tylung Sarlee.—The Mehitra merely receives first in entertainments the sandal and Pan.

Konkunee Goulee.—At marriages the Mehitra has his feet washed, and receives with his wife rice, dal, wheat, flour, ghee, goor, sooparee, Pan, a cocoanut, the turmeric and red mark on the forehead, lamp soot (kajil, a substitute for antimony for the eyes), chiksa, a composition put in women's hair at the Nahun (first appearance of puberty), consisting of almonds, &c., Goolal, red colour thrown on the clothes at the Hoolee, a Phunee, or comb, papuru, koolwundee, and other dishes.

Simpee.—At all caste assemblies the Mehitra is invited to the house of the party where the festival is held, and thither invites all the guests; at marriages he receives koolwundee, Papuru, Telchee,. Polee, &c. The girl's parents going to fetch the bride, carry her rookhwut (fifty kinds of dishes and sweetmeats, of which the Mehitra receives a part, and his wife a slice of cocoanut, an invitation to the festival, Pan, &c.). Occasionally he receives a turban. The Mehitra's rank, however, is less than the *S*ettee of the peth or village.

Marathe Telee.—At Magune, the caste with the future bridegroom's parents being assembled at the bride's father's house, the guests divide Pan, and the Mehitra takes it first; his wife has priority in receiving the sandal, &c. At the Dewuk Gondul (entertainments on occasion of family worship two days before marriage), the Mehitra and his wife are invited, and receive sandal and eatables.

More or less of the above Huks and privileges are enjoyed by Mehitras of the other castes; among the presents received may be added sugar-cane, copper pots, &c. The Mehitras of the Mhar and Mang caste besides are exempted from Ghur Puttee (house-tax).

The right of, or precedence in, tying and throwing the Polee at the Hoolee festival, and making Pooja thereon, is the frequent subject of judicial dispute or personal combat.

Ahir Goulee.—At marriages and Pats the Choudree receives two rupees. In all caste assemblies he receives a double allowance of eatables and Pan. At the Hoolee and Devalee, the Choudree gives his caste two rupees for sweetmeats, occasionally more.

Kamatee Tylung.—The Mokuddum is entitled to one-fourth of every fine levied on offenders at a Gotaee, and to precedence in receiving Pan, &c.

Ghisaree.—The Chouhan, &c., receive no Huks whatever, and merely conduct the business of the caste.

Burhaee.—The Choudree receives Sandal, and Pan, and double eatables. The Sukhee has no Man-Pan. The Bughut receives a Dhotee, Pan, and Sandal on occasion of a Gondhul or Bundara (given by Byragees and Gosaeens).

Hulalkhor.—The Gooroo of the Goojrathees, and the Sur-Mehitra of the Dekhunees, receive fees in money, &c., at marriages, &c. Of the forty rupees fine levied in cases of adultery, twenty rupees go to the caste, five rupees to the seizer of the defendant, five rupees to a clever manager in the caste, and ten rupees to the Mehitra. The Mehitra of the two peths (Mongulwar and Bhowanee) of Poona have also Huks and precedence, and two and a half rupees in cases of adultery.

Moolamgar.—At marriages the Choudree takes five rupees in the name of the caste, which sum is kept in deposit and expended at his pleasure.

Dakote Josee.—The Singar, Guroor, &c., merely are entitled in receiving Pan to priority.

Rawul Jogee.—Suntojee receives pan and sandal before others at marriages. He enjoys exemption from payment of house-tax and shop-tax on shops for sale of tape and strips of cloth for Cummurbunds. He receives annually from the Desmookh of Poona two sheep, and from the Koolkurnee, Mahajun, and Sette of Poona a one khun Cholee annually, who also invite him to dine with them on the festivals (Eeds). In the Peshwa's time, they used to give at the Dussera five Khun Cholees and Hulud Koonkoo.

All the other castes who have head men have given the particulars of their respective Huks and privileges which are on record in Mahratta. It has been thought sufficient to give above an English translation of the most remarkable. Much difficulty was often found in obtaining the answers, there being disputes subsisting in many cases between the head man and his caste. In such instances the rights of the former are held in abeyance pending the decision.

4.—*Appointment of New Holders.*

1. In our caste, should the Mehitra die without heirs, several men of intelligence, from age and experience, with the concurrence of the caste, appoint a successor.

[17.] Koshtee, Gooruwu, Sootar, (2) Patrawut, Malee, Bhat Byragee, Tylung Sarlee, Koombhar, Simpee, Kahar Bhoee, Lonaree, Purit, Booroor, Dohor, Mhar, Mang, Lukhuree, Kykaree.

2. As in (2), substituting the Choudree for the Mehitra.

[17.] Burhaee, Lohar B., Johuree, Konkunee Goulee, A. Goulee, Hulwaee, Chuppurbund, Mewafurosh, Buldee Koombhar, S. R. Koombhar, Ling. Goulee, B. Telee, R. J. Telee, Rungaree, Purd. Chambhar, Sultungur.

3. Hitherto we have had no Mehitra in Poona; should the caste think proper to appoint one, they will do so.

[3.] Sarlee, Lodhee Purdesee, Punchum Wanee.

4. Should the Patell of our caste die without heirs or abscond to another country, the caste (with the advice of several men of intelligence) appoint one of his relations, or Gotru, his successor.

[3.] Surwude Josee, Kachee Boondelee, Kachee Nurwuree.

5. Should the Naikwaree of our caste die without heirs, the caste may appoint a successor.

[2.] Marathe Bhoee, Ramosee.

6. A new Mehitra can only be appointed at the general assembly of the caste at Sreesuptusring (a temple of Parwutee, fourteen coss from Trimbuk).

[1.] Kantaree.

7. New Settees, or Karbarees, are appointed by the caste, in case of the old one refusing to be guided by their wishes.

[1.] Kasar bh. Kurunar.

8. Should it be necessary to appoint a new Mehitra, the Desmookh, Despande, Patells, and Mehitras of several sur-

rounding villages are assembled, and, with the concurrence of the caste, appoint a successor, giving information to the Sirkar.

[1.] Nhawee Kusbekur.

9. Should a *S*ettee die without heirs, a successor is appointed by the caste from among his relations, selecting a man of intelligence with the concurrence of the Desmookh, Despande, and Koolkurnee.

[1.] Punchal Sonar.

10. Should a Patell or Chougola die without heirs, or son by a slave-girl, or Gotruj, the appointment of a successor will rest with the Desmookh, Despande (to whom are often escheated estates of Patells and Koolkurnees dying heirless), and the Sirkar.

[1.] Koonbee.

11. A new Mehitra is appointed (on occasion of an old one dying heirless) by the Desmookh, Despande, Sette, and Mahajun, with the concurrence of the caste, should it be thought advisable.

[1.] Marathe Telee.

12. The caste has authority to appoint successors to the Gunnacharee or Karbarees dying without issue.

[1.] Gondhule.

13. The Desmookh, Despande, and caste appoint a successor to a Mehitra Wuttundar, dying heirless.

[1.] Mar. Chambhar.

14. The Patell, Koolkurnee, Andil, Mahajun, Chougola, with the concurrence of the caste, appoint successors to those officers dying heirless.

[1.] Wotaree.

15. The caste appoint a successor to a Mokuddum dying heirless.

[1.] Kam. Tylung.

16. Do. to a *S*ettee of the caste do.

[1.] **Bungur Wanee.**

17. Do. to a Mehitra dying heirless, or refusing to obey the wishes of the caste, with the concurrence of the Koolkurnee, Mahajun, *S*ettee, De*s*mookh, and De*s*pan*d*e, and the inhabitants of the Peth or village.

[1.] **Dhungur Kartik.**

18. Do. to a Mehitra or Patell dying heirless.

[1.] **Hulalkhor.**

19. No new appointment takes place of a Singar, Guroor, or Pachung Row. A Naik is appointed by the three Wuttundars with the concurrence of the caste.

[1.] **D. Josee.**

20. The caste would give a son in adoption to Suntojee or the Choudree, being without heirs.

[2.] **R. Josee, Moolamgar.**

5.—*Arrangement in Case of several Co-Heirs.*

Should there be several sharers in the office of Mehitra, the elder will take the duties of the office and the Man-pan, and all the sharers will divide the proceeds among them. The Mehitra-pun is not held year and year about, like the Wuttun of a Koolkurnee.

[20.] **Koshtee, Gooruwu, Sootar, 2 Patrawut, Nhawee Kr, Malee, Ty. Sarlee, Konkunee Goulee, Koombhar, Dhungur Kartik, Marathe Telee, Lonaree, Purit, Booroor, Chambhar, Dohor, Mhar, Mang, Hulalkhor.**

2. As in (2), substituting the term Choudree for Mehitra.

[13.] **Lohar B., Johuree, A. Goulee, Hulwaee, S. R. Koombhar, Mewafurosh, Ling. Goulee, B. Telee, R. Telee, J. Telee, Rungaree, Chambhar Purd., Sultungur, Lukheree, Moolamgar.**

3. As in (2), substituting the Patell and Chougola. The former generally enjoys the Enam land called Pachoree.

[5.] **Koonbee, Kamatee Tylung, Surwude Josee, Kachee B., Kachee Nurwure.**

4. As in (2), substituting the *S*ettee; but the younger sharers receive nothing.

[2.] Bungur Wanee, Punchal Sonar.

5. Do. substituting the Naik.

[2.] Mar. Bhoee, Ramosee.

6. Do. substituting the Patell, Chougola, Koolkurnee, Andil, and Mahajun, the five *Mankurees* of the caste.

[1.] Wotaree.

7. Do. do. Gunnacharee and Karbarees.

[1.] Gondhulee.

8. As in (2), substituting the Sukhee, Bhugut, and Choudree.

[1.] Burhaee.

9. Do. do. *S*ingar, Guroor, Pachung row, Naik.

[1.] D. Josee.

10. The Choudree is not a Wuttundar; whoever has most intelligence in the caste, he is Choudree.

[1.] Kykaree.

11. The elder of the family of Suntojee enjoys the Manpan.

[1.] R. Josee.

6.—*Duties of the Head-man.*

1. The duty of a Mehitra is to answer the summons of the Sirkar or the caste, to assemble the latter, and, with their concurrence, to settle affairs of general or individual importance, as marriages, festivals, and meetings to exclude and readmit offenders. The Mehitra or other head-man of a caste must have the express concurrence of men of intelligence and experience in the caste.

[20.] Koshtee, Gooruwu, Sootar, (2) Patrawut, Nhawee Kr, Malee, Tylung Sarlee, Konk. Goulee, Koombhar, Dhungur Kartik, Marathe Telee, Lonaree, Purit, Booroor, Mar. Chambhar, Dohor, Mhar. Mang, Hulalkhor.

2. The duty of Choudree is to answer the requisitions of

the Sirkar, to settle disputes among individuals of the caste (if sufficiently intelligent); otherwise to assemble three or four others, and, with their assistance, to put an end to the quarrel, to assemble the caste at marriages, arrange the entertainment, and receive Man-pan, and generally to manage all the affairs of the caste.

[16.] Lohar Boondelee, Johuree, A. Goulee, Hulwaee, S. R. Koombhar, Mewafurosh, Ling. Goulee, B. Telee, R. Telee, J. Telee, Rungaree, Purd. Chambhar, Sultungur.

[4.] Lukheree (including correspondence on arranging marriages).

Kykaree (including furnishing begarees at the requisition of Govt.) and Moolamgar.

3. As in the foregoing, substituting Patell, Chougola, &c. These officers appear to possess more authority than headmen in other castes.

[5.] Koombhar, Kamatee Tylung, Surwude Josee, Kachee B., Kachee Nurwure.

4. Do. do. do. Settee.

[2.] P. Sonar, B. Wanee.

5. Do. do. do. Naik. His duty includes the assembling men of the caste at the requisition of the Sirkar.

[2.] Mar. Bhoee, Ramosee.

6. The Patell's duty is to perform the foregoing duties of the Choudree; the Koolkurnee writes the papers and documents necessary for the caste; the Mahajun, &c., are assistants of the Patell.

[1.] Wotaree.

7. As in (3), substituting Gunnacharee and Karbarees.

[1.] Gondhulee.

8. The Bhugut, Sukhee, and Choudree assemble the rest of the caste through the Nhawe. Their other duties are those of the Choudree in (3).

[1.] Barhaee.

9. The Choudree assembles the caste through the Kotwal. He has other duties, &c. (*See* 3.)

[1.] Bhat Byragee.

10. The duties of the Powar, Chouhan, Salokhe, and Pudwulkur are those of a Choudree (3).

[1.] Ghisaree.

11. The duties of a Mehitra are to assemble the caste, obey their orders, distribute pan, and put sandal on the forehead of the guests.

[1.] Simpee.

12. The Singar and Naik together submit all matters relative to the caste to Pachung row and Guroor, obey their orders, and settle disputes.

[1.] D. Josee.

13. Suntojee performs these duties, though without the appellation of Choudree.

[1.] R. Jogee.

V.

In whom is Vested the Authority to Expel and Readmit to Caste Privileges.

1. The caste has authority to expel from caste, and to readmit after the prescribed expiation has been performed by a Brahmun; those who are of experience in affairs from age or intelligence assemble the caste, and with their concurrence pass sentence on the offender.

[56.] Goluk, Komtee, Khutree, Kantaree, Wys Sonar, Ahir Sonar, Konkune Sonar, Lar Sonar, Dewagun Sonar, Kanure Sonar, Purdesee Sootar, Lohar Kasar Wiknar, and Kurnar, Patrawut (Salkur and Punkur), Nhavee Gungateerkur, Pahar Malee, Bhat Koonbee, Sarlee, Kamatee Tylung and Kanuree, Gondhulee, Lodhe Purdesee, Chupperbund, Bhurbhoonje Kirar, Buldee Koombhar, Purdesee Koombhar, Sekwuttee and Rajwuttee Koombhar, Dhungur Koontekur, Douree Gosawēe, Simpee Wiknar, Ahir Simpee, Tilelee Wanee, Punchum Wanee, Koonbee Wanee, Maratte and Kuhar

Bhoee, Telee Rathor, and Jyshwur, Rungaree, Johuree, Ghisaree, Sungur, Kolee, Booroor, Kolartee, Purdesee Chambhar and Dohor, Kast, Brahmunjaee, Lukheree, Ugurwalee, Kykaree, Holar, Bruhmukshutree (consulting Brahmuns).

2. The whole caste assembled with the Mehitra have athority to expel and readmit.

[15.] Koshtee, Gooruwu, Sootar, Nhawee Kusbekur, Malee, Sarlee Tylung, Konkune Goulee, Koombhar, Dhungur Kartik, Mahrattee Telee, Lonaree, Purit, Chambhar, Mhar, Mang.

3. The whole caste with the Choudree have authority, &c., as in (1).

[6.] Burhaee, Purdesee Lohar, Bhat Byragee, Johuree, Ahir Goulee, Hulwaee, Mewafurosh, Lingaet Goulee, Batree Telee, and Sultungur.

4. The Patell (both of the village and caste, Chougole, Wuttundars, &c.), and men of experience in caste, with the assembled caste, &c.

[6.] Koonbee, Surwude Josee, Wotaree, Kachee Boondelee, Kachee Nurwuree, Hulalkhor.

5. With the concurrence of the Gooroo and Mutputtee, after performing the penance required by them, an offender may, with the consent of the caste, be readmitted.

[2.] Jungum, Punchum Wanee.

6. Should a Brahmun lose caste, those of his caste who from their intelligence are worthy of giving their opinion, expel him altogether from caste privileges, in the event of his having murdered a Brahmun or killed a cow, or committed other Maha Patuk, first informing the Sirkar thereof, should it be a matter of which the Sirkar takes cognizance. Should the offence be expiable (after intimation to the Sirkar if a matter cognizable by it), the superior men of the caste assembling the rest, with their concurrence prescribe the penance to be performed by the offender by the hands of the Wywharee Josee. Or, in some cases, offenders receive puri-

fication by private arrangement, performing penance at the hands of a Brahmun.

[1.] Wywharee Josee.

7. The *Settee* or Mahajun assembles the caste, and with their concurrence does what is necessary.

[1.] Punchal Sonar.

8. With the concurrence of the Chitnees and Potnees, what is necessary to be done is done by the assembled caste.

[1.] Purbhoo.

9. In our caste Gumbeer Row in the Gungturee Prant, and Prutap Row in the Balaghat, are of supreme authority; what the Brahmuns determine as necessary penance with their concurrence being performed, offenders are readmitted.

[1.] Wunjaree.

10. The Dut Gooroo, with concurrence of the caste, has authority to expel and readmit.

[1.] Jyn.

11. The Naik, with the concurrence of the caste, has authority to expel and readmit.

[1.] Ramosee.

12. The Punch of every Muhula, under which are from 200 to 300 men of the caste, have this authority.

[1.] Marwarree.

13. The Singar and Naik, with the caste, have authority.

[1.] Dakote Josee.

14. The Gooroswamee, with the caste, do.

[2.] Goolwee Wanee, Kacharee.

15. Suntojee Poonekur, with the caste, has this authority.

[1.] Rawul Jogee.

VI.

Penance and Subsequent Readmission to Caste Privileges.

1. Penance is enjoined for the following crimes :—

Bruhmuhuty, comprising offences considered of equal guilt as killing a Brahmun, such as striking or abusing him, &c.

Streehuty, killing or severely beating a woman.

Balhuty, killing a child.

Ubhuksha bhukshun, eating prohibited food.

Kreea Kurum Ukurm, abstaining from performing funeral rites of deceased relations.

And other great offences of a similar kind. After performing the penance as enjoined by a Brahmun, the offender will be received into his caste as purified.

[90.] Wywharee Josee, Goluk, Purbhoo, Komtee, Khutree, Koshtee, Gooruwu, Kantaree, Wys, Ahir, Konkunee, Lar, Dewagun, Punchal, Kanaree Sonar, Sootar Burhaee, Purdesee Sootar, Lohar, Tambut, Lohar B., Kasar Bhandee wikunar, Kasar Bhandee Kurunar, (2) Patrawut, Purdesee Koombhar, Sekwuttee Rajwuttee Koombhar, Dhungur Kartik, and Kootr., Douree Gosavee, Simpee, A. Simpee, Koonbee Wanee, Mahratte Bhoee, Kahar Bhoee, Mar. Telee, Nhawee G. and K. Koombee, Malee, P. Malee, Bhat Byragee, Bhat Koombee, Ty. Sarlee, Sarlee, Kamatee Tylung, Kamatee Kanure, Surwudee Josee, Wotaree, Gondhulee, Johuree, Konkune Goulee, A. Goulee, Hulwaee, Lodhee Purdesee, Kachee B. Chuppurbund, Kirar, Mewafurosh, Koombhar, Buldee Koombhar, B. Telee, R. J. Telee, Rungaree, Ghisaree, Sungur, Lonaree, Kolee, Wunjaree, Purit, Boorood, Ramosee, Chambhar, Purdesee Chambhar, Dohor, Sultungur, Mhar, Mang, Hulalkhor, Kast, Brahmunkshutree, Brahmunjaee, Lukheree, Kacharee, R. Jogee, Kykaree, Moolamgar, D. Josee, Goolwe Wanee, Holar.

2. Penance is prescribed by the Jungum to offenders above mentioned, and they are readmitted after such purification. To the above list should be added—

Soorapan, drinking spirits.

Matragumun, incest with a mother.

Goorootulpuk, connection with a Gooroo's wife.

[5.] Jungum, Tilele Wanee, Punchum Wanee, Bungur Wanee, Lingaet Goulee.

3. Offenders above named, together with persons eating with men, or having connection with women, of another lower caste, are readmitted after giving the caste a meal with sweetmeats.

[1.] Kolartee.

4. Offenders named in (1) are readmitted on performing penance enjoined by a Brahmun; persons eating (unuwiwhar) or having connection (Gumun) with a lower caste are not readmissible.

[1.] Kachee Nurwuree.

5. Offenders of all kinds are readmissible on performing the penance that may be enjoined by our Mookhy Swamee.

[1.] Jyn.

6. Among dancing girls (Kulawunt), should a girl be disobedient to her parents, or quarrel with her husband on account of the possession of her child, she would be excluded by a Punchaet, and prohibited to wear her ankle-bell; she is readmissible on payment of a fine.

7. Offenders guilty of a great crime are not readmitted on penance. For a slight offence, as eating with persons of another caste, the offender is ordered to feed Brahmuns, or make ablution in the Gunga, and feed the caste, or beg pardon of the assembled caste.

[1.] Ugurwale.

Inferred from the answers of eighty-four castes before named.

1. Children born previously to their parents losing caste may, provided they have not ate with Mhars or Moossulmans, be received into caste on performing penance or feeding the caste, otherwise they remain excluded. Children born subsequently to their parents losing caste follow their example, whether readmitted or excluded. The Purbhoos profess to be guided by the *Sastrus*.

Readmission into caste generally depends more on the ability of the party to pay fine, or provide an expiatory entertainment, than the enormity of his offence; but long association with very low castes, or castes not Hindoo, is stated to be a bar to the readmission of parents and children.

2. Children who, after the period of their infancy, leave such parents and reside with a relation (as their maternal uncle), may be readmitted. If, after years of discretion, they continue to reside with their parents, they remain excluded with them.

[1.] **Marwarree.**

3. The caste may readmit to caste privileges the children of excluded persons on their petition and on investigation into the case.

[3.] **Goolwee Wanee, Dakote Josee, Lukheree.**

4. The caste readmit children under eight years of age (ten*) if their parents lose caste in a time of famine or tyranny. Not above that age.

[3.] **Kast, Bruhumkshutree,* R. Jogee.**

5. Do. with limitation of age.

[2.] **Holar, Moolamgar.**

6. Do. (The Gooroo, Muttaputtee, and caste.)

[1.] **Kacharee.**

7. Children of excluded persons remain excluded.

[1.] **Ugurwale.**

8. Do. as in (1), in case only of their having associated with low-caste individuals.

[1.] **Kykaree.**

VII.

On Permanent Exclusion from Caste Privileges.

1. A man who eats and resides with Moossulmans or Mhars for a considerable period is not readmitted into caste.

[85.] **Wywharee Josee, Goluk, Komtee, Klutree, Koshtee, Gooruwu, Kantaree, Wye Sonar, Ahir, Konk. Lar. D. P. Sonar, Sootar,**

Koombee, Joharee, 2 Patrawut, Burhaee, P. Sotar, Lohar, Purdesee Lohar, Kasar bhandee wikunar, Jyn, Nhawee K. and G. Malee, P. Malee, Bhat Byragee, Bhat Koombee, P. Sarlee, Sarlee, Kamatee Tylung and Kan, Surwudee Josee, Gondhulee, Konk. Goulee, A. Goulee, Hulwaee, Lodhee Purdesee, Kachee Boond, Chuppurbund, Kachee N., Burbhoonje, Kirar, Mewafurosh, Koombhar, B. Koombhar, Purdesee Koombhar, S. Koombhar, Dhungur K. and Koontekur, Douree Gosawee, Simpee, A. Simpee, Jungum, Tilelee Wanee, Bungur Wanee, Lingaet Goulee, Ling. Wanee, Koombee Wanee, Mar. Bhoee, Kahar Bhoee, Mar. Telee, Batree Telee, Rathor Telee, Jyshwur Telee, Rungaree, Ghisaree, Sungur, Lonaree, Kolee, Wunjaree, Purit, Booroor, Ramosee, Kolatee, Chambhar, Purd. Chambhar, Sultungur, Dohor, Mhar, Mang, Hulalkhor, Kast, Bruhmukshutree, Brahmunjaee, Ugurwale, D. Josee, G. Wanee, Kacharee, R. Jogee, Lukheree, Kykaree, Holar, Moolamgar.

2. Murder of a Brahmun, of a woman, or of a child, disqualify the offender from being readmitted into caste.

[1.] Kanare Sonar.

3. For a first offence, the offender is prescribed a pilgrimage or other penance, and a repetition disqualifies him, if the crime be heinous, from being readmitted into caste.

[1.] Wotaree.

4. Keeping a woman of another caste, and eating at her hands (as of the castes Chambhar, Bungee, &c.); Gotruhuty, or killing or striking one of his own family name; incest with a son's wife, daughter, brother's wife, or his daughter-in-law, or mother's sister; eating [constantly] with one of a low caste; such are the causes of exclusion from the caste by a Punchaet. A man so offending is, in some instances, readmitted, on Teerthyatra, or other penance; a woman never.

[1.] Marwarree.

5. Penance, and absolute exclusion from caste on account of feeding with other castes, &c., are not practised among dancing girls.

[1.] Kulawunt.

For other offences a fine is usually levied on the offender, which is expended on feeding the caste, if imposed by them, or taken by the Gooroo, if he have passed sentence. The offender also undergoes various degrees of penance, such as pilgrimage, branding, fasting, pricking the tongue, drinking the Punchguw, shaving the moustaches, &c. The relative guilt of the offence is in estimation various. Under Ootumpatuk (crimes of the highest supposed guilt) are legally reckoned murder, especially of a cow, a woman, a child, or a Brahmun, incest, stealing gold, drinking spirituous liquors. The guilt of adultery is estimated according to the relative caste of the parties, and the means used to compass the object. Robbery and striking are also amenable to caste punishment; eating the numerous kinds of prohibited food, associating with or touching persons of low caste, and disobedience to the orders of the Gooroo, or head of the caste, are subject to different degrees of penalty.

During the period of exclusion from caste privileges, the offender is not allowed to eat with his caste, nor, frequently, to enter* their houses; persons associating with the excluded person are all liable to fine and penance. Fines and penance are, in the first instance, imposed by Brahmuns, in most castes, the Hindoo ceremonies being in general performed by them only on payment of customary fees.

Puschatap or repentance is followed by Prayuschit, and is held the chief requisite in procuring expiation. Prayuschit is specified in the *Sastrus* for every imaginable offence, and it is apparently from the unwillingness of the party to submit to it, rather than from that of his caste to readmit him on such condition or its equivalent, that long association with Moossulmans or Mhars and Christians (*see* Castes, 122)

---

* A restriction occasionally dispensed with in favour of men of rank or talent.

is the only offence which involves utter degradation from caste privileges.

In the Hindoo criminal law, higher caste, and sometimes rank, entitle the offender to a diminished rate of punishment, except in cases of theft. Offences against the peculiar ordinances of the Hindoo *S*astrus are classed as of equal enormity with breaches of universal morality. The oath is, in fact, a trial by ordeal, characteristic of a superstitious people.

Of their punishments, some are prescribed on a principle of retaliation, others on a supposed analogy to the crime. There are, however, some precepts which denote considerable refinement in legislation, as in the scale of punishment to instigators, participators, and frequent offenders; in modifying rules by the sex and abilities of the injured party, and in prescribing compensation for various injuries in persons and property.

It may be observed that offenders denying their guilt are, on proof, to be punished in a greater degree, while confession is encouraged, by showing less severity towards those who plead guilty.

The prevalence of falsehood among the Hindoos is consistent with its legal permission for particular objects, although false evidence, generally, is stigmatized as a crime of the greatest magnitude.

Although the Hindoo criminal law and judicial procedure have been modified and improved by the regulations of Government, the opinions of the people are, as may be supposed, in many respects in accordance with the principles laid down in their religious books.

Answer from Khandesh. A person does not, by exclusion from caste, forfeit property or right of inheritance.

Answer from Satara. Do. But a holder of an office of religious service as a Hindoo, would forfeit it by changing his religion.

VIII.

Rules of Intermarriage and Eating Together (Pungut).

I. There are no subdivisions in these castes. Persons belonging to each intermarry and eat with their own caste only.

[66.] Goluk, Purbhoo,* Komtee, Khutree. Koshtee, Goorawu, Kanure Sonar, Wys, Ahir. Konk. Lar, Dew. Punch, Kan. Sonar, Sotar, Purdesee Sotar, Lohar, Purdesee Lohar, Kasar Bhande Vikunar, and Kur, Jyn, Nahwe kusbekur and Gungatilkur, Malee. Bhat Byragee, Bhat Koonbee, Wotaree, Gondhulee, Purd. and Ahir Goulee, Lodhee Purd., Chuppurbund, Burbhoonjee, Kirar, Mewafurosh, Koombhar, Buldee Koombhar, S. Rajwutee Koombhar, Dhungur Kootekur, Douree Gosawee, Simpee, A. Simpee, Jungum, Tilelee Wanee, Bungur Wanee, Ling. Goulee, Ling. Wanee, Koombee Wanee, Mar. Bhoee, Kahar Bhoee, Mar. Tilelee, B. Rathor, Jysh. Telee, Rungaree, Ghisaree, Lonaree, Wunjaree, Purit, Booroor, Kolartee, Ramosee, Chambhar, Dohor, Mhar, Mang, Hulalkhor, Kast, Brahmunjaee, Bruhmukshutree, G. Wanee, Kacharee, Moolamgar, Holar.

II. Persons belonging to these castes will eat with other castes of an equal or superior rank to themselves, but intermarry with families of their own caste only.

[18.] Wywhare Josee 1;† Burhaee 2; P. Malee 3; T. Sarlee 4; Sarlee 5; Kamatee Tylung 6; Kamatee Kan. 7; Surwude Josee 8; Konkune Goulee 9; Hulwaee 10; Kachee Boondele and Kachee N. 11; Koombhar 12; Dhungur Kartik 13; Sungur 14; Kolee 15; Purd. Chambhar 16; Sultungur 17.

2. Many of this caste practise as Sootars, will eat with Koonbees as superior to themselves, not with Sootar castemen. 3. This caste eat in the houses of Koonbees and Malees; the Koonbees will eat in theirs. 4. Eat with the Sarlees of Hydrabad, none of whom reside here. 5. Eat with Soot. Sarlees. 6. Eat with Koonbees and Malees. 7. Eat

---

* This refers to the only division of the Purbhoos' name resident in Poona. They are called by themselves Chundrusenee, and by others Kayusth.

† The answer must be understood with reference to the ten subdivisions of the Brahmun caste. Four of these (Drewir, Tylung, Kurnatuk, Maharashtr) will not eat with the Goojrathee, the remaining one of the Punchdrewir.

with Koonbees. 8. Eat with the other five Josees, Douree Josee, Dukoonjee J., Sahadeo J., Merhe J., Hoopenee J. 9. Eat with Koonbee Mahrattas. 10. Eat Pukarusaee (sweet milk, prepared Ghee, &c.) with the Hulwaee Kanojee, Hulwaee Tuskaree Putwe, and Hulwaee Beerkur Kucharusee in their own caste only. 11. Eat in the houses of Brahmuns and Phool Malees. 12. Eat with the Buldee Koombhars in their house; the latter will not eat in theirs. 13. Eat with other Dhungur castes. 14. Eat with the Dhungur Kootekur, Dhungur Hootkur, Koonbee, and Malee. 15. Eat with Malee. 16. Eat with Eerwar and Paradosh Chambhar. 17. Eat with Byragees and other superior castes. The Johurees have two subdivisions, Dusee and Bisee; they do not intermarry, but eat together. The Koonbees state that children by their domestic slaves go by their name, but they do not eat nor intermarry with descendants of such children for several generations.

The Patrawut Punkur and Salkur do not eat nor intermarry.

The Marwarres comprise numerous sects. Those among them of higher caste profess to eat and intermarry with those of high-caste descent (oothum usul) only; of other castes, they consider Brahmuns highest in estimation, next Mahajun, Kshutre, Rujpoot, and Kayust; after them Ahir, Malee, Simpee, Kasar; lowest of all, Bungee, Dhobee, Bulhaee, Chambhar.

It appears from a Punchaet case in Khandesh (No. 7), that Telees are admissible into the Koonbee caste.

The Kykarees have two subdivisions, Koochare and Bootewale. The latter call themselves Kykarees, but there is no intermarriage or eating together between the two.

The Ugurwale and Lukheree eat Pukarusaee (curds, sweet milk, &c.) with some other castes; they eat Kucharusaee and intermarry with their own caste only.

The Dakote Josee eat in the houses of Koonbees, Malee,

Simpee, and other higher castes. They have as subdivisions J. Nuggurkur, Dabholkur, J. Taskur, Geerwul J., and Lasoorkur J., all of whom intermarry and eat in company.

IX.

Oaths most Binding in each Caste.

1. In these castes the most binding adjurations are by their gods (either naming a particular deity or the whole); 2, by the feet of a Brahmun; 3, by a cow.

[10.] **Purbhoo, Ahir Sonar, Kon. Sonar, Lar Sonar, Punchal Sonar, Nhawee Gungatilkur, Pahar Malee, Koonbee Sarlee, Kamatee Tylung, Dhungur Kartik, Simpee, Ahir Simpee, Marathe Bhoee, Mar. Telee, Wunjaree, Kolee, Purit.**

2. In these castes it is the custom to swear by the goddess Bhowanee Karlee (a name of Parwutee).

[10.] **Koshtee, Kantaree, Wys Sonar, Dewagun Sonar, Kansar, Bhandee Vikunar, Kasar Bhandee Kurnar, Wotaree, Gondhulee, Mhar, Mang, Kykaree.**

3. By the god Ballajee or Venkoba (a name of Vishnoo). The great temple of this deity is near Cuddapah (Kurpa).

[10.] **Sonar Purdesee, Ahir Goulee, Bhat Byragee, Hulwaee Purdesee, Kachee Boondele, Kirar, Purd. Koombhar, S. R. Koombhar, Purd. Chambhar, Sultungur, Ugurwale, Lukheree, Moolamgar.**

4. By the River Gunga (understood by natives on this side of India as the Godavery).

[10.] **Purd. Lohar, Lodhee Purdesee, Chuppurbund, Burbhoonje, Mewafurosh, B. Koombhar, Kakar Bhoee, Batree Telee, Jyshwur Telee, Booroor.**

5. By the god of the family, whoever he may be (Koolswamee or Kooldeo).

[9.] **Wywharee Josee, Goluk, Khutree, Burhaee, Jyn, Kanuree Kamatee, Koonbee Wanee, Kolartee, Hulalkhor, Bruhmukshutree.**

6. By the god Samba (a name of Mahadeo, or *Siw*).

[9.] **Gooruwu, Malee, Tylung Sarlee, Koombhar, Douree Gosawee, Tilelee Wanee, Rathor Telee, Sungur, Dohor.**

7. By the god Kundoba (an awatar of Mahadeo), or by taking up the bel (creeper) and bundhar (pounded roots of the turmeric plant), both sacred to him.

[8.] **Bhat Koonbee, Kachee Nurwuree, Dhungur Kootekur, Rungaree, Ghisaree, Lonaree, Ramosee, Ghambhar, Holar (by Kundoba and a Brahmun).**

8. By the Gooroo of their caste, by the Jungum's feet.*

[6.] **Komtee, Surwudee Josee, Jungum, Bungur Wanee, Ling. Goulee, Ling. Wanee, Goolwee Wanee,* Kacharee.***

9. By the father or ancestor (Moolpooroosh), viz. first of the family.

[2.] **Sootar, Nhawee Kusbekur.**

10. By their caste.

[2.] **Lohar, Konkunee Goulee.**

11. As builders and adorners of temples, descendants of Wishwu Kurumu,† the Kanure Sonars swear by him.

[1.] **Kanure Sonar.**

12. By Nath Sahib, Gooroo Nanuk, and Gooroo Govind Sahib.

[1.] **Johuree.**

13. By our veracity (Eeman) and caste custom (Dhurm).

[1.] **Marwarree.**

14. Dancing girls swear by the god of their caste, if Hindoo; if Moossulman, on the Koran.

[1.] **Kulawunt.**

15. By the cow and the Brahmun.

[2.] **Kast, Brahmunjaee.**

16. By the Gayatree.

[1.] **Rawul Jogee.**

17. By Mahadeo.

[1.] **Dakote Josee.**

---

† Signifying ability to practise any act whatever. It is the name of the carpenter and artificer of the gods.

III.—EXISTING CUSTOMS.

III.

EXISTING CUSTOMS.

MARRIAGE.

I. The ceremonies prescribed by the books are by no means universally observed at the present day. With the exception of those performed at birth, marriage, and death, at the Moonj of males, and the maturity of females, the Sunskar rites are often neglected even by Brahmuns and the higher castes who imitate them. The expense of feeding Brahmuns and providing an entertainment usual on all such occasions naturally operates to abridge the frequency of their occurrence; although a man of any caste does not scruple to incur a ruinous load of debt in obtaining funds for an extravagant display at a marriage, or, occasionally, at a funeral in his family. **Of the Sunskara.**

II. The first species of marriage mentioned in the books, or Bruhm, is the only one now practised among the higher castes. There are some trifling distinctions in a man's first and second marriage. The lower castes often receive money on the marriage of their females called Hoonda, which is the characteristic of the fifth (Usoor) variety; and it is suspected that Brahmuns occasionally, in the present avaricious generation, incur sin on this account. All the lower castes admit the second marriage of wives in particular instances, and of widows, the ceremonies at which differ in many respects from those at a first marriage, as hereafter detailed. **Different kinds of marriage.**

12 *

Betrothment. Time. II. Among the Brahmuns, Purbhoos, Sonars, &c., the betrothment is termed Wagnischya. It takes place shortly before marriage, after full inquiry into the caste and family of the parties, and hence is seldom retracted, although the promise is not considered irrevocable until after the Hom sacrifice has been performed (P. D.).

According to some castes, a simple agreement only is necessary. (*See* the Replies from Dharwar in the Appendix.) Cocoanuts and other articles are sometimes given. Asses are given in the Johuree caste, P. The intervening period before marriage is undefined in many castes (P. S.), often three or four years (D.). It is short among the Johurees, who betroth after maturity. In the Ugurwale caste, presents are sent to the intended husband at the Magune, which takes place immediately before marriage (P.).

The engagement may be dissolved and the parties married to others, in the event of its being discovered, 1, that either party has lost caste, or is of a lower caste; 2, that on an astrological calculation of their birthdays the conjunction is unfavourable; 3, that the man is impotent; 4, that the parties are of the same Gotr (87 castes, P. 51. C. P. 1 & 2); 5, the same result takes place if the parents withdraw their consent (25 C. P. consulting the caste); or 6, if the man becomes incurably blind or diseased (Marwaree), Do. 1, 3, 6, D. Do. 1, 3, 5, K. Do. 1, 3, 6; and 7, if just before marriage any near relation die; or 8, if a former betrothed is still living, S.

How broken off. In the case of betrothment to one, and marriage in his absence to another, the girl may, in the Koonbee and lower castes, be given up to the first if the signs of puberty have appeared; or the first may formally resign her by giving a Chhor Chittee to the second, K. The same case may occur from avaricious motives of the parents, B. S. S. D. A Punchaet would generally make the girl over to the first, sometimes even after she has had children. Occasionally, however, she remains with her last betrothed or married husband, she with her children losing caste, D. In this case the girl's parents pay the marriage expenses of the first, 4 C.P.K.D.S. (unless there has been neglect on his side, S.). On which ever side the fault is proved to be, that party returns to the other the jewels and money advanced. No divorce takes place till after marriage.

The caste levy a fine on a man causelessly breaking off an intended marriage, 3 C. P.

It is not customary among the Brahmuns, Purbhoos, and fourteen other castes (P.) to give jewels before marriage. On a dissolution of the engagement, the jewels and presents given are returned to the man (56 C. P.), but not if his caste be deficient (13 C. P.), or the fault, generally, be on his side (8 C.P.).

The engagement is indissoluble, and the jewels are not returnable, 5 C. P. It is dissoluble only by an order from the Suptusring goddess, 1 C. P.

In a Punchaet case in Khandesh (No. 1), the plaintiff had agreed to marry his son and daughter to the daughter and son of the defendant. Defendant's daughter afterwards died, and defendant did not claim plaintiff's daughter until after the time fixed for the marriage. The Punch decided that the agreement was properly valid, but as the girl's mother had threatened to destroy herself and her daughter if the marriage were persisted in, they declared it void, and directed that plaintiff's daughter should be given in marriage to whomsoever her parents might choose, K.

IV. A male may be married, among the Brahmuns, at any time after the Moonj; and among other castes, at any age, S. K. Age of marriage.

The female's age on marriage should be less than that of her husband (53 C. P. D.). She should be married before the signs of puberty have appeared (rootoo, nahun, shanee), except from unavoidable delay (45 C. P.); in that case being liable to penance (18 C. P.) or exclusion (10 C. P.). Brahmuns, Bunyas, and other castes, marry their females under ten, otherwise they undergo penance (K. D.). Brahmuns, Senwees, Purbhoos, Sonars, Bunyas, Komtees, Rajpoots, and Maratha chieftains are positively forbidden to defer the marriage of their females till their shanee, on pain of exclusion, S. The high castes irretrievably lose caste on discovery, and the female is to be exposed and considered as dead, D. Less strictness exists in Poona on this point; seven castes stated that girls might be married after maturity, P.

In the Koonbee and lower castes females are sometimes not married till twelve or sixteen (K.); but such marriage after puberty is disreputable, and generally the Nikah, or widow's marriage ceremony, is performed, D. In the Lingaet and other castes betrothment before puberty is sufficient, D.

Sometimes parents defer a daughter's marriage, when the relations interpose with the Gooroo or Head-man of the caste, D.

Whose consent necessary.

V. The consent of the parents on the girl's side is essential, and on the boy's it is considered necessary on a first marriage, and is always advisable, K. Otherwise, the nearest relation present, or friend acting as guardian with the concurrence of the caste, gives the necessary authority for a girl's marriage, P. A marriage concluded without the consent of parents is not annulled, 5 C. P., if concluded with the consent of other relations, with persons of proper caste, and with the regular ceremonies, 12 C. P. In the father's absence, the mother—on the death or insanity of the parents, the uncle—give a girl in marriage, K. D. The girl has no voice, K. But in the Koonbee and lower castes, a girl after maturity is at her own disposal, K. There are contradictory opinions from D. as to the validity of a girl's marriage without her parents' consent; one states it to be valid if concluded by her own choice. So also the Ugurwale caste, P. And if married by compulsion, the offending party would be finable by the Sirkar.

To the consent of parents is added the opinion of the Sastree as to a legal intermarriage, S., or that of the Gooroo and caste, D.

Among the caste or profession of dancing girls, a son is always married; a daughter may either be married to a Moossulman or Hindoo, or be introduced at once to her profession at her parents' pleasure. Marriage is concluded according to caste custom, and the wife may remain in private creditably under her husband's protection. A girl born of such marriage is under the orders of her parents, and need not follow the profession unless from choice, P.

VI. The parties must be of the same caste, and different Gotr or family stock, P. Brahmuns are prohibited from intermarrying with all Supindu relations, and descendants of their Rishi's brothers, and connections within three or four degrees,* P. Intermarriage with cousins and nieces is prohibited (53 C. P.), but occasionally takes place from poverty, P. D. So with aunts and their children, Sugotrus and Suprubhurs, and of course with daughters, mothers, and sisters, D. A brother's children may, however, marry a sister's children, not being Sugotr, D. First cousins intermarry in the Wys caste, D. Komtees give their children to nephews and nieces, D. Other exemptions in particular sects of Brahmuns and other castes are mentioned, P. D. Some distant affinity is, however, preferred (D), as intermarriage with families who have intermarried for several previous generations, 20 C. P.

Restrictions in selection.

VII. In all the castes, it is the object of parents and

Order of marriage in a family.

* *See* Appendix.

relations to secure the marriage of the young females of the family; from poverty or other causes the marriage of boys is frequently deferred till a late period, and sometimes altogether omitted. The elder is first married, agreeably to the *S*astrus.

Period at which the marriage ceremony can be performed.

VIII. Marriages are celebrated during the months Margsirsh, Magh, Phalgoon, Wysak, Jesht, or (specially) a few days after Jesht, P.; also during Asha*r* if the Mithoon (Gemini) *S*unkrant fall within it, and to the north of the Godavery, if the Mesh *S*unkrant fall within it, K. The Mang and Mhar castes marry in Asha*r* and *S*rawun only.

Marriages are not performed on the 1st *S*ood, nor for two or three days after the 10th Wud, nor on the 30th Wud* of the month, P. K. Nor when the planets Jupiter and Venus are invisible, P. S. Nor during the Si*n*hust year, when Jupiter is in the Lion Constellation, once in thirteen years, P. Nor after the sun has passed the Ardra nukshutr, in Gemini, P.

Ceremonies at the time of marriage.

IX. These are detailed in the replies from P., and especially in those from D. (*See* Appendix.) The chief appear to be, among Brahmuns, the Lugunputrika, Suptapudee, and Hom sacrifice. Other castes modify the Brahminical ceremonies, which are performed by Brahmuns, or, in a few, by caste priests. The girl is given away, oil and turmeric are applied to the parties, prayers for their happiness are recited, and general festivity ensues, often occasioning extravagant expenditure, S.†

Presents in jewels and money. Personal service.

X. The payment of Hoonda is not customary in some castes, 28 C. P. It is generally paid by the girl's family, if rich; if poor, they receive Hoonda, though the practice, con-

* Every month is divided into fortnights, the days in which are numbered consecutively. The first is termed *S*ood, the second Wud.

† The expense of a marriage may be as low as twenty-five or as high as many lacs of rupees, averaging from 100 to 2,000. The expense of a pilgrimage to Benares, or of a Moonj, may be half that of marriage. The average charges at funeral are 20 to 200 rupees, but may extend to any amount.

sidered in the light of a purchase, is held disgraceful, P. D. Presents in jewels and clothes or furniture (the former more especially), held the wife's property, are common in all castes according to the parties' ability, P. The nonpayment of dowry agreed on does not affect the legality of a marriage, D. A poor family, to avoid the disgrace of receiving Hoonda, will sometimes marry their daughter into a family of similar circumstances; or an intermarriage may be agreed on on both sides.

Marriage on condition of personal service is not customary in 69 C. P. Occasionally a marriage may take place between a resident orphan and his master's daughter, 60 C. P. It is customary in 26 C. P.; but though the father have no son, such Ghur-jowahee would be entitled only to gifts, not to inherit his father-in-law's property, 4. C. P.

Period of cohabitation.

XI. The girl's residence is usually at her father's house during this period, P. D., her duties remaining those of an unmarried daughter, K. According to the *S*astrus, the husband may compel his wife to reside with him after marriage, K. D.; and in all cases after her maturity, D. Mutual assistance is occasionally given from affection, but it is not usual for parents to contribute to their daughter's maintenance after she quits them, D. Cohabitation before the Shanee is punishable by *S*astru (K. S. D.) with penance, or an absolution at the Gurbhadan, S. It is, however, common, except in the Brahmun caste, D. The husband maintains his wife, and a child then born is supposed to be the husband's, unless he has been absent, when it is held adulterous, D.

Consequences of an irregular marriage.

XII. If the husband refuse to receive his wife, the jewels previously given remain on the girl's person, except in the event of her criminality, when they are given up to the husband, 97 C. P. So in case of the husband being hard pressed by creditors, 3 C. P.

If the parents refuse to send her to him, the jewels remain with the girl so long as she remains virtuous, 85 C. P. They are given up to the husband, 12 C. P. The caste generally settle such disputes, 4 C. P. The husband has a right to the wife's jewels in all cases, assigning her a maintenance in case of disagreement (Brahmuns, 3 C. P.).

The validity of a marriage is not affected by failure of a contract to pay money, nor by omission of ceremonies at the Shanee, nor by a girl's representing to her Gooroo that her marriage was performed without her consent, or by compulsion, K. D. Nor by a discovery before the Shanee that the astrological conjunction was unfavourable, 72 C. P.

Among the Brahmuns and higher castes, if it be discovered that the parties were of the same Gotr, or different castes, the marriage is annulled, the wife being maintained by the husband, but connection would be deemed incestuous (the husband must maintain her as a sister, 2 C. P.) S. D. The woman and her children are permanently excluded from caste, D. Minor omissions of ceremonies are followed by penance only, D. In the lower castes, in which previous inquiry is not so strict, if the discovery be made before the girl's Shanee, or even before the birth of children, she may be married to another by *Pat*, S. D. The marriage is not annulled by the discovery that the parties are of the same Koolee, 70 C. P. If the husband be discovered to be of a lower caste, both are excluded temporarily, and readmitted on paying a fine to the caste, only in case of his caste being a little lower one. If the wife be of the lower caste, she is alone excluded; and if not readmitted, is only entitled to maintenance, P. K. S.: as if the discovery be made after the birth of children, D. Otherwise, in castes which allow *Pat*, the husband may at his option give his wife a Chhor chittee, and she may form *Pat* with another; but this is not customary after the Shanee or birth of a child, D.

On the discovery of the husband's impotence before the Shanee in the Brahmun and other higher castes, the wife remains with him, K. D. In the lower castes she may, with the concurrence of the caste, perform penance, and form Pat with another man, 77 C. P. D.

In the three previous cases, the caste must be consulted before annulment, D. Marriage expenses are to be paid by the party who is the cause of the annulment, K. Presents already given are not returned; Hoonda promised to be paid is on the annulment sometimes paid, sometimes not, 44 C. P.

If, before the Shanee, either party die, among Brahmuns, &c., the jewels remain with the husband or his relations, 6 C. P.; with the survivor, 94 C. P. Hoonda, if already paid, is not repaid, and if unpaid it is not exacted, 58 C. P. If a wife die before the payment of her dowry, it must be paid to the husband or children, or expended in charity (K.). To the children, D.

In this case the husband is at liberty to marry again; the girl can only form Pat (79 C. P.), and that not among the higher castes (Brahmun, and 16 C. P.).

Should it be discovered that a girl has been married before, the first marriage is binding, the second null,* S. D. The caste of the girl is not affected, but her parents repay the

---

* In a Khandesh Punchayet case (No. 3) plaintiff married defendant's niece and left the country; afterwards her father died, and her mother sold her to a Despande (as his mistress). On his death her release was procured. But the plaintiff's father refused to receive her, and gave a Chor-chittee on his son's behalf. The girl was married therefore again, and lived with her second husband till his death, twelve or fifteen years after. Plaintiff then agreed to take her back as his wife, but absenting himself for two and a half years under pretence of consulting his relations, she married a third husband.

Punchayet decreed that the plaintiff's consent was necessary to the Chor-chittee given by his father; that his marriage was not thereby done away with; and that he should therefore receive back his wife from her third husband, on paying that person the expenses he had incurred on marrying her. Failing to prove that defendant received money from the third husband, that claim of plaintiff was disallowed.

second husband's marriage expenses. Should it not be discovered until after connection, the woman is excluded, maintaining herself by manual labour separately from both, and her parents pay the first husband's marriage expenses, D.

Failure of a contract to pay dowry does not affect the validity of a marriage, D.

Polygamy and second marriages of women.

XIII. A man may marry as many wives as his inclination or circumstances allow, P. K. S. D. Marriages in succession, in consequence of the death of a former wife, are very common (P.); but polygamy is not usual, except on account of the barrenness, &c., of the first wife, K. S. It is practised in the Koonbee castes, P. The ceremonies are the same (K.), but the festival is greater on a first marriage (D.). On marrying a second wife during the life of the first, there are some peculiar ceremonies. The conciliation of a man's parents is not so essential on his second marriage as that of the second wife's relations, and of the first wife and son, if any, D.

In a Punchayet case at Nugger (No. 39), in which the plaintiff was brother-in-law of defendant, both Koonbees (the Punch consisting of two Brahmuns, one Moossulman, and two Koonbees), plaintiff claimed the value of jewels taken away by his wife on her going to reside with her brother in consequence of his second marriage. Her funeral he had since performed. The claim was allowed by the Punchayet, deducting for expenses of medicine furnished by her brother, and subject to future examination as to the value of the jewels.

Among the lower castes, widows and wives under certain circumstances are allowed to form the inferior contract termed Nikah, *Pat** (P.), or Oorkee (D.). These circumstances are— if the husband prove impotent, 76 C. P. S. K.; or the

* Called Natra in Guzerat and among the Parsees.

parties continually quarrel (72 C. P.); if the marriage were irregularly concluded; if by mutual consent the husband break his wife's neck ornament, and give her a Chor-chittee, K. P. After which divorce, with the concurrence of the caste, the wife may form Pa*t* with another man, S. Sometimes, even without their concurrence. And if after twelve years' absence a husband continue unheard of, his wife may form Pa*t*. Should he afterwards return, she must return to her first husband, or live with either at her option, the party deserted being reimbursed his marriage expenses, K. D.

On a woman's forming Pa*t*, she gives up all her property and jewels to her former husband's relations (P.), except what had been given her by her own parents (K.), in default of which her second husband may be compelled to give up such property to the creditors of the first, K. S. The children, except infants, are given up to the first husband or his representative, P.

Ceremonies of Pa*t* are different from those of marriage, P. S. A widow's Pa*t* is considered more honourable than a wife's, K. Women forming Pa*t* are excluded from preparing food at sacrifices and festivals, and from being present at marriages, even of their own children, S. P. But children by Pa*t* are equally legitimate with those by marriage, S.

The castes in which Pa*t* is admissible are specified, K. S. D., and those in which women cannot remarry include Maratha chiefs, S. K. 9 C. P.

In the caste or profession of dancing girls, girls of beauty and accomplishments are made Naikins by the ceremony of applying Misee (a powder made of vitriol) to their teeth; cardamums are distributed to the guests; turmeric is put on the girl's person; after which a religious ceremony is performed in honour of the gods, or Peers. The caste are feasted, the Misee is applied by several Naikins, one of whom, of hereditary office and repute in the caste, takes the girl on her lap, and presents her with a Saree. A girl of another caste may be made a Naikin. In general, expense is incurred by obtaining the sanction of creditable Naikins. The Misee of a daughter precedes that of a Paluk-kunya, or adopted girl.

The ceremony seems distinct from the Shanee, at which period a few guests or the caste are feasted; also at the first connection. But no Deodhurm, or religious ceremony, is then performed, P.

Precedence among wives.

XIV. The wife takes the husband's rank, K. S. The first married wife is head of the family, and has a right to precedence on religious festivals and entertainments, P. K. The others are of equal rank.

Relations of husband and wife cohabiting.

XV. The custom is analogous to the law, with, of course, individual exceptions of harshness and infidelity. On a small fault the wife would not lose title to receive maintenance and presents. By expulsion from caste, a woman loses all title to property, K.

Constancy on both sides is commanded by the *Sastru*, D. It is not, however, considered criminal in a married man to have connection with a slave-girl, Kusbin, &c., K. D., though penance would be incurred by keeping a low-caste mistress or any concubine, 23 C. P. D. A wife has no right to complain of her husband's inconstancy, K.; nor to demand payment of presents made by her husband to a kept mistress. A virtuous wife will not leave her husband on any account; a wife may, however, demand a separate maintenance if her husband ill-treat her on account of a favourite wife or mistress, but she has no right to claim a divorce on account merely of her husband's inconstancy, S. But the wife's chastity and dependency on her husband are essential virtues, K. D.; and her inconstancy is punishable, according to her caste and circumstances, with loss of caste, repudiation, or penance.

The husband is answerable for the wife's offences against caste, K.; not for a criminal offence, S. (as prostitution, murder, robbery, D.). She must perform any service directed by her husband, K. D. He may beat her for faults (K. S.), or other reasonable cause, not wantonly, D. A husband is bound to maintain his wife while faithful, and if sick or disabled from performing her domestic duties, D.

XVI. A wife cannot be sued separately in a civil suit, nor can husband and wife be evidences for each other. Contracts for her subsistence, or that of her children, made by her are valid, K. While a woman resides with her parents, they are responsible for her debts; and after she resides with her husband, he is responsible, S. D. Mutual evidence.

It is disreputable for a husband and wife to complain of each other, D. But a husband may be judicially compelled to assign maintenance to his wife, if faultless, P.

XVII. Murder of either by the other is an equal crime, K. The murder of the husband by the wife is the greatest possible crime, D. A husband may kill his wife found in the act of adultery, according to the *Sastru*, but in no other case; an exception not allowed to the wife in similar circumstances, D. Murder of either by the other.

XVIII. Among the higher castes, the husband may repudiate his wife for parricide or other great crime, adultery with a low-caste man, eating forbidden food; but not on his mere pleasure on account of her being disagreeable to him, D. Separation between husband and wife.

A man committing great offences against caste sometimes retains his wife; otherwise she, with her children, remains pure, D.

Separation by mutual consent occurs even among the higher castes; but the husband pays for his wife's maintenance, P. K. D. He may demand her jewels, K. He is not bound to support her if she leave him without his consent, nor on loss of caste, K. He generally does so, unless she is incurably vicious, D. If he refuse to do so, she may resort to any means of subsistence authorized by her caste custom, K.; not to prostitution or thieving, D. The husband maintains his wife with food and clothing in all cases (except loss of caste), Brahmun, 12 C. P. Do. only while she lives virtuously, though separated, Koonbees, 4 C. P.

Repudiation and consequences of adultery.

XIX. On repudiation for parricide, adultery with a low-caste man, or other great crime, the woman loses caste, and her funeral ceremony is performed (S.). She cannot form a new connection, but remains in her husband's house on the footing of a slave, D.

A wife may be repudiated for homicide, poisoning, offences against caste, adultery with a low-caste man, or entertaining designs against the life of her husband or children, P. D. Adultery with her own or an equal caste man is generally punished with chastisement and penance, D., and she is then readmitted to caste and to her husband's society, P. If habitually, with a low-caste man, and after admonition by her Gooroo (D.), she loses caste and property, K. D. (even presents given by her parents, D.); and, except in the Brahmuns and higher castes, receives no maintenance from her husband, K. He is not bound to pay her maintenance debts, unless he afterwards retake her, 48 C. P.

In the lower castes, at the husband's option, the wife is allowed to receive from him a Chor-chittee and form Pat with her paramour, P. The paramour is to pay the husband's marriage expenses, 38 C. P. This is not universally enforced, P. The caste may levy a fine, P. In case of seduction by a low-caste man, the woman might remain out-caste and the paramour be fined; but a wealthy seducer of the same caste may, with the concurrence of the husband, caste, and Sirkar, obtain a divorce, paying the husband's marriage expenses, without affecting the caste of the woman, D. Or the ceremony of divorce may be performed by the Gunnacharee, the husband and caste receiving money, D. In the Kykaree C. (P.) the caste oblige the paramour (if of higher caste) to give three asses to the husband and two to the wife, when he may retake his wife. If of another caste, the woman must perform penance and give alms. If the paramour be of low caste, she is excluded; he pays nothing, P.

In the lower castes, besides adultery, &c., above mentioned, the husband's impotence, or simple disagreement of the parties, even against the advice of the caste, is sufficient to cause a divorce, D. The husband breaks his wife's Mungulsootr and tears her saree, when she is at liberty to form Pa*t* with another, K. P. D.

The husband accuses his wife before the caste, or Gooroo, as among some sects of Brahmuns before the Dhurm,adhikaree, P.

Effect of the children.

XX. On a separation between the husband and wife, infants remain in the mother's charge, P. Children born previously to divorce remain with the father, K. S. If the wife lose caste, the children remain with the father, P. K.; if the husband, with the mother—she and her children remaining pure in charge of the house and family, P.

Case of absentees.

XXI. Among the higher castes, if a husband remain absent without being heard of for twelve years, his wife puts on the appearance of a widow and performs Kreea. Should he afterwards reappear, penance is necessary before readmission to caste, K. D. And the husband's *S*unskar ceremonies are to be reperformed, D. If the corpse be not found, the referees in D. mention twelve, fifteen, or twenty years as the period before which Kreea should not be performed, D. The Kreea should not be performed until certain intelligence of the man's death have arrived: 19 C. P. 17 C. mention twenty-five years, 8 C. 24, 20 C. 15, and 36 C. twelve years as the limit. But as to the lower castes, *see* 13.

Duties of separated wife.

XXII. These are the same as prescribed in the books: she

may resort to any means of subsistence authorized by her caste custom, K.; not to prostitution or thieving, D. Exceptions will of course occur.

Duties of a widow.

XXIII. Among the Brahmun and higher castes, in case of the husband of a woman dying after marriage, though before the Shanee has occurred, she is considered a widow, and cannot remarry. Her head is shaved immediately, or on the Shanee occurring, nor does she wear the Mungulsootr, D.

Widowhood is considered by all castes less honourable than the married state (D.); but it is respectable, so long as the woman conforms to her caste customs (K.) as to continence, and especially performance of religious duties, D.

Suttees.

XXIV. A widow about to become a Suttee is entitled to give away all her husband's property, K. She cannot resume it should her resolution fail. Kokunust Brahmuns of the *S*iw persuasion are the principal Suttees at Poona. The wife of a Teloe burned herself in 1825. The Desust Brahmuns, it is understood, are averse to the custom, which is not so common to the southward of the Krishn or Kistna river.

Rights of a widow as to property.

XXV. Should the husband have left no brother, father, or sons of age sufficient, in the house, the widow is head of the family and manager, K. S. She should be guided by the advice of her brother-in-law and husband's male relations, if any, D. As manager, she may collect the produce of property, through her servant or sons; appoint a Goomashta to perform Wuttun service, and may sign documents, though this last is not customary, K. She may treat for her children's marriage, K. The eldest son, on becoming eighteen or twenty, becomes head of the family, if they remain in common, his mother resigning to him authority and property, and he being bound to support her, S. The son has no absolute right to succeed to a father's authority on coming of age, but if the family do not separate, he may provide for his brothers' and sisters' Moonj and marriage expenses, K.D.

Each widow is guardian of her own children, and may after separation live with any one of her sons *ad libitum*, K. Among several widows, the wife first married is the head of the family, and has charge of the property. Among several widows of sons, the widow of the eldest son has that authority, K.: and a mother-in-law living with her son's widow takes the management, though they are joint-heiresses; and should the latter refuse to reside with her mother-in-law, she can receive a maintenance only, K.

Should a husband die while living in community with his father or brothers, they take the property, and provide for the widow, K. She, however, retains sole right and control over gifts made her by her parents or husband, K. Do. as to her own property (Sonars), 3 C. P.

Should she have a child, the relations will give her her husband's property in charge for her son; and if she wish to live separately, she may claim a half share, K. There is no regular share given. The sons of the deceased (being co-heir and co-partner with his brothers at the time of his death) would share equally his portion of the joint stock, S.

Should she have no sons, the widow is entitled to a provision for life only, her husband's share reverting to the joint stock of the family, S. She can only claim food and clothes if she have no child, K.

In case of the husband having made partition with his relations before his death, and dying without sons, the widow (or widows jointly) is heiress to the husband's personal property. She holds the real property for life, appointing a Goomashta for it, but not having the power of alienating it, K, S. She may adopt one of her husband's relations, with their concurrence and that of the caste, who will be her heir, S. Otherwise the husband's brother or relations on her death pay her daughter's marriage expenses, and take the property and settle who is to be her heir if she die without children, K.

Among the Brahmuns, &c. (P.), the husband's brothers take his share of the Wuttun, maintaining his widow and daughters, and providing for the marriage expenses of the latter. The widow may, however, adopt, if ordered to do so by her husband before his death (Brahmuns, P.), and give money away in charity (out of the produce of the Wuttun). Neither is she to forfeit her right to maintenance by living separately (Do.).

Among the Sonars (P.), after deducting the daughters' marriage expenses, the widow takes the deceased's share of the family Wuttun. The widow is heiress, 18 C. P., M.,* &c., until she form Pa*t* with another man, 58 C. P., Do., and may give away a house or other property to her daughters (Purbhoo, P.). She may adopt a son, and give away any part of her husband's relations as to immovable property, 24 C. P. She may give the Wuttun to one of her husband's brothers, or direct him to perform service on her behalf.

The widow is entitled to give away a small part of her property, 7 C. P., Do. M., she being under her brother-in-law's authority; such as presents in Dhurm, alms, &c. (Brahmun, and 8 C. P.).

If a widow live separate, she is only entitled to a maintenance (18 C. P.), forfeited by her leaving disorderly, Do. A woman cannot insist on a provision if her husband have willed away all his property, K.

PARENTAGE.

Parental authority.

XXVI. A father may chastise his son by beating at any age, commonly under twelve; he is either educated at home by a

* The letter M. denotes the replies of the Marwarrees, subsequently received.

Koolgooroo or by the village Puntojee,* K. A father sometimes gives a son property to be at his separate disposal, even while living together, K. D.

XXVII. At an age not precisely limited between fifteen and twenty-five, when a son is able to conduct the affairs of the family or acquire his own livelihood, he may sign documents and attestations, 50 C. P. An infant is entitled to share property, 50 C. P. K. Two castes (P.) mention twelve and fourteen; Brahmuns and three others sixteen; 20 C. twenty years of age, P. The age of majority is sixteen, D. A boy or girl is considered of age at sixteen; a father cannot turn a son out of his house before the age of sixteen, nor is he bound to maintain him after that age, unless incapacitated by natural imbecility, in which case the parents must maintain their child for life, K. If a son separate from his family, his father need not give him a stipend. A boy may make oath at twelve, and at sixteen may manage his own affairs and be answerable for debts and promises, K. In the higher castes, a woman is considered to be always under tutelage. Age of majority.

XXVIII. This is practised in seasons of famine and distress to a great extent, as a means of preserving the lives of parents and children. Parents may not sell their children unless reduced to the last extremity. The latter are well treated by the purchasers, and are considered as redeemable slaves. *See* Slavery, K. Sale of children.

XXIX. A father can prevent his son's enjoying hereditary property during his own life (16 C. P.), and may deprive him Deprivation of inheritance.

---

* The proportion of educated to uneducated boys in Khandesh appeared by returns made in 1825 to be one to eighteen. Of the 2,022 scholars, 311 were Brahmuns, who were taught to read the Veds and *Sastrus*; 65 Moossulmans were instructed in Persian; and of the remainder attending elementary schools, 486 were Brahmuns and 267 Bunyas or shopkeepers. The general state of education was at a similar low ebb throughout the Dekhun.

of a part of the inheritance (K.), but not of the whole, P. K. The father is bound to pay his son's debts (those for maintenance with interest) while living with him, unless incurred after warning on his part to the lender, D.

Liability to pay debts, &c.

XXX. A son must obey his father's commands, whether living with him or separately, K. He is bound to defray the father's debts, especially those incurred on account of the maintenance or necessary ceremonies of the family, P. He ought to take charge of the family affairs if his father become prodigal, insane, or otherwise misconduct himself, 1 C. P. D. If the father become poor, his sons are bound to support him; and if by agreement a sum is assigned for the father's income, after the death of one, the survivors must defray it, K. D. *See* Money Debts and Interest.

On the father's death, the sons owe obedience to their mother and respect to their father's other wives. It is absolutely necessary to provide for the subsistence of the former, K. A son does not pay interest on sums borrowed from his mother, unless under special agreement, D.

A son is bound to receive and maintain his mother applying for his protection, though she have quarrelled with his father and taken away her jewels, K. D. On his attaining majority, the eldest son does not absolutely succeed to his father's authority, but it is his duty to assist and maintain his mother, manage the family, and provide for the Sunskar expenses of the younger branches of the family, K. S.

Precedence among sons.

XXXI. The son of the wife first married, though born subsequently to a son by the younger wife, is entitled to the privileges of the Bu*r*epuna, 85 C. P. There is a discrepancy on the point both according to *S*astru and custom. Brahmuns (P.), 14 C. P. state that the first-born son is entitled.

The same discrepancy exists as to the eldership of twin sons. Brahmuns (P.), 71 C. P. state that the last born is entitled to the Bu*r*epuna, 26 C. P. give the privilege to the first born, and 2 C. P. to the son whose face was first seen by his father.

These privileges vary with different castes (*see* Appendix A.). They are, the right to hold and place the family idols, to sign an attestation first in order, to possess the right side of the house, to take first share on partition, to enjoy precedence in receiving Pan, &c., at marriages and other festivals. The law of primogeniture in inheritance prevails only among a few families, and some district Wuttundars, and confers on them rather a right of supreme management and of making assignments of maintenance than an exclusive title to the whole property. In the D. Josee caste (P.), the elder is entitled to three rupees in addition to his share.

Illegitimate children.

XXXII. Posthumous children receive their share of inheritance, S. They are not reckoned illegitimate unless born above ten months after the husband's association with the wife, K. The same limitation of time is applied to the case of absentees, K.

Children by Lugun or Pa*t* enjoy equal shares of inheritance, but the former are entitled to the Burepuna and Man-Pan; 87 C. P. 9 C. P. do not allow the practice of Pa*t*. Children by Lugun and Pa*t* are equal in all respects, K. 8 C. P. The child by regular marriage receives three rupees more than the child by Pa*t*, 1 C. P.

On mutual separation of the parents, *see* para. 20.

Children by kept women are not entitled to share property, nor to sit with the family at meals, nor (in general) to caste privileges, 35 C. P. Do. K., if the father be a Brahmun, &c. They can only receive presents from their father, 19 C. P.; and are considered as slaves not purifiable in caste for several generations, 3 C. P. But it is usual to leave legacies to mistresses and their children, S. The father is obliged to support his natural son, he performing the duties of a servant, K. In some cases, where the parents are poor and have no other son, the natural son succeeds to the property, K. He is treated as a child, 1 C. P. 26 C. P. stated that the custom is unknown among them.

Natural children are maintained by the father (55 C. P.), who pays their marriage expenses, after which they must maintain themselves, K. Such maintenance to the children depends on the good conduct of the mother, 15 C. P. It is the father's duty, but the mother may do so, 1 C. P. A natural child cannot, in the Brahmun and higher castes, demand maintenance from his father's married wife, nor in general from his heirs, unless during youth, K.

In case of a legitimate daughter and illegitimate son living under the same roof, either succeeding to the property must give a share to the other, K. Lower castes give natural children a share of the property, K. They inherit the mother's property only (Brahmun), 10 C. P. They inherit the father's only in case of there being no other heirs (57 C. P.), after paying the father's funeral expenses and feeding the caste, 3 C. P. They may acquire property, and the father has no right over their acquisitions, K.

Illegitimate children are of the mother's caste, 62 C. P. Do. if the mother be of low caste, otherwise they are purifiable, 3 C. P. Girls only, 1 C. P. If the mother be of low caste, the children are burun-sunkur, of mixed caste. A child by a slave has no rights of property, M. and 2 C. P.

Children by an irregular marriage are considered the illegitimate children of whichever parent was of lower caste, and their offspring to three generations do not regain the caste privileges of legitimate children, S.

Children of a woman living in adultery have no caste, 49 C. P. On the mother's readmission they may regain caste, 13 C. P. If the mother remain excluded, the children are so also, and are considered as the offspring of slaves, 23 C. P. They are of their father's caste (5 C. P.), or considered the

"Goluk" of their father's caste, K; and are excluded from inheriting the property of their mother's husband, K.

Children of dancing girls are of their mother's caste, and are entitled to inherit her property and settle her debts. During her life, the mother has a right to the daughters' gains. They have no claims on their father, though occasionally the girl's husband or paramour will provide for them, P. But a son is heir in preference to a Paluk-kunya or adopted girl. The latter is heiress if neither son nor daughter is alive, P. Daughters inherit the mother's property in preference to sons. They cannot inherit other property, but may acquire it, K. If one in a family die, leaving a young child, the rest provide for its maintenance until of age and understanding sufficient to conduct affairs.

Foundlings.

XXXIII. The parentage of exposed children should be if possible ascertained; otherwise they would be held of no caste, nor would any one be obliged to maintain them. They may serve in a temple or Muth, K., or obtain maintenance as slaves. *See* Slavery.

Children are never emasculated in this country, K.

ADOPTION.

Why adoption is permitted.

XXXIV. Adoption is allowed in order to secure the performance of obsequies after death, the succession to Wuttuns and property, and assistance during old age, 98 C. P. Nine castes have not the custom of adoption.

It is allowed in case of a begotten son becoming out-caste (Brahmun, 2 C. P.) or insane, or otherwise becoming incapable of conducting the family affairs, 38 C. P.; such adoption is in the name of the son, 1 C. P. A madman is, however, seldom married, and an out-caste is often readmitted, 2 C. P.

No son can be adopted during the life of a begotten son, K.

(not disqualified as above). No son can be adopted if a begotten son have no natural disability to succeed to property. *See* Inheritance.

Two kinds of sons.

XXXV. The only distinction now observed is between the Ourus-pootr or begotten, and the Dut-pootr or adopted son.

Disqualifications.

XXXVI. An insane man cannot adopt without the consent of relations. An out-caste man cannot adopt (Brahmun and Sonars), 7 C. P. Neither can adopt (Purbhoo), 2 C. P. His wife, if free from such disability, may adopt, 10 C. P., with the consent of the caste, 72 C. P. Previous insanity is no bar, if reason afterwards return, M. An unmarried man cannot adopt, D.

Age of the parties.

XXXVII. The age of the adopter is unlimited, P. It should be above forty, or the period of begetting children, M. The adoptee should be young, on account of the mutual affection of the parties, 5 C. P. M. He should be adopted previously to the performance of his Moonj (Kan. Sonar. Purbhoo, P.) or marriage, at least if not a near relation (Purbhoo), P. His age should be between five and twelve, 7 C. P.; any period between one and twenty-five, 47 C. P.; under twenty, 21 C. P.; between five and twenty-five, 5 C. P.; under thirty, or even fifty, 3 C. P. There is no limitation as to age (Brahmun), 3 C. P. The adoptee should be not older than the adopter.

Preference in selection.

XXXVIII. The following relations are to be selected in order:—1, Brother's son; 2, Paternal first cousin; 3, Paternal second cousin; 4, One of the same Gotr; 5, One of the same caste, P. Should the party first in order be refused by his immediate family, the caste may advise; and if they fail to persuade the party, another boy is, with their concurrence, to be adopted, P. In case of Surinjamdars, &c., the consent of the Sirkar is necessary, P.

The son of the nearest relation is to be adopted; but should his father not consent, a stranger may be adopted with the consent of several respectable persons, K.

A daughter's son is sometimes adopted, with the consent of relations, D.

XXXIX. Of three sons, the second is to be adopted in preference to the eldest and youngest, P. An only son is not to be given in adoption, 60 C. P. But an only son may be given in adoption to his uncle, in order to secure succession to his Wuttun (Brahmun, 2 C. P. M.) or acquired property, 18 C. P. An only son may be adopted with the concurrence of both parties, 10 C. P.; but such adoption seldom takes place, K. D.

Who are not adoptible.

XL. The free consent of the parents of the adoptee, at least of his father, is necessary, P. S. Also of the adopter's brother if before partition (5 C. P.). The signature of the relations should appear on the adoption deed, K. The consent of the near relations is necessary, 51 C. P. Also of the caste (43 C. P.) or inhabitants of the place (5 C. P.). Should the proper party refuse consent, after an ineffectual attempt on the part of the caste to persuade him, another boy, being the relation next in order, may be adopted with their sanction, 11 C. P.

Consent of whom necessary.

The consent of the Sirkar is necessary to adoptions by Wuttundars, 3 C. P. K. Purgunnah Wuttundars, 3 C. P. The *S*astrus should also be consulted, 3.

Enamdars, exclusive of dancing girls, in making adoptions, must obtain the consent of the representatives of the granters, or if the Enam land were granted by Government, of the Sirkar. Nuzzurs were paid to the native Government on occasions of granting permission to adopt, P.

XLI. It is not customary to adopt a second son during the life of the first adopted, 14 C. P. K. Only one can be adopted, S. If two were adopted, they would share equally (45 C. P.), the first adopted taking tho Burepuna (Sahookars of P.). Such an adoption was permitted by the Peshwa on one occasion only, when he received a Nuzzur of some lacs

Successive adoptions.

of rupees; but it gave great offence to the Brahmuns, being in opposition to the *S*astrus, Do. P. A man may adopt two sons, one to each wife (Wys Sonar, P.).

A boy maintained in the house, married and advanced in life, whether a son of a relation or stranger, is called a Paluk Pootr, and is not entitled to share in any property *de jure*, P. *See* Paluk,kunyas, 43.

Form of adoption.

XLII. At an adoption a festival is held, to which are invited relations, friends, and leading men of the caste. Presents are distributed among the head men of the caste, village officers, relations, and guests. The fact of distribution of sugar, cocoa-nut, and Pan is evidence of an adoption, P.

In the Brahmun and other castes, in which the *S*astru ceremonies are performed, the placing the boy in the adopter's lap is considered an essential ceremony, P. Occasionally an adoption deed is signed by those present, or an entry is made in any books* which the parties may have, 1 C. P. P. Adoptions may also be proved to have occurred by ascertaining the relations in the new and old families whose Kreea and Puksh have been performed by the adoptee.

Adoption how annulled.

An adoption concluded agreeably to the *S*astrus is not annullable, 49 C. P. S. It is not retractable among Brahmuns after the Hom ceremony has been performed, nor among lower castes, K.

But if concluded contrary to *S*astru or caste custom, unknown to the caste at the time, it is afterwards annullable by them, 70 C. P. Examples: Adoption of one older than the adopter, or of a father's brother, 25 C. P. Or of a sister's son, or a cripple, or one deficient in understanding, or of one adopted without the consent of his parents or relations, 5 C. P. Or of one adopted without the established ceremonies performed by the Oopadya Brahmun, 1 C. P. Or

* Not account books.

the adoptee is afterwards excluded from caste, K.; Sonars, P. Also if he is afterwards proved to have been of a lower caste.

Though the adoption be not annulled, yet should the adoptee not perform his filial duties, he separates from his adoptive father, receiving some share of the property, K., Sonars, P.; as one-tenth of the property, not being liable to pay debts, Ling. Wanee, P. He receives a maintenance only if he turn out of dissolute habits or unfit to manage the property, Purbhoo, P. *See* Separation between father and sons.

The adoption of a Paluk-kunya as a dancing girl may be annulled if she does not conduct herself at the pleasure of the adopter, P. *See* 43.

The Ugurwale stated, that in case of a man maintaining a relation's child, writing a deed to the effect that he should not be heir, and afterwards adopting him, the subsequent adoption would bar the effect of the deed, and the adoptee would be heir, not the widow, P.

Rights of an adopted son.

XLIII. An adoptee performs the ceremonies of Kreea and Puksh for his adoptive father and relations only in case his natural father should die without any other son or near relation, when he would perform them as a Dhurmpootr, S. (Sonars, 19 C. P.). An adoptee performs Sootuk for his natural family according to their adoptive relationship, P. K. D.* In other respects, he is on the footing of a begotten son, S. P.; even if, contrary to custom, more than one boy should be adopted.

Adoptions are sometimes made by nuncupative will at the point of death: such an adoptee sometimes receives a part only of the deceased's property, D.

The caste is competent to decide on the question of a legal

* Example: If a nephew is adopted, should his natural father die he should perform the Sootuk prescribed for an uncle; if a stranger is adopted, no relationship is held to exist after adoption between him and his natural father, P. K.

adoption, P. If unsettled by them, it may be referred to the Sirkar, B. S. P.

Among the caste or profession of dancing girls, Palukkunyas are sometimes given from friendship, or taken on receiving a present. Their Misee is performed after that of born daughters, but in other respects they have equal rights with the latter, in a manner analogous to adopted sons, P.

The adopted son receives whatever the adoptive father gives him during his life, obeying and kindly treating him, and succeeds to his property on his death, being answerable for his debts, P. He can only inherit from his natural father, in default of other heirs in previous order of succession (49 C. P.), in virtue of his adoptive, not his original relationship, S. He cannot intermarry with either his natural or adoptive Gotr, D.

After the father's death, an adopted son is bound to provide for his mother in food and clothing: she is not entitled to a share, Ugurwale, P. In the lower castes a partition sometimes occurs, but the adoptee is heir to his adoptive mother, and generally manager during her life.

Consequences of a son afterwards born or appearing after supposed death.

XLIV. In this case, both the begotten and adopted son would inherit the father's property in equal shares, but the former would be entitled to the honour of primogeniture (Burepuna) and (78 C. P. K.) precedence (Man-Pan); the latter being considered as a younger brother, S. The begotten son would be entitled to a larger share of property, 8 C. P., even two-thirds of the whole, as in the case of his reappearing, 1 C. P. He is considered superior to the adoptee (Purbhoo, P.); sharing the father's bad as well as good fortune, M. The adoptee is entitled to Man-Pan, 1 C. P.

In some places, the two boys share all property equally; in others, the former takes two-thirds; in others, three-fourths; in others, the father, on the birth of his begotten son, gives the adoptee a present according to his ability, and separates him from the family, and in consequence he takes no share; in others, the adoptee obtains nothing without a complaint to the Sirkar. The former is entitled to management of hereditary property, and if an Enamdar or Wuttundar, to the Dustkhut (right of signature), Sikka (seal), Naonagur (mark or signature of a Patell), and other privileges of eldership. Sahookars of P.

XLV. A wife, in case of her husband's continued absence, when no hope remains of child-bearing, may adopt by his written order, P. K. Or after the period has expired, when she puts on the appearance of widowhood, she may adopt as his widow. *See* Widowhood. **Adoption by females.**

A widow is permitted to adopt, if by her husband's order, and after consulting his relations, Brahmuns, P. In default of the husband's order, the consent of relations and caste is necessary (79 C. P.). The last requisite is not universal.

A widow without heirs may adopt (42 C. P.) with the consent of her caste (40 C. P.). The Brahmuns stated that she must have her husband's order, and must consult his relations previously to adopting, P.

A widow whose husband has died before her puberty may adopt, if she have her husband's order, and after consulting his relations (Brahmuns), or with the consent of the caste (4 C. P.), or with both (1 C. P.). Five castes mention the consent of relations as essential. The same, if no other heir (4 C. P.). To preserve the succession to property and a wuttun (5 C. P.), such immature widow may adopt, if not desirous of forming Pat; the adoption should then be celebrated after her Shanee (38 C. P.). Do. with the consent of her relations and caste (33 C. P.).

Of two widows, the elder is to adopt. Should she not listen to the advice of the caste, the younger may adopt with their concurrence, 73 C. P. The elder is to adopt, but the younger does so in some places, Brahmuns, P. The elder has the right, but in the event of her living irregularly

(1 C. P.), the younger may adopt; or both, by the husband's order, 4 C. P. Either may adopt (by mutual consent), 2 C. P.

The adoptee is bound to provide the widow in necessaries, K. She retains, during life, the right over her own property, but the adoptee is heir to his adoptive mother, K.

See Separation between father and sons. A son adopted by a widow would be entitled to a greater share of management of property on a separation with her, than in case of a separation with a father; but Farikhuts of partition are unusual between parents and children, P.

All the above rules as to selection, consent, age, ceremonial, &c., are applicable to widows' adoption.

In a Nuggur Punchaet case (No. 46), in which both parties and Punch were Brahmuns and Koolkurnees, the widow of an adoptee obtained a decree for the possession of a wuttun given to him by the adopter, in opposition to a claim set up by the nephew of the latter according to blood. The Bukshishnama or deed of gift was in the names of Venkajee, the adopter, and his brother's wife, being in community. It contains the names of the parties, their gotrus, and their fathers' names. It states that Venkajee having no son, and having given in marriage his daughter, a son was necessary to manage his worldly concerns and perform his funeral ceremonies: he had therefore requested Ramajee (defendant's grandfather) to allow him to take on his lap his youngest son (plaintiff's husband), in return for which he grants to his said adopted son Jeewajee his wuttun of Koolkurnee, with his house, bullocks, cows, buffaloes, iron and brass utensils, jewels, gold, silver, &c. The adoptee to receive and pay all debts, enjoying the property for himself and his descendants; all connection as to property being in consequence broken off between the adoptee and his natural father. This deed is written by the Koolkurnee, and attested by the district Wuttundars with the mark of a plough. It was decreed that defendant should keep the property inherited from his grandfather, and that only.

In a case decided in 1190 Fuslee, under the superintendence of Ramsastree of Poona, Rugoohet Bhu*t*, an Ugneehotre Brahmun, claimed his rights as son of Kakun Bhu*t*, who had been adopted by Gune*s* Bhu*t* with the consent of Babun Bhu*t* and others, defendants. Defendant asserted that Kakun had been adopted forcibly, and that his party did not perform the customary Sootuk at the death of Gune*s*, &c. It appeared, however, from the evidence of the villagers, taken in the Temple by a Karkoon deputed for that purpose, that the signature of Babun was on the adoption deed—that he and the others did perform Sootuk on Gune*s*'s death—and that when, on the death of Kakun Bhu*t*, they refused to perform it, the more distant relations refused to eat with them in consequence. It was decreed that defendants should undergo penance previously to obtaining purification for this neglect, and that plaintiff should continue to perform the duties and receive the dues attached to his office.

GUARDIANSHIP.

Guardianship of children.

XLVI. Should a wife be living with her husband at the time of his death, separately from his relations, she is the guardian of her children, and each widow of her own; if she have previously separated, she has the option, K. The mother of course takes charge of infants, though separated from her husband, K. A son of due age may also superintend the ceremonies and marriage of his younger brothers and sisters. *See* Widowhood.

But should any of the widow's husband's brothers be

living with him at the time of his death, he becomes guardian of the children; or any other qualified relation. A guardian is afterwards responsible for his trust, K.

Should there be no parents, or paternal relations, whether the father died during community or after separation, by his verbal bequest, in presence of several witnesses of the caste (58 C. P.), children may be placed with their property under charge of their maternal uncle; or father-in-law (4 C. P.); or more distant relation, or trustworthy friend or servant, 84 C. P. The arrangement is made by the caste (5 C. P.), who are guardians, 1 C. P. If no other, the Patell and Koolkurnee will fulfil the office, 4 C. P. Two Yads or inventories are made out of the property when the caste arrange the guardianship, of which one is kept by the guardian and one by a man of repute in the caste, Ugurwale, P.

If no natural guardians are alive, others may be appointed by relations, or by the Gooroo, or by the father before his death. The former cannot be set aside, except on a refusal to act. It sometimes happens that there is one guardian of the person, and another of the property, K.

Relations of guardian and ward.

Guardians are entitled to emoluments if agreed upon, or afterwards fixed by Punchact. They may be called to account by any interested party. They may not manage their ward's property for their own benefit, but may sell or borrow on his account to defray his Moonj or marriage expenses only, with the consent of the relations, K.

Orphans cannot during tutelage dispose of any part of their property without their guardian's consent, K. Tutelage terminates at sixteen, or, if a female, at marriage, K. On the ward's coming of age, the guardian must prove his Talabund accounts by vouchers to his satisfaction, D.

Cases of in-

Insane persons are often put under the care of a near

relation, and taught by gentle means the knowledge of some customs of their caste, D.

sanity, absence and prodigality.

After absence for several years, and in some cases of profligate expenditure, family property may be put in deposit by the relations for the benefit of the children, or otherwise beneficially employed, D. A father sometimes before his departure on a long absence puts his property in deposit, settling a sum for the expenses of his family, D.

In a Punchaet case (No. 1), N., in which the Punch was composed of one Koolkurnee (Brahmun) and three Patells (Koonbees), it appeared from depositions that the Wuttun claimed (Mokuddimee of a Patellship) had always been enjoyed by the defendant's family (caste Koonbee) until his father's death, when a relation during the defendant's minority and absence assumed the title of Mokuddim, and received, on account of the Man-Pan of the Wuttun previously to his return on the expiration of his minority, 65 rupees, which he deposited with a Marwarree and paid over to defendant. Decree in favour of defendant's right to the Wuttun.

In another N. Punchaet case (No. 74), in which the parties and Punch were Brahmuns, two youths claimed from their mother jewels and papers the property of their deceased father, a Sahookar in Nuggur, deposited with her in a locked chest by their late brother. The mother objected that her husband had no property on partition with his own family, that all his property had been gained in trade, through money brought by herself at and since her marriage. It was decided that the shop and trade should be carried on in the name of the sons, by them conjointly with a Goomashta appointed by three members of the Punch, and daily accounting to them and to the mother for all the trading transactions. The keys to be given nightly by the Goomashta to the sons; the latter to sign Hoondees.

The family expenditure was fixed at 1,020 rupees per annum; the second son's food and clothing not to exceed 25 rupees per month each; the mother and elder son's wife together being allowed 35 rupees.

Expenses of *S*raddh and Puksh to be defrayed from the trade. Marriage of the younger son to be defrayed by consent of both. Expenses of a pilgrimage to Benares to be allowed to the two females, if they wish it.

Mooneem or Goomashta's salary fixed at 200 rupees per annum, writer's at 100, four servants of the shop (collectors of cash, &c.), 50 each.

Expenses of paper and ink, sweetmeats, oil, alms, &c., 200 rupees per annum. Expenses, after examination, to be allowed for Dhenge (gifts to Sahookars on the Deepwalee and Dussora festivals), Ahir (gifts of a turban, &c., to relations on a marriage), and Siddhy Khurch (a day's food to Brahmun mendicants).

Should the brothers not attend to the trade, their Nemnooks to be reduced one-half. The deceased brother's widow to live with the mother, and should they disagree, to live separately on an allowance settled by the latter. No one to appropriate money or effects besides the assigned Nemnooks, it being the Goomashta's duty to see every debt and profit collected on account of the trade.

It does not appear whether the Punchaet in this case were relations of the parties. In the absence of relations, the decision of several of the caste is, in disputed cases, final.

Spiritual guide and pupil.

XLVII. Similar in many respects to the relation of adoptive father and son, is that of Gooroo and pupil, recognized in the *S*astrus, and at present customary among devotees of the Brahmun, Lingaet, and Jyn castes, as well as among Gosaens and Byragees.

Apprentices, &c.

If a servant engage himself on condition of being taught

a trade, and learn it, and afterwards misbehave, the master should dismiss him. If a master agree for a certain sum of money to teach a servant a trade, he may turn him off before he is completely qualified, receiving a portion of the money, according to the number of days he has been with him, K. No restriction exists similar to the English law of apprenticeship. The term for learning a trade is not fixed, nor are new comers prevented from commencing trade in a different village from that in which they have been hitherto educated and resident. The best intelligence, however, subsists among individuals of a trade as to the state of the markets, and the advantages derivable from combination are, it is believed, well understood. The trading classes are far more acute than the cultivators; the Ryuts, unable to read or write, are often at the mercy of the Koolkurnees and Sahookars, to the latter of whom many of them are largely indebted.

SERVICE AND SLAVERY.

Relation of master and servant.

XLVIII. Personal recommendation, and not a written character, is usual among natives in engaging a servant, nor is there any system of registry. The sum payable monthly, and the food, clothes, &c., to be given, are settled previously to the party being entertained. No definite period as to warning is usual, though it is the interest of both parties to delay a few days after the communication of either to the other that he wishes to terminate the contract, S. The same custom does not hold good for servants of all ages. A servant cannot go to his village without giving notice, but an old servant would not have his wages deducted for doing so, unless he made a long stay, as a month or upwards, K. A servant may quit his service

Warning.

without warning if his wages are not paid, but should he give warning, the master is not to maltreat him. A servant committing a fault frequently after admonition may be dismissed without further warning, K.

Wages. The ordinary wages of a labouring man are from twenty to twenty-five rupees a year, and his victuals twice a day. He comes to his work ordinarily at sunrise or half an hour after, and goes home after dark. During the day he has two intervals of half an hour or an hour each, to eat his food, S. K.

Time of labour.

Neglect and injury. If a labourer run away after performing half his work, he forfeits his hire, but cannot be otherwise punished. If the master order an indispensable work to be done, which the servant neglect to do, the master may make the servant answerable for the damage ensuing. If a servant injure anything of his master's, he must pay the damage, K.

Chastisement. The master may have his servant chastised for lying, carelessness, drunkenness, quarrelling, and fighting with other people, or other irregularities common to the lower classes. He cannot, however, stop his pay unless he neglect to come to his work, on frequent repetition of which he will be discharged also, S. A master may deduct his servant's wages during the time he gave him displeasure, and according to his rank may abuse, strike, and beat him, K.

A servant cannot be compelled to accompany his master wherever he goes, unless such has been the agreement, K. But if so, and if the servant at setting out refuse to go, he may be compelled to go, or find a substitute; and if he desert his master without leave, he may be punished, unless he can give sufficient reason, S.

Loss of deposita. The value of a thing lost through carelessness, after having been entrusted to a servant, may be deducted from his wages, but he ought to be excused if the loss occurred accidentally. If he strike wantonly cattle put under his charge, he must pay the damage, K.

If a master entrusts his goods to a servant, and the latter sell them without his master's knowledge, his master can make him refund the sums he received; so also, should it exceed in amount the sum specified by the master as that for which he was to sell the articles. Should there be a great defalcation, the servant is answerable for it; he may even be prosecuted for theft after selling articles entrusted to him. A servant sending to a friend articles entrusted to him by his master, whereby they become injured, the master may indemnify himself in money from either of them, K. The servant may recover wages or money that he is entitled to, having laid it out in purchases by the master's order, S. *Sale of deposits.*

In proportion to the length of a man's service, one-third or one-fifth of his wages are deducted when incapacitated from an injury received in the service for further duty. If the injury be to the extent of a hand or foot, in war, the servant being sent on important duty, the master, according to his means, should support him for life. If other servants or hired labourers on a trifling business get their arms or legs broken, the master should give them money, K. The servant may demand a maintenance during any accidental injury sustained while in the performance of any dangerous work, S. *Pensions and presents.*

The duty of a servant is to obey and protect his master, and resent any ill-treatment to which he may be exposed; a servant, after joining his master in a fray, would be exonerated from blame, even should he kill one of the opposite party, S. *Duty towards a master.*

There is no fine or punishment for enticing away the servant of another, though it is improper. A servant seducing other servants from their duty should be dismissed, K.

The master is not responsible if the servant, without his orders, commit any crime, or set fire to a house by neglect; nor is he responsible for his servants' debts. If a servant die leaving property without heirs, the master should expend a *Responsibility as to servants' acts.* *Servants' property.*

part in charity, and the rest go to the Sirkar. The master has no right to succeed to it, K.

Responsibility as to servant's purchase.

A master in the habit of sending his servant for goods to a shop (not merely occasionally) is answerable for payment of the goods delivered. If the master have not pointed out to the shopkeeper the servant as a trustworthy man, the shopkeeper is answerable, K.

The master may defend a servant who has committed no wrong, K.

Dhors, Mangs, or Mhars.

The duties of village menials are to watch against robbers, and trace stolen property; to clean the horses of strangers, watch by their baggage at night, and accompany them on their journey as guides to the next village. They hold Wuttuns, of which they are particularly tenacious, being entitled to land or huks in grain from the village cultivators. As guides, they do not object to carry a trifling load, but the practice of begarries was, until checked by the orders of the English Government, prevalent, especially among public servants travelling, or during the march of troops. Such compulsory and gratuitous labour, even of cultivators, would naturally prevail occasionally as one of the abuses of despotic power.

See custom of Sahookars as to responsibility of clerks, &c., and hire, on responsibility of carriers.

Slaves of different kinds: male and female prisoners of war.

XLIX. Prisoners of war were seldom enslaved by a humane prince; they would be liberated on a slight ransom on entering his territories, D. K. No distinction appears to have been made between those who yielded and those who were otherwise taken. Unclaimed females so taken, and children, became the slaves of their protectors, unless found to be of a respectable caste or family, when they would be given over to their parents, D.

Female convicts.

A woman convicted of murder, attempt to poison, procuring abortion, sorcery, theft, adultery, beating her family or husband (he not being willing to maintain her), was sentenced to slavery; but was sometimes liberated on the payment of a fine by her relations. The condemnation of prostitutes to slavery, not being sanctioned by the *Sastrus*, may be considered characteristic of an arbitrary government, D. It has not been customary, K. It was considered discretionary to ransom a prisoner of war or not, but posterity of criminals were never enslaved, D. Nor criminals (K.), except for a very heinous crime, D.

Female prostitutes.

Male criminals and their posterity.

Insolvent debtors occasionally discharge the obligation by service to their creditor. He is allowed to treat him under such circumstances as he would any other slave, but the period is temporary in proportion to the amount of the debt. Should the debtor die before the expiration of the contract, his son takes his father's place. His wife does not become the creditor's bandhee, but in the event of no male of his family remaining, the females must discharge the debt by money or service. It is discretionary with the creditor to accept or refuse ransom offered during the period of service. In some parts of the Kanura and Mysore country, it is customary to enslave even the posterity of a debtor, if a Mhar. The native Government did not enslave debtors for balances due, D. K.

Temporary service of insolvent debtors.

Famine and poverty often oblige persons of every caste to sell both themselves and their families. But in general Brahmuns are not enslaved, and Mhars, &c., are from low caste incapacitated from acting as household slaves, S. In periods of distress owners of slaves also sell their slaves, D.

Children and others sold for slaves in times of famine, or kidnapped.

Wandering tribes (Brinjarrees, Kykarees, &c.) and Gosaens, not unfrequently steal children strayed, and sell them. Such children are recoverable by their parents, if boys, before fifteen or sixteen, and if girls, before their pregnancy, by paying a fixed ransom, or on simply claiming them, if their servitude has set off the debt of maintenance, D; as after twenty-five years, in case of foundlings, K. The same rule exists as to children sold by relations, whether to obtain money or to get rid of their prior claims to property, S; and to foundlings, D. K. *See* 54.

Persons never sell themselves as slaves unless dying for want of a maintenance, when caste is a secondary consideration. Pending slavery, a man is not considered of equal respectability with a freeman of his caste, but he may after the famine be readmitted to his caste on the usual penance. He performs the services allotted to him with reference to his caste; not forfeiting it unless from the commission of a caste offence, D.

Caste of the slave.

Of the above descriptions, those recognized as slaves in (S.) are, purchased slaves, foundlings, illegitimate children, and children born of slaves. Those in (K.) are, children sold during a famine or taken in war, and children born of a female slave (except Brahmuns and Bunyas), foundlings being there treated as domestics, according to their competency, and not degraded as slaves. Apostates are not enslaved, D. K., but called Bohast, K.

Conditions of Hindoo slaves.

L. The whole of these are treated more like adopted children than slaves; most persons who can afford it maintain and clothe them better than domestics, providing for their marriage expenses, affording them more or less their confidence, according to their intelligence and ability, and frequently before their death emancipating them or giving them some property. So universal is this kind treatment, that a poor family in times of distress consider it an advantage to get one or two of their children so well provided for. Among the upper classes, almost all the females who perform the drudgery of the house are purchased slaves. However, the labour of hired servants is found much more effective, in consideration of maintenance and the trouble of teaching a slave. Slaves seem to be kept up in rich families more from ostentation than use, S. They were treated with more harshness than at present under the native Government, D.

Emancipation.

A slave-owner may at his option receive ransom for a purchased slave, whether tendered by himself or a third person; but insolvent debtors should be emancipated whenever the amount of the debt may be forthcoming, D. The Sahookar must be indemnified; sometimes the Government will interfere and emancipate the debtor, D. Slaves taken in war or purchased in a famine must be emancipated on ransom offered: children born of a female slave or otherwise purchased need not be so. In the first case, the children of the slave are emancipated also; in the others, not unless their ransom also is paid, K. The owner or buyer may at his option accept as a substitute the child or relation of the emancipated slave, D. K.

A master may apprehend a fugitive slave wherever he meets him, whatever be his caste, K. Absence, however long, does not alter the relation of master and slave; but if the slave be not found till after the master's death, he is not the slave of his heir. And in case of the slave having been allowed by his master during absence to marry a woman of better caste, his posterity in the ninth generation rise in estimation, D.

A slave-owner may emancipate his slave at any time, by so expressing it in his will, and may make him perfectly independent of his heirs, D. K. The manumission of private slaves by the Sirkar, in opposition to the owner's wish, would be arbitrary, K. D. If, after being manumitted, the slave should be unable to procure subsistence, the master may receive him again as a slave, D. Slaves, if separating from their masters, generally do so by mutual consent. If he save his master's life, he can claim no right of being freed *de jure*, D. He and his family are freed, K.

Responsibility for offences.

Slaves are responsible for the crimes they may commit, but the owners are so for slight breaches of the peace in which the former may be concerned, D. A master is answerable for debts contracted or crimes committed in his house only if done with his knowledge, K. Slaves cannot contract debts except with their master's sanction and at his responsibility, D.

Adoption of slaves.

A man of the *S*oodru caste may adopt his slave, if he have no children of his own, K. Mahrattas and Moossulmans, if without children, adopt those by their Bandhees. Such children are held of inferior caste with their posterity to several generations. They, however, superintend the property, and are nearly on the same footing as children, D.

Girls purchased by dancing women.

Female children are often purchased on a Khureed-putr, or deed of sale, by dancing women for the purposes of public exhibition and prostitution. It is not usual to take such girls from the Brahmun or Syed Moossulman castes, P. They are taught the usual accomplishments of the profession, and sometimes eventually rise to the head of the establishment. They cannot leave their purchasers without consent of the latter, and the parties generally live harmoniously together. Sometimes the mistress and the slave exchange the appellations of mother and daughter, the latter supporting the former; sometimes the girl's liberty is purchased by an admirer. At others, from rivalry, ill-treatment, or attachment to a favourite lover, they abscond, and the mistress, becoming a loser in consequence, complains to the Government authorities. Under the native Government the girl was restored, with remuneration for the injury sustained, to the person who had from infancy maintained and clothed her, unless a compromise was entered into by the seducer, which in the event of his being a man of rank, was not difficult, S. P. A purchased girl is under the orders of the daughters and Karbaree. Naikins may purchase girls, their age and number not being limited. All property acquired by them is taken by their mistresses, though one purchased girl sometimes is heiress, to her companion. The son or daughter performs the Kreea of a purchased girl, P. In default, the caste, who also purchase a girl and establish her as successor to an heirless Naikin, with the ceremony of lighting a lamp in the house. The property is not taken by either the caste or the Government, P.

Rights of the slave as to evidence and property.

LI. A slave is not considered infamous either as a witness or in any other judicial capacity (S), if otherwise competent, K. P. From Dharwar, opposite opinions were received in answer. The labour a slave performs for his master is an understood exchange for his food and clothing, S. If he realize money when not required by his master, the latter could not with propriety demand it of him, though at his death, without children, it would revert to the master, S. Slaves may inherit and bequeath property which, by their master's consent, they have possessed. On his death the master would become entitled to the whole, as, strictly, he was during his life, but the slave's wife would enjoy it during her life ; and bequests to any person or caste, slaves or others, would generally be carried into effect, D. A slave may acquire property, or inherit it, or take bequests : should he die without children, the master inherits, K. A slave may serve as a soldier (K.), if otherwise competent, and when permitted by his master, D. Should slaves own slaves, the profits of their labour go to the master, D.

Rights over the slave.

LII. In case of a slave complaining against his master, not for insufficient food and clothing, nor on account of his marriage not being provided for, but for severity of punishment for disobedience, he should not be listened to; and on unfounded complaint should be delivered over to his master for punishment, P. A slave cannot make a complaint against his master; Government should punish him for so doing, K.

Should a slave be obstinate or insubordinate, his master may punish him by depriving him of his accustomed food, K. D.; or otherwise, or may turn him out of doors, K.; but may not take his life, D. The owner is bound to support in age the slave who toiled for him in youth, K. D.

A master may on his departure assign land to a particular slave, and take all the others away, K. Such slave cannot be turned out of it except by their master's losing right of possession. Slaves cannot be obliged by their masters to emigrate with them, if not stationary on their Wuttuns; but slaves of Government Ryuts accompany their owners wherever and whenever they emigrate, D.

Offspring of slaves.

LIII. Children of female slaves (Bandhees), of foundlings, and of persons who voluntarily yield their freedom, are hereditary slaves, D.

Female children of slaves are given in marriage; hence their lot and that of their children of both sexes is preferable to that of the male children of slaves not so favoured. Children of Bandhees by illicit intercourse become slaves; but their descendants rise in estimation in the seventh generation. Children of Bandhees married to male slaves are the slaves of the father's master. Should, contrary to custom, a free woman marry a slave, the offspring, if enslaved, are the slaves of the father's master; the woman, too, loses caste. Generally, however, neither a free woman nor her children are enslaved. A freed Bandhee marrying a free man, the offspring are free, but are of inferior caste to the father. A free man may purchase a Bandhee as a kept mistress, and the offspring are his slaves, generally acting as servants in their father's house. Bandhees are often so kept, or live as prostitutes, &c., D.

Children of purchased females are slaves, and the master

may sell them; but as they regain caste in the third generation, the grandchild of a purchased slave cannot be sold. Children of male slaves are not considered slaves, but are a kind of apprentices for an unlimited period, S. The son of a male slave is a slave like his father, K.

In case of a slave-owner acknowledging as his own the child of his female slave, such child would generally be employed as his confidential servant, take precedence of the children of other female slaves, and be maintained and married in common with the family. The mother would become free, D.; though not *ipso facto*, D. The father ought to manumit both the mother and child, K. A person voluntarily becoming a slave is treated more as an adopted son than a slave, and is considered respectable in society while conforming to his caste customs, D.

LIV. Parents may dispose of their own children in time of famine, and a man may dispose of his brother's or sister's children as well as his own, D. But should a person be sold by another who has no right by custom to sell him, the former must be immediately emancipated, and the seller made to refund the value received and be punished; and if he cannot ransom the slave otherwise, he must do so by his own personal service, D. It is wrong to sell one of a man's own family; but if sold during a famine, a father is not punished, and he may emancipate his son after paying the charges of maintenance, K.

Sale of children by parents.

COMMUNITY OF PROPERTY.

LV. Private property is of the following kinds:—

Different kinds of property.

1. Land originally granted by Government or acquired by an individual, and which by long prescription has obtained the title of a hereditary Wuttun. The Purgunna Wuttun-

Wuttun.

dars, or Zumeendars, under the late Government superintended the cultivation and revenue accounts, as head Patell (Desmookh) and Koolkurnee (Despande) of the district. They also witnessed contracts and settled disputes. Nuzzurs were levied from them by the late Government. Their Wuttuns consist of, 1, Land, waste or cultivated, usually let out to cultivators on an agreement to pay the landlord a share of the produce; 2, Umuls and Huks, shares of Government dues, or periodical or other payments from the cultivators in money or kind. This property is in some places held free of rent, in others it is chargeable with a rent or tax of one-third to one-half that of the ordinary ground of the village, either payable annually or at prescribed intervals.

Statement of the estates of village Wuttundars in the district of Poona, varying in different places.

Patells. They enjoyed enamland, freehold, or subject to Joree or Tizaee enam; Meeras land; house freehold; besides Huks, viz. Teewara or Kawee, right to a portion of grain from each field at threshing time; Googree, one wun of grain from each Chahoor of 120 beegahs; Parlbhara, a man's or Tattoo's load of grain from each field when the crop is ripe; Wanwura, one or two strips of garden land, planted with vegetables; Pasoree, a piece of land or money given for a pachoree (cloth for dress); Sirpao, a turban from the Sirkar at the Jummabundy; right of taking, daily, from the shops, Pan Sooparee, oil, and tobacco; right of taking Fuskee, a handful of grain, &c., on bazaar days; right to a portion of grain, &c., imported into the village; Lugun tuka, a present on the marriage of an Oopuree or Mohturifa; dues from travelling merchants, who pay per night four pice to the Patell, four pice to the Ramoosses, and one pice to the Mhar for every tent.

Lowazima, viz. right to the service of a Kolee in bringing water for domestic purposes; to that of a Mhar in bringing wood to that of the Hujam in shampooing. The Patell also claims of the Dhobee a Puchoree to sit on during dinner, and a Saree on his daughter's marriage; and it is the Naik's duty to precede him on days of ceremony.

Man, viz. right to give Nuzzurs to Government, precedence in receiving sugar at marriage, right to receive Pooja at the consecration of the village god (once in one or two years). His wife receives a cholee, and his son and daughter take precedence in marriage processions. The Patell conducts the ceremonies at the Holee and Dussora festivals. On all occasions he receives Pan and Sandal first in order.

Naonagur, right to sign and mark with a plough, khureed putrs (deeds of purchase) of Meeras land or village wuttuns.

The customs of sharing these Huks, &c., vary in different places; in some a greater proportion is received by the Mokuddum, or elder of the family. The amount and value of course vary with the population of the villages.

Koolkurnees, or village accountants, do not in general enjoy Enam land; in some places they have Meeras, or a money salary varying from 10 to 400 rupees in amount; their Huks are, Mooshara, right to receive one or two seers of grain per beegah from every field; Kagud*baha*, do. a sum in money payable from the Gaonkhurch or fund for village expenses; Bikulmache huk, a fee of one rupee on writing deeds of sale, &c. Googree, Parlbhara, Wanwura, are similar to the Patell's Huks. The Koolkurnee's Pan Sooparee and Palkee are equal to one-half the Patell's Huks. The Lowazima of the Kolee, Mhar, Hujam, Dhobee, Naikwara is the same as the Patell's. The Man-Pan is the same as the Patell's, but the latter has precedence. The Wuttun of a Koolkurnee is generally enjoyed in turn, year by year, by all the family claiming shares in it. In some places the elder takes the Huks, and the land is equally shared, P.

Enam. 2. Land and dues granted in free Enam by Government, or independent Jageerdars, or Enamdars, to individuals.

Enams were given under the late Government from personal favour to chieftains, Mootusuddies, *S*astrees, Josees, physicians, Brahmun priests and devotees, Gosaens and mendicants, Sahookars, dancing girls, artisans, sons-in-law, friends, dependants, &c. The subjects of Enam grants are the Sirkar revenues, or portions of them (as the different Umuls of Mokassa, Babtee, &c.), due from villages, and Government land, formerly subject to the discretionary levy of Nuzzurs on alienation, &c. These grants were hereditary, and generally freehold. All the sovereign princes and great chiefs gave Enams out of their own territories, and generally obtained the confirmation of the supreme authority, P.

Dewusthan. 3. Land granted rent-free to Brahmuns and others for officiating in temples, or granted in Enam to the deity of the temple, styled the Dewusthan. The Dewusthans also enjoy Wurshasuns and Nemnooks (fixed payments from the treasury), and Huks or local dues varying in nature and amount. Prescription of twenty years has been held sufficient to allow a possessor of such land to have appropriated part of the land, &c., to purposes not intended in the original grant. Heirs of the grantors of Enam to a temple have right of superintendence, P. If the Dewusthan be large, a Karkoon on the part of the Sirkar superintends the revenue and expenditure. In small temples, the Poojaree superintends the expenses, and the Moamlutdar occasionally sends a Karkoon to examine the accounts. It has been usual, pending disputes and trivial claims, to resume the revenues *pro tempore*, appointing an officiating Poojaree on the part of the Sirkar. The Sirkar would appoint a relation (should there be one) successor to a Poojaree convicted of a crime against the purity of his caste, P.

Meeras. 4. Meeras, under which tenure cultivators have a hereditary and exclusive right of cultivation, with the power of transfer to another, subject to the payment of a settled Government rent or tax. The shares of village land, probably originally divided equally (sthuls or thuls), have become, by the long process of the law of inheritance, of variable extent and quality. The Meerasdars enjoy Man-Pan after the Patell and Koolkurnee. Oopurees are tenants-at-will, without the power of alienating the land which they agree to cultivate. There are others who cultivate land in other villages called Pykarrees and Wywankurees. No cultivator can convey manure beyond the limits of the village in which he resides, though he should have a field of another village close to it, S.

Dues of Bulloota.

5. Dues of the Bullooteedars, consisting of grain, &c., are received by the village blacksmith, carpenter, astrologer, &c., on different occasions.

Houses.

6. Houses.—After a house has been built on land given by Government, it becomes the property of the grantee, with power of alienation (K.), and resumption after any interval, provided no new building has been erected. The purchaser of a house is liable to all the usual taxes, not paying them in arrears. Special taxes and licenses of course do not affect the house, but the trading occupant, and are levied on him as a shopkeeper, S. K.

Shops.

Jageer and Surinjam.

7. Grants by the native Government in Jageer were either Fouj Surinjam, subject to the performance of military service; or Jat Surinjam, personal Jageer. The subject of these grants were the whole or particular portions of the revenues of villages belonging to the Sirkar.* Besides military chieftains, Jageers have been given to Sahookars, relations and friends of the prince and others. Usually the

* Mokassa, Babtee, Sahotra, Sirdesmookhee, Kusur, Neem Choutaee, Nuzzur, Ghasdana, Hoozoor Choutaee, Zilhe Umul, &c., varying as to name and amount in different places. Land was also given, dry, garden, or pasture.

grants depended on the pleasure of the sovereign and the fidelity of the grantee, and were liable to the payment of Nuzzurs on succession, partition, adoption, and alienation; and it was customary to take a part of the money necessary for the equipment of the contingent, if the military force was not required. They were not in general hereditary; sunnuds seldom exist; on the first grant it was usual to give the grantee a khut or order addressed to the Government officers of the district.

Nemnooks and Wurshasuns.

8. Grants from the Hoozoor or district treasuries to individuals in money were called Nemnooks and Wurshasuns. The grantees were generally religious characters, or performers of civil and military services. Sometimes a Nemnook was given in commutation of Surinjam or Enam. These grants were of the nature of annuities, but not necessarily hereditary.

Movables.

9. Jewels, clothes, household utensils, domestic animals, and money, are included under the general head of movables.

Rights of the manager and alienation of common property.

LVI. Should the elder of a family (*i.e.* the father, eldest son, widow, or her husband's brother, &c.) be unfit for the management of property, one of the other relations of sufficient skill is chosen in his stead. He generally receives presents of greater value on ceremonial occasions (64 C. P.), but no greater share on partition, 101 C. P. In a Nugger Pt. No. 16, a younger brother of superior intelligence was manager; and accounts being passed in joint names, no partition was held to have taken place with the elder.

In Enams granted on account of religion, a greater share is in some places assigned to the elder of the grantee's family, on account of the expenses of management, sacrifices, &c. In some places the proceeds of land and huks are shared, in others the land is shared definitively. Example: Of the early grants to the Chinchore god (a supposed ncarnation of Gunputtee, hereditary in a Brahmun family for eight * generations), one-half is enjoyed by the god, and managed by the elder of the elder branch, who offers Pooja and receives the profits; one-half is shared equally by the relations. All the latter grants are managed and enjoyed on the god's account.

In the villages of Teoor, Ranjan, and Siduk, called Sumusthans, from being supposed to be under Divine protection, one practice is that descendants of the grantees should share equally the old and new grants, and bear an equal share in the god's expenses; another, that the elder should receive a large share on account of expenses, the rest sharing the remainder equally,† P.

In alienations of family property by a manager during community—

The consent of the rest of the family is necessary, 24 C. P. Do. unless they are incapable of giving it from infancy, or other cause, 14 C. P. Do. in alienating immovable property and movables above the value of one or two hundred rupees, 11 C. P. Do. in alienating immovable property (Sonars), 6 C. P. Do. for sale, not for mortgage. Desmookhs and Despandhes, P. Do. the money being wanted for the necessary expenses of the family, 4 C. P.

The right is vested in the manager, but he should acquaint the rest of the family, or the most intelligent of them (Brahmuns), 50 P. M.

The manager is at liberty to alienate property without the consent of the rest, 24 C. P. Juniors are bound to respect and obey the elder, M. But they have a right to object if

---

* The term was originally fixed at seven descents; but the present, who is eighth in succession from the original pretender to Divine energy, is still in repute in Chinchore and the vicinity.

† Authorities: Sam Row Pingule, of Poona, Venkut Row Nana, Gopal Row Despande, and Ragopunt Tuthe.

he make self-interested bargains, or appropriate an undue share to himself, P.

Of widows, she is manager who is of greatest ability and experience, B. S.

The consent of the rest is necessary to alienations made by one of a family, 29 C. P. So also in the alienation by sale or gift of Wuttun property of Desmookhs and Despandhes, P., including pledge of other Wuttuns, 13 C. P. An exception is, however, made should the rest of the family be absent, or the party distressed for funds for his necessary family expenses (Brahmuns), 6 C. P.

The consent of the manager is sufficient, 24 C. P. With the same exception as to absence of the rest, and pecuniary exigency, 21 C. P. Other castes limit such alienation of family property, in any event, to movables of one or two hundred rupees value (Sonars), 19 C. P. Descended property is considered entailed, but one of several may alienate his own share, K.

Property not saleable without the consent of heirs may be recovered by them, the seller being obliged to indemnify the purchaser, K.

Property acquired by one in a family before partition.

LVII. Wuttun or other property acquired by an individual's exertion during community is brought into the common stock and enjoyed by all, 89 C. P. Zumeendars, P. Enamdars, P. The acquirer, before partition, can alienate his own share only, K.

At a subsequent partition, if a district Wuttun, all the relations share equally, in general, especially if they have contributed money or aid towards acquiring the new Wuttun (as under the native Government, by payment of Nuzzurs, &c.). In some cases, the acquirer and manager being brothers, the elder would receive the privileges of Man-Pan and Burepuna as usual, and both would share equally on partition. But in some cases the sons of the acquirer take a large share, P. In the D. Josee caste, the elder takes three rupees more than any other, P. One of a family of district Wuttundars may alienate property acquired by himself, and his relations cannot bar its sale or gift, P. But even acquired property should not be disposed of except on an emergency, K.

In Enam property an acquirer would take a larger or smaller share on partition of his own acquisitions, in proportion to the amount of assistance derived from his family. Example: If he have taken a small part only of the family property, he would receive one-half the acquired Enam, and his relations take the remaining one-half. If a larger sum, the shares would be two-fifths to the acquirer and three-fifths to the family. Of those three-fifths a larger share might be assigned to the manager, with the obligation of superintending the family at home. Generally, however, if the acquirer have received no aid whatever from his family or paternal property, he would keep the whole himself, or his elder son would take it, assigning Nemnooks for the maintenance of his younger brothers and relations, P.

Property so acquired during community is on a subsequent partition shared equally (Brahmuns and 3 Sonars), 78 C. P. The acquirer is entitled to a larger share (Purbhoo, Kan. Sonar, P.). Do. but the amount is not defined, S. Both customs are extant, M. The acquirer takes a larger share of immovable property acquired and the Burepuna, 6 C. P. Do. the Burepuna only, 2 Sonars, P. The heirs have the right of pre-emption, in case of such alienation of acquired Enam or Meeras land, or service, S.

In the case of a son acquiring property while living with his father, the latter has no claim on it, nor is it answerable for a father's debts in general, K. D. He can only alienate it in part, or in pledge, D. Or in cases of urgent necessity, K. The father sometimes gives his son separate property to be at his own disposal, the parties still residing together. The father and son ought to act reciprocally for each other in Wuttun and other services, K.

One of several unseparated relations frequently places money in Sahookar's hands for the exclusive benefit of his own children, unknown to the rest: but the latter would claim a share if the fact ever came to their knowledge, 12 C. P. One of several unseparated relations sometimes leaves his family and acquires property abroad, which descends to his own children, the latter neither claiming anything from their relations nor giving them a share of their own property, 1 C. P. Such absence effects a virtual separation. In a case decided in Fuslee 1189, under Ramsastree's superintendence, two brothers (Gosawees) being in community, one of them obtained an Enam of two villages, and afterwards borrowing 1,000 rupees, went on a pilgrimage to Benares with his father, and separated from his brothers. On his return he obtained a re-grant of the Enam (it having been resumed in his absence), with additional land and Umuls in other villages. It was decided that the son of the acquirer in question should enjoy one-half of the old and the whole of the new grant on account of his own share, defraying the expenses of the god in the Muth as by custom established, and almsgiving; that the two sons of the acquirer's brothers should receive the remaining one-half of the old grant between them; that the three cousins should defray in equal shares the debts on account of the Benares pilgrimage, but that a debt incurred in recovering the Enam, and another on account of the god, should be defrayed one-half by the acquirer's son, one-half by his two cousins in equal shares: Khuts were delivered to the parties accordingly. In another case, settled in Fuslee 1185, a similar distribution was made of Enam property among four Gosawees, brothers; the elder receiving one-half and engaging to perform the religious services; the others receiving the remainder, chargeable with deductions on account of the god.

In a Punchayet case, N. (No. 66), the Punchayet were five Brahmuns, and the parties an elder and younger brother, Sonars engaged in trade. The elder had obtained certain jewels, of which the younger got possession. Afterwards the parties separated, and Farikhuts were taken. It was decided that the younger should have no share in these jewels, on the ground that the elder was manager, and had incurred charges in paying debts to which the younger had offered interruption.

PARTITION.

Period of partition.

LVIII. Partition of property is not general between father and sons; it occasionally occurs, owing to the extravagance of one party, or undue partiality shown by the father to a younger wife, or one of his sons. Sons are entitled to what the father freely gives them, and one son may receive property from his father and separate, the rest remaining in community, 96 C. P. The father sometimes gives a larger amount to a favourite son under pretence of providing for his marriage; or keeps a larger proportion himself under pretence of an intended pilgrimage, D. No majority is necessary, S. P.

Partition between brothers may occur from the quarrelling of their wives, the appropriation of an undue share by one, the Karbaree's partiality to his own wife or children, or the refusal of one to listen to the advice of the rest, 101 C. P. If brothers are young, they should remain in their father's house with their mother, under her management; after they are grown up, a separation may take place, K.

Proof of partition.

LIX. Partition is proved to have taken place by the parties

cooking and eating separately, and by separate performance of religious domestic ceremonies (Nywedy and Wys Deo), Brahmuns, 2 C. P. Or by Farikhuts, and attestations, 83 C. P. Farikhuts or acquittances are universally customary in the Komtee, C.; not usual, in 2 C.; and described as not universal, S. The distribution of earthen pots to the caste is evidence of a partition, 1 C. P. If the parties eat and carry on trade separately, they are held to be separated, though no Farikhut have passed, M. But between a father and son, if they separate, a Farikhut must pass, M.

Disputes would be settled by the mediation of relations, by a Punchayet, or by the Sirkar, K.

In case of a Surinjam or Sumusthan, the debts are generally divided with the other effects; should the manager during community have paid debts, he will recover them from the sharers on partition, D.

Separation of one, and re-union.

LX. One of several relations may take his share and leave the family, the others remaining with their joint property in community as before, P.

Several relations occasionally agree to live together again (29 C. P.), on the settlement of the expenditure of each proportioned to his share, 45 C. P. Such reunion occasionally takes place from poverty, 4 C. P. It is not customary in nineteen castes, P. The shares may remain, as before, divided, the new acquisitions or family revenues being appropriated for family subsistence, and the surplus divided in the shares before determined, 3 C. P.

Reservations on partition.

LXI. Previously to partition, provision is made by Nemnook or otherwise for the parents, if living, and for their funeral ceremonies if dead; for the expense of building a temple or other religious or charitable expense directed by the father, M.; or agreed upon by the surviving partitioners (1 C. P.), as well as for the marriage and other ceremonial expenses of the younger branches of the family,

53 C. P. The amount of the latter may be either placed in deposit or given to the parties in addition to their shares, K. Girls also receive clothes and jewels from their parents or brothers as gifts, D. Brothers also make provisions for a widowed sister residing with them, P. Or other female relation. In a case decided under the superintendence of Ramsastree, Fuslee 1173, four brothers and a cousin living in community, one of the former died, leaving a son without any widow. The survivors agreed to give her a house, a Nemnook of 150 rupees per annum, and a saree each; the Nemnook to be reduced to 100 rupees should they receive no income from the Sirkar as at present, and the widow to retain her jewels.

Partition is not customary among dancing girls, a daughter of ability conducting the affairs of the family: sometimes a son is Karbaree. Should one of the family separate, the rest provide maintenance. In gifts, sales, and pledges of property, it is customary for the Karbaree to consult the Naikins before concluding the engagement, P. A family consisting of a mother, son, and daughter, on separation take Farikhuts; the girl living separately provides for her own subsistence, but if in distress, her family will assist her. A temporary separation sometimes takes place. A mother dying and leaving a son and Paluk Kunya, they may separate, sharing debts and property, but it is usual for a family to live together, P. Debts of all daughters contracted on account of Sunsar during community, are defrayed by the rest, P. Dancing girls.

LXII. Generally, a Wuttum is not divided until the father's death, when, if the family separate, the brothers receive equal shares, the eldest enjoying Burepuna, 52 C. P. Separation between father and sons.

The father, being manager, has the power of dismissing a son for ill-conduct, but not of disinheriting him, 52 C. P. On quarrelling, he may give the son what he pleases, 86 C. P. The father is absolute as to his acquired property, M. K. Enam lands may be divided at the father's option, K.

The son has no right to demand partition from his father, so long as he conduct himself properly in the management of the family property, 82 C. P. If the father were, however, to act extravagantly—for example, give it away to a stranger—a separation might take place, P. Or should the father be incapable of managing the property, the son does so in his name, for the preservation of it in the family, 78 C. P. Should the elder son have been dismissed, and the younger manage the property, he may continue to enjoy it exclusively, being, however, chargeable with the payment of the father's debts, 52 C. P. A son so put in charge of a Wuttun by his father has no power to alienate it, 1 C. P. So also whether remaining with his father, or born subsequently to the dismissal of an elder brother, the son takes what remains on the father's death, paying his debts, 26 C. P. On the father's death, the debts and inheritance would be equally divided between a son separated, and one born after such separation (Brahmuns), 12 C. B. The son with whom the father has lived is entitled to a larger share. Should a son be born after partition, the divided property ought to be re-collected, and after adding that acquired since, there should be a new distribution, K.

On a partition of descended property, a father's and son's shares are equal, 2 C. P. Purbhoo. The father has a greater share of that acquired by himself; and the sharing is at his option. *Vide supra.*

If the parties choose, the property may be sold and the produce divided, K. Services are often performed by the parties in turn year by year, and Huks are annually divided, D. Each may collect the produce of his divided share, or each may take his share of the annual produce;

as, of a life estate, or of the profits of land held in pledge, K.

It is usual for provision to be made for the payment of a father's debts previously to partition, but sons are always bound to pay their father's debts according to their ability, if incurred for necessary purposes, K. P. M. But a son being grown up is bound to pay the principal only of debts contracted by his father without his permission, and each son especially is bound for debts contracted on his own account, D.

In Fuslee 1176, a partition of property was determined under Ramsastree, between a father and his son by the elder wife. It appears the parties had disagreed in consequence of the father's second marriage, and the birth of a son by the younger wife.

The family property consisted of, 1, The Mokassa Umuls of twenty-nine villages. These were divided in the proportion of one-half to the father, one-fourth to the elder son separating (the villages being specified from which he was to receive his share of the Umuls), and one-fourth to the younger son remaining in his father's family. 2. Wuttuns, viz. one-half share of a Mokuddimee or Patellship (being Dhaktepuna, or attached to the younger branch), half of the Koolkurneeship of the same village, and one-half of the Mokuddimee of another village (being the Burepuna, attached to the elder branch). It was settled that the elder son should manage the Patellships, and receive the Man-Pan thereon, giving his father two shares of the produce, and keeping one himself; that on the same principle the father should manage the Koolkurneeship two years, and the elder son one year, by turns. 3. House, and Meeras, and Enam land. The house was to be divided between the two brothers, a wall being run up the middle. It was determined that all the property on the father's death should be equally divided between the brothers.

Partition between brothers.

LXIII. The general custom is for co-heirs to take equal shares, 95 C. P.; and if some time have elapsed after a succession to joint-stock property, the parties share on the principle of representation, sons receiving among them their father's share in the event of his previous death, S. In the D. Josee caste, the elder receives three rupees in addition to his share, P.

In case of hereditary offices, equal sharing is also most usual. But in some families it is customary to set apart one-fifth of the whole for the head of the family, dividing the rest equally; and in others the elder or selected manager takes the whole as head of the family, providing for the rest, S. These three modes are in use in Desmookh's Wuttuns. In those of Despan*d*hes, the duftur and enjoyment of the Wuttun are also taken in turn, year by year, P. So also in a Nugger Punchayet case, No. 29, in which the parties and arbitrators were Brahmuns. There had been no regular community nor partition in the family for above forty years. After partitioning equally all property not acquired by individual exertions, it was determined that the family right of visiting, as Bhuts, the Brahmun householders at marriages, &c., should be in future exercised by each in successive years: all dispute about roosums already received was waived by both parties.

In case of an acquirer of Enam property dying encumbered with debt, it may happen that the elder of his two sons retains a small part of it only, while the younger, taking the remainder and superadding new acquisitions of his own, disencumbers the property. The heirs of the younger would then take the property, exclusive of the portion originally retained by the elder, P. *See* Community of Property (Dewusthan).

Brothers living together, but trading separately, are answerable for each other's debts, but not for the debts of one of them contracted while separated altogether, K.

In general, debts are distributed in proportion to shares of property partitioned, 95 C. P. Should the assets be small and the debts large, a dividend is accepted by the creditors, as in cases of bankruptcy.

Brothers in community.

On the death of one relation in community with others, his creditors demand payment of the manager, 74 C. P. The debts of one being defrayed by the family, or after partition, by the members of it equally, M. Debts incurred after partition are not payable by the former coparceners, M.

Widows.

Widows are responsible for their husband's debts if they receive property through him, K.

Sisters.

Sisters living together are bound to pay the debts contracted by either for subsistence or other purpose, K.

Dancing girls.

Dancing girls pay sunsar debts of sisters (whether ourus or paluk-kunya) contracted while living together.

Enam grants by Dan-putr to a son-in-law or friend are not shared by the relations while the family property remains in common. On a partition, it is optional with the grantee to give them a small portion, P. Their consent to the gift is, however, here presumed. After partition, a gift to a son-in-law would bar claims of lineal descendants on it.

In case of one brother living separate, from a desire to procure a maintenance, or in consequence of a quarrel, without partition of a hereditary Wuttun, his descendants, after 100 years, may claim their share in such hereditary Wuttun, first paying their quota of Nuzzurs exacted thereon in the interval, P.

Case proposed.—A father and son divide property; two other sons are afterwards born in the father's house, when he dies, and the three brothers make partition. Answer.—After deducting for the expenses of marriage, Moonj, and other ceremonies from the movables, the two sons in the house share equally the remainder; although the eldest son may have been in the habit of visiting the family, and must

1. Movables

2. Immovable property

perform his father's Kreea, he does not share, after having taken his share before; and if he before took so large a share as one-half of the hereditary descended Wuttun, a new partition is made, in three equal shares. The father may appoint his two younger sons (to the exclusion of the first) heirs to a Wuttun or Enam acquired by himself, before three or four witnesses in writing, in default of which appointment the three share equally. Whatever property each of the brothers may have acquired, it is not shared by the other, P.

In a Punchayet held under Ramsastree's superintendence, Fuslee 1187, the father of plaintiff had by his own exertions obtained an Enam grant; some of the papers, however, bearing his brother's name, and he having given to one brother one of his acquired villages, it was held just that he should assign an equivalent to defendant, son of the other brother. The two brothers had reserved on a partition the share of plaintiff's father; another village was assigned to plaintiff's mother for her maintenance during life.

Farikhuts of partition frequently contain arrangements for the set-off of debts of account, houses and other property being in consequence unequally divided. From the constant partitions among co-heirs, houses, &c., become subdivided, so as to render pecuniary arrangements necessary for mutual convenience between the sharers. Wells, if not assigned to individuals, are shared in due proportion by specifying the number of *pruhurs* per diem during which such party is allowed to draw water (Nuggur Punchayet, No. 7). Sunnuds remain in the possession of the elder of the family, with liberty of inspection to the rest when necessary; copies only with the rest (Do. No. 29).

In a Nuggur Punchayet case (No. 13), in which the parties were Koonbees, before a Punch of two Patells and three Koolkurnees, it appeared that the elder (Mokuddum of a Patell's Wuttun) had unfairly divided the patrimony with his two younger brothers, giving them 82½ begahs of Meeras land instead of 22½ begahs of Wuttun. In compensation, it was determined that the former should not in future receive from the latter his Googree on the land so given, nor his dues of Sooparee and cocoanuts on marriages in their houses, nor his roosums on goods coming to them from other places.

In a decision under Ramsastree, Fuslee 1169, two cousins signed a Suntoshputr or amicable compromise, in which it is stated that the elder (as his father had done before him) held the Bu*r*epuna while he with his younger cousin were in community, but that on account of the expenses consequent on the residence of one party at a distance, they had separated, taking equal shares.

Form of a Discharge of all Demands given by one Brother to another on the Occasion of a Separation and Division of Property (*S.*).

I and my revered elder brother, Ramjee, and my esteemed younger brother, Sudasheo, being all full brothers, have up to this period lived together as one family. It has now appeared desirable that each should take his share and separate. Accordingly, of the property which descended to us from our forefathers, and of that which has since been realized, the following share has come to me :—

1. In the Pergunna of Waee, the sixth portion of the perquisites of the Despan*d*eship belongs to our family; whatever balance of these perquisites remain after paying the necessary expenses, shall be equally shared between us three. The duties of the office and the management of the concern shall be conducted by our elder brother, Ramjee.

2. The office and perquisites of Koolkurnee of the villages of Balgaum, Pimpulgaum, and Chinchore also belong to our

family, the duties of which and the management of the concerns of which we entrust to our elder brother, Ramjee, reserving to ourselves the right of exercising the said duties and realizing the perquisites of the said office annually in succession.

3. In the village of Balgaum is a piece of Enam land, measuring one chowhr, belonging to our family; of this one-third share has been transferred to me in proprietary right.

4. The house belonging to our late father at Waee shall be made over to our younger brother, Sudasheo, and the house in Balgaum shall be occupied half by me and half by my elder brother, Ramjee.

5. The bipeds, quadrupeds, specie, grain, jewels, clothes, ornaments, house, furniture, &c., &c., have been equally divided in shares, of which I have received my proportion.

6. Of the money due to the family I am to receive my share when the debts are realized.

7. Of the sums due I agree to pay according to the share which I have received.

8. There is Luxmy, the widow of our late brother, Gunesh, whom we are all bound to support by turns, if she chooses to live with us; if not, and she wishes for a separate establishment, she shall receive 100 rupees annually from each of us. If she wishes to go on a pilgrimage to Benares, she shall receive 500 rupees from us, of which I agree to pay my share.

9. Our late father having dedicated a temple to Sree Vishnoo in Waee, at the anniversary of which he expended 100 rupees, I agree to pay my share annually for the performance of this ceremony.

10. The household gods have been, as usual, left in the possession of our elder brother, Ramjee. According to the above I have received my share, and am satisfied. I am therefore henceforward separated from my other brothers,

and I have no further demands on them of any description, for which purpose I have given this paper of acquittance.

Witness
JUNARDHUN BULWUNT, (Signed) ANUNDRAM,
Koolkurnee of Waee. Despande of Waee.
This fourth Ashar Vud suke 1745, at the town of Waee.
RAMJEE HUNMUNT,
Inhabitant of Waee.

Discovery, &c.

LXIV. In case of fraudulent concealment, or accidental discovery of concealment of property at the period of partition, the parties aggrieved would be entitled to a new partition, or to such adjustment of the former one as may effect a *bonâ fide* fair division of the property on the principles above detailed.

Impartible property.

LXV. Modifications of the rule of equal division are not uncommon, though varying in particular cases. *See* paragraph 71. The partition of houses, and of the right to take water from wells and tanks, is usually laid down with great nicety. It is customary also for parties to retain possession of articles which they have hitherto used, arranging an equivalent.

Separate title by partition.

LXVI. Sons or brothers who may after separating from their relations acquire property, individually retain it; nor do sons re-share their divided property on the subsequent death of their father. The partition solely refers to the patrimony, or to their own common property, P. N. So à Zumeendaree Wuttun, acquired by a man's individual exertions, after his separation from his family, and without assistance from them or connection with them, is divided among his sons or their representatives in equal shares. It may, however, happen (as stated in paragraph 63), that the descendants of one brother living separately without a partition, may, even after the lapse of 100 years, claim their share of a hereditary family Wuttun, on payment of their quota of charges on the property during that period, P.

INHERITANCE.

Exclusion from inheritance.

LXVII. Insanity is a ground of exclusion only while the party remains unmarried, 72 C. P. The wife or relations may manage the share or Wuttun proceeds of an insane or blind person (Brahmuns), 13 C. P. But if without understanding, and having no wife or children, he is entitled to maintenance only. Blind persons, if married and having a family, may take their shares, 83 C. P., their relations managing for them. 2 C. only state that they are excluded from inheritance. Lame or deformed persons are not excluded, 1 C. P., nor are the deaf and dumb, K. Impotence is not a cause of exclusion, 37 C. P. Such a man sometimes receives a maintenance only, 36 C. P., or presents, 4 C. P. If possessing understanding, his relations may manage his share, 6 C. P. Hermaphrodites are excluded from caste and inheritance, K.

On loss of caste, the delinquent is generally readmitted on paying fine, when he is not debarred from his share of property, 39 C. P. Or his family are not excluded with him, in which case they would receive it, 35 C. P. His relations manage the property for the benefit of his family, 10 C. P. But a permanently excluded person would receive no share, 12 C. P.

No such cause of exclusion is recognized, 2 C. P. M. An insane or other person incapable of managing his own affairs cannot be debarred from his right of inheritance, K. If married, such persons would receive their share; if not, according to circumstances, 12 C. P.

A father has not the power of debarring his son from inheritance, 76 C. P.; though he may limit the amount of property enjoyed by him during life, 16 C. P. A father can prevent a son's enjoying hereditary property during his own life (16 C. P.), and may deprive him of a part of his inheritance (K.), but not of the whole (P. K.).

On the father's incapacity, the son becomes manager. *See* Antea, 52 C. P. All persons, except the sovereign, can prevent their son from inheriting the whole, but a father cannot deprive his son of a share in a future partition, K. Two castes stated that a father may prevent his son's inheriting his property, P.

The only case in which an heir is deprived of his rights is that of a successor to a religious office entirely losing caste by change of religion; in which case, though he would not be excluded from inheriting movables and immovables, and offices of a public nature, he could not enjoy the emoluments, nor (like a female incumbent) appoint a Goomashta to perform the duties of such religious office, S.

A man entirely losing caste by changing his religion from motives of avarice, has no right to share in the partition of family property, unless he did so in return for a grant to the whole family of a Wuttun, &c., when he would be allowed a share. If the change of religion were operated by force, the relations might at their option reserve to the party a maintenance, P.

LXVIII. On the death of a man, whether separate or in community, the duty of performing his funeral, and subsequently the monthly and annual ceremonies of purification for the dead, devolves on his heir. In default of his eldest son, the youngest son should perform the funeral; 3, brother; 4, brother's son; 5, any heir, as the sister's son, or Sugotr, P. M. Should the son not be on the spot, the nearest relation present may perform Kreea. The Supindu should be performed within the year, if possible, and on the spot where the father died, and only by the son, or the relation who performed the Kreea, S. Should the party be disabled

Performance of the deceased's funeral rites.

by sickness, he may appoint a sister's or daughter's son of the deceased to perform the ceremonies in his stead, 1 C. P. The eldest son defrays the expenses of the Kreea out of the common property, or if after partition, he performs the ceremonies at his own charges. The others would contribute to the expense at his requisition. All might perform the monthly and annual ceremonies at their separate charges, if after partition, as other religious ceremonies, P.

An heiress is subject to the same rules, but she appoints a relation or Dhurmpootr* to be the actual performer of the ceremony, P. K. S.

The non-performance of Kreea, Sraddh, and Sootuk, does not affect the party's right to inherit, only his religious purity, P. S. M. Nor does the actual performer (as a Purgotr, 45 C. P.) become thereby entitled to a share, but merely receives a present as hire, P. S. If not the heir, such performer is punishable, after being ordered to desist, S. The Kreea is usually performed by the Josee's orders, the expense varying with the amount of property, S. K. An entertainment to the caste is usual, 55 C. P. If the deceased left no property, from five to ten rupees only are expended (K.), the rites being performed by a Dhurmpootr, appointed by the caste. After paying the deceased's debts, and providing for an entertainment to the caste, the remainder is given away in charity, in the event of a man dying with distant relations only, 3 C. P. In this case, or on the refusal of the next heir to perform a man's Kreea, he may give his property to another on condition of his performing the ceremonies, and the survivors cannot dispossess such conditional heir, 3 C. P. A Wuttun service is often given to a stranger if there are no near heirs. The distant relations then perform the rites for their own puri-

* This term is also applied to the person appointed by an heirless widow, being a Suttee, to light her funeral pile.

fication, 1 C. P.; and to ensure the supposed happiness of the deceased in another state of existence, P. S. Hence, if the individual whose duty it is to perform the rites refuse, he is subjected to fine before readmittance to caste privileges (45 C. P. K.), without being precluded from receiving the property (38 C. P.). The Kreea is, however, performed at his charges, 3 C. P. His share may be given to his son, Brahmuns, 2 C. P. The Sirkar may have the Kreea performed out of the attached proceeds of the descendant's estate.

Among Marwarrees, the Oswal and Surawugee sects do not perform Kreea.

Heirs are bound to comply with requests of the deceased as to his funeral (S.); if consistent with caste custom, K.

Among Brahmuns, children who have not yet got their teeth (P.), or who are under two years of age (K.), are buried. Sunyasees are sunk in water or buried (S.). They are buried in salt after the brain has been extracted, P. All other Brahmuns are burnt. Bunyas and other castes sometimes bury their dead, but burning is preferred by many. Bhils, Mhars, Mangs, &c., always bury, K. Jyns bury for the first year, then burn the bones, S.

Dancing girls.

The Kreea of a purchased dancing girl, if not performed by the son or daughter of the family, is performed by the caste, P.

Nuzzurs.

Under the native Government, it was customary to levy Nuzzurs of indefinite and discretionary amount (averaging 52 per cent. on the annual value of the estate, and varying from 2 to 182 per cent.) from Jageerdars, on direct and collateral succession to their estates, on partitions, alienations, and adoptions; as well as fines for neglect, contumacy, and disaffected conduct. The Sirkar's grants in Surinjam and Jageer were held under a less certain tenure than Enams, still less than Wuttuns, being liable to conditions of furnishing military aid, either specified or unlimited, and not, unless under special grant, hereditary. Nuzzurs were not levied on succession to Enams, only on alienations by sale, to the amount of one year's value of the estate. The Zat Surinjam often yielded a few rupees only annually. The Fouj Surinjamdars levied small Nuzzurs from their dependants. Sahookars and Mahajuns also paid Nuzzurs. It is the only direct mode in which these opulent classes paid taxes, and it had a good effect in checking partition. Nuzzurs to the amount of 50 per cent. on the annual value of the estate were levied on Zumeendarees and village offices descending to collateral heirs, not in direct succession unless the estate were a large Sumusthan similar to a Jageer. On adoptions by widows and redemption of heirless shares, Nuzzurs of 125 per cent. were sometimes levied.

Custom regarding absentees.

LXIX. A man's Kreea ought only to be performed after certain intelligence of his death has been received, Brahmuns, 19 C. P. Other castes state that after twelve years (33 C. P.), fifteen years (20 C. P.), twenty years (Sonars, 8 C. P.), or twenty-five years (Purbhoo, 8 C. P.), have elapsed without receiving intelligence of an absentee, his Kreea may be performed and his property shared, &c.

Representation.

LXX. Law and custom agree in this principle and to the same extent. Among collateral relations, each family takes the share of ancestral property to which their head would be entitled if living, S.

Inheritance of property. 1, Sons.

LXXI. After a man has separated from his father or brothers, his property on his death is shared by his sons, in equal shares, provided they prefer a partition to living in community, 89 C. P. The eldest son has some privileges (mentioned in parentage), but, so far as regards property, his chief advantage consists in a right to become manager, unless incapable of the trust.

The law of primogeniture prevails in some families of Sattara both as to real and personal property. These are, the Bhonslas of the house of Sattara, the Chowhans of Duflapoor, the Nimbalkurs of Phultun, and others, S.

Among Desmookhee Wuttundars, in some places the eldest in like manner takes the whole property, giving to his brothers and relations villages, shares of villages, Huks or Nemnooks, for their subsistence. In others, the eldest reserves to himself a larger share, with the privileges of Burepuna and Karbharee or management, giving the rest a smaller share each. In others, the eldest merely takes the management and Burepuna privileges, all sharing the property equally, P.

Among Despandhe Wuttundars, one custom is for the eldest to take the Duftur, Burepuna, and a larger share, or even the whole property; another, for all to share equally, the eldest being manager; another, for the eldest to take the Burepuna only, the Duftur and Wuttun being held by all in turns, year by year, P.

Among Patells, the eldest in some places holds the title of Mokuddim, the Enam land attached to the Wuttun, the Huk, Lowazimah, the Pasoree field, Naonagur, and other Man-Pan; the younger sons taking equal shares with him of the Meeras land, houses, and other property. In other places the relations share equally the Enam land; in others, the Huks also; and in a few the Pasoree field also. In some villages, should the eldest be unfit to manage the office, the most intelligent of his relations would take that duty, receiving occasionally shares in Huks, P.

Among Koolkurnees, the usual practice is for the relations to perform service and enjoy the salary, land, or huks attached to the office, year by year, in turns. In some places the land only, in others the huks also, are shared by the relations equally; and if the eldest is incapable of management, he may appoint a Goomashta; or one of the relations acts as his substitute, receiving one-half his dues, P.

Equal partition is usual among Enamdars, P. In regard to hereditary offices, it is customary in some families to give the elder one-fifth of the property, with the Sikka and Dustkhut, or the elder as manager takes the whole, providing for the rest of the family, the marriage of the girls, &c.; movables being shared equally, S.

There is no difference as to inheritance between the half or whole blood, natural or adopted sons, or posthumous children, S., or children born before or after a partition, D. If a man die leaving three sons by an elder wife, and two by a younger, the five sons would take equally, 93 C. P. But 6 C. P. and Wys D. state that the three would divide one-half and the two the remainder. *See* Case, in Partition. 2. C. P. qualify this answer by the condition "should the mother be living at the time;" and generally, a son separating from his father loses advantages in inheritance, even should the father not exercise his right to make unequal distribution.

Case proposed.

Three brothers enjoying hereditary and acquired property in common, the first dies childless, and after him the third dies, leaving two sons. The second has no children. In sharing the property between the surviving uncle and his two nephews—

Of the hereditary property one-half is to be given to the uncle, one-half to the nephews; of that acquired by the first brother, do. do.

Of acquisitions by the second brother (by his own independent exertions), a larger (two-thirds) to the uncle, a smaller (one-third) to the nephews.

Of acquisitions by independent exertions by the third brother, a larger (two-thirds) to the nephews, a smaller (one-third) to the uncle.

Among dancing girls, a daughter has a prior claim to inherit her mother's property, paying her debts. The purchased girls have no claim on it. A son is heir in preference to a paluk-kunya, but the latter takes the property in the event of there being no son or daughter, P.

LXXII. On the death of a man without sons, leaving a widow and daughters— 2, Widows or brothers.

A Wuttun is inherited by the brothers of the deceased, providing out of its proceeds for the maintenance of the females and the marriage of the daughters, and performing the Wuttun service and the deceased's Kreea (Brahmuns), P. In the Brahmun and Bunya castes, the widow succeeds to the personal property, K. The widow receives a fixed maintenance while living virtuously, and may adopt in order to preserve the Wuttun hereditary, 1 C. P. She is entitled to her personal jewels, and may even take a share if her husband's property were not extensive, Ugurwale P. Immovables.

A Zumeendaree Wuttun may be enjoyed by the widow for her life, but she has not the power of alienating it, unless her subsistence is not provided for by the relations. Should she not adopt a son (which is generally allowed), the deceased's next heirs take the property at her death; otherwise the adoptee. The widow is at liberty to give her jewels, &c., to her daughters, P.

The widow succeeds to the Wuttun, or the partitioned share of it belonging to the deceased, providing for the marriage of daughters, and perofrming her husband's Kreea through a Dhurmpootr or adoptee, 20 C. P. She can only make gifts to a small amount without the consent of the next heirs. She has no right to alienate a Wuttun, but should appoint a Goomashta or agent, as, one of her husband's brothers, 1 C. P., for its management, and to perform the service attached, receiving her maintenance from him, K. On her death, it reverts (if no adoptee) to her husband's brothers, parents, cousins, or Sugotrus; in default, to her own brother or cousins; in default, to her husband's Gooroo; in default, to the Sirkar or, if a Brahmun, to his caste, K.

Widows of Enamdars are at liberty to give to their daughters or in charity part of her husband's share. Where the Enam revenues are still enjoyed in common, the consent of the relations is necessary to such gift. Widows may also adopt, with the consent of the representatives of the granters of the Enam, P.

A widow becoming a Suttee, without children, may give away all her husband's property, K.

Movables. The widow succeeds to the personal property, with power of disposal of it during her life, 60 C. P. K. M. Out of it she may give presents to her daughters, and provide for their marriage expenses, 3 C. P. She may give what she pleases to her daughters, even a house, Purbhoo, P. Or she may adopt, except in 2 C. P. And her jewels descend to her daughters, P.

Two widows will be joint heiresses to their husband's property; but no widow can insist on a provision in case the husband has willed away all his property, K.

On the death of a childless widow the relations generally meet and appoint an heir to her property, K.

The widow's enjoyment of property is conditional on her living virtuously. In a case decided by Ramsastree, in Fuslee 1175, a separation of property had taken place between two brothers, after which the elder died, leaving a widow. After his funeral, the younger carried off all the property from the house, and the widow went to Benares. It was decided that the brother should pay the widow the whole of her late husband's property, after deducting the funeral expenses defrayed by him. It seems the parties were Brahmuns: the deceased left no children.

In a Nuggur Punchayet case (No. 110), in which the

parties were Koonbees (Patells), and the Punch consisted of Brahmuns, a widow had resided for several years with her daughter and son-in-law, and before her death had given several presents to her daughter. These were allowed; but all her remaining property was assigned to her son.

Case proposed:—A man dies, leaving in his house two widows, with two daughters by the elder, and two sons by the younger. After deducting future marriage expenses, the sons share their father's property equally; should he before his death have desired them to give their elder sisters anything, they will fulfil his wishes. The two widows keep their jewels for life; should they prefer living separately (though in this case the younger would in general prefer living with her sons), the sons assign them a Nemnook, *i.e.* monthly or annual pension for their expenses of food, clothing, alms, &c. They are at liberty to give during their lives their jewels, &c., for charitable or other purposes, and what remains at the death of the elder is shared by her two daughters; of the younger, by her two sons, P.

In a Khandesh Punchayet case (No. 6.), the gift of money by a woman (though by Dan-Putr) to her son-in-law on his marriage with her daughter was declared improper; but "as some consideration should be paid to the deed in the grantee's favour," the Punch decided that the money should be divided between the sons-in-law and the woman's husband's brother, and clothes, metal utensils, &c., left at her death should be made over to the latter as her heir, K.

3, Brothers and daughter

LXXIII. On the death of a man without sons or widow, whether before or after partition, leaving a daughter—

The brothers of the deceased succeed to his property, providing for the daughter's marriage expenses, P. The daughter has a right only to such property (movables) as may have been given her by her father or paternal uncle, P. The brothers may give presents of movables to a grown-up sister, 12 C. P. The daughter has a right to have her marriage expenses defrayed, even out of the real property; after deducting which, the whole property goes to her father's brothers, parents, &c., in order of succession, K.

Should there be no near male relation, a distant relation performing the deceased's Kreea might share with the daughter; in default of whom, the daughter would take the whole (or daughters in equal shares), paying a substitute to perform their father's Kreea, either their son, or some other not their husband, P.

4, Brothers and father.

LXXIV. On the death of a man without a widow or children—

His father will succeed to his property in preference to his brothers, 43 C. P. His father and brothers will divide his property (3 C. P.) equally (Purbhoo, P.), the father receiving a larger share (2 C. P.). His brothers will succeed in preference to his father, 50 C. P. Either in different cases, 2 C. P. If no near male relation exist, the sisters of the deceased would share his property with a distant relation performing the Kreea, P.

In a dispute between two Kasar's, before a Punchayet of five Koonbees (N. No. 35), it was decided, on the evidence of the Patell and Barakaroo of the village, that neither party was entitled to the Meeras land claimed, on the plea that one-half was directly descended, and one-half the property of an uncle who had died heirless; but as both appeared to be descended in equal degree (three generations) from the great-grandfather, and as all other relations had fled the village, they were pronounced to be entitled each to an equal share.

It is understood that the law of the *Sastru* forms the basis of the rules of inheritance among the higher castes, but the strictness of its rules is often infringed by native arbitrators, in favour of parties connected with the deceased by ties of mutual assistance and long association, to the prejudice of nearer relations in the prescribed order, who may have deserted their kindred or be otherwise provided for.

V. On the death of a man without heirs—

His caste will take charge of his property, and after paying his Kreea and charitable expenses in his name, will expend the remainder in an entertainment to the caste, 32 C. P. K. S. And after paying his debts, 4 C. P., the head man of his caste will appoint a successor to his village Wuttun, or obtain the Sirkar's confirmation of the appropriation, 5 C. P. Patell's Wuttuns go to the Desmookh; Koolkurnees' to the Despandhe.

The Sirkar will succeed after the Kreea and debts of the deceased have been provided for, 42 C. P. Enamdars, P. Provided the property were sufficiently extensive, 1 C. P. The deceased's house should be given to a caste-man, K. 2, 3. But the Sirkar cannot succeed while any relation of the deceased can be found, Brahmuns, P. And an entertainment to the caste should be provided for, 3 C. P.

If the deceased left no bequests, after his funeral, half of his property, with the exception of village Wuttuns, should be taken by the Sirkar, and half by his caste for religious expenses, K. Annual stipends revert to Government, S.

Heirless property goes to the Gooroo, 3 C. P. To the goddess Suptusing, 1 C. P.

Dewusthan property never reverts to Government as (Nirwans) heirless, P.

In an investigation into the proprietorship of a Tikan by order of Ramsastree, in Fuslee 1185, it was decided by him that for a series of years it had been possessed sometimes by one party, sometimes by the other, generally by persons unconnected with either, and belonged to the Sirkar: he therefore took a Nuzzar of Rupees 250 from the plaintiff, and gave him a Meerasputr for the future right of occupancy, copies of which were given to the Soobah of the district, to the Zumeendars, to the village, and to the plaintiff.

Lands given in Enam on failure of heirs revert to the granter, whether Government, or an individual Jageerdar, &c., K.

Inheritance of an unseparated brother's property.

LXXV. The law and custom here correspond in principle; generally, however, the brothers assume the guardianship of the deceased's family, and his property continues in common as before until a partition take place.

Streedhun.

LXXVI. All a wife's property is her husband's, 80 C. P. S. Even her clothes and personal jewels, K. His pleasure must be consulted in gifts made by her, whether residing with him, with her father, or separately, 77 C. P. (Purbhoo, Sonars). A wife is allowed to make small presents for good and charitable purposes (Brahmun), 8 C. P. By custom, she may dispose of presents given her by her own and her husband's relations, D. Do. even immovable property given by her parents, even while in her husband's house, or on his death, K. Whether the husband die before or after connection, the wife retains her dowry, and her parents take charge of it if she is in their house (K.), or her brother-in-law, if she is in her husband's, P. The husband is the wife's heir, P. A husband may dispose of his wife's jewels* if in difficulty (K.), and borrow them without interest; but it must be done with the wife's concurrence, D. And he may demand them on separation. But this does not extend to a wife's hereditary property, which is not confiscable by a husband's creditors (?). A wife cannot receive immovable property from her husband, and all he has given her he may resume at pleasure, K. Do. all her property, S.

---

* The wedding locket, nose and earrings, and rings of the second and fourth toes, are especially the wife's property, D. The wife is allowed greates latitude if separated and receiving a stipend from her husband, as to gifts of movables to her daughter, or in charity. *See* P.

After the husband, a wife's property on her death descends to her children, or, in default, to her mother or nearest relation. Presents given by her husband, or property realized by her living virtuously, though separated, descend to her children, or mother-in-law. Presents given by her own relations, to her daughters. The caste would meet and decide, K. A wife's property descends to, 1, husband; 2, children; 3, brother-in-law and nephews; 4, parents; 5, brothers and sisters. If no husband or children, it may be given in charity, or afterwards to the grandchildren, D.

LXXVII. Alienation of Wuttun services, and religious services, is never made but from extreme poverty, Brahmuns, 2 C. P. If held in common, they are not alienable without the written attestations of all the heirs to the deed of transfer, K. A portion of property must be left to each relation, equivalent to their share; a man cannot, while in common, alienate such property, even to his son, to the exclusion of other relations being heirs, K. Such a grant would only hold good during the grantor's life, and for his own share, 20 C. P. A Wuttun, or a share of it, can only be transferred to one of the relations, Brahmuns 3 C. P. The relations have the right of pre-emption, K., and may appoint Goomashtas to perform the duties, K. S. Should there be no son, the other relations would not consent to alienate a Wuttun; an Enam field, or a house acquired by the party, might be given away with the relation's consent, Ugurwale P. Acquired Wuttuns and religious services, being personal grants (K.), not rendered hereditary, nor hereditary in the family from which it was purchased, but granted by Government on condition of personal services (S.), may be alienated at the pleasure of the acquirer, K. S.

Limitation to the right of alienating property by gift, will, or in pledge.

Grants to a temple, enjoyed by a Poojaree performing religious services, are not alienable by him without the consent of Government, K. An old incumbent, however, having no son, and being himself incapable from age or infirmity of performing the duties, may, unless the heir protest at the time, alienate for ever his right to receive huks or proceeds of land, subject to the performance of the customary religious services by the new acquirer, S. K.

Grants of descended property must, to be effective, have the consent of all the relations. The father's Danputr, attested by the heirs, is essential to gifts of immovable property generally, as a hereditary Wuttun or land, P. There are instances of gift or will of Wuttun services (as a Patellship), where no near heir was on the spot, S.

The custom of wills is not general in the Dekhun, K. S. As bequests are generally disputed, gifts are usually made during a man's life, S. Verbal and written wills are, however, valid, if made with the attestation of three or four relations, heirs, and several of the caste, K. Houses, and other bequests, if made verbally in presence of the heirs, or if they are not present, before credible witnesses, are fulfilled by the heirs, Purbhoo 6 C. P. Without an attested Danputr the grant would hold good only during the grantor's life, 2 C. P. A man may give property according to his circumstances by an attested Khut, 3 C. P. A will properly attested would hold good in favour of one yet unborn, K.

In gifts of movables, the consent of the immediate heir is sufficient, K. A son is bound to attend to his father's expressed wishes, 6 C. P. It is his duty to fulfil verbal bequests of movables, though no compulsory measures are adopted to compel his performance, 2 C. P. A refusal would subject him to reprimand and even exclusion by the caste, 6 C. P. A son is bound to fulfil his father's bequests, but not to the extent of alienating his whole property, M.

Nuncupative bequests of movables to children, relations, or attendants are sometimes made on a death-bed, S. The amount of property directed by law to go to each relation may be varied at the testator's pleasure, K. Heirs have no right to object to gifts of movables, Purbhoo P.

After a man's death, should any one claim a bequest not known by the heirs to have been made by the deceased at the time, they are not bound to fulfil it, 73 C. P. Even a son is not bound to fulfil bequests of money, if he were grown up and his father had not made them with his concurrence, 4 C. P. The claimant must produce the father's Danputr, Sonars K. P.

A Punchayet of relations has authority to settle the distribution of the deceased's property, should his will be unattested, or its validity disputed, K. A Punchayet would set aside wills made contrary to *S*astru and custom, alienating descended or immovable property to the prejudice of the heirs. Even if a large portion of movables acquired were given to a friend or companion, not a relation, a part of such property would be demanded and probably received by the heirs on a Punchayet, S.

Verbal directions are common previously to a man's death respecting living in community, the widow's provision, maintenance of helpless children, funeral and charitable expenses, and the management of the property; which are usually fulfilled by the heirs, P.

Wills made by women verbally or in writing before several respectable witnesses, are obligatory on the heirs, so far as their own property, given or settled on them at marriage. Jewels given to favourite wives are kept by them, K. *See* Widowhood and Inheritance.

The attestation of relations is in like manner necessary to a Gahun-putr of all property pledged, if the pledger is in community; and of immovable property and houses, after partition, P. The Khut should be written by the Koolkurnee (47 C. P.), and attested by the village and district Wuttundars, 20 C. P. The attestation of strangers is sufficient to a pledge of movables, 4 C. P. Annual stipends can only be pledged during the life of the stipendiary; other property cannot be touched by the heirs until the original debt is liquidated, S.

CONTRACTS—DOCUMENTS.*

Capacity to contract.

LXXVIII. There is no absolute restriction as to the incompetency of aged persons to make contracts; but should a man, from age, or anxiety, or disease, cease to have control over his understanding, and constantly talk childishly, he would not be allowed to be a witness or sign papers.

What contracts null.

LXXIX. No document is allowed to be annulled on account of alleged force or violence at the time of its execution, provided it has been attested. Theft and adultery are primâ facie probable, and the asserters of innocence are not to be believed in accusations of those crimes; but in documents the presumption is in favour of truth. So also a Khot-putr† given by a party convicted of wrong or falsehood before a Punchayet, is to be believed in spite of his assertion that it was extorted. On the other hand, should a dependant of a powerful chief produce a deed of purchase as evidence of his just title to a Wuttun violently seized, or a receipt in proof of his having discharged a debt, should there be no collateral evidence by accounts, &c., the documents on alleged extortion are not to be trusted as evidence. The same remark applies to a Khot-putr extorted by a relation of such powerful dependant from his opponent in a civil dispute, which would not be held good evidence unless corroborated by other oral,

* Authorities: Sam Row Pingule, Atyaba Wukeel of Wareekur Jadoo, Govind Row Nene, and Siddheswur Sastree, P.

† Acknowledgment of wrong.

written, or circumstantial evidence; to a Tumsook or receipt given on the faith of the grantee's paying money, which he afterwards failing to do, nevertheless insists on the validity of the documents thus fraudulently extorted; and to Tumsooks and acknowledgments of the correctness of accounts either signed by a Gomashta, or to which the Gomashta had obtained his principal's signature; such signature being fraudulent on the part of the Gomashta, and the principal being young or insane, or unable to attend to the whole matter, and the Gomashta therefore vested with general trust. In this case the principal, on subsequently investigating into the facts, will be entitled to call the Gomashta to account for any fraud or deficit, but has no claim on a third party, unless he is an accomplice with the fraudulent Gomashta. The following case has happened: several associates agree to share the profit in certain proportions of a Moamlutdarship formed from the Government, and one of them is appointed manager from an opinion of his trustworthiness. Should he afterwards attempt to defraud the children of a deceased partner, arbitrators would decide on an examination of general evidence. A Tumsook without collateral proof would not be of itself sufficient evidence to enforce payment of money, the party against whom the claim is made asserting that the money had been repaid, and that the bond had not been returned owing to delay and fraud on the part of the present holder; especially if the original parties to the loan are dead, and the dispute exists between their descendants. A Tumsook is sometimes written, and after the expiration of some months the debtor gives the Sahookar another Tumsook for the accumulated principal and interest, without having the former returned to him.

A Tumsook for payment of money, or deed of pledge of a Wuttun accepted by a Sahookar from a young member of a family, who is not of full age nor has the management of the family property, would not be acted on, and be declared null on an investigation. Advances made to a wife without the consent of her husband, being of sane mind, cannot be claimed of him by the Sahookar, and any bond signed by the wife would be annulled; but documents signed by a wife of full age, and manager of a family (her husband being insane or unfit to conduct his own affairs), would be valid. Documents signed by a young widow, or by her with consent of her young son, would be invalid, the consent of the manager (whether a relation, a trustee appointed by arbitrators, or a trustworthy Gomashta, often, in large families, a hereditary office) being essential to such contract. Documents written by a person under the influence of Bhung, opium, or intoxicating drugs or liquor, would not be held valid.

DEPOSITS.*

Responsibility of the bailee.

Deposits for custody, if lost.

LXXX. In case of goods deposited for custody, it is not customary to reimburse the owner if they are lost during the plunder of a town, or seized to answer demands of contribution by military violence of an enemy or the State (Rajkrant), not even if the depositee has preserved his own goods in safety, provided the loss in the way stated is proved, or the depositee agrees to give the amount, on future proof of his having appropriated the goods. Should the depositee's property be confiscated by his Government for crimes, he is bound to reimburse the owner, regard nevertheless being paid to his means of doing so. The depositor is not reimbursed in case of his goods being proved to have been plundered in a gang robbery (Durora); nor in case of proof

* Authorities: *see* Documents, P.

of their having been destroyed by fire while in the depositee's house. In failure of proof the depositee is responsible.

Where neglect of care is proved against the depositee, he is bound to reimburse the owner, but without interest.

Where the depositee's own goods have been accidentally destroyed or plundered, and the depositor's preserved, it is usual for the latter to make the former a present in acknowledgment of his fidelity, or exert himself in lessening the calamity, if induced by plunder or confiscation, by obtaining the restoration of a part.

A depositee of goods for safe custody is at liberty to expend their value only in view to avert a vital calamity. Should he otherwise make use of them on his own account, he is bound to repay the depositor with interest, P. It is usual to enter them in the account-book or Wuhee, or give a bond to deliver on demand, receiving hire or insurance, when the Sahookar is responsible for their loss if robbed. If packed, sealed, and deposited without entry, the owner bears the loss; he receives it back with unbroken seal, and pays no hire (D. S.). There is generally a particular agreement. Travellers putting up in a Sahookar's house for the night, bear their own loss if robbed, D. Deposits for custody if used.

A person deposits several thousand rupees with a Sahookar or friend, telling him to make use of the money, but to return the amount to him on demand, without interest. Should he then lend the money on interest without informing the owner, and lose the principal, he would be bound to repay the owner with interest at the rate of ½ per cent. Should the depositee's house be destroyed by fire, he will be bound to reimburse the owner; but if poor, he may be allowed to do so by instalments. Should the money be lost by theft in the house, he will be bound to reimburse the owner, but without interest. The case is otherwise in regard to Rajkrant, or Durora. The deposit having been made in cash when the Deposits of cash for use.

Sahookar pays interest, must be reimbursed by him if stolen, K. So also jewels deposited and entered in the Wuhee on interest by Jageerdars or rich owners, K. *See* Deposits with Sahookars.

Shawls and silks for custody.

Shawls or silks (Pushmeena Summeena) deposited for safe custody, must be delivered to the owner *in statu quo*, and he must be reimbursed to the extent of the injury sustained, if any. If deposited with liberty to use them, they are retaken, unless unfairly injured.

For use.

Metal pots, jewels for use.

Metal pots, of gold and silver, jewels, and articles not injured by use, may be, if deposited, reclaimed, and if not forthcoming on demand (having been in use for a wedding, &c., in the depositee's or relation's house) their value according to the list made out at the time of the deposit must be repaid with interest. If their value is not stated in the list, the articles are to be appraised. Such articles, if injured by fire, are to be produced without reservation before the owner; but if such injury or loss is proved, the owner is not reimbursed to the extent of their loss of value, neither is he reimbursed in case of Rajkraut or Durora.

If lost.

Pearls.

If damaged in use.

Pearls, however, are more liable than metals or precious stones to injury: the wearer therefore is answerable if they are seriously damaged by bathing, anointing, &c., while so held in deposit.

Houses for use.

The value of a house left in charge of a person (with liberty to reside), afterwards destroyed by fire, or (being old) by the rains, is not paid to the proprietor, except in case of the resident having received money from the proprietor to put it in repair, and the house having fallen previously to his doing so.

Land deposited and pledged.

In case of land left in charge of a person and pledged by him previously to gathering the crops, should the owner redemand the land, the pledgee is to be first reimbursed by sale of the crops, and the land being given over to its proprietor, an arrangement is made between him and the person left in charge.

Or sold,

In case of sale, the owner recovers his property, the person left in charge reimbursing the purchaser. In case of resumption or confiscation by Government (zubt) for a crime committed by the person left in charge, the Sirkar would not on explanation seize such land. In case of gardens and trees left in charge with liberty to enjoy the produce, if proved to have been plundered by an armed force, the owner is not reimbursed the damage: it is otherwise if the person in charge has cut down wood for building, &c.; if he has sold to another the water of a well, or from negligence has allowed such well to lose its supply of water, and the trees around it have thereby died, the person in charge must reimburse the owner. He has in fact no right to sell or pledge garden land or its produce without the owner's consent.

Or zubted, Or plundered, Or waste committed. Or well water sold.

Animals for use.

Bullocks, horses, and mares, camels, or buffaloes may be placed in charge of another, the latter feeding the animals, and putting moderate loads on them. Should they die on the road from disease, or accidentally lose their road and fall into a well, &c., or be seized by gang robbery or armed violence, on proof of the fact the owner need not be reimbursed (K.). Should, however, the person in charge have immoderately loaded them, or given them insufficient provender, or marched them too far, and the animals have died in consequence, he must pay their value, unless such excessive march was made to avoid plunder, &c. Where carelessness is proved the loss should be divided, D. Separate agreements are usually passed relative to mares in foal, cows, &c. Such person in charge should pay the owner a part of any large sum he may collect by letting the animals to hire. The money received from the Sirkar on account of horses for Sowars in public pay, after deducting all expenses of feed, is to be given to the owner. The owner should be reimbursed damages resulting from harsh treatment of the animal while

If hired.

let in hire by the person in charge, or the hire will be stopped (D.). Sheep and goats are left in charge during the owner's absence: if the person in charge cannot prove his assertion of their death, &c. (having unwarrantably sold or ate the animals), he must reimburse the owner, P.

As to young produced.

The young animals produced during the period of their remaining in charge, and the milk and other proceeds, are generally divided (by sharing the quantity, or alternately milking) between the owner and the depositee, or taken as an offset to charges of maintenance according to agreement, D.

Persons of great respectability would not demand compensation for injuries to their animals while lent or put in charge: inferior people would obtain their full value, especially if neglect or wilful injury is proved.

Deposits for a time certain not returned on demand.

Should the person in charge of property for a time certain be unable to restore it on demand by the owner after that time, from loss by fire, Rajkrant, &c., he is excused, being of course responsible if fraudulent retention is afterwards proved against him. The same remark applies to unavoidable losses pending an agreement, after the demand of the owner to restore the property in a short time certain. But should the time expire without restoration, the person in charge must reimburse the owner all damages accruing after the period from any cause whatever. Money in cash, animals, land, and houses, if placed in charge on an agreement to allow them to remain so for a time certain, cannot be demanded by the owner within that time. Jewels and clothes may be demanded by the owner on occasion of a wedding in his house, &c., though within the time. Money, too, may be given back for a necessary cause; but should the owner have promised a certain sum per mensem as reward for the care taken of the property, such sum must be paid for the whole period during which the property was stipulated to be kept, P. *See* Deposits with Sahookars.

PLEDGES.*

LXXXI. In the pledge of land, gardens, houses, animals, male and female slaves, and carriages, it is understood that the pledgee is to make use of the property, and enjoy its produce or proportion thereof, or produce of labour. Shawls, cotton cloths, and silks are usually, if in any quantity, pledged in a packed state; if few in number, by special agreement, the articles may be worn. Jewels pledged are not worn by the pledgee, nor metal pots, nor weapons, but are merely kept as security (P.), and are not saleable without the owner's consent, nor so long as interest is regularly paid, S. Except money, corn is the only article on the loan of which interest is regularly calculated, as where a ryot receives for food or seed a quantity of grain, promising to give a larger quantity of other grain yet unripe when cut (Moobadila), the quantity of the second varying from 25 to 100 per cent. on the first (Suwaee, Deerhee, Donee). But interest on the money loan varies according to the pledge, viz. security.

Pledges for use. Land and houses, animals, slaves, carts. For custody. Shawls. Jewels, metal pots, weapons. Interest on money and grain only.

If there is a probability of repayment of the money within a week or a fortnight, it is usual to advance large sums on pledges of smaller value. If within a year, the pledge is generally 25 per cent. higher in value than the loan.

Value of the pledge as to the loan.

A house may be pledged with an agreement that the owner should pay an annual sum towards the repairs: on his failing to do so, and the house being destroyed by the rains, the pledgee is not responsible. The latter is bound to rebuild the house and reinstate it, if so destroyed by the rains subsequently to the owner's having sent the money, the pledgee appropriating the same. A house may be pledged with an agreement that the pledgee should make the

Repairs of houses pledged.

---

* Authorities: *see* Documents, P.

necessary repairs, and that the owner should be charged with the expense whenever he should settle the debt. If the pledgee should fail to repair the house, and in two or three years it should fall down, he is bound to pay the expenses of reinstating it. But after the period for settling the original debt has expired for several years, the pledgee is no longer so bound.

If the owner has agreed to repair the house and pay the Government tax (Puttee), should he from absence or other cause avoid doing so, the Sahookar (pledgee) will pay the money and charge it accordingly in his account, with interest. The Sahookar will be responsible if he does not make necessary repairs to a small amount: as to heavy expenses, he should write to the owner and act accordingly. He is not responsible if the repairs absolutely necessary would involve a great expense, nor is he obliged to incur a heavy charge, even if directed by the owner to do so, on promise to allow the charge in settling the account, if inconvenient. In case of a house being burnt down, the loss would fall on the owner: enquiry might be made on suspicion of its having been wilfully or maliciously set on fire.

Hoondabhara. Hoondabhara is where a house is pledged as security for a debt, the rent of which is supposed to equal the annual interest, when no account is necessary. On the repayment of the principal, the house is given up to the owner. In such cases it is usual for the owner to agree to make the repairs.

In case of agreement that the pledgee should live in the house paying no rent, and the owner be charged with no interest on the money lent him by the pledgee, repairs to a moderate extent (as 10 rupees) may be defrayed by the latter; and if the house should fall through his not doing so, he is responsible. The charges of rebuilding walls and other heavy expenses are paid by the owner.

A Gahunputr is not always taken in small pledges, for which an entry in the Wuhee is sufficient. The former contains a description of the property pledged, the amount of the debt, the rate of interest, and the period of repayment; concluding (if a house) with a special agreement as to the rate of hire, the amount to be annually devoted to paying off the debt, the charge of repairs, &c. It is signed and witnessed by neighbours, and written by the Koolkurnee. Private contracts of mortgage are also entered into. Mortgage deed.

Property pledged with an agreement to take great care of it, if destroyed by neglect of the pledgee, must be restored in value to the owner. If pledged property is proved to have been lost by gang robbery, by fire, by flood, or by military violence (unless under special agreement), it is not restored in value. Property proved to have been lost by thieves is to be restored by the Sahookar (presuming negligence), K. If a slave dies from disease, his or her value is not restored; if from bad food given by the pledgee, he is responsible. Animals not provided with proper food or medicine, and dying in consequence, are to be restored in value. Camels, horses, bullocks, overloaded, and thence injured, are to be restored in value, unless in order to escape plunder, &c. Animals accidentally killed by tigers, falling into wells, or plundered, or dying by disease, are not restored in value. The pledgee hires out pledged cattle at his own risk, and reimburses himself for their keep, S. Cattle are seldom pledged, or at least remain in the owner's possession, K. So also horses, K. The pledgee is bound to make up to the owner of a garden pledged the injury to trees from not giving them sufficient water, or cutting them down; not if they accidentally die. If jewels worn by the pledgee or his dependants, or let out to hire by them, are lost, the owner is to be reimbursed, according to the

Responsibility of the pledgee for losses.

Slaves.

Animals.

Garden.

Jewels.

value fixed in the yad of agreement at the time of pledge.

Shawls. Shawls being benefited by wearing, the owner is not reimbursed on account of their becoming dirty; if burnt or torn through the wearer's carelessness, they are to be replaced; not if eaten by worms or rats. There may be special

Grain and cloth. agreement in these cases, P. Cloth and grain damageable by delay would be generally sold by the pledgee, or the pledgor must bear the loss, S. Money taken from a sealed

Women. bag is to be returned, principal and interest, D. Women are not generally pledged: if made to work contrary to agreement, the pledgee is debited with hire, D. The pledge of women or slaves is unusual, K.

Weapons. In the pledge of swords, guns, and other weapons, the Sahookar is not responsible if they are damaged from neglect to rub them with oil, &c., from time to time, P.

Carts and bullocks. The use of bullocks or carts is generally a sufficient offset to interest. If the pledgee feed the cattle, he is not responsible for damage incurred during ordinary work: if the debtor feed them and pay interest, the pledgee must pay hire, and be responsible for damages not accidental, D.

Horses and animals. In the pledge of horses and animals, it is usual to fix a valuation and write it down at the time of payment. It is generally agreed that the Sahookars should be at the charges of feeding and tending the animal for three or four months, and be reimbursed by the owner at the time of settling the debt. If during this period the animal die a natural death, or run away, or be seized by military followers, &c., the owner must reimburse the Sahookar according to the value specified, or give a new pledge to the amount. But should the Sahookar neglect to have the animal fed, he will be responsible to the owner for the loss. The animal may be sold when the charge of maintenance, &c., exceeds the amount of the debt. If on sale his value should be diminished by natural disease, the owner is to reimburse the Sahookar;

if from neglect of the latter, he is responsible to the owner.

In the pledge of jewels or any other articles, should fraud or substitution be proved on the part of the owner, he would be fined, and obliged to return the principal and interest, receiving back the article; if on the part of the Sahookar, the debt would not be recovered by him, and he would in addition be fined, P. Jewels.

Books wilfully destroyed while in pledge are generally restored in value or new ones written; or the remuneration for keeping them is forfeited; or the profit from the use of them is debited to the pledgee, D. Sahookars are answerable for damages to books while in pledge, K. Books.

In case of sugar pledged, a deficiency of one or two seers is not reckoned on return; if five or ten seers, the Sahookar is answerable, K. Sugar.

Movables are always taken away by the pledgee at the time of advancing the money. Movables kept by the pledgee.

Should immovable property be mortgaged successively to two persons, and contrary to general custom the owner continue to enjoy the land, the latter is bound to settle the debts with both; should he be absent, or from poverty unable, the two mortgagees would possess and enjoy the land between them; otherwise, the earliest mortgagee would enjoy the whole, even though his Gahanputr had not the Despandhy's, Koolkurnee's, and other usual attestations, it being proved that he had advanced the money, and that the owner could not at the time settle the debt. In the event, however, of one of the mortgagees holding the house in possession, and both having regularly attested Khutputrs, the party in possession retains the house without regard to priority of contract, and the other is left to claim repayment from his debtor by other means; and this even should the owner be unable from poverty, &c., to repay either. If, however, the first mortgagee Successive mortgage of land to two.

[were unable to possess the house from being obliged to] go to a distant country, on his return he would be entitled to turn out a second mortgagee, and enjoy the house himself, especially if he had enjoyed the property for a long period before his departure, and the second had enjoyed it for a much shorter time, or both. Mortgagees may by agreement enjoy the property for equal successive periods.*

If the second pledgee is proved to have known of the former contract, he must give up the article pledged to the first, on his demanding possession. So also if the second pledgee have been in possession long enough to have repaid himself his advance to the owner; if after the owner's death the first return from absence in a distant country, the latter is entitled to immediate possession, having made a large advance still remaining unsettled. In case of property pledged to one person verbally, and subsequently to another by regularly attested deed, the latter is entitled to possession, P. Both pledgees would demand payment, K.

In case of the owner, after mortgaging immovable property to one or two, selling it to a third person, with an agreement in the Khureedputr (deed of purchase) that he will answer any claims on the property, the purchaser pays the owner the purchase money; the mortgagees then putting in their claims, the purchaser is obliged to give up the property to them, and comes on the owner for repayment. Or, the deeds of mortgage and sale being regular, the owner repays his debts to the mortgagees out of the purchase money, and gives over possession of the property to the purchaser. In case of the owner having retained possession, or having spent the money advanced on the two mortgages, together with that received from the purchaser, and become unable to pay, or having fled the country, the mortgagees and

* There appears no certain rule on this point.

purchaser (neither having enjoyed the property) on comparing their deeds sell the property and divide the proceeds in equitable proportion: or, the owner having mortgaged his property to two persons without regularly attested Gahanputrs, and afterwards sold it to another by a Khureedputr publicly attested by the villagers, &c., the mortgagees cannot come on the purchaser after he has had possession for six months or a year, unless at the time of the sale they had given notice of their claims on the house to him: their debts would be considered simple contract debts. But if the mortgagee gave notice before a witness, the Khureedputr is void, and the purchaser comes on the owner for repayment.

Delay in demanding settlement of a mortgage.

In case of the mortgage of immovable property and its subsequent sale by the mortgagee to a third person; after such purchaser has enjoyed the property upwards of sixty years, the original owner has no claim thereon, except he have frequently from time to time given notice of his *right of ownership* to the purchaser. In this case the latter is said to have the Suwedhbhogy, or imperfect right of enjoyment, in contradistinction to the Nywedhbhogy held by a proprietor *de jure*. Arbitrators would restore the property in case of Suwedhbhogy to the original proprietor proving his title at any period, adjusting the claims (Torjor) by allowing interest on the purchase-money, hire for the house, &c., and cost of improvements.

Limits to time of property remaining in pledge.

It is not customary to allow property to remain in pledge for a long period, as for the life of the pledgee, or his descendants. If from poverty or absence of the owner the pledgee's descendants have continued in possession for several generations, they are bound to restore immovable property to the pledger's representative on demand, it being proved that they have received repayment of twice the amount of the original advance (Dam Doput) from the property enjoyed. Should no demand be preferred for one hundred years, the

Improvements during pledge.

possessor becomes proprietor *de jure*. In the event of restoring property, the value of improvements made and buildings erected by the pledgee or his descendants must be allowed to them, settled by arbitration.

Case of mortgagee of land not entering into possession.

If the mortgagee neglect during five years to enter into possession of a village he cannot do so: he will receive the debt, if proved by the Gahan-putr, with interest, whether he has enjoyed the village or not—unless he has been prevented from possessing it by force on the part of the mortgagor, or has in the interval made Tukaza on the latter demanding possession, or at the time of entering on possession was compelled by the Sirkar to fly the country.

Transfer of mortgage of land.

The mortgagee for (say) Rupees 5,000 having entered on possession, remains in enjoyment for a number of years, when, the owner not making his appearance (or his being in the country, remaining unknown to the first mortgagee), the latter transfers the mortgage to a second, receiving 10,000 rupees from him. Such third person receives the Gahan-putr, &c., with a memorandum of the new contract on the former one, and with a provision that whenever the owner should arrive he should be at liberty to enter on possession, the second mortgagee giving up the village to him on receiving the principal and interest borrowed, viz. 10,000 rupees, from him, while the owner comes on the first mortgagee for the difference. Even should the second mortgage be made as if the right of proprietorship were solely vested in the first mortgagee, the owner will come on the first mortgagee, and through him settle the debt with the second; if he is unable to do so the owner will himself repay the debt to the second, and redeem his village.*

Mortgage of a village, with agreement as to casual losses.

A village is mortgaged under an agreement that a sum amounting to the usual revenue of the village, deducting

* It hence appears that the right of property is less fully vested in the owner after mortgage among the Hindoos than among us.

expenses of salary, &c., should be annually applied in discharge of the debt and interest, with exception in case of loss of crops or exaction. In the event of failure of the crops from want of rain, or the village being plundered, the actual collections only will go in discharge of the debt; and should the Sahookar (mortgagee) oppress the ryots, and future loss of revenue be thereby incurred, he would be responsible.

Whenever the amount of principal and interest equals the value of the pledged movable, according to the period previously fixed for the settlement of the debt and redemption of the property, the pledgee is to give notice to the owner, and in default of redemption he is then at liberty to sell the property and reimburse himself. Until after the expiration of a period generally fixed in the Tepnama, it is not usual to sell horses, jewels, or swords pledged, on account of their variable price. In the event of no bond for repayment at a particular period having been passed, arbitrators would determine the amount chargeable to the pledger on account of principal and interest (seldom exceeding Damdooput, or equal amount of each) with regard to his circumstances, and the article is either returned to him on payment, or it is sold; and sometimes he gives a promissory note to the pledgee that he will pay the particular outstanding balance against him by instalments, or whenever his future ability may allow. A Chithee on the settlement of the debt is usual, and in cases of poverty the debtor is excused some part of his debt. Redemption and settlement. Movables.

Immovable property is generally redeemed by the payment of the principal debt only, it having been agreed that the enjoyment of the property pledged should be an offset to the interest. Immovable property is never sold, P. Sometimes the time of possession is prolonged to the pledgee, on account of losses from want of rain or Rajkrant; Land.

unless such causes of deficiency have been expressly exempted in the original agreement by some phrase, as "Bin Afut Binfitoor," &c. And in the event of the proprietor flying the country before the expiration of the Mukta, or fixed time for redemption of the produce of the property, the proportion payable to the Sahookar, his tenant, and the proprietor, are fixed by arbitration.

Houses.

Houses pledged are given up to the proprietor at the time specified, when the interest and amount fixed as rent equal each other. The pledgee in possession has agreed to make the necessary repairs, but he is not obliged to rebuild the house if destroyed by fire, heavy rains, or other misfortune (Asmanee).

Metal pots, shawls, clothes, or jewels.

In the pledge of metal pots, shawls or clothes, and jewels, should the period for redeeming the property expire, after waiting a few days, the articles may be sold before arbitrators, and on the arrival of the owner he would receive or pay the balance, whether on the price received or on the principal and interest account. Should the owner be prepared to redeem his property, and in case of its not being forthcoming, should referees fix the value too highly (as proved by their subsequent production), the referees' decision would not be set aside, unless on special agreement. The pledgee is to make up the loss (unless there were an agreement at the time) occasioned by the articles through his fault not being forthcoming on the demand.

Case of the pledgee not producing the pledge according to Yad of deposit.

Besides the Gahun Chittee, the Sahookar (pledgee) keeps a Yad of the articles pledged, specifying their number and weight (if jewels) and value: this Yad is referred to in case of losses from fire and flood, and Rajkrant and Durora. If the pledgee sell the articles for more than stated in the Yad, or for more than the value as verbally settled or determined by referees, he must give up the surplus of his debt and interest to the owner. Such unavoidable causes of loss are comprehended under the general title of Afut Asmanee-Sooltanee. On proof of false assertion of loss, the pledgee would be bound to restore the whole value, in default of special agreement, either according to the Yad, or as otherwise deposed.

Interest on loans secured by pledge.

Interest on a debt secured by pledge is lower than on simple contract debts. In case of the pledge of land, or horses, or swords, interest varies from eight annas to two rupees per cent. per mensem, without Munotee or bonus. If grain, or clothes, or jewels, the same interest is required; and on the latter, Munotee at the rate of eight annas to two rupees per cent. on the value of the pledge is besides paid at the time of the advance. Larger interest is taken according to comparative risk and mutual agreement, P.

If the pledgee refuse to deliver over the property after the interest and principal debt have been liquidated, he is liable to fine, D.

Pledges not to be repawned or sold without the owner's consent.

Without the consent of the pledger, no pledge can be repawned or sold, K. The pledgee ought not even to use the pledge without the pledger's consent; should he do so, he must pay the damages and expenses accruing. He cannot repawn or sell it without the owner's consent; nor, on his delay and refusal to redeem his property, by the adjudication of arbitrators, K.

Or used.

Exception.

Under-mortgage.

In under-mortgages the owner or first mortgagor may sign the under-mortgage-Khut; or the name of the second mortgagee is substituted for the first in the original Gahunputr; or the first mortgagee may have agreed at first to restore the house to the owner *in statu quo*. Punchayet case, N. (No. 2.)

HIRE.*

Responsibility of the hirer.

Articles hired on a marriage.

Glass.

Metal utensils.

Jewels and ornaments, clothes.

LXXXII. In case of articles hired on occasion of a marriage, and lost while in the hirer's possession by theft, their value must be repaid to the proprietor by instalments, &c., K. If plundered by Rajkrant or Durora the proprietor is not reimbursed. Articles of glass, if broken, are to be made good. Metal utensils are weighed when taken by the hirer, and any deficiency in weight is made good on returning them. Jewels and gold and silver ornaments are valued, and any deficiency is made good on returning them, unless occasioned by Rajkrant or Durora. Cotton cloths burnt or torn while in the hirer's possession are to be made good, allowing time to the party if his premises were destroyed by fire, P. Houses accidentally burnt are not chargeable to the tenant (S.), who pays the rent up to the time it was burnt down, K. If he or any of his people set fire to the house they are responsible. A tenant is not responsible for movables left in the house rented or premises not rented by him, unless expressly deposited in his charge, S. K.

Houses.

Animals for carriage.

In case of animals hired for carriage, if the owner accompany them on the journey he is not reimbursed for any losses whatever; if not, the hirer must repay the value of animals dying, or stolen, or injured by his neglect, not if plundered by Rajkrant or Durora. The owner is bound to replace accidental deaths if he accompany the hirer, and if he have agreed to convey the party to a particular place, P. S. The owner of the cattle pays damage done to the bullocks and trappings, the owner of the goods damage to the goods, unless arising from the carrier's neglect, K.

If the animals are stolen by robbers or lost through care-

---

* *See* Documents, P.

lessness, the owner not being with them, the hirer generally defrays half the value (K.). There is generally a special agreement, D.

In case of a person hiring land for a period of (say) ten years, and afterwards improving it by building a house, digging a well, or planting trees, on the expiration of the lease the owner takes the improvements at a valuation, otherwise the lessee is entitled to carry away the materials (this is in default of any specific agreement between the parties). A man living in his father-in-law's house would not be entitled to reimbursement for buildings erected for his own pleasure, if turned out; but if he has improved the house so as to get rent for it, his expenses must be repaid, K. If from building a well the produce of the ground have increased two or three-fold, and the Sirkar rent have increased in proportion, arbitrators would assign to the lessee annually after the expiration of the lease either the whole or part of the net increase on account of the well, deducting current expenses of labour, until he shall have been repaid the expense of building it; the land and well remaining in the owner's possession. The same principle of settlement is adopted in other improvements, as bringing in water-courses, or planting trees, or raising bunds, or manuring the ground, P. So in case of the real owner appearing after the ground had been rented by a false claimant, K.

Improvements of land rented.

Agreements for hiring lodgings vary in terms, and are generally made verbally before witnesses; the payments are usually in arrears. Warning of a month at least is given if the rent is to be increased; as to other warning, there seems no established rule. If a man rents a house from month to month without any definite agreement, the landlord can turn him out at four days' warning, K. The landlord's heir may turn the tenant out at fifteen days' warning, K. If the tenant improve or repair the premises, the landlord some-

Hire and lodgings; warning.

Improvements. times agrees in writing not to increase the rent so long as he occupies them. Death of lessor. In case of the death of a landlord it is optional with the heir to make a new lease, or continue the tenant, or reject him after due warning; Do. lessee. so if the tenant die his heir may insist on not quitting before the expiration of the lease, but it is optional with him to fulfil or not the engagement of the deceased, S. K.

Repairs. The tenant of a house rented for ten years pays for ordinary repairs. Expensive repairs are defrayed by the landlord, or may be deducted from the rent, K. The landlord's consent must be asked in repairs, K.

Contracts for work in time certain, with materials given, according to plan of the hirer. In case of a man contracting to perform a particular work by a particular time, if paid by the day, his wages are not diminished by failing to finish it by the time stipulated. Agreements to manufacture a particular article according to muster must be strictly kept: if the party fail with the materials given he must find others, taking those spoilt after completing the article. But a builder failing to build a house according to a particular plan is not responsible for the failure; nor is, in the former case, the manufacturer, if the failure is at all attributable to the hirer, P.

Contracts for work. Weavers. Cloths not properly woven are returnable to the weaver contracting, the owner receiving back his advance, K. Dhobees. Dhobees are answerable for damage to clothes washed, but a man of respectability would not press for remuneration, K.

Rent of houses and land. In case of four persons renting a house and three absconding, the fourth will be answerable for the whole rent, unless he give notice to the owner or his servants, K.

If a piece of ground is rented with a specification as to its quantity, the rent may be diminished on the quantity proving less than specified, otherwise not, K.

Two persons rent a house or land jointly, one of whom pays his rent regularly, the other dies indebted to the owner;

in this case the former is not answerable (unless on special agreement), K.

The landlord cannot without the leave of the tenant live in the house until the expiration of the lease, K.

A man renting a house from month to month may either give a written receipt or a verbal one. A man renting a house for a year before witnesses must pay rent for the whole year, though obliged to leave the country two months after concluding the contract, K. His wife or relations living in the house would continue to pay rent, K.

Rent of land.

The usual terms of land (either Wuttun or Enam, freehold or liable to quit rent) rented to cultivators by private proprietors are either to pay in money two-thirds of the Government rent, or to give a portion of the crop, not unfrequently one-half, after deducting seed and sundry other expenses. The value of land of course varies with the fertility of the soil, the facility of irrigation with greater or less labour and expense, and the proximity to the village.

Mutual loan of cattle and husbandry implements.

In case of farmers borrowing each other's cattle, should the animal be accidentally injured, the village sometimes decide that the owner should be reimbursed if he is poor and cannot afford the loss, otherwise not. If the animal strays or dies of ill usage, the hirer is responsible; if he uses it well and it dies of disease, the loss falls on the owner, K. Implements of husbandry lost during loan are generally replaced. Except under special agreement hired cattle cannot without the owner's consent be hired to another, K. S. Young animals would belong to the owner, paying expenses of keep, K.

Carriage of goods; responsibility of the carrier.

In case of goods engaged to be conveyed to a particular place for a certain sum, should they be lost during the carrier's casual absence, having left them in charge of an unknown person, as on a necessary occasion, his neglect being implied, he is to reimburse the owner; so, if lost while the carrier is asleep; so, if articles of glass were broken by his falling asleep, or other neglect; so, if metal utensils were damaged by being thrown down; so, if the carrier without authority pledge or sell the articles on the road. But a very young person would be excused from responsibility to this extent; and in all cases the owner is not to exact repayment of the value of the article without proof of the carrier's neglect, nor to exact it with severity as to amount of damage or time of repayment, but to have regard to his means, P.

Such carrier is not responsible if the goods were seized by gang robbers, himself being alone; nor if dropped accidentally into a well while he was drinking; nor if seized by Rajkrant; nor if consumed by fire; nor are his family responsible if the carrier himself were devoured by a tiger, &c., Do. S. K. P.

The carrier is not responsible for breakage unless he gave a special agreement to deliver those articles safe on larger amount of hire. The responsibility of the carrier extends to the delivery of the packages to the persons directed as made over to the carrier by the owner, S.*

Carriage in time certain.

A deduction may be made from the line agreed on if not delivered within the time specified, provided the delay arose from neglect and not from accident or disease, P.

DEBTS AND INTEREST.†

Rates of Munotee and interest.

LXXXIII. The amount of interest in the ordinary state of the money market varies according to the security given, or the probability that the principal and accumulating

* *See* Insurance.

† Authorities. *See* Documents and Hoondees, P.

interest will be repaid. The lender receives on advancing the money a bonus of from 1 to 2, or even 5 per cent. on the whole, called Munotee. Interest on loans to Sahookars, or on pledge to substantial ryots, varies from ½ to 1 per cent. per mensem, but loans from one partner to another often bear no interest, D. Large Sahookars would take 6 to 12. Even 48 per cent. is taken, K. The rate to petty traders varies from ¾ to 1¼, and to grain dealers, Zumeendars, Moamlutdars, and Khooshbash individuals, from 1 to 2½.

Larger interest is paid in particular cases according to private agreement between the parties. Sometimes the borrower receives only 95 rupees in every 100 nominally borrowed (the deduction of 5 per cent. being on account of Gunesee 2, Kichree 2, and Dustoree 1), and promises to pay 125 rupees in one or two years by instalments. Loans to petty bazaar traders, on whose credit the Sahookar has little confidence, are sometimes contracted for on an agreement for the trader to pay one pice per week on every bazaar day for every rupee advanced,* P. Even so high as 1 anna, or 6¼ per cent., payable weekly, has been known, S. Ryots sometimes mortgage a proportion of their crops (as from ½ to ¾ of the produce of a particular field). In this case the Sahookar takes his chance of the season, or he agrees to give a certain quantity of grain (as from 1 to 3 Pylees of rice, ragee, til, &c., per rupee lent), or if not grain, he gives an equivalent sum of money at the bazaar rate of the time. Advances are made by Sahookars to ryots of grain for subsistence, to be repaid at the close of the year at the rate of 1¼ to 2 Muns of grain for every Mun advanced, P. D.:

The bonus is equal (on good security) to about double what the interest would amount to, S.

Ryots' mortgage of crops, and payment in grain.

In the Dees of Poona interest is one Pylee lower.

Advances of grain.

In the Mawuls the Mun contains twelve Pylees or forty-eight Seers.

In the Dees 16 p. or 64 s.

* Or a deduction is made of 25 per cent., and 10 per cent. paid monthly for a year till paid off; this is called Khistee lean, S. Or the trader gives a Khut for 32 rupees, to be paid at the rate of one anna per diem, receiving an advance of 25 rupees only, P. Daily interest is, however, thought excessive, D. K.

25 per cent. more is given on grain advanced for subsistence, and 50 if for seed, S. But the lender cannot reject payment of the grain in kind at the expiration of the time, S.

If from failure of crops the ryot fail to perform his agreement, the grain is to be received at a future opportunity at the price it bore at the time it was to have been delivered, with interest from that date, D. K. In grain advances the maximum demandable by the creditor is three times the original advance (Triput), S.

Advances for cotton.

So in advances for cotton, the repayment is generally fixed in money at the price of the time of the advance (if in cotton a larger quantity being given in lieu of interest or premium). If the creditor refuse the article according to agreement, he can only receive the principal without interest at the price of the time of the advance. If he decline removing the grain or cotton, though warned by the ryot, he bears the loss; though accidental losses are generally participated. A Sahookar cannot insist on repayment if the grain he lent for seed does not come up at all; at least great indulgence is due to the ryot, D.

Do. for cloth.

Advances are sometimes made to receive cloth at a stipulated rate and period. If the contract is not performed, the advance bears interest from the period, unless from unavoidable causes; if the non-performance was with a view of profit, the creditor may claim either his interest or the debtor's profit made, D.

Do. for Goor.

In advances by a Sahookar to a ryot on condition of receiving a quantity of Goor from sugar cultivation, in the event of a bad year the Sahookar abides the loss, K.

Do. for personal labour.

Advances are sometimes made to Brahmuns to be repaid in labour, viz. in bringing water, cooking, or writing, reckoning the wages at 2 or 3 rupees per mensem. The borrower in this case receives his maintenance. Servants of other castes may receive money to be repaid by labour without maintenance. A ryot sometimes contracts to serve as a labourer from three to five years, receiving food and clothing during that period, in consideration of an advance of Rupees 30, P. Artificers and others agreeing to work out debts by personal service can only be obliged to perform duties consistent with their caste, D.

Compound interest.

Compound interest is not usually specified, but from the custom of making up accounts at the Deepoulee, and entering the balance of principal and interest as a total sum bearing interest in a new account, it is in fact paid, S. K. There is no limit to the amount of interest, but Punchayets award a sum according to the debtor's circumstances, either taking off interest of a particular period, K., or reducing it to 1 or 2 per cent., or striking off the excess of double amount of principal (Dandoput*), and decree that it shall be recovered by instalments. In case of poverty, the principal only, or a part of it, is accepted by the creditor, P. D. K.

Deductions on interest account.

No distinction of castes (contrary to *Sastru*) in trading and interest (82).

Contrary to the *Sastru*, all castes, even Brahmuns, trade in any articles except leather, meat, and spirituous liquors, and take interest at the rates above specified, without regard to the caste of the lender or borrower, D. S. K.

Liability of a son to pay his father's debts (26).

A son is bound to pay his father's debts with interest; but the principal only of debts if contracted by the father without his consent, he being grown up, D.

Of heirs and widows.

Heirs, including widows, are bound to pay the debts of the deceased out of the property inherited, and widows and sons, if at a future time they possess property. Brothers in community are responsible for the trading or other debts of one

Of brothers in community.

* In debts of long standing it is generally understood that if double the amount of the principal has been paid the debt is cancelled, S. When the interest has quadrupled the amount borrowed, the parties come to mutual agreement, K.

of their number dying before partition; and for debts incurred by a brother separated, if he afterwards reunite with them and all trade on joint capital, but not if he return in debt, and live with them, not as a trading partner, D. After a partition brothers are only bound to defray funeral expenses.

Of brothers after separations.

Of a father to pay his son's debts.

A father is bound to defray his son's debts whilst living with him, especially for maintenance (with interest), unless he have given notice or warning not to trust the son. The son would not pay interest on advances for immoral purposes, D.*

A father's debts are to be paid, both principal and interest, K., whether the son receive the inheritance or not. This does not apply to other heirs; but if the debtor is poor, the interest is not allowed to exceed the principal, in which case, as before explained, he is said to give Damdoput; if exceedingly poor, on his earnest entreaty, he is allowed to pay the principal only, P.

Liability of a grandson to debts of grandfather.

Money debts descending from a grandfather are paid by his grandson, if capable of doing so, but to the extent of the principal only. If unable from poverty, the creditor agrees to take a part only of the principal, to the extent of from one rupee to one anna, or 20*s.* to 1*s.* 3*d.* in the pound, P. A grandson and great-grandson are bound to pay debts contracted for the pilgrimage of the family, and no other, K.

Deduction.

Rates of interest and Munotee on loans to minors.

In loans to minors, payable when they may obtain possession of their property, a bonus of from 5 to 10 per cent. (Munotee) is at first deducted, and the interest varies from 8 to 12 per cent. per annum. On coming into possession land is often made over to the Sahookar, with a promissory bond to pay the principal debt by annual instalments, the produce of land being a set-off to the interest, S. Fathers sometimes give warning to Sahookars not to advance money to their sons, &c., after which they would not be responsible, K.

* *See* Parentage and Partition.

Sahookars to whom Bunyas are indebted sometimes stop the sale of their stock in trade, and take the whole in pledge: in this case the trader cannot remove his trade to another bazaar without giving security to the Sahookar, K.

Attachment of goods.

The custom of Tukazu under the late Government was of various kinds. If the parties were Sahookars, or the debtor a man of fortune, it was usual for the creditor to demand payment verbally, or bring the debtor to his own house, D. K.; then to send a Goomashta to his house to demand payment; then to seat a man near his house: and should the debtor not request his creditor to take him off by a Munnachithee, he would be obliged to comply with the man's demand for daily subsistence (4 annas, &c.), the owner fasting the whole time, from morning till evening, and accusing the debtor as the cause thereof. Should the debtor still persist in not coming to some agreement, the dun would forbid any water to be brought inside the house, and subsequently plant several hired men of the debtor's caste at his door, who would forbid the cooking of food within the house from morning to evening, and receive their hire from the debtor. This practice continued daily until the parties came to some settlement of the debt, P. D. K. In Tukazu the creditor cannot exercise violence towards his debtor, nor dun his wife or family, nor take away property without his permission, K.

Tukaza.

On Sahookars and men of fortune.

This variety only of Tukazu exists at present.

Among Tylung Brahmuns and Gosaeens it was not usual to place any hired person at the debtor's door, but the creditor himself remained on the spot, fasting, abusing him, and demanding payment; or he stood with a stone placed on his head, or his *Sendee* (lock of hair unshaven) platted and fastened to a peg at the debtor's door; he even threatened to hang himself, or confined the debtor in a room. The sin of these self-inflicted acts is considered to rest with the debtor, who is the cause of them; nevertheless men in

Among Tylung Brahmuns and Gosaeens.

power would repel such attempts to obtain payment by violence, P.

Confinement in gaol for default in paying debts was not practised under the Mahratta nor under Tippoo's government, D. Debtors confined should be allowed to give security, and be temporarily released for performance of religious ceremonies, D., and for food, K.

Or military chiefs.

It was usual in demanding payment of debts from Sirdars and military chiefs, to plant at their houses ten or fifteen Sipahees, and demand daily on their account 25 to 150 rupees, according to the circumstances of the debtor, but not to prevent his taking food, although themselves remained fasting, P.

Payment of Jemadars of horse by assignment on a village.

Jemadars of horse under the native Government were paid by Tunkahs drawn by Sirkar officers on particular villages or Amils. If the Amildar were discharged before the bill was honoured, or if it were unpaid, the drawer was held responsible, unless the delay arose by the Jemadar's consenting to receive the money some time after the bill became due. If the ryots gave a bond on which a Sahookar paid the Tunkah, the new Amildar would pay the Sahookar and recover the amount gradually from the village, D. A new Moamlutdar would continue an assignment on a village to support horse, K.

Responsibility of the Jemadar.

By custom a Jemadar entertaining Sepoys or horsemen was responsible for all promises of pay, &c., to them, notwithstanding his services were not subsequently required from the Sirkar (D.); in case of written agreement, K. On advances to Sepoys paid irregularly under the late Government, and horsemen (providing for their horses out of their pay), the Sahookar generally deducted a bonus of 1 per cent. at least, and charged 12 to 24 per cent. interest, or received the bonus at the first receipt of pay. In Hydrabad the rate of interest has been known as high as 72 per cent.

High rates of interest to Sepoys.

per annum, and among the Arabs in Khandesh 10 per cent. a *month* for arrears of pay was commonly given, S. But sepoys enlisting on a tacit agreement only received what the Jemadars could give them, and sometimes put up with loss of pay altogether, K.

Mortgaged Surinjamee afterwards resumed.

In case of the mortgage of villages, &c., by a Surinjamdar or Sumusthan for the payment of Sirkar dues or expenses incurred on account of Government, in the event of the Surinjam being resumed by Government, the Sahookar would be allowed to remain in possession of part of the land until repaid; if the debt were contracted on private account, the loss falls on the Sahookar if the Surinjamdar has no other means of payment, D. Do., Zumeendars, K. Government would settle the Sahookar's debt out of the land attached (K.) if on account of Government. If incurred on account of charity or a marriage, &c., the Surinjamdar would be answerable, K.

A Surinjamdar is responsible for the whole of debts contracted by him, notwithstanding the subsequent resumption of his Surinjam, or a part of it, by Government. Payment would be made by instalments or deductions, according to the circumstances of the debtor, D.

Mortgaged Zumeendaree.

Petty Zumeendars' estates are often completely in the hands of Sahookars, who pay them an annual sum for expenses, discharge the Joree or other dues to Government, and receive the whole surplus, D.

Jageerdars bound by acts of Karbaree.

A Jageerdar is bound to pay every debt contracted in his name by his recognized Karbaree, or manager, K.

Village debts.

It has been customary for villages to borrow money from Sahookars in order to pay their balances due to Government at from 12 to 24 per cent., K. Where a verbal agreement is made with the ryots jointly,* or a bond is given by the Mo-

* The usual expression is, "On our account;" sometimes the debt is entered as a private debt of the village officers. They include their own private debt in the village debt, and hence due investigation is necessary.

kuddum and head ryots on the part of the village, defaulters' shares are made up by a Puttee on those who are able to pay, exclusive of new ryots who were not in the village at the time the loan was contracted (inclusive, if on account of Government, K.). Where a number of ryots sign a bond, each is answerable for his own share only and his heirs (K.), but he is bound to aid in recovering the money from absentee defaulters. It is better that the Government should levy the money from the village and pay the Sahookars, K.

Bankruptcy of the Sahookar.

In case of a Sahookar receiving money from a village and becoming responsible for a larger amount of their balances, and afterwards becoming bankrupt, the ryots must not be called upon to pay any money twice over, if not recoverable from the Sahookar's estate: the part already not paid by the villagers only must be collected from them, D. K.

Loss of revenue from the village.

In case of a Sahookar becoming responsible for village balance, and paying them, after which the village is plundered, or the crops fail, he must recover the amount from the village by gradual instalments. The Sahookar pays the amount to the Amildar *pro tempore:* the new Amildar recovers on his arrival outstanding balances from Sahookars, Durukdars, Patells, and villages, and if they produce Chorchithees from the former Amildar, he is of course responsible for what he has not brought to account. The new Amildar is responsible only for public and ex-officio debts of his predecessor, D. K. In case of a Sahookar taking a bond from ryots to pay a contribution, the ryot may afterwards recover any sums proved not to have been paid, K.

Change of Moamlutdars.

Mortgage of Government lands for village debt.

It is not usual for villages or head ryots to mortgage Sirkar lands: it occasionally happens if the debt is contracted to defray Government balances, or with the consent of the Government officers; in which case the mortgagee would enjoy the lands, and the ryots collectively pay the Kists due thereon, D.

Enam lands are sometimes mortgaged for a short period to pay village debts, the Enamdar recovering the amount gradually, D. Government should aid in releasing them, K. Mortgage of enam land.

Under the native Government, ryots were generally obliged to pay all bonds extorted or otherwise, if on account of Government Puttees, however unjust such enforcing contracts made under fear of personal injury, Tullee, &c., might have been, D. Extorted bonds and village debts.

It was not usual to keep vouchers for money paid as douceurs to men in power under the name of Durbar Khirch; of course the amount of bonds for advances on that account was repayable to the Sahookar, D. Durbar Khirch.

The ruinous system of lending money to ryots or grain for subsistence and seed is very general. A bond is generally given by the unfortunate cultivator for all outstanding balances and interest at the end of the year, so that he is bound to the Sahookar as a slave to his master, mortgaging the crop to him, or selling it at one-fourth, one-third, or one-half its price in a fair market. Meantime the rents to Government are regularly paid, and the ryot finds the advances of the Sahookar necessary to enable him to continue his occupation, S. Advances to ryots.

Under the late Government it was customary to purchase the Moamlutdarship of a district, paying the money in advance, and sub-renting villages, &c., to other individuals. In case of such Moamlutdar being dismissed before the period for which he contracted had expired, he was not expected to repay the advances made by his sub-renters unless he received his own from Government, including principal, interest, and Munotee, D. Advances for the purchase of a Moamlutdarship.

Amildars under the native Government and those employed by Sumusthans, Jageerdars, &c., are precisely on the same footing, K. The profits of the latter are, however, less, D. They have a small fixed salary, and much arbi-

Death of the purchaser.

trary power of exaction. In case of the purchaser of an Amil dying before the expiration of the lease, it was usual to continue his heir, if capable of managing the trust (K.), otherwise to return a part of the purchase-money to the heirs, or allow a pension, or give presents to the females of the family, D. K.

Exactions committed by him.

In case of a purchaser of any Moamlutdarship committing exactions, &c., to a great amount, breaking cowls, and resuming Enams, the oppressed individuals generally received some redress from the new Amildar. If the extortions were in order to pay the amount due to Government, Government would excuse the ryots the sum of their bond debts, D.

Responsibility for debts contracted during office.

A Moamlutdar would be obliged to repay all borrowed money actually spent by him on private and public account before losing his Moamlut, principal and interest, K. And if Government had sanctioned a loan from one Sahookar to him, he could not recover interest on forming another contract with another Sahookar, K.

Proof of debts.

A debt to a Sahookar may be proved in the absence of Tumsook or bond, and pledge, by entry of the payment in the Sahookar's Wuhee, supported by one or more Kuboolat Chitthees* signed at different periods by the debtor for the principal and accumulating interest, though without a regular bond or Tumsook. It may be proved by such Kuboolat Chitthees, if witnessed, even in the event of the Wuhee having been lost. And if not witnessed, yet if the Kuboolat Chitthee is proved to be in the debtor's handwriting by comparison with other known handwriting of his, it will be sufficient proof of the debt. Such Kuboolat Chitthee is in the following form: "Rajsree (name of the Sahookar and of the debtor) who acknowledges to have

* Notes of acknowledgment of the debt.

received from——Rs.——at——per cent. interest, to be repaid on——." Then follows the date, signature or mark, and attestations. Koonbees, or persons of low rank, write as follow: "Waidee Roka—date—name of Dhunkonam (creditor) Rajsree—and of Rinkonam (debtor). I acknowledge to have received from you——Rs. at——interest, to be repaid———." Then follow mark and attestations. Sahookars and persons of rank write as follow: "Yad of account between———and———. I acknowledge," &c. as before.

A debt to a Sahookar may be proved by the mere entry in the Sahookar's Wuhee, if he be of a respectable character, even without any Khut, Tumsook, or Kuboolat Chitthee; or if the money were paid through a third person, the debt may be proved at the Deewalee ka parwa (annual settlement of Sahookars' accounts on or about Kartik Sood 1) by inspection of his Wuhee, even should no entry have been made in the books of the actual creditor. Should the parties be unable from absence to come to a settlement for several years, it may be made on meeting on the above principles. The Wuhee consists of, 1, Kucha-khurd, or rough day-book; 2, Puka-khurd, or cash-book, into which the entries in the first are copied fair: these two are kept in order of date; 3, Khutawunee, or ledger, the entries of which are called Khat; this is kept in order of names, and contains the accounts of the Sahookar with all his constituents. All these should be compared in seeking evidence of payments, whether from the party, or by transfer through him. **Sahookar's account book alone sufficient evidence.**

Should a creditor abstain from offering Tukazu to his creditor for any number of years, it matters not how long, the creditor may exact payment on proof of the debt. But should a debt be of very long standing (50 to 75 years), it may be settled by arbitrators, who annul the debt on the **Delay in demanding payment.**

Deduction on settlement of old debts. debtor paying the creditor a sum equal to double the original principal (Damdoput), if the debtor is a man of substance; if poor, on his paying 75, 50, or 25 per cent. on the principal together with it, or even less than the principal, in the proportion of (12, 8, 4) annas, or even 75, 50, 25 per cent., or 6. 25 per cent.—1*s.* 3*d.* in the pound. Such abstaining from Tukazu is *primâ facie* a suspicious circumstance, but the relative condition of the parties is to be inquired into, as, if though living in the place the creditor could not demand payment, his debtor being a man in power; or did not do so, on account of the poverty of the debtor. In assigning a debt to a third party, the creditor should give up his bond to the second, and take a receipt; the parties being Sahookars, an entry in the Wuhee is sufficient, P.

Assignment of debts.

SURETIES.

Different kind of sureties.

LXXXIII. There are four kinds of bail or security customary; 1, Mal-Zamin, where the security binds himself to pay a certain sum in default of the others not paying it; 2, Fael-Zamin, where the security binds himself to be responsible should the other commit any prescribed offence, as rebellion, &c.; 3, Hazir-Zamin, where the security binds himself to produce the other when required; 4, Sunklee-Zamin, where any number of persons bind themselves jointly as security for each other. In the first case, should the security die, his son is still responsible (K. D.), and the money must be paid, if necessary, from the family property by the Karbaree, whoever he may be. The son is responsible in the other two cases, if living with or near his father at the time of his death, and of sufficient age, P. D.

Responsibility of heirs of sureties.

A father and son, husband and wife, brothers during community, teacher and pupil, are inadmissible as securities for each other. A recluse (Sunyasee) is not admissible, nor, in general, an agent or Gomashta, D. Nor women, K. **Inadmissible sureties.**

The surety need not be annoyed if the debtor is present; in case of his absence, the surety is allowed from one to six months before payment of money is enforced, D. **Claim how enforced on the surety.**

Debtors generally give a premium or Munotee, a per centage on the amount of the debt, to their securities, but Punchaets seldom enforce more than payment of principal and interest, D. **Munotee payable to sureties.**

In case of joint security of two persons as Mal-Zamin, the expressions in the bail-bond being "Of the whole sum I will pay half, and half you will receive from him," the whole amount is not demandable from either, whichever may be capable of paying it, but each is responsible to the extent of one-half. Should one fly the country, the other is answerable only to the extent of a share. But if it is expressly stated in the bail-bond that "In default of payment, we will together settle the debt," the presence of both is requisite before enforcing the conditions, P. Unless under special agreement, joint securities are only answerable to the extent of their individual shares, D. **Joint sureties.**

In case of a writing being produced with the names of two joint securities thereon, and one of the security alleges that he was not present, that he cannot write, and did not intend to become security, it will be necessary to prove that he was present and gave due consent before his quota of the money can be declared payable by him, P.

Mal-Zumeendars sometimes pay interest as well as principal in case of a Sahookar proving a defaulter; it is not usual in general, D. The surety agrees to pay the money by a fixed time, on failure of which, interest is chargeable to him, K. **Interest payable by sureties.**

Villages surety for debts.

Villages sometimes become collectively responsible for debts to Sahookars, and the Koolkurnee writes the names of the Mokuddum or head Patell as security. The money is to be collected by a Puttee from the village officers and such ryots as are capable of paying, the richest paying the largest quota of subscription. Inquiry must be made whether the village officers, as sometimes happens, have drawn up the deed fraudulently for their own benefit, in which case the ryots of course are not responsible, P. *See* Money, Debts, and Interest.

Security for Moamlutdar.

Under the late Government, if a Moamlutdar or farmer paid Munotee to a Sahookar on his becoming his security, in the event of another security being afterwards chosen, the Sahookar merely returned his deposit money, not the Munotee, unless he was not accepted by the Sirkar at the time, or withdrew his security himself.

PURCHASE AND SALE.

Receipt of purchase-money without giving up the articles sold. Jewels and precious metals.

LXXXIV. A seller of jewels, or gold and silver (articles not damaged by time), receiving the money without giving up the articles, is liable to give up either one or the other with interest, at the purchaser's option.

Cloth or damageable goods.

If the articles contracted for were cloth or damageable goods, the seller, on failing to perform his contract, must provide an equal quantity of undamaged cloth. So in

Grain altered in price.

grain; but if the price have altered much in the interval, the option of giving an equal quantity of grain is not

Animals.

allowed. Horses and animals must be transferred in the state they were in at the time of the contract, or the buyer receives back his purchase-money with interest. Male and female slaves are never retained a day after the contract, P.

If the articles are not according to sample.

Jewels returnable within one year.

If goods are not according to the sample, they may be restored, or the advance bears interest, D. Jewels may be returned within six months or a year on the discovery of a flaw or any great fraud in the amount of the purchase-money agreed on. On suspicion of excessive price within a week, the books of the jeweller may be examined to discover the original purchase-money, when, if proved, the jewels may be returned and the money repaid.

Gold and silver articles one week.

Metal utensil four days.

Houses, animals, arms, slaves, grain at the time.

Gold and silver articles in the same way are returnable within a week, if found to be alloyed, or to bear excessive price; other metal utensils, if found to be cracked or old, are returnable within four days. Houses, animals, arms, slaves, and grain are only returnable at the time of the contract, or in case of a cow sold under the assurance of being with calf or giving so much milk, and afterwards failing in both particulars, K. S.

Cloth eight days if fixed trader.

An animal taken away without any verbal agreement cannot be returned, K. Cloth discovered to be damaged, or of short measure, is returnable within eight days (provided the trader is a regular shopkeeper) or a month, S. Travelling Bunyas and village weavers (S.) will not retake goods accepted, after the time of purchase, P. But any casual deficiency of length in one bale, or injury by vermin of one or two pieces, would not affect the bargain.

Case of brokerage.

Cloth may be returned even within six months, if undamaged in the interval, S. Cloth sold to a person deputed by a Sahookar to purchase cloths, afterwards ordered by his principal not to do so, are not returnable to the seller, K.

Butter or Ghee much mixed with flour, oil with much dirt in it, milk half mixed with water, wax mixed with honey, unproductive seeds, &c., may be returned at the periods mentioned, or new articles of good quality may be given in exchange, K.

Land.
Do. responsibility of seller.

Land is only returnable by mutual consent, especially if a house or well is built, and afterwards found unsuitable. Whoever sells land or houses before four witnesses is answerable to the rightful owner, K.

(See note on transfer of mortgage land.)

A person is tenant of a house, the owner of which having been absent for many years returns after the tenant has sold the house to another; in this case the tenant might retain quarter the purchase-money and give the owner the remaining three-quarters, K.

Articles not demanded by the buyer.

Articles purchased and left with the seller, may be resold on the purchaser's non-appearance for eight or ten days (if at hand), otherwise, should he live at a distance, he must wait a month, K.

Responsibility for losses.

Articles purchased and left to be delivered by the seller's people; if accidentally lost on the way, the loss falls on the purchaser, K.

Oil trade.

Ryots extract oil from the castor-oil plant in their own houses. Cocoanuts are bought in the bazaar. All other seeds from which oil is extracted are brought by the ryots to the oilmen,—the latter extract the oil in their own press and with their own bullocks, receiving one pice per seer of oil-seed brought, and returning the oil-cake to the ryots, or retaining half the oil-cake in lieu of hire; the oil is then sold to travelling traders, or shopkeepers, often by agreement that the price received should be divided between the ryot and oilman. Sometimes the oilman buys oil-seed in the bazaar and expresses and sells the oil on his own account.

Names of Oil-Seeds.

4 Seers of	Karule Til	—yield 1 Seer of oil	—hire 4 pice.	
,,	Red Til	1½	,,	,,
,,	Kuraee	½	,,	,,
,,	Ambaree	⅜	,,	,,

4 Seers of	Mal Kanguree*	yield 1	Seer of oil—hire 4 pice.
,,	Jorwus	1	,, ,,
,,	Moohuree (Raee)	1	,, ,,
,,	Khuskhus	1½	,, ,,
,,	Bhooeemookh	1¼	,, ,,
,,	Kurjee †	1	,, ,,
1 Seer of	Kobra	yields 8	Seers of oil, P.

New or old oil may be known by the smell; oil is not affected by cold or heat (P.), but the seeds vary from the effects of damp, S.

Oilmen usually agree on inspection of the nut to give so much oil per seer or pylee of 8lbs. of nut, the oil-cake belonging to the oilman if not otherwise stipulated. A merchant hiring the press and workman with cattle pays heavily, S.

Frequent embarrassing questions arise unless the bargain is made in writing, which it seldom is. Adulterations frequently take place, but are seldom discovered at the time, and are always difficult to prove, S.

If the oil plant give less oil than agreed on, on account of rain, the loss falls on the purchaser. If it give more than agreed on before pressed, the excess goes to the oilman, K.

Many ryots have not sufficient capital to manufacture their own sugar. The cane is often bought up on the field, the ryots cutting it and bringing it to the boilers. If the cane turns out less good than was expected, the manufacturer often accuses the ryot of neglecting to water the cane sufficiently after the contract of sale, S. Sugar.

The whole labour in the boiling is performed by the

* This affords no oil-cake; it is used medicinally by external application.

† The oil-cake is useless for feeding cattle.

farmer and his men; the merchant or a superintendent merely inspecting the process, and receiving all the manufactured produce, molasses, Goor, or sugar, S.

Molasses and Goor improve by age, grow darker in colour, and lose weight, hence the price is greater by weight for old Goor. Sugar does not alter in this respect, but it becomes heavy in damp weather. In all cases of litigation on account of loss of quantity, &c., these circumstances should be considered, S.

Cattle, &c. In the sale of animals, it is common, if the purchaser and seller are unacquainted with each other, for the seller to give security, or a Khureedputr, in which he binds himself to answer all other claimants (P.), and to give various warranties, S.

Draught bullocks are generally taken on a week's trial (unless bought from a stranger); cows on several days' trial as to the milk; horses are also taken on trial for three or four days, P. Of animals dying accidentally while on trial, before payment of purchase-money agreed on, the loss falls on the seller, S. K. P. Of those dying before the payment of purchase-money, a time being specified after trial, the loss falls on the purchaser, K.

If the purchase-money remain unpaid after the period fixed by agreement (say two months), interest is chargeable. The original owner may oblige the purchaser to sell the animals to a third person in order to defray the debt, but it is not customary to charge hire for the period (P.), nor to demand payment for forage, S.

Calves taken from the cow at one year old are pastured for three years, when they are sold, and the produce equally divided between the owner and pasturer, P. S. In the interval the farmer is not responsible for the death of the young animal, nor can he in that case recover expenses of keep, S. K. Colts are pastured in the same way for one or two years. A mare in foal or a cow in calf is pastured for a year, then returned to the owner, and after the expiration of another year the calf is given to the pasturer. The same kind of contract is made with regard to goats and sheep. If an abortion occur, the mare or cow is exchanged for another, or sold and the produce divided. Should the cow die accidentally, no money is paid on either side, P.

In carrying home cattle, lucky or unlucky days are consulted. If earnest have been paid and the animal die even while in the stall of the vendor, the purchaser must bear the loss, S. Unless their death is caused by the vendor's neglect or ill-treatment, K.

The rules regarding the sale of cattle do not appear very definite, nor even everywhere the same, S.

Land and immovable property.

In the transfer of land, &c., the situation, extent, and nature of the land, the tenure by which it is held, and the consideration for which it is made over, are described in the Khureedputr. With the land are also transferred water, grass, trees and their produce, dry wood, treasure, and stones to be found thereon. The village officers and others witness the deed, which is generally written by the Koolkurnee, S. P. Land is not resumable by the granter if he give an Enam Putr, K.

Sale without ownership.

In case of the sale of any articles by a broker or shopkeeper generally known, afterwards discovered to be the property of another, the purchaser informs the owner who the seller is, and the seller is bound to reimburse the owner, the property remaining with the purchaser. In the event of the seller not being discoverable in the bazaar, or the price given for the article having been below its value, the articles must be given up to the owner; and the purchaser can only recover his money from the seller wherever recognized.

PRESCRIPTION.*

Right of proprietorship by undisputed possession of Wuttun for 100 years.

LXXXVI. In case of a Wuttundar's running away, and another possessing his Wuttun (by permission of the villagers, &c.) without interruption or dispute by any one for a period of 100 years, the descendants of the original Wuttundar cannot claim possession. If, however, such acquirer (Jura) has had his claim disputed in the interval by a sharer (Tukseemdar) of the Wuttun or resumed by the Sirkar, he must give it up to the owner on proof of his claim, keeping a part in consideration of his having paid charges on (Kusala) and preserved the Wuttun for so many years.

Do. interrupted.

Do. in case of a Goomashta in possession.

In case of a Goomashta preserving a Wuttun and paying its expenses, though the papers belonging to the Wuttun are not in his possession, after possessing the Wuttun for 100 years without interruption, he becomes proprietor. Should he only have had *suwedh bhogy*, he or his representatives would be appointed Wuttundar or hereditary Goomashta, or would have a pension assigned to them payable from the Wuttun after delivering it up to the proprietor's descendants. The possession of the papers confers the right to proprietorship.

Do. interrupted.

In case of a Goomashta or Jura Goomashta of a proprietor personally unknown to the village possessing a Wuttun for a long period, and the proprietor selling it to another, the purchaser should continue to transact the business of the Wuttun, as the signing and sealing papers, Doomalaputr (deeds of transfer signed by Zumeendars), &c., through such Wuttunee Goomashta, though he has power to dismiss him if he act in disobedience to his orders.

Possession by a lessee for 100 years.

A proprietor lets a house for a stipulated rent, and goes abroad. The lessee and his descendants then enjoy the property without paying the rent, but keeping the premises in

* Authorities. *See* Documents, P.

repair. After 100 years the representatives of the proprietor may claim the property, but not the rent, in case the expenses of repairs nearly balance its amount, calculated to the period when the claim was made. In case of the lessee having built expensive additions to the house, &c., if the proprietor cannot defray their arbitrated value, the lessee has a right to carry away the timber and materials.*

Boundary dispute. Uninterrupted enjoyment for 100 years bars a judicial decision.

In a boundary dispute, where Nirwedhbhogy, or uninterrupted enjoyment of the land, is proved on one side for a period of 100 years, a trial by ordeal is not admissible. If within such period the land in dispute has been partially enjoyed by another, or resumed by the Sirkar, or has been the ostensible cause of village disputes, it is matter of judicial investigation, P. In a Punchaet case in Khandesh (No. 3), no witnesses or documents were produced by either party in a boundary dispute, and both were ready to make oath. It was decreed accordingly that the land in dispute should be equally divided, K. *See* Ordeal.

TREASURE TROVE.†

In house of hereditary proprietor in possession.

LXXXVII. In the event of treasure found in the house of a man whose family have been in repute and lived in the house for several generations, and there existing no other probably just claimant to the property, the possessor takes it. Occasionally a part is given to the Sirkar.

Do. after sale by him.

On a house sold by the proprietor to another, treasure found by the purchaser is to be given to the original proprietor, deducting one-sixth to Government, K. Should the

* *See* Pledges and Rent.

† Authorities. *See* Documents, P.

house be in the possession of a family for several generations, and afterwards be sold to a stranger, who on pulling it down finds treasure concealed, he is bound to give three-fourths of it to the heir of the former proprietors, and keep one-fourth himself; should he through avarice keep the whole, he would be obliged to give it up to the heir on subsequent investigation and proof. The first case depends on an omission of the word treasure in the conveyance.

On land newly granted by Government.

Of treasure found on the site of ground newly given to cultivators or other proprietors by the Sirkar, three-fourths is to be given to the Sirkar, and one-fourth to the new proprietor. It is customary, in giving an Enam putr, to mention, as included in the grant of land, water (Jul), trees (Turoo), grass (Trin), dry wood (Kasht), stones (Pashan), and treasure (Nidhee), in which case the donee would of course take the whole.

On Government land.

Treasure found on Government land by a ryot (whether Meerasdar or Oopuree) in the jungle, on the bank of a river, on a road, or in drains (Moree), belongs *de jure* to the Sirkar, but the Sirkar would usually grant a part of it as a recompense or free gift to the ryot or finder.

On boundary between two houses.

Treasure found on the boundary between two houses is to be given to the owner, as proved by investigation; as, whether the description or name of the vessel in which the treasure was found is known to either occupant, whether either has any knowledge of the treasure having been buried, under which house are found the marks of a hole having been dug, or of chunam lining such hole, whether the ancestors of one were rich, of the other poor, &c., if the ownership is proved by neither, they are to divide the treasure; but if it appear probable that the ancestors of neither concealed it on the spot, the Sirkar may take the whole.

In a house rented, &c., by a tenant.

Treasure found in a house by a tenant not a proprietor is to be given by him to the proprietor.

Treasure or property of any description to which there is no heir is to be given to the Sirkar. If found on the site of heirless property given by the Sirkar to a new proprietor, it is to be given to the Sirkar, the proprietor receiving a present thereout. In the Peshwa's time, it was usual to give the whole of treasure-trove to the finder if a Brahmin, Sahookar, or Sirdar.

Heirless treasure and treasure found on heirless property.

EVIDENCE.*

LXXXVIII to XCII. It is not customary to receive the evidence of a boy under fifteen years of age, his understanding not being supposed sufficiently matured. In Wuttun deeds, persons under twenty-five years of age do not sign as witnesses. The evidence of a Goomashta or servant is not received in a matter in which their principal is concerned, unless absolutely necessary, and is always suspicious. The evidence of an old or deaf man who has become imbecile in understanding, or of an insane person, is not received. Nor of a shameless quarrelsome individual (or low caste, D.) always engaged in disputes. Nor of an avaricious man, careless of the means of acquiring wealth. Nor should the witness be a great friend of the party, or have money dealings with him, or be otherwise interested in his favour by relationship, &c. Nor is it usual to admit a woman as evidence. Nor should the witness be prejudiced against the party by enmity, &c.; or a constant eater of opium, bhung, &c., or drinker of intoxicating liquor. The above rules apply to disputes of Wuttun, debt, &c. But the evidence of bystanders would be taken in all cases of homicide, assault, robbery, &c., P. D. The evidence of a child is receivable in cases of murder, D.

Incompetent witnesses.

* Authorities. *See* Documents.

And the evidence of witnesses of doubtful credit (including females) would be received in all cases as *confirmatory* of other unexceptionable evidence, but would not be admissible unsupported. A single witness is not admitted, unless of established veracity.

In cases of theft, where it has evidently been committed by persons within the house, all relations and servants are admissible. Circumstantial proof is brought in aid of the *vivâ voce* evidence, and occasionally the parties undergo some ordeal with the view of discovering the theft. Under the late Government it was usual to beat and otherwise ill-treat and alarm prisoners in order to obtain confession; such confessions were not, however, considered good proof, unless confirmed by some circumstantial or other collateral proof, P.

Number of witnesses.

Two respectable witnesses at least are generally necessary in every case; one witness of extraordinary character for veracity would be sufficient. Where no other person was present, one witness is admissible for proof. No objection exists to receiving the evidence of a man of one caste against a man of another; respectability of character is the great requisite, D.

Accomplices and interested witnesses.

The evidence of accomplices in criminal matters, as of persons interested in civil disputes, should not be received against the party in one case, nor in favour of him in the other, D.

Written evidence.

Documents should be proved genuine by comparison of the signature, &c., with other handwriting of the party. The account-book of a respectable Sahookar is good evidence, provided his character for honesty is established, P. D. The different parts of the Wuhees, and balances brought forward, should be compared, P.

Witnesses should be admonished, examined separately, and fined or disgraced on giving improper or untrue evidence, according to the circumstances of the case and the caste or rank of the offender. False evidence is held right if given to save a life, promote a marriage, &c., not if given to prevent the punishment of a criminal, D.

A witness is bound to answer all queries, whether they criminate himself or no, D. Under the native Governments it is customary to flog or otherwise harass prisoners with the view of making them confess.

On other points relative to evidence, the opinions given accord with the English practice. A physician's or Wukeel's evidence is admissible, but a man violating his professional confidence would lose estimation in society, D.

ORDEAL.*

LXXXIX. Oath or ordeal is demanded by a party suspicious of another's veracity in the last resort, and in default of other written or oral evidence, 1, In a boundary dispute; 2, In a dispute between brothers or relations as to family property entrusted to one during the absence of the other; 3, In a dispute as to the proprietorship of a Wuttun; 4, In disputes of debt and accounts; 5, In cases of theft; 6, Of homicide; 7, Of suspicion of any crime.

Ordeal is of various kinds:—1, Tuptgola, in which the person submitting to the ordeal, after first stating his innocence, or giving his deposition, takes in his hand, unhurt, a hot iron ball of the weight prescribed.

2. Tupt Rawa, in which he plunges his hand into a pan of boiling or heated oil, and takes out a piece of money placed therein.

3. Kucha gura. He has to fill an unbaked earthen pot

* See page 155.

with water from a river, &c., and bring it back on his head unbroken.

4. Bel-bundar. He goes to the temple, and brings away therefrom the sacred Bel or creeping plant and Bundar (turmeric roots ground), or from the household god in his own house.

5. Gunga. He stands in the river Godavery, and gives his deposition.

6. Dewul. He stands in some temple which has a high character for Kuramut (power to dispense good or evil) under the bell, and before the idol, and gives his deposition.

7. Gou. He gives his deposition holding a cow's tail.

8. Brahmun. Ditto, laying his hands on the feet of a religious Brahmin, who duly performs his ablutions, &c.

9. Siw. In boundary disputes between villages, the village officers assemble both parties, who by common consent name in writing an individual, according to whose deposition the decision is to be passed on one or the other side. He then bathes in a sacred stream (if any near), puts the Toolsee plant round his neck, or other sacred flowers, goes before some god, applies sandal to his forehead, and gives his deposition. Afterwards he proceeds to the boundary, and walks over the disputed ground. The line traced by him is fixed on as the true boundary thereafter. But if any calamity happen to him or any of his family within a certain period (the particulars being before prescribed in writing), the deposition is considered to have been a false one, and decision is passed in favour of the opposing party, P. Or he carries on his head an oil-cake (sacred as the food of cows), when, if it breaks, the deposition is considered a false one, P.

CUSTOMS OF SAHOOKARS.

Tumsooks not usual between Sahookars.

It is not the general custom to take Tumsooks in money transactions between Sahookars, especially if they are of credit and importance. Entries in the Wuhees are considered sufficient security. Tumsooks are taken from petty Sahookars and traders, ryots, and persons not engaged in trade, in which case a memorandum to that effect accompanies the entry in the Wuhee.

In the former case, it is usual to send a man in the evening of the day on which a payment has been made to a Sahookar, to inquire whether it has arrived and been accounted for; it is not necessary for the Sahookars themselves to meet, or see the entry made.

Entry in the Wuhee.

The entry in the Wuhee stands thus: "Date ——— Huste (by the hands of) ——— belonging to ——— received ——— rupees." Wuhees of both parties may be compared by either at any time, but such comparison and settlement of accounts is most usually made at the Deepoulee.

Mode of opening accounts.

When a Sahookar of credit opens an account with another, his name only is written in the Khate or ledger entry. When the person who opens an account is not a Sahookar, it is customary for him to procure another Sahookar who will give verbal security for him, being responsible (should he be bankrupt or overdraw his account) to the extent of 1 or 2,000 rupees for a specified time, as, till the next Deepoulee. The account is then opened in the Khate: Widyuman, or Nisbut, or Marifut, † or Jumma—Sahookar. No other document is necessary, but the Khatree or security must be renewed after the time limited has expired.

---

* Authorities. *Vide* the replies on the subject of Hoondees, P.

† So the Marwaree and Goojrattee. The Mahratta Sahookars say Atmaram, Jumma or Khatree, Bapoo Moonee. The term Nisbut is generally applied to Goomasthtas signing "on the part of."

Annual settlement at the Deepoulee.

On the settlement of accounts at the Deepoulee, the balance on one side or the other, if not paid, runs on in a new account for the following year, where it appears with the rate of interest determined on as a balance brought forward from the last year. (Ootar Pan sal Goozushta.)

Rate of interest between Sahookars.

The rate of interest as determined on is specified in the first entry at the time the money was advanced. If the Sahookar is one of credit to whom the advance is made, the interest is from 4 to 8 annas per cent. per mensem; if the money is advanced to a smaller trader, or person not in trade, from 8 annas to 1 rupee. If to Moamlutdars, Jageerdars, &c., 1 to 2 rupees, or even above that rate, according to agreement between the parties.

3 to 6 per cent. per annum.
6 to 12 per cent. per annum.
12 to 24 do.

Verbal agreement.

The rate of interest is sometimes neither specified in the Wuhee, nor in a Tumsook, but merely settled by verbal agreement between the parties. The contract therefore rests for validity on their honour only.

Payment through a Goomashta.

Should a sum of money be paid by one Sahookar to the Goomashta (or shopman in the service) of another, and the debit be made in his Khate "Huste, Nisbut, &c.," the Yejman or principal of the Goomashta will be answerable at the Deepoulee, even should the Goomashta have fraudulently received the money and converted it to his own use. The Goomashtas of Sahookars being personally known to each other, it is not usual for them to bring orders of payment; and a further security exists against fraud in the custom of sending every evening to make inquiry. In the above case the money is debited to the Goomashta's principal, there being an account current with him at the time. If, however, the same entry is made to the debit or account of the Goomashta himself, the Sahookars advancing the money can come on the latter only; and so also in the event of there not having been an account current between the two Sahookars before the money was paid to the Goomashta and debited to his principal, unless the payment was allowed by the party sending a man in the evening, or entered in the Wuhees on both sides.

Effect of the annual balance or interest.

The custom of bringing forward balances unpaid at the Deepoulee, with the rate of interest at which the old balance (principal and interest together) is to run on, has of course the effect of compound interest, annually estimated.

Division of the Wuhee. Day-book. Journal. Ledger.

The Kuchakhurd, called also Rozkhird, Phurd, Roznishee, is the first division of the Wuhee. It is a rough cash or day book, from which the entries are transcribed into the Puka-Wuhee (cash-book or journal), and thence (under the separate names) into the Khutawunee* or ledger. The entries in the latter are called Khate. Some Sahookars have no Kuchakhurd. The balance in hand daily struck is called Silk-jhara, and the particulars of the coins in which it consists, Nanamel. These with the Jumma Khurch, are all entered in the Kuchakhurd. The Jumma Khurch alone is entered in the Puka-Wuhee.† Hoondees drawn or presented for payment are copied and entered in a separate book called *Nugul-Wuhee*, or Nama-Wuhee (by the Goozrattees). The Marwarees enter Hoondees in a Kucha-Wuhee when sent off, and in a Puka-Wuhee on notice of payment having arrived.

Nugul-Wuhee for Hoondees.

Jangur-Wuhee for brokerage.

The Jangur-Wuhee is an account-book in which articles given to a broker for sale are entered. The entry consists of the broker's name, a description of the articles, and their value.

Chitnoud or letter-book.

In the Chitnoud, or Chitha-Wuhee, are entered the particulars of letters from correspondents and others relative to the trade, also of Hoondees, and consignments of goods. The date and abstract are sufficient.

* There are sometimes a Kucha and Puka Khutawunee.

† Called Awerra by the Goozrattees, and by the Marwaree Roznamon.

Wyaj-Wuhee for interest.

In the Wyaj-Wuhee are entered statements of interest due, as agreed on by the parties after inspection of the account. This is not, however, universally kept; the entry may be made in the Phurd. And, generally, the account-books universally kept are the Wuhee and Khutawunee, Kucha and Puka.

Should, in the progress of time, the Wuhee appear to be of insufficient size for probable entries of the year, or the unwritten part be damaged by oil or ink thrown over it, new paper may be added, but it is not customary to make a copy of a Wuhee once written from any of these causes.

Clerks and servants to Sahookars.

The names of persons in the service of Sahookars on account of trade are—

1. Mooneem, whose duty it was to receive and pay money, take charge of deposits and pledges, superintend purchases and sales, sign Hoondees, and generally to give orders to entertain and dismiss Goomashtas, Parkhees (Suraffs), &c. But the Kilee-wala (in charge of the keys) is generally appointed by the principal at the same time as the Mooneem, and is liable to be dismissed by himself.

2. Goomashtas, who write the accounts, Hoondees, and perform other duties abroad or at home. Occasionally the Mooneem also makes entries in the Wuhee.

3. Kilee-wala, who is in charge of the keys, and by the Mooneem's orders opens the chests for receiving or giving out money or other articles—unless appointed by the Mooneem, which is unusual. He does not give him the keys every evening.

4. Parkhee, who shroffs the coins and states the daily balance.

5. Gure-manoose, who are sent in the evening to inquire whether money payments have been received; despatched on Tukazu, &c., &c.

The number and description of these clerks vary according to the extent of the trade; in some, the Mooneem performs the office of Suraff and key-bearer; in some shops the key-bearer shroffs the coins.

The salary of a Mooneem varies from 100 to 1,000 rupees per annum, but he generally contrives to make money on deposit, pledges, &c., either by the death of the depositor, or false entries in the accounts. Salaries of Goomashtas vary from 150 to 500 rupees; of the key-bearer, from 200 to 750 rupees; of Parkhees, from 75 to 200 rupees per annum. Gure-manoose receive monthly wages of from 5 to 8 rupees.

The key-bearer may open the chests, &c., at his option and replace the articles, but in all transfers of property to strangers or receipts of property from others, the order of the Mooneem is essential. It is not customary to put seals on the locks.

Security given by them.

If a Goomashta or other servant is not trustworthy, it is usual to take on his account Malzamin, Hazir-zamin, and Faelzamin (the last, however, merely binding the security to produce the party in the event of his committing or concealing fraud): a Zamin Khut is taken, but after six months or a year, the party having become trustworthy, the Khut is withdrawn. Should the party commit frauds, &c., the money (if Malzamin) is paid by the security or his heirs; and if he died after having become Hazir-zamin, his son, being of age to conduct business, will answer for the party. The son either verbally may continue his father's security or enter into a new bond, or refuse, when the party must find another surety until his employers have confidence in him.

Pensions to their families.

Wives and families of Goomashtas and servants dying after many years' service, receive, at the option of their employers, a certain part of the allowances, which are continued to them. The amount and period to which such allowances is continued vary in different cases.

And presents.

In case of the death of a Goomashta while carrying his master's property from one place to another, whether such were his regular occupation or otherwise, by violence, as gang robbery, &c., his master sometimes gives a present to his surviving wife or family. The party himself, if wounded, may receive a present of a turban, &c. But these are not universal customs. A stranger so occasionally employed would not appear to have any well-founded claim.

Responsibility of Goomashta or servant as carrier.

A Goomashta or servant losing property committed to him to carry from one place to another, if by neglect, is punished; if by Rajkrant, or such unavoidable misfortune, he is excused. It is not customary to oblige him to repay the value in any case except fraud, when the whole is recovered from the party or his surety. The recovery may be made by stopping half his pay and allowing the party to remain in service and receive the other half for his subsistence.

Duties of the Mooneem.

Responsibility of the principal.

As to Wuhee debts.

The Mooneem Goomashta being vested with the general superintendence of the trade,—for whatever debts he may incur on its account, and which he may afterwards be unable to repay, his principal is responsible. The latter, however, is not bound to repay debts incurred by the Mooneem on his private account, if not entered in the general, but in his own private, Wuhee. If, however, not entered in the Wuhee from forgetfulness, or the Goomashta giving notice by letter of the deposit to the principal, the latter is responsible as to the Wuhee debts. The principal afterwards recovers from the Mooneem, whether money expended on his private account or debts contracted during sickness or insanity, or from his heirs, in the event of his death.

Deposits.

In the same way the claims of depositors, though the

deposit were made without his express consent or knowledge, are settled by the principal if entered in the Wuhee, in the event of the Goomashta's death, or insanity, or inability to do so, and the principal afterwards recovers from the Mooneem or his heirs.

The principal is responsible for losses or insurance contracts entered into by the Mooneem, the latter being solely responsible for any money of his own which he may have risked in the investment. Insurance contracts.

The Mooneem Goomashta receives, besides a yearly salary of from 100 to 1,000 rupees (varying according to the circumstances of the principal Sahookar and the ability of the Mooneem), presents of clothes and money on marriages and festivals (the Dusserah, *Deepoulee*, or Gooreekee Parwa—Chytru Sood 1st). Salary of the Mooneem.

The principal is bound to account for all Hoondees drawn according to custom by the Mooneem in his name. The Mooneem signs his principal's name at the top of the Hoondee or Khut-putr, and his own at the bottom, unless it is signed by the principal only. The principal's signature is alone necessary in dismissing his Mooneem, should he himself superintend the business. Mode of drawing Hoondees.

The Mooneem, in drawing on his principal, if the Hoondee has not been paid for, writes to that effect to his principal; and the bill remains *Kuhree* until he hears from the Mooneem that the money is or will be paid. The principal pays a bill drawn on him by his Mooneem, before the arrival of (Lahune) consignment to answer it, if the Mooneem writes to that effect.

The Mooneem and principal are sometimes in partnership, otherwise all gain and loss on trade affects the latter only. Trading can only be undertaken by the subordinate Goomashtas on their own account. Partnership of Mooneem and principal.

The Mooneem, if placed at the head of a shop in another

Mooneem manager of separate shop.

place, has the whole superintendence of the trade in his own hands, writing and signing Hoondees, Khut-putrs, &c.

It is usual to make up his accounts and send them to his principal at the Deepoulee, but in cases of limited confidence, the principal may require them to be sent at shorter intervals.

Principal responsible.

Even should the Mooneem cease to write his principal's name, and accounts between the firm and other Sahookars be written in the Mooneem's name, the principal (if really continuing to employ the Mooneem in charge of his capital) is responsible for all debts and contracts, and the creditors come on him and not on the Mooneem or his heirs. The principal afterwards settles his own account with the latter.

Partnership of a capitalist and Mooneem.

Of two individuals entering into a trading partnership, one advances capital, and the other officiates as Goomashta, under agreement to receive a salary of 100 rupees, or in lieu ¼th of the profits: for several years he receives ¼th accordingly, the total profits sometimes a little exceeding, sometimes falling short, of 400 rupees. A year of loss following, he receives nothing. Afterwards following a year of unusual profit, the capitalist partner would be bound to give ¼th of the profit to the Goomashta. The latter is in this case a partner, and has been treated as such in the year of loss.

Mooneem's office often hereditary.

It is customary, but not universally, to continue in his father's place the son of a faithful Goomashta, if capable of conducting the business allotted to him, or to give a Nemnook for life to his childless widow. Also to give a Nemnook to a Goomashta wounded by robbers, or rendered incapable of further service in the course of his duty.

Fraud by the Goomashta.

In case of a Goomashta concealing any deposit or statement of account favourable to a constituent on the latter having a civil dispute with his principal, and receiving as the price of such concealment a douceur of half the amount, on discovery of the fraud after the Goomashta's death the principal would not be allowed to recover the half so given from the Goomashta's heirs.

In appointing a Mooneem Goomashta, it is sometimes usual to present him with a cocoanut, saying, "This is my head which I have given into your charge, to preserve or to destroy." Sometimes the principal writes a Khut-putr, specifying the salary and the trust, advising caution, but without any limitations as to the trade to be carried on. Mode of appointing a Mooneem.

Should the Goomashta, having been instructed to keep a certain number of Gure-men, keep fewer in view to appropriate the amount of their wages, and afterwards property be lost on the road owing to an insufficient escort, the principal would be justified in dismissing the Goomashta on proof, but he would not come on him for the amount of the loss. The Goomashta is not answerable for property sent by the principal's order, though in charge of a friend or casual person, and afterwards lost while in their charge. Goomashta not responsible for losses by neglect.

Should, contrary to custom, the principal prohibit the Goomashta, verbally or in writing, from trading in a particular way, in the latter case only the Goomashta is responsible for the loss :—and not even then, should he advise his principal of this intention so to trade, on a probable estimate of profit. Prohibitions by the principal.

Should money be sent for from a Sahookar by the hands of a subordinate Goomashta, and its amount afterwards entered in the Wuhee of his principal, having been paid on a chittee of the principal to the Mooneem, or on a chittee written by the Sub-Goomashta in the name of the principal or Mooneem, and in the evening found to have been received by the Sahookar's messenger, the principal is responsible; but should a Goomashta be discovered to have made fraudulent entries in the Wuhee, &c., he would be dismissed, and notice of his character be given to all other Sahookars, in order to prevent his further obtaining money from them. Goomashta how responsible for fraud.

A Goomashta is answerable to the Sirkar for treacherous intrigue and acts detrimental to its authority; also for acts contrary to its orders on account of his principal. But if the principal ordered him to do so, or replied to his letter consenting thereto, or even abstained from forbidding him after receiving a letter with advice of what was going on, the principal is responsible. Fines on account of adultery, theft, assault, fraud on his own private account, or on account of his relations, and for acts of treason against the State in opposition to his principal's order, are to be paid by the Goomashta.

Fines imposed by the Sirkar in an investigation connected with the trade, are defrayed by the principal.

Mooneem's appointment of substitute.

Should the Mooneem be desirous of placing a substitute in his room, he writes to his principal for permission before doing so, mentioning that the person is trustworthy. After the answer has arrived, the Mooneem will not be responsible for losses: even should he, contrary to custom, place a substitute without acquainting his principal, the losses would fall on the latter. The Mooneem, indeed, has a right to place such substitute if intending ten or twelve days' absence only, instructing him to collect and pay money, enter it in the Wuhee, &c., and drawing blank Hoondees for him to fill up as many as will in all probability be required; and all losses during the Mooneem's absence will fall on the principal.

DEPOSITS WITH SAHOOKARS.*

Interest.

Interest on a deposit of cash with a Sahookar is never higher than eight annas, and if the deposit is made by a Sahookar, lower, varying from one to eight annas. Under

* Authorities. *See* Hoondees.

an agreement to draw for cash when required, the depositee (banker) pays three or four annas per cent. per mensem.

Property may be deposited without interest accruing to either party; as where an officer of Government places one or two lacs of rupees in a Sahookar's hands, the former charging himself with the payment of Sebundees, &c. (as may have been agreed on), entertained for the safe keeping of the treasure, and being allowed to draw for cash when required. Or the deposit may be made for security, without receiving interest, or paying charges. Without interest.

An entry in the Wuhee is generally considered sufficient to secure deposits of cash; but if the depositor fears the loss of the Sahookar's books (from Rajkrant) or doubts his credit, the latter gives him a Yad specifying the sum, rate of interest payable monthly or annually, signed by the Sahookar, or a Khut signed by both, and generally attested. Entry in Wuhee. Yad.

If the parties agree that the Sahookar is not to be responsible for losses by Rajkrant, Durora, fire, or flood, he will not; but they generally determine that any articles afterwards recovered will be restored to the owner. If no agreement have passed, a deposit of cash entered in the Wuhee, lost by the above four means, is to be recovered from the Sahookar; not so a deposit of cash merely placed in amount without such entry. Responsibility of the Sahookar. Cash deposits.

Jewels, gold, silver, metal pots, and cloths are not recovered in whatever way lost; but as the former articles are only partially injured by fire, what is recovered by the Sahookar must be restored to the owner. Jewels, metals, and cloth.

If the Sahookar's property be confiscated by the Sirkar through a crime of his, the Sirkar will give up deposits, on proof of ownership, to the owner; and if a fine be imposed on the Sahookar, he will be obliged to give up deposits to the owners. If the Sahookar's property, confiscated.

Deposits recoverable on demand.

Deposits recoverable on demand, if refused to be restored, are chargeable with interest from the day of such refusal, according to agreement. Interest, however, is not claimable if the depositor agreed to give two or three days' notice of his intended demand, and, failing to do so, the depositee delayed returning the amount.

Unclaimed cash deposits.

With deductions according to mutual agreement.

Cash deposits remaining unclaimed for many years, owing to the depositor's going abroad, may be re-demanded with interest by the son of the depositor after his father's death, even should the interest amount to double or treble the amount of the original deposit. Should, however, in the interval, the depositee send a written notice to the depositor that he should withdraw his deposit, and prove* his having forwarded such notice (so as to render it evident that the deposit was left in his hands merely to raise the interest balance), he will only be called on to pay the principal and interest up to the day on which the depositor received the notice—even should the distance be great, and there be no means of drawing a Hoondee.

Cash deposits with a Sahookar of high credit, if remaining unclaimed for ten years, nevertheless accumulate at compound interest, the statement of the principal and interest being annually made up at the rate agreed upon. After ten years it accumulates at simple interest only; but should the depositor in the interval have made a false charge against the Sahookar, afterwards disproved, he can only receive compound interest up to the period when such charge was first preferred.

The following articles are generally deposited with Sahookars: money in cash, jewels, gold and silver, silk

---

* It is not sufficient in such proof for the depositor to produce a memorandum in his Wuhee that on a certain day he sent off the notice by Tappal; but if he enclosed the notice in a letter to a friend, and the latter states that he delivered it, the proof is adequate, and a verbal (attested) notice is sufficient.

and cotton, cloths, houses, lands, metal utensils, and grain.

Time for receiving deposits.

Deposits brought to a Sahookar within ten Ghurees after sunrise are received, and interest for that day paid. Hoondees are subject to the same regulation: if not received till after the time specified, that day is not reckoned in the period for its payment.

Customs prevalent at the Deepoulee.

The Deepoulee festival commences Aswin Wudy 13th, and ends at Kartik Sood 5th. The first day is called Dhuntryodusee, on which Sahookars open all their chests, perform Pooja to their wealth, and take account of gold, silver, &c., therein. The Ghee lamp lighted on that day is allowed to burn till the Prutipudha in the Jamdarkhana, and oil-lamps are lighted on the outside of the shop. On the Chutoordusee it is customary to rise three Ghurees before daylight, bathe, and anoint the person with oil, before eating. On the Ahmawasyu, in the dusk of the evening, gold and silver coins are brought out, Brahmuns invited, and the Lukshmee Pooja performed; sandal, &c., are placed on the new Wuhee, and Pooja is performed before the old and new Wuhees, and the papers, pens, ink, and scales appropriated for the new year; Dukshuna is distributed to the Brahmuns, festivities are usual in families at this season, and presents are given to women, relations, and dependants, as well as to Bhikshook and Josees, brokers in connection with the trade, private friends, and Sirkar servants. Pansooparee and Lahee (a dish of rice) and Buttasee are presented to the guests. On the Parwa, or several days after, Sahookars send to each other five or ten rupees by way of opening the accounts of the new year. These are called the *Sukoon* rupees. A Goomashta is sent out by rich Sahookars for this purpose, with a Yad of the names, among whom the money, Lahee, &c., are to be distributed.

In the Mungulwar-Nana, and especially in the Bhowanee-

Peth of Poona, reside wholesale traders in grain and Kirane received from travelling Bunyas, and sold to retailers in the city. It is the custom for these *Urthes* on the day of the Pooshy Nukshutr—falling generally on Kartik *S*ood 6 (Gubar Moort)—to make Pooja before their Wuhee, &c.

From Bahadrupud *S*ood 1st to the Deepoulee, during about two months, Sahookars send to their creditors demanding payment, and collect their debts. From Aswin W. Ahmawasy, Karkoons, &c., are sent to the houses of their constituents to compare and settle their accounts, principal and interest. It is not usual to enter the amount of interest except under the debtor's personal inspection. If the balance is unpaid, it is entered as a "balance brought forward" in the new Wuhee.

PARTNERSHIP.*

In what trade customary.

Partnership implies joint trade and joint liability to gain or loss thereon. It is usual in the sale of cloth, in transactions of mortgage, deposit, and Hoondees, in the purchase and sale of Ghee, spices, Goor, turmeric (Kirane), &c., in the purchase and sale of grain (Bhoosa), in the purchase of houses and timber, in brokerage, in money-changing, and in agency of Hoondees.

* Authorities:—These are translations of replies from the following Sahookars in Poona to queries proposed by Sam Row Pingule, of Poona, in aid of the present abstract: Motee Bhaee, on the part of Dyaram Atmaram; Bapoo Moonee; Shesuna Naik Padshapoorkur; Bapoo Kumlapoorkur, on the part of Hureswur Bhaee; Eswunt Naik Joonurkur, Goomasta of Sudasew Rungnat Wanwule; Venkoba Naik, Goomusta of Dutram Moteechund; Himmut Row, on the part of Wurjulal; Doolubdass Tribuwundass, on the part of Doulut Ram Gumbheer Mul; Sukharam Goojur, on the part of Gokulset; Hureechund Becher; Myachund, on the part of Koosal Ramchunder; Nanchund Goojrathee, on the part of Ramchundr Busta; Joomkha Rungeela.

Agreement of partnership is generally concluded on personal knowledge of the party, seldom with a stranger. It is not customary to write security Khuts on entering into partnership. A partnership trade is carried on by several under the name of one, who is the head of the firm.

Security Khuts not usual.

Name of the head of the firm.

There is no limit to the number of partners: each takes a certain share in the trade, in the proportion of half-anna, two, four, or more annas (the whole being reckoned as one rupee), and occasionally by consent of all a small proportion of the profits (say half-anna) is reserved for expenses in honour of some god. It is not usual for a working partner to receive a proportion of the profit and not be responsible for the loss, but it may so occasionally happen.

Proportions of profit and loss.

Reservation to some god.

Every subordinate partner usually writes a Surkut-nama, or partnership deed, addressed to the head partner, in which he states that he "has become partner with him in the proportion of ——, has deposited —— rupees, on which he is to receive —— interest; and besides is to pay or receive whatever loss or gain may accrue." If no money is deposited the former part is omitted. Then follows the subordinate partner's signature, and occasionally also those of two witnesses. Each party keeps a copy. Verbal agreements of partnership are sometimes made, and sometimes an entry is made in the account-book to the same effect. Occasionally one joint deed is drawn up by all the subordinate partners, expressing the money deposited, and proportion of loss or gain accruing, addressed to the head partner.

Partnership deed.

The duties to be performed by each partner are prescribed either by the head partner, if the trade is carried on on his capital, or by common agreement, if all contribute capital. The interest account on capital advances is kept separately. Partners also carry on trade on capital borrowed from a Sahookar, either on bond or joint or separate debit of their names in his books;—or the head partner borrows the money

Duties of each partner.

Interest.

Borrowed capital.

on his own responsibility. A partner either contributes capital or labour, or both.

Bankruptcy following borrowed capital.

In cases of bankruptcy following trade on borrowed capital, as it is the most general custom for one person to borrow on his own account, the subordinate partners would not be liable to pay their quota of loss unless they had jointly borrowed the money and made themselves jointly responsible: this is sometimes done by two traders. But if any one of the partners, not the head, borrow money from a Sahookar under the name of the head partner—*i.e.* of the firm—and the sum is entered as such in the partnership accounts, all are responsible (on a bankruptcy) according to their respective shares. The entry is thus made in the Sahookar's books: "Paid to ——— (huste) by the hands of ———." Tumsooks are not usual, unless in cases of weak credit, when a Khut is drawn up in the name of the head, or of all the partners, or of each of them.

Duties of the head partner.

The duties of the head partner are to superintend the important purchases, sales, mortgages, and deposits connected with the trade, to be answerable to the Sirkar when called on, and to overlook the whole establishment. His share in the trade is generally greater than that of the others. Of subordinate partners, one agrees to write and keep the home accounts, another to travel to make purchases and sales, another to collect money, &c. Each has separate duties.

Of the accountant.

The partnership account-book is one: all the working partners superintend the manner in which the accountant performs his duties; and those partners who advance capital only, without actively engaging in the trade, receive their shares, confiding in the integrity and intelligence of the rest. Errors in making out the profit and loss account are not usual, and are settled at the time, should they occur; and on the error or fraud being discovered, the party guilty is made responsible.

Mokhtyarnama not usual.

It is not usual for the head partner to take a Mokhtyarnama from the subordinates, nor for them to agree verbally to what he may in future propose. It is a system of mutual confidence; the head partner on all matters of consequence asks the advice of the rest.

Deductions of charges of trade. Hire, salaries, and shop expenses.

Expenses of salaries to Goomashtas, hire of shop or premises, charges for oil, paper, &c., wages to servants, charges incurred by the partners on account of the trade, are deducted previously to a partition of the profit or loss. Sometimes a charge on account of personal servants is allowed to the head partner. A head Goomashta, or several Goomashtas, are entertained by the head partner after consulting the rest, and the expense is of course deducted as above. Also charges on account of vows by any partner to pay money to the shrine of a particular deity, if entered into for the benefit of the trading partnership, are deducted as above. Also fines imposed by the Sirkar on any one of the partners for an offence connected with the trading partnership.

Vows to a particular deity.

Fines.

Settlement at the Deepoulee.

The accounts are examined every year at the Deepoulee, viz. a few days before or after Kartik Sood Prutipudha. According to the profit or loss which then may appear, the several partners either receive or pay their proportions at the time, or, making a statement of the account, carry it on as before. Only in the sale of houses and money-changing a settlement of accounts may take place daily, or on settling every separate contract.

Purchases abroad.

A head partner may either send a Naik (head Goomashta) or go himself abroad and purchase goods, &c., but he must be guided by the amount of the joint capital, otherwise, by his extravagance and speculation, those at home will undergo loss or ruin.

And should such absent partner purchase goods abroad on account of the firm, and clandestinely send them for sale to his own house or elsewhere, such fraud will be matter of inquiry, and those concerned in it will be responsible. If, however, he agreed first with the rest to make the excursion on his own private account as well as on that of the firm, they cannot complain. The profit or loss accruing in consequence of a person sent by the head partner affects all the partners.

Receipt of deposits and pledges.

The head partner receives deposits and pledges: it is not necessary for the depositor to advise the rest. An entry is made in the Wuhee of the deposit and the object of it; should the firm thereafter become bankrupt, all the partners are responsible according to their proportions. Inquiry must, however, be instituted whether the head partner was a fraudulent bankrupt or otherwise (Wastuwik): in the former case, the defrauder is alone responsible.

Reservation of share of profits for the god Ballajee.

It is customary, whenever the trade of the year has been profitable, to set apart a portion of the gains as the share of Ballajee (whose temple is at Triputee in the Kurnatuk) or Venkoba (a name of Vishnoo). Some set apart on this account one-third, one-fourth, others one-eighth or one-sixteenth, others five per cent. This money is set apart, and expended in alms and charitable expenses by the head partner, with the consent of, and as agreed on by, the rest, and is kept in his charge.

Partition of losses.

Losses by Government confiscation or Rajkrant, by theft, or by fire consuming the shop and premises employed in the trade, fall on all the partners. Also losses by fire consuming the dwelling-house of the head partner, if adjoining the shop, not otherwise. If fraud be suspected, an investigation is held into fraudulent deposits or transactions for the party's own personal profit. In the same manner losses on the road accruing to one of the partners (from Rajkrant, neglect, forgetfulness, or fraud of another) travelling with money or goods, if not fraudulent, are defrayed by all the partners according to their shares.

Should such travelling partner be killed on the road, the loss falls on all the surviving partners. If he have left a son capable of attending to business, his father's share is continued to him; and accounts of interest, profit, and loss are made out, if necessary, by arbitration. Should the son be incapable, or should the deceased have left no son, it is usual for the survivors to pay a sum, without strict calculation, to his family, and take a Farikhut or release in full.

Case of travelling partner killed on the road.

Such travelling partner being sent to purchase cloths, he receives on departing a Jabta or Yad, specifying the articles and prices. So in purchasing Kirane, the Jabta specifies the quantity and prices. Verbal directions are also customary. An intelligent traveller is allowed to make unspecified speculations, which are afterwards approved by the rest, if entered into with due regard to the capital of the firm.

Responsibility of subordinate partners on death of the principal.

Should a head partner die, the surviving subordinates are bound to pay balances due to the creditors of the firm, even though they were not known to have been in the partnership, but only according to their respective shares. The remainder must be paid to the creditors out of the deceased's estate.

Servants or poor relations.

Persons who bring water or cook food are not in partnership, unless allowed a small share (one-half anna) of the profits as a maintenance by the head partner, being his relations, but unfit for any other duty. Should the trade be unprofitable, their small proportion of loss would be defrayed by the head partner, or they may receive settled wages, from three to five rupees, or be paid in both ways. The other shares are distributed as at first settled, and without regard to comparative diligence, &c.

Fraud of the head partner solely managing trade.

Should a head partner carry on the trade singly (his other partners supplying capital only and not attending to the business from confidence in him), and afterwards fraudulently open another trade on his own private account, transferring losses and bad debts to the partnership account, and profitable transactions to his own, on an investigation he will be obliged to repay the losses so occasioned. This species of fraud is not unusual.

Division of profits in lieu of salary.

Four partners trading together—one advancing capital, one acting as head partner, and two performing the business of the firm, the former having agreed to give the two latter one-fourth, or four annas, of profits that might accrue in lieu of salary (rozmurra)—after the first year the two working partners receive each 75 rupees, on a profit of 300 rupees; after the second, 25 rupees on ditto of 100 rupees; then after the third a year of large profits (say 5,000 rupees), the former would not be allowed to pay them only 75 rupees as in lieu of salary, but must act either strictly on the letter of the agreement, or on the same principles as they had done in the two former years.

Two partners with two shops.

Two partners commence trading, superintending shops in different places, but advancing equal capital, and agreeing to share profit and loss equally: the profit and loss of the trade of each shop must then be estimated, and the whole gain or loss equally divided. Should one of them admit other partners, with the consent of the other, the new partners share the whole gain or loss with the two original; if without the other's knowledge, they of course only share in the profit or loss falling to their principal, and have no connection with his original partner.

Settlement of accounts on the death of a partner.

Should one or more of several partners die, arbitrators and respectable persons would decide, on an examination of accounts, what balance is due to the family, and Farikhuts are given on receiving it: after such full investigation, the accounts would not be demandable by a son on growing up, nor would a different estimate be admissible. But should the surviving partner receive a Farikhut merely on his own statement, the son on growing up has a right to inspect the accounts, and to receive any small balance that may be proved not to have been paid to his family.

Absence of one partner.

Should one of several partners absent himself on his own affairs in another country, it is customary for him before his departure to leave his son, brother, or other person in his place, responsible for him. Should he not do so, but write a Farikhut of separation, or verbally state that from that day forward he and his former partners would have no dealings in partnership, it is of no consequence; from that day, or from the following Deepoulee, his partnership ceases, and he may receive the balance due to him whenever he may return. Should a partner, after speaking with the head partner, absent himself for a stated period, and exceed the time settled by several months, the partnership nevertheless goes on. On his continued absence, the head partner would write him a notice of its termination, should he not return by a certain time: should he not send any reply, the partnership account would be closed from the day of his receiving the notice. Should no notice be written, the partnership would continue at least till the period fixed on at departing for his return; but the absentee might, in the event of his capital advanced not being repaid to him, claim interest and principal on his future return up to the day of its payment.

Should a partner absent himself without consulting the head of the firm, the latter would write to him a notice that their partnership account would close by a certain period: if then he return by a day specified by himself, he continues in partnership; otherwise he ceases to be a partner from the following Deepoulee,* and the remaining partners, with respectable arbitrators, inspect the accounts, and fix the amount payable.

* So the Kirane Sahookars. The Kaprekure Sahookars state the day on which he went away as that from which partnership ceases, in case of his having advanced no capital.

Should a partner be detained by violence—for instance, seized by the Sirkar* on any matter connected with the trade, as for refusing to pay a Dund, or contribution, his partnership account would be allowed to continue till his return at liberty; but should it be proved that he had, after obtaining his release, lived without restraint for a long period, his claims on the partnership would cease from the day of his obtaining such release. Should he be apprehended on a matter of personal concern, as for any crime, the head partner writes him a notice, and should he return no reply, the partnership account ceases after the expiration of a year.† Should he be absent at that time, his wife or brother, &c., receives the balance due to him of profit, with principal and interest, as may have been settled by arbitrators, and gives a Farikhut. Should he have no relations, the amount remains settled by the arbitrators as to profit or loss, and on his future return he may receive his capital and interest up to the time of his return. He is entitled to a year's profit or loss on his return, whether or no there have been any arbitrated settlement.

Should a partner go on a pilgrimage after fixing a period for his return with the other partners, and should he delay such return for a long period, either party may write to the other fixing the present year as the period for closing the accounts. Should neither write, the accounts of profit and loss (exclusive of interest) should be made up to the Deepoulee ‡ of the year in which the return was fixed.

Should a partner, after consulting with the rest, go on an absence of a month or two, and should it be prolonged by sickness, &c., to a year, if the parties agree by letter, the

* These and similar replies of course refer to the practice under native Governments.

† See the above note as to the Kaprekure Sahookars.

‡ *Ibid.*

partnership account may go on; if, however, he have no capital in the firm, the others will not agree to such prolonged absence, but will give him his share of profit and loss up to the specified period of his absence, and not beyond: in some cases, however, indulgence is given on this point, by favour of the head partner, &c. Should he engage in trade while absent on such understanding, his profit or loss will be considered part of the common stock, and shared among all.

Bankruptcy from extravagance of the head partner.

It sometimes happens that a head partner expends and consumes the gains of the whole concern deposited with him by the rest: on a bankruptcy then occurring, all the partners come on the head partner; and should he have no effects, they incur loss to the extent of the deposits.

Advances to Sahookars to receive share of trading profits.

It is customary for a man to advance money to a Sahookar on a written agreement to receive a small proportion of profits thereon, as part of the Sahookar's capital, without being answerable for loss, and without receiving interest thereon. Such sum is to be repaid at the time specified, but is not demandable except at the period of the Deepoulee.

Dissolution of partnership.

It is customary on dissolving a partnership for the party leaving to write a Farikhut, or deed of acquittance, to the rest, which is sometimes witnessed. It expresses the amount of capital, interest, proportion of profit and loss, &c., and states that from that day the one party has no claim on the other. If no Farikhut is written, the party signs an entry in the Wuhee to the same effect.

New partners.

In introducing a new partner, the consent of all is of course necessary. It sometimes happens that a head partner persuades a person to advance a sum under the idea that he is taken into partnership, and makes an entry in the Wuhee of the receipt of ——— rupees, with or without interest: the advance would, nevertheless, be considered a debt payable with or without interest. But if such entry in the Wuhee specifies that the person paying the money is admitted as a partner, the others, in the event of their not objecting to it at the time, would be bound to consider him as such.

Claims on the heir of fraudulent Sakookar.

Should a Sahookar make away with his constituents' money and keep no accounts, and after his death his son obtain wealth, the creditors of the father must prove their debts by bond, &c., proved by comparisons of handwriting before arbitrators; and should it appear that the debts are just, and the accounts were fraudulently destroyed, the son would be bound to defray the whole debts, with interest. Some deduction may be made in the event of a long period having elapsed.

Intimation to Sakookar on opening partnership.

In opening a partnership, it is usual to assemble some respectable traders and inform them who are the parties; but it is not usual to mention the amount of the shares. If required, such information may occasionally be given. It has never been usual to acquaint the Sirkar. In small partnerships of brokerage, &c., the above intimation is unnecessary.

Period.

No particular month is prescribed for commencing a partnership, but it is necessary to do so at a propitious moment, astrologically determined.

Two partners borrow ——— rupees from a Sahookar, and make a profitable speculation. The Sahookar himself then enters into partnership with them, after which a bankruptcy ensues. In the event of one of the two subsequently making money, the Sahookar can only come on him for payment of a share of the money he may have advanced as a debt, with the interest thereon: if he agreed to advance money on chance of gain or loss only, or to enter into the trade on the chance of gain or loss on his former advance, or in view to receiving share of profit only without interest, he cannot come on them.

Should one partner die while absent on a pilgrimage to Benares, having left a Goomashta in charge to receive money, &c., on his account, after writing to ascertain the fact, and waiting six months or a year, the deceased's relations in order, or if none, his caste or the Sirkar (according to the custom of the caste), will be entitled to the balance of his property remaining in the Goomashta's hands. Arbitrators of the caste would collect all the proceeds of the deceased's estate, pay the Goomashta his salary (Wetun), and deliver over the balance to whom it may be determined. Deceased' effects.

Two brothers, being in community, put 5,000 rupees into a Sahookar's hands in one payment (Khate), or in two separate equal payments from each, and a dispute afterwards occurring between them, should one charge the Sahookar not to pay over the other's share without his consent, it is not customary for the Sahookar to pay such share. Should the Sahookar afterwards become bankrupt, on the settlement of the dispute between the two brothers, if the one who gave the charge to the Sahookar is proved to have had a just claim, he will pay his brother his share of the deposit that may be recovered from the bankruptcy only; if his claim was disallowed, he is bound to pay him the half of the original deposit, viz. 2,500 rupees, with interest.

Partnerships in brokerage, Suraff trading, and house-selling may be terminated by one party at any time at his option, he receiving his capital, interest, and share of profits. But in partnerships of Kirane and cloth-selling, it would incur a loss to the trade were a partner to leave the firm at his option at any period: he is desired to leave a Goomashta to act for him in the interval, and at the following Deepoulee the accounts are made up, and he receives his share. Otherwise, on his refusing to do so, a valuation of all the goods Dissolution of partnership in brokerage, &c.

is made, the debts and credits are set down, and the advance of capital made by the separating partner is repaid him in goods, or by Howale* on some debtor of the house. He would probably incur great loss on such arrangement, P.

Advances to the relations of a partner.

Advances by partners to their own relations and dependants are not, except by special usage, or with the consent of all, entered in the joint account, D.

Prohibitions to make particular speculation.

In all partnership transactions the loss and gain are equal, unless in case of one partner at a distance expressly prohibited from making a particular speculation, D. K.

Responsibility of partnerships for each other's trading debts.

Partners are liable for each other's debts incurred in trade; but they have no concern with the domestic affairs of each other, K. Should a man contract debts before entering into partnership, his partners are not liable; but his creditors may demand from them his share of the concern, unless he can compromise the matter in some other way, S.

INSURANCE.†

On carriage of goods.

The term Wima is applied to a per-centage on the value of articles conveyed from place to place, and insured against their loss or damage. It is also used to signify the articles insured. The insurer has not only to reimburse the owner for such loss or damage, but to subsist one or more attendants to accompany the goods on the road for their protection; and in the carriage of gold, silver, jewels, or cash, it is cus-

* Draft on a third person indebted to the drawer.

† Authorities :—Translations of replies to queries proposed by Sam Row Pingule to Motee Bhaee, Pomasa Mansinh, Hureekurrun Ruveekurun, Wurjulal Doolubdas, Bapoo Moonee, Mohun Lal Laljee Mul.

tomary for the insurer to pay all expenses of carriage also; there being in general, owing to Hoondee transactions, no necessity to send the whole. The carriage of jewels is a trifling charge, and there are no land customs levied on those articles. Insurance is also paid at Poona on the carriage of cloths, cottons, silks, and shawls, merely against losses, and exclusive of cattle hire and land customs, respecting which the owner must make a separate arrangement. Insurance is also paid on the carriage of cattle, grain, metal pots, &c., but not, here at least, to so great an extent. Losses insured against are: plunder by military bodies or robbers, damage or loss incurred by fire or water, by the carrier's negligence, by his being carried off by a tiger, drowned in fording a river, or dying from epidemic disease: the charge of the attendants is enhanced by scarcity prevailing in the particular country; on all which accounts the amount payable as insurance varies according to the comparative freedom of different roads from such dangers or probable losses. More attendants are of course necessary where plunder may be anticipated.

Rates of Insurance payable at present on the Carriage of Articles from Poona to

		Per cent.
Hyderabad . .	On the value of gold and jewels, including all expenses of carriage	1 to 2½
	On do. cash and silver, including all expenses of carriage .	3 to 5
	On do. cottons, silks, and shawls, exclusive of hire of carriage, bullocks, and customs . .	3 to 5
Benares, Lucknow, Bithoor, Oude, Mutra .	On gold and jewels, including all expenses as before, ad val. .	5 to 7
	No insurance on other articles.	

		Per cent.
Jypoor, Gualior, Ajmeer . . .	On gold and jewels, including as before	3 to 4½
	On cash and silver . . .	4 to 5
	On cottons, &c., exclusive of bullock carriage and land custom	4 to 5
Surat	On gold and jewels, including expenses	1¼ to 2
	No insurance on other articles.	
Ahmedabad . .	On gold and jewels, including expenses	3 to 5
	On cash and silver . . .	4 to 6
Baroda . . .	On gold and jewels . . .	2 to 4
	On cash and silver . . .	3 to 5
Burhanpoor . .	On gold and jewels . . .	1½ to 2½
	On cash and silver . . .	2½ to 3½
Indoor, Oojein, and Maheswur	On gold and jewels . . .	2 to 3
	On cash and silver . . .	3 to 4
Nagpoor . . .	On gold, &c.	3 to 5
	On cash, &c.	4 to 6
Oomrawutee . .	On gold and jewels . . .	1¾ to 2½
	On silver and cash . . .	2½ to 3½

	On gold and jewels.	On silver and cash.
Meriz, Kolapoor, Punderpoor, Solapoor, or Nasik	1 to 2	2 to 3
Narayunpeth	3 to 4	3 to 5
Ahmednuggur, Kurar, Sattara, and Mahoulee	½ to 1	½ to 1½
Dharwar and Hooblee . . .	1 to 2	1 to 3
Bellary	1½ to 3	1½ to 3½
Madras or Cheenaputtun, Seringapatam, and Mysore . . .	2 to 3	2 to 5

	On gold and jewels.	On silver and cash.
Soorapoor	2 to 3	3 to 5
Masulipatam or Muchleebunder .	3 to 2	3 to 5
Tanjore	2 to 3½	2 to 4
Aurungabad, Jaulna, Yewla, Pytun, Chandore, Malligaum . . .	1¼ to 1¾	1¾ to 2½
Bombay	½ to ¾	1 to 1½

Sikh country: shawls are insured from thence at 6 to 10 per cent. ad valorem. They are not otherwise procurable. Cloths, &c., are insured at the same rates as silver and cash, exclusive of bullock hire and land customs.

Insurance is not undertaken for a longer distance than 100 coss (200 miles), unless on property of a greater value than 1,000 rupees. Within that distance the value of goods whose safe carriage is insured varies from 100 to one lac rupees.

The charges to the insurer are less if the owner or persons on his account accompany the goods; they are enhanced by the number necessary as an armed escort. Exclusive of such charges, the principal sums defrayed by the insurer are on account of loss and damage to the property insured.

Partnership in insurance.

Persons may act as partners in receiving insurance premiums, being responsible for losses and charges in the proportions agreed on.

Payment of damages and losses.

The valuation of the goods is made previously to their being sent, and in the event of their being lost, the sum so fixed is paid to the owner (without interest), and after deducting 1¼ to 2 per cent. thereon. The valuation fixed by the owner, whether greater or less than the real value of the goods, forms the basis of reimbursement in the event of loss or damage accruing. But greater than one-fourth excess or deficiency of the real value is not allowed on gold and jewels. A still greater conformity to the real value is necessary in insuring money or silver. It is customary among the Hindoostance Sahookar insurers to make the valuation verbally, the owner presenting his packages to the insurer packed or sealed, with a Yad of the contents kept by both parties. Among the Poona insurers, there also prevails the custom of opening the packages and making a correct valuation of the articles.

The Sahookars of Poona who are insurers make no insurances on the carriage of goods by sea; nor is the custom known here of insurance of houses, &c., against fire, nor of life-insurance.

Insurers are bound to defray loss or damage, if they possess the means of doing so, even should their property have been partially confiscated by the Raja.

Proof of losses where the owner's people are carriers.

In case of property being sent, not by the insurer's people, but carried by the owner himself, with or without associates on the part of the insurer, he would be required to prove, by a letter from the Patell and Koolkurnee, &c., of the nearest village, the fact of his having been robbed, or of having lost his property in the mode stated by him, before receiving the sum to which amount he had made the insurance.

Yad and receipt from the correspondent.

It is usual to enclose in the package a letter to the insurer's correspondent in the place to which it is to be sent, or a Yad of the articles, and the reply or receipt is afterwards shown to the owner. The premium is paid either on sending off the articles or on hearing of their safe arrival.

Loss by theft of the carrier.

The packages are sealed with the seal either of the insurer or owner, in order to prevent their being opened on the road. If, however, the carrier should contrive to extract some part of them, if the insurer previously inspected all the contents, he must defray the loss, and replace the articles; if he merely received a Yad of the contents, as of a certain number of jewels, he must replace any deficiency in the number on the arrival of the package, according to the valuation set by the owner on the lost jewel: if the insurer did not see the package closed and sealed, but received it in that state from the owner, he is not bound to reimburse him for any loss incurred by the exchange of the jewels sent for others of less value, or similar fraud committed by the carrier.

Traders in cloths, &c., often travel in large companies: all of them do not insure their property, but the insuring Sahookars pay the losses of those only who pay their insurance on departing, either on inspection of the goods, or simply on the statement of the trader as to their value, and the sum to the extent of which he intends to insure. The insuring Sahookar sends with the traders from five to ten men of his own, or as many as are necessary. Losses incurred from neglect, delay in moving from a halting-place, and subsequent robbery, are reimbursed by the insurer; but the matter is investigated, and if it should be proved that the owner had made a false statement of loss, or had buried or otherwise concealed the property with a fraudulent intent to appropriate the sum insured, he would not, of course, receive anything. **Insurance of cloth traders.**

No money is paid to the owner in the event of any of his people losing their lives on that account.

It is customary on some occasions for the owner to make a contract with the insurer for the latter to pay him the value of the property (say jewels), either as settled on inspection or submitted to the valuation of others, being himself chargeable with insurance-money. The jewels on their arrival are sold by the owner's correspondent (Urthee), and the produce paid to the Sahookar's correspondent. In this case losses on the road fall on the Sahookar only. Should the value of the jewels be Rs. 5,000, and Rs. 2,000 only have been paid to the owner, whether damage or loss happen on the road or not, the Sahookar is bound to pay **Dam Wima.**

22 *

the owner the balance, deducting two per cent. on the whole. This species of contract is called Dam Wima.

Responsibility on losses.

In common insurance, it may happen that the insurer, having seen the package closed and sealed, and received a Yad of the contents at the owner's house, does not take it away with him on account of the lateness of the hour, but promises to send for it on the following morning. Should it happen to be stolen during the night, or lost while in the owner's possession, or while in charge of his servant carrying it to the insurer, the insurer is not bound to defray the loss. It is not, however, customary to take a Yad until the package is deposited in the insurer's house. If lost while in charge of the insurer's servant, the insurer is responsible.

It is customary to make an entry in the Wuhee at the time of despatching insured packages of their description and amount to which they are insured: if, after the owner's depositing the packages, and before such entry in the Wuhee, one of them should be lost by the negligence of the Mooneem, or other Goomashta of the insurer who has the duty of receiving goods, the insurer would defray the loss to the whole amount insured of the particular package, without deduction. Of course his servants would be responsible to him for their individual neglect. Should all the packages be insured for a certain sum as the value of the whole, the insurer would on the complaint of the owner send for the two packages back from the place to which they were sent and keep them himself, paying the owner the whole sum insured. In this case the insurer takes his chance as to the proceeds of the packages not lost.

Insurance from a place.

Property coming from a distant place (say Dharwar) may be insured by the owner (at Poona) on advice from his Goomashta or correspondent, giving a Yad or statement of the property coming to him, and fixing the amount to which he will insure its safe carriage from the place where his Goomashta or correspondent resides. Whether a servant of the insurer is sent to take charge of the property or the owner's people bring it, the insurer will (on clear proof of the loss or damage) pay for the same, deducting 2 per. cent. or less, as before stated.

After intelligence has arrived of the departure of the property from Dharwar uninsured, should a report be brought of its plunder or damage, the owner may if he please insure its value at 50 or 60 per cent. on the value, the insurer taking his chance of the report proving a false one, or of paying the value on its proving true, with the usual deduction.

In insurance to a place for time certain, interest when payable.

In common insurances of property despatched from the place where the insurance is made, it is customary for the insurer to fix a certain period for its arrival, and to agree to give interest on the amount insured at the rate of from ¼ to ½ a rupee per cent. per mensem for the time that period may be exceeded. This is in compensation of loss to the owner on account of delay: damages on the road are of course provided for by the insurance.

Damages to embroidery.

Should gold embroidered cloth be stolen on the road and afterwards found with the embroidery cut off, if the damage is repairable by sewing it together the owner must retake his property, otherwise the insurer takes it, and pays the sum insured.

Insurance to a part of the value.

Property may be purchased from a Sahookar and sent to another country for sale, the value of the whole being Rs. 5,000. The purchaser, insuring its safe carriage to the value of Rs. 2,500 on his own account, receives the amount of losses up to that sum: if he agreed to pay premium on Rs. 2,500, the Sahookar and himself taking equal shares of losses, such contract also would hold good. This last is termed a partnership insurance.

HOONDEES.*

Different bills of exchange.

There are several kinds of Hoondees or bills of exchange usual in this country.

Dhuneejog, where Atmaram pays a sum of money to Bapoo Moonee, Sahookar at Poona, previously to his journey to Dharwar, receiving a Hoondee drawn by Bapoo Moonee on his correspondent or Urthee, Krishnajee Sahookar, at Dharwar, payable to himself or order.

Shahajog, where Atmaram pays the money to Bapoo at Poona, receiving a Hoondee drawn on Bapoo's Urthee at Dharwar in favour of his (Atmaram's) correspondent or nominee (Dyaram) there, being the bearer.

Nishajog, where the person to whom the money is made payable (Dyaram) is described in the body of the Hoondee, not being known to Krishnajee.

Dursūnee,† where the Hoondee is made payable at sight.

Bundee Moodut, where it is made payable at so many days after date.

Letter of advice.

It is not customary to draw bills in sets, but merely to send a letter of advice by the Dawk following that on which the Hoondee was sent. Advice from the correspondent (Dyaram) or Goomashta (or partner) of Atmaram of payment of the money at Dharwar is called Jowab-i-Hoondee; on account of which Atmaram pays to Bapoo Moonee 8 annas to 2 rupees, according to the distance of the place, per cent.

---

* Authorities:—Translation of replies to queries proposed by Sam Row Pingule, to Motee Bhaee, Hurreekurrun Ruveekurrun, Bapoo Moonee, Sheshupa Naik Padshapookur, Doulut Row Gumbhun Mull, Bapoo Kumlapoorkur Nisbut Hureshwur Bhaee, Krishnajee Tookaram, Bapoo Chiplonekur, Kaseepunt Bhow Nisbut Ramchunder Naik Gokle.

† These are generally drawn and accepted by the Aurungabad Sahookars, &c. They are not general in Poona.

It is not customary to allow days of grace, as with us; the money is to be paid on the day specified.

After the Hoondee has been drawn at Poona, it may be sold in Poona to another Sahookar, instead of sending it direct to Dharwar. Such purchaser indorses it (Bechana) with his signature. After undergoing several sales and indorsements, it reaches the correspondent of the drawer, Krishnajee, who accepts the Hoondee, and on the money being paid, the payee writes a Parvutee Chithee (or receipt) on the back of the Hoondee. The Hoondee is then returned to the drawer, Bapoo Moonee, and remains in his possession. Sale of Hoondees.

Should the drawer have no partner or Goomashta at Dharwar, he fixes on some trader there as his Urthee or correspondent: it is customary to allow him 1 to 4 annas per cent. on the amount of the Hoondee. This is called Hukshaee. Hukshaee or commission to the correspondent.

When the drawer, in order to answer his Hoondee, sends gold, silver, or cash to his correspondent, such articles are called Lahune. This is said to be a general custom. No other articles are sent to answer Hoondees. In some cases, the balance of debts and credits would render such carriage of bullion and coin unnecessary. Sometimes the drawer (Bapoo) sends to his correspondent (Krishnajee), in lieu of Lahune, another Hoondee drawn on a Sahookar of (say) Hyderabad, a debtor of his, payable to the order of Krishnajee, who then sells it in Dharwar for the amount, and the purchaser (indorser) obtains the money from the Hyderabad Sahookar on its being presented there for payment. Such Hoondee is termed Desawurchee Hoondee, Budulee Hoondee; and sometimes Bapoo Moonee has credit with Krishnajee to a certain amount by agreement: till his Hoondees drawn on the latter exceed which it is unnecessary to send Lahune (or Budulee Hoondee). Hoondees answered by consignment of cash or bullion. Balances due. Bill transactions. Or credit.

The correspondent is entitled to his Hukshaee or commis- Hukshaee in all the above cases. sion whether he receives bullion and cash, or Budulee Hoondees to answer Hoondees payable by him. In the latter case, a bill-broker is often employed to sell the Budulee Hoondee, who receives a brokerage (Dulalee) of 1 anna per cent. on the amount of the Hoondee. The Hukshaee and Dulalee is chargeable to the drawer.

FORM OF A HOONDEE.

Sreekar.

Mark.

(Signature of the principal.) "Likhitum Bapoo Moonee pay on this Hoondee Rs. 500." Or, Dustoor Goomashta (Mooneem) Swustusree (Dharwar) Mahasiwusthan, poojeradhee or *sreepad*, or bhaee or rajmund raj*sree* *Krishnajee*, to him (from Poona) *Bapoo Moonee*, having performed the sashtangnumuskar (if a Brahmun), or Johar and Ram Ram (if a Marwaree), or Jygopal (if a Goojrathee), writes to this effect:—"I have drawn on you from hence, on account of money paid by raj*sree* *Atmaram* (or through Ballajee Naik) to me to the amount of Rs. 500, the half of which, being 250 Rs. doubled, you will in 4, 4 [viz. 8] days after sight pay to *Dyaram* or Shahajog (viz. the bearer), or to the Dhuneejog (Atmaram being the bearer), or to the Nishanjog ——, of —— height and breadth, and —— complexion. This Hoondee is bin-a-jabta (viz. of the payment no advice is necessary), or Jab-i-Hoondee, or Durs*u*nee, &c. Date of writing (Lilewutee) Suke 17 Magh wudy 9 Gooroowar. ——lines (of writing.)" *

If the principal does not sign himself, Dustoor —— Goomashta of Bapoo Moonee.

(Mark.)

Indorsement. What we should call an indorsement is written at the top

* This entry is not universal. On the back is written pay four times the half of half, or 125 rupees.

of the Hoondee, below the word Sreekar. It runs thus: "Bichanlikhitum —— to ——," if a Marwarree or Goojrathee; "Wikule —— to ——," if a Mahratta Sahookar.

Should the Hoondee be dishonoured—viz. sent back from Dharwar without payment—the drawer must pay Atmaram Bapoo Moonee interest at 8 annas to 1 rupee per cent. per mensem from the day on which the Hoondee was drawn on Atmaram's payment to that on which it was returned; and besides interest a per-centage called Nukraee, varying according to different places on which the Hoondee was drawn, and from which it was returned.

Dishonouring.

Charges in consequence.

On Kashmeer, 5 rupees per cent.

On Delhi, Calcutta, Agra, Benares, Bruhmawurth, Lucknow, 4 rupees per cent.

On Jypoor, Oudepoor, Ahmedabad, Baroda, Madras, Mysore, Seringapatam, Masulipatam, Gualior, Jumboosur, Peeranpatun, 3 rupees per cent.

On Hydrabad, Surat, Burhanpoor, Indore Oojeen, Myheswur, Nagpore, Ajmeer, Oomrawutee, Dharwar, Soorapoor, Bellaree, Tanjore, Narayenpeth, Hoobly, 2 rupees per cent.

On Dhoolia, 1½ rupees per cent.

On Aurungabad, Pytun, Chandore, Malligaum, Yewla, Nasik, Ahmednugur, Bombay, Jaulna, Punderpoor, Meriz, Kolapoor, Solapoor, 1 rupee per cent.

Besides interest and Nukraee, the drawer of a dishonoured bill, if returned from within 20 coss of Poona, has to pay 1 per cent. on the amount of the bill, under the name of Azora (hire of carrier); if within 40 coss, 2 per cent.; within 60 coss, 3 per cent.; and so on.

Although it is not customary to draw Hoondees in sets, on hearing of the loss of a Hoondee on the road by theft, &c., it is customary to write a *Pet* to this effect: "On ——— I gave a Hoondee on you for ———; in consequence of its having been lost, I have written this *Pet*. You will therefore give

Pet or second Hoondees drawn on supposed loss of the first.

Rs. ——, as written in that Hoondee." Should the Pe*t* be lost, it is usual to give a Pur-pe*t*, written in the same form, mentioning the Hoondee and Pe*t*. And on the three first being lost or stolen, a Jab, mentioning the Hoondee Pe*t* and Pur-pe*t*, to the same purport. The bearer of the Hoondee, before receiving payment from Krishnajee, must prove his identity with the payer mentioned, by producing an evidence thereof (Khatirjumma), or Zamin. If on such apparent proof Krishnajee should pay the money to the wrong person —the thief for example—he must nevertheless pay the bearer of the Pe*t* or Pur-pe*t* the money specified, and come on the person to whom he paid the money for reimbursement. If he cannot find him or his security, the loss falls on Krishnajee.

Pur-pe*t*.

Should Dyaram, on account of the delay of the Hoondee on the road, request Atmaram to send a Pe*t*, on his doing so, the holder of the Pe*t* does not by custom sell it. Should he do so, and the new holder present it to Krishnajee for payment (Krishnajee having before such presentation paid the money on the Hoondee itself presented by Dyaram), he would not pay it again on the Pe*t*, unless from excessive carelessness, or not taking Khatirjumma; but in any case the loss, if any, falls on himself, not on Bapoo Moonee. Krishnajee would come on the bearer of the Pe*t* for the principal, with interest at 8 to 12 annas, and the loss of the latter would be a punishment for not having known or acted up to the custom of not selling the Pe*t*.

Consequence if no Lahune arrive or credit exist.

It is not customary for Krishnajee to decline paying the Hoondee at the time specified if the credit of the drawer is well known to him; but if the drawer is unknown, he would require Lahune, Budule Hoondees, or other Khatirjumma before payment.

If Krishnajee is a smaller Sahookar, and the Lahune consignment should be delayed beyond the time fixed for paying the Hoondee, he requests the delay of a day or two. On the

Lahune not arriving, from inability or unwillingness to pay, the Hoondee would be returned to Dyaram, by him sent to Atmaram, and by him to the drawer. Otherwise, on its arrival, the money is paid to Dyaram, with interest for the days which have elapsed above the time fixed in the Hoondee at 8 annas to 12 annas per cent. per mensem, and Krishnajee afterwards recovers the money from the drawer, Bapoo Moonee. But should the Hoondee have been forwarded as drawn by Bapoo Moonee through a Goomashta of Krishnajee resident at Poona, whatever its amount may be, and whether or not accompanied by Lahune, Budule Hoondees, or Khatir-jumma, Krishnajee is bound to pay the sum to the payer Dyaram, having merely ascertained that Atmaram had paid the original money in Poona.

Discount on bills payable at sight.

In Dursunce Hoondees, payable at sight, it is customary for the drawer to allow his correspondent 8 annas per cent. on the sum which he is called on to pay; but this is optional between the parties.

The rate of exchange varies chiefly on account of the different coins current in the respective countries.* Their relative estimation varies according to the quantity of precious metal contained in the coin, and its freedom from alloy; at least those particulars form the standard to which the estimation of the coin approximates.†

Daily advices.

The rate of exchange on different places is known by the letters daily received by the Sahookars from those places, specifying the rate there.

* The allowance on account of different coins is properly speaking Butta, but the Butta is included in the Hoondunawul, or rate of exchange. Exclusive of Butta, Hoondunawul varies on account of the distance, expense of carriage of the Lahune consignment, its insurance, interest, and other charges attending the contract. In the interior, besides the balance of trade, Government remittances often greatly affect the rate of exchange, so as occasionally to counteract the Butta on the coins.

† It is stated that the common people prefer particular coins at certain periods, without regard to these, to us, essential qualities.

Coins in which Hoondees drawn at Poona on different places are paid there.

Hoondees on Hydrabad, Soorapoor, Narrayenpeth, Hoomunabad, are written in the Goonmutkul Nagpooree, Govind Buksh, Narayenpeth, Sikundur Jah, &c. rupees. These rupees are all at the same rate in those countries: their rate is 1 to 2 annas in the rupee lower than that of the Chandwar or Ankosee rupee, and 1½ to 3 annas in the rupee lower than that of the Sikka rupee. For 91 to 95 Chandwar rupees, or 83 to 87 Sikkas, paid in Poona, 100 of any of the above rupees would be paid in those places.

107 to 110 Ankosee for 100 Jarsye, 99 to 104 Sikkas.

Hoondees on Aurungabad, Pytun, Jaulna, Dhoolia, Yewla, Chandore, are payable in the Toore rupee. Its rate is from 1 to 3 rupees per cent. higher than Ankosee, and 3 to 6 per cent. lower than the Sikka.

Hoondees on Jypoor and Ajmeer are payable in the Jarsye and Jypooree Sikka; the rate of both which is 2 annas in the rupee higher than the Ankosee, ½ anna in the rupee higher than the Sikka.

107 to 110 Ankosee for 100 payable there.

99 to 104 Sikka for 100.

Hoondees on Oudepoor and Gualior are payable in the Sindesye Chandwuree rupee, the rate of which is estimated higher than the Chandwuree of Poona.

98 to 100 Ankosee for 100 of ditto payable there.

94 to 96 Sikka for 100.

Hoondees on Ahmedabad, Peeran-patun, &c., are payable in the Sekye rupee, or Ahmedabad. It is of less value than the Chandwuree, the Butta being half an anna in the rupee on it, and 2¼ annas in the rupee on the Sikka.

Ankosee 98 to 100 for 100.

Sikkas 94 to 98 for 100.

Hoondees on Surat and the neighbourhood are payable in the Soorutee rupee: the Butta is from 1 to 1¼ annas in the rupee; its value is therefore greater than the Ankosee.

Ankosee 105 to 109 for 100.

Sikkas 98 to 101 for 100.

Hoondees on Benares, Calcutta, Bruhmawurt, Luknow, &c., are payable in the Kuldar rupee or Furrukabadee. It s Butta is 1 anna on the Chandwuree and 2 to 2½ per cent. on the Sikka.

Ankosees 108 to 112 for 100.

Sikka 98 to 102 for 100.

Hoondees on Burhanpoor are payable in the Burhanpooree and Haleesikka rupee. Its rate is about 1 anna higher than the Chandwuree; it is at par with the Sikka.

Ankosees 108 to 110 for 100.

Sikkas 98 to 103 for 100.

Hoondees on Indore, Maheswur, Oojein, &c., are payable in the Indooree Sikka, Maheswuree rupee, or Oojeinee Sikka. The three rupees are current in all the places mentioned: their rate is ¾ to 1¼ annas on the Chandwuree, and 1 to 3 per cent. on the Sikka.

Ankosees 105 to 108 for 100.

Sikka 95 to 102 for 100.

Hoondees on Nasik are payable in the Jureeput rupee, which is at par with the Chandwuree: the rate is 2 annas below the Sikka.

Ankosees 100 to 102 for 100.

Sikkas 93 to 95 for 100.

Hoondees on Nuggur and Punderpoor are payable in the Ankosee rupee, which is equal to the Chandwuree.

Chandwuree 99 to 101 for 100.

Sikkas 93 to 95 for 100.

Hoondees on Bombay are payable in the Soorutee and Bungalee rupees. The rate of the former is 1 to 1¼ annas above the Chandwuree.

Ankosees 107 to 109 for 100.

Sikkas 97 to 101 for 100.

Ditto on Oomrawuttee, in the Oomrawuttee Sikka: rate equal to the Hydrabad rupee.

Hoondees on Seringapatam, Bellary, Cuddapah, Mysoor, and the country beyond the Toombuddra, are payable in the Gare or Name rupee, the rate of which is 1¼ to 2 annas higher than the Chandwuree, and ½ to 1 anna lower than the Sikka.

Ankosees 110 to 115 for 100.

Sikkas 98 to 100 for 100.

Hoondees on Dharwar, Hoobly, Shahpoor, are payable in the Shahpooree, which is equal to the Chandwuree.

Ankosees 101 to 103 for 100.

Sikka 93 to 95 for 100.

Hoondees on Merij are payable in the Merijee rupee, which is less than the Chandwuree. Butta 1 to 2 annas; 2½ to 3½ annas on the Sikka.

Ankosees 90 to 94 for 100.

Sikkas 82 to 87 for 100.

Hoondees on Kolapoor are payable in the Punalee Goonolee rupee, which is much less than the Chandwuree; 2 to 3 annas and 3 to 5 annas on the Sikka.

Ankosees 85 to 90 for 100.

Sikkas 75 to 90 for 100.

Hoondees on Solapoor are payable in the Ankosee rupee.

Ankosees 99 to 101 for 100 payable there.

Sikkas 93 to 95 for do.

Hoondees on Baroda are payable in the Baroda, Sikka, and Babasye rupee; they are less than the Chandwuree. Butta from ¼ anna to 1 anna, and on Sikkas 1½ to 2 annas.

Ankosees 94 to 98 for 100.

Sikkas 85 to 91 for 100.

Special deduction on Shahajog Hoondees.

It is customary for the bearer of a Shahajog Hoondee, on presenting it for payment, if at either of the three places, Aurungabad, Hydrabad, or Benares, to receive 2 annas to 3 annas on every 1,000 rupees, under the name of Sukraee.

Discount on

The bearer of a Hoondee payable after date may receive

the money on presentation and advice before the period fixed in the Hoondee for payment, deducting interest (discount) at the rate of from 8 annas to 1 rupee per cent. per month. If paid after the period fixed, the bearer does not receive interest, unless the payment has been deferred at the request or by fault of the Sahookar who pays the amount, not from his own delay, from sickness, or other cause. present payment.

Memorandum in the correspondent's Wuhee.

The correspondent, after paying a Hoondee, writes a memorandum to that effect in his account-book on the day following that on which the Hoondee becomes due—or *Pet*, &c., as the case may be—debiting the drawer of the bill to the amount paid.

It is usual to write the same time of payment in the Hoondee and the *Pet*; hence, on the presentation of the latter, the money is immediately paid, unless the time is not yet arrived.

Loss on Nishanjog Hoondees.

Nishanjog Hoondees can scarcely ever be paid to the wrong person: should such ever happen, the loss falls on the Sahookar who has paid it. If he cannot come on the first payee, he would be obliged to pay the person in whose favour the bill was really drawn on proof of his identity.

Hoondees drawn through agency.

In case of Hoondees drawn by Bapoo Moonee at Poona on Dharwar, the amount of which he has agreed to receive from Bhikajee through (*Marifut*) Atmaram, Bapoo Moonee can only come on Atmaram, and he on Bhikajee. The latter pays Atmaram Hukshaee or commission at the rate of 2 annas per cent. on the amount of the bill, in consideration of his procuring him the accommodation. Should the drawer Bapoo Moonee become bankrupt, Bhikajee will lose his money: he cannot come on Atmaram, unless Atmaram had not paid the money received from him to Bapoo Moonee.

Notice of Hoondees being Kuhree, viz. unanswered by consignment or credit.

It is usual, in the event of a Hoondee being presented for payment to Krishnajee before any letter has been received from Bapoo Moonee desiring him to pay the money without delay, or before the arrival of Lahune, or other Khatirjumma, for Krishnajee to state to the bearer of the Hoondee that his bill is "Kuhree," viz. standing over. If time pass on without the arrival of Lahune or Khatirjumma, the Hoondee may be returned to the bearer without payment; but it is usual to fix a time, called Kuhree Moodut, as "4½, 4½," viz. nine days, within which, should the Lahune or order for payment arrive, the return of the Hoondee is rendered unnecessary. This custom has arisen within the last ten or fifteen years; formerly no Hoondee was paid until the arrival of the Lahune, &c.

Purchase of Hoondees by correspondents.

It is not customary for a correspondent in Poona (Bapoo Moonee) to purchase bills on Hydrabad and send them to his correspondent in Dharwar whenever the rate of exchange is favourable, unless they have a specific agreement to that effect, or a particular order for bills is sent from Dharwar with a consignment to answer it. If, in case of such agreement, but before the receipt of such particular order, Bapoo Moonee should purchase bills on Hydrabad from Atmaram, send them to Dharwar, and they should be afterwards returned dishonoured from Hydrabad, owing to the bankruptcy of Atmaram's correspondent there, Bapoo Moonee would be entitled to claim from Atmaram the principal, interest, Azora, and Nukraee. Should Atmaram be bankrupt, and Krishnajee's name have been written in the Hoondee as the Rakhile (or person on whose account the Hoondee was drawn, and from whom the money for it had been received), his will be the loss, even though he should have written no specific order on the occasion in question.

Payment to

Should the bearer of a Hoondee payable to himself die on

the road, or the payee die before receiving the money, his heirs should be discovered, and the money paid to them. If within two years they can be nowhere found, the Sahookar who has received the amount of the Hoondee should build a temple or expend it in charity. Should he keep the money himself, he will suffer the consequences of sin :- such money would not be taken by the Sirkar. the heirs of the person in whose favour drawn.

Should a Hoondee not presented for payment be after two years returned to the drawer, the original payee (Atmaram) having in the interval died, the money should be paid to the heirs of the latter, but without interest, unless Atmaram's correspondent (Dyaram) should have agreed to allow the money to remain in deposit in Krishnajee's hands, when the amount would be debited in Krishnajee's accounts to Bapoo Moonee, and Krishnajee would alone be answerable for the subsequent payment. Otherwise the Hoondee remaining unpresented (Koree), Atmaram's heirs would come on Krishnajee, and in default of his paying the money, on Bapoo Moonee, P.

The drawer is responsible if, with a view to profit, he draws for more than he is authorized to do, and the Hoondee is lost, or in consequence dishonoured, D.* Case of responsibility of the drawer.

BROKERAGE.†

Rates of commission on the sale or purchase of gold and silver, if above 1,000 tolas, 1 rupee per 100 tolas; if a smaller quantity, ¼ to 1 anna per tola. Rates of commission.

---

* Hoondekurees are contractors for the carriage and payment of land customs on imports and exports between different places. They have not necessarily dealings in bills of exchange.

† Shesuppa Naik, &c., and Sam Row Pingule.

Jewels, pearls, diamonds, &c., set in gold, &c., 2 rupees per 100 rupees value.

Cloth—1 to 1½ rupees per 100 rupees value.

Ghee—1 to 1½ rupees per pulla of 130 seers; Kirane Jins (oil, sooparee, sugar, cocoa-nuts, Goor), 1 rupee per pulla of 120 seers.

Hoondees—1 anna per 100 rupees.

Exchange of coins, if the rupee is much in use, 4 annas per 1,000 rupees; if the rupee is more scarce, 1 anna per 100 rupees.

On Hoons exchanged for rupees, 4 annas per 100 Hoons.

Profits on wholesale trade in grain.

Sahookars purchasing grain of the ryots at from 4 to 6 pylees per rupee, put on the resale a charge of 4 to 8 rupees per pulla of 120 seers, called Urthee. It is customary in Poona for retailers to purchase grain and other articles from these Sahookars, and not directly from the ryots.

The brokerage on the sale of horses and other animals, also on ginger, dates, and spices, depends on mutual agreement. It is an immemorial custom not to levy brokerage nor custom duties on cows.

Persons negotiating a marriage, if successful, often receive from 100 to 1,000 rupees, according to the difficulty of the case and the circumstances of the parties.

Responsibility of brokers retailing property.

Brokers employed by Sahookars to retail property are answerable to them for the purchase-money of all articles transferred to them, and are entitled to any excess they may obtain over the price agreed upon with their employer.

Fraud of do.

Should the broker, through neglect or roguery, sell any goods not intended for sale, the owner has no claim for restitution on the purchaser, but the latter must prove the sale by accounts or witnesses.

Sale without ownership.

The owner of property, on discovering it to have been sold without his consent in the bazaar or elsewhere, may oblige the seller to point out the person from whom he purchased it, or restore the property, provided the seller has no commission as broker or agent, P.

There are three sorts of Dulals—one who receives a per-centage (say 2½ per cent.) on bringing the purchaser and seller acquainted; another, who actually makes the purchase, receiving about 1 anna, or 6¼ per cent.; a third, who brings customers and holds himself responsible for the payment: the last receives a higher premium in proportion to the risk he incurs, S. Different kinds of brokers.

A Sahookar agreeing with a man to procure him articles on a per-centage, cannot refuse to take them on account of delay in delivery occasioned by rain, &c., though if occasioned by neglect of the contractor he is answerable. Goods purchased through such contractor would not be returnable to the seller on the Sahookar countermanding his commission, K. Delay in delivering goods purchased by contract.

Sahookars and Suraffs sometimes enter into partnership, the latter engaging to deposit their bags of coin every evening with the former. Should loss occur by carelessness in the house of either, they would be responsible, without interest: losses by robbery in the street would be borne equally. A special agreement is usual, D. Partnership of Sahookars and Suraffs.

Suraffs make great profit in selling pice. They purchase pice at the mint at 73, or from gardeners, oilmen, and petty traders at 79 per rupee, and sell them at 72. Ryots and others selling their gold and silver ornaments to Suraffs receive less than the ordinary price, often 2 rupees per tola of gold (15 for 17 rupees), and are paid in silver coins of less current value. Butta on the different coins is another large source of profit; but Suraffs have generally to pay interest and Munotee on borrowed capital, besides the hire of a shop, from 4 annas to 8 rupees per mensem, Bytuk payable to the Sirkar (1 pice per diem), alms to Fuqueers, &c., P. Profits on exchange of coins.

In exchanging copper for silver, large Suraffs charge a *Dumree*, $\frac{1}{256}$ of a rupee, and even an *Adela*, $\frac{1}{128}$. The price of copper, however, constantly varies with the supply and demand in the market, the former of which is carefully regulated by those interested. In receiving payments, they take one Dumree or Adela above the price of the day; in making payments, they give one less. They refuse coins with the slightest blemish, or take them at a lower rate, paying away the same coins at par. The great Suraffs advance copper to the smaller money-changers, who receive 1 pice, or $\frac{1}{72}$ of a rupee, for giving change. These are, in fact, subordinate agents of the larger houses, receiving from 20 to 25 rupees' worth of copper at a time. Loans to shopkeepers are frequently made repayable weekly in copper; a fund is hence raised for the traffic of the money-changer.

The evils resulting from this system will always continue so long as there exists no standard coin in general circulation, S.

BANKRUPTCY.*

Causes of unfraudulent bankruptcy.

Inability on the part of Sahookars and traders to pay their creditors arises in this country from numerous causes independently of fraud. Such are the destruction of property by fire, flood, or shipwreck, the loss of property uninsured on carriage, the failure of trading speculations, the falling in price of goods kept for sale. Under the native Governments, advances to chiefs and Sirdars, either on account of warlike equipments and enlistments, or for other expenses,

* Authorities:—Shesuppa Naik Padshapoorkur, Bapoo Moonee, &c., P.

were frequently not repaid at the time agreed on, if at all, under pretence of the failure of the military expedition and the non-performance of the Sirkar's promises to themselves. Rich Sahookars were also on frivolous accusations obliged to pay fines to Government, or furnish them with forced loans. Advances made to Moamlutdars, inferior officers and ryots, often remained unpaid on account of failure of crops, plunder, and exaction.

Fraudulent Sahookars under the native Government, after neglecting their accounts or wilfully making false entries and balances, drawing Hoondees afterwards dishonoured, and receiving large deposits as bankers, absconded with the money and took refuge with a powerful Sirdar. **Fraudulent, &c.**

It has been customary for the Sahookar himself (in the former case) to represent the constant Tukazu he underwent to Government. The Sirkar authorities then placed men in charge of the Sahookar's property and house, for the collection of his debts, and the payment of all or a proportionate part of the claims against him. **Interference of native Governments in the former case.** A man becoming bankrupt signifies his inability to answer demands by placing a light on a small mound of cow-dung at his door, himself leaving the house, but not his family. **Acts of bankruptcy.** If he shut himself up in the house and deny himself to his creditors, give bills on merchants which are afterwards dishonoured, and refuse to pay the amount when protested, or continue to evade payments of money due, the creditors assemble and make arrangements for the collection of debts and assets, and dividing the amount, S. By Government authority all the bankrupt's books, papers &c., may be seized, and his house broken open for that purpose, S. The creditors, or several of the most respectable of them, then assemble, and calling the bankrupt before them, inquire into his debts and assets and the causes of his insolvency. **Meeting of the creditors, settlement of debts and assets, and dividend of the balance.** All mortgages are if possible paid off, otherwise pledges are generally sold, D. If not redeemed, the pledgor can only share the proceeds with the other creditors, S. Deposits of cash are accounted for. If necessary, the creditors would make Tukazu on the individual with whom the bankrupt has taken refuge, the expense to be borne by agreement among the creditors sending after him, P.

If, on full investigation, the assets appear sufficient to answer the debts, a Punchaet would show a preference to priority in contracting them; but, in general, debts are paid according to the degree of Tukazu enforced, or priority in establishing a claim, D.

Acquittance to the bankrupt.

If the assets are insufficient, the creditors (and Wukeels of absent creditors) then take a dividend or per-centage on the amount of their respective debts, and give an acquittance (Farikut) to the bankrupt, by which they forego all further claims on him or his property in future, P. D. K. If the assets are sufficient to pay off principal but not interest of the respective debts, at various rates, the interest on all the debts is reduced to the same rate (K.); but should there be a surplus, the creditor at higher rate of interest receives a larger proportion on that account, D.

Different rates of interest.

Caste no source of distinction.

Indulgencies to the bankrupt.

There is no preference in paying the creditors to those of higher caste, as prescribed in the *Sastru*, D. P. A bankrupt becoming so by misfortune is allowed to keep necessary articles of furniture and wearing apparel, S.

Deposited shares of absent creditors.

If one creditor is absent on a pilgrimage, his share is to be kept in deposit till his return, D. K.

Creditors refusing dividend (and in case of absconded bankrupts) come on future acquisitions of the bankrupt.

Any of the creditors refusing to receive the dividend, or any absentees whose shares may not be kept in deposit, take their chance for future payment from any property the bankrupt may subsequently acquire, P. The same rule holds on the bankrupt's absconding. His person is also liable to be seized on his return, S.

Disposal of

Movables of the bankrupt are generally sold, sometimes

shared. Even the wife's jewels are not exempted, contrary to the *Sastru*. But a Wuttun or immovable property belonging to the bankrupt is not sold or mortgaged; the annual proceeds only are given up in discharge of debts, P.

the bankrupt's property. Movables, wife's jewels; Wuttun or immovable property.

It has been customary, on proof that a Sahookar requires time to collect money due to him, for Government to prevent Tukazu upon him for a time, on his complaining with that object, P.

Time given to collect property.

Decisions of Punchaets on what is afterwards proved to have been a feigned insolvency may be set aside by Government, D. Fraud is punishable by fine, by authority of Government only, at the recommendation of creditors or Punchaets, S.

Decisions on feigned insolvency afterwards set aside.

Persons not trading becoming insolvent from want of property cannot benefit by the customary rules in cases of bankruptcy, unless by consent of their creditors. Without an acquittance, in either case the insolvent is liable to be sued again for the balance of the debt, though generally for the principal only, from the day on which the goods were seized. If property is expected to be forthcoming, the creditors may procure the continued imprisonment of the debtor, S.; though this was not usual under the native Government.

Insolvency of persons not in trade.

Under whatever name the trade is conducted, whoever pays and receives profits is the responsible master. Money spent by his Goomashta in another place on his private account is never recoverable, and the Goomashta would be punished; but the master must pay trading debts contracted in consequence (K.), and be answerable for the Goomashta's acts of bankruptcy.

Responsibility of the principal for bankruptcy in consequence of a Goomashta's extravagance.

APPENDIX.

APPENDIX A.

ON THE CUSTOMS OF PARTICULAR CASTES OF POONA.

(3.*) On the Betrothment.

1. After the Wagnischya or Magune the marriage must be concluded, unless either of the parties prove of lower caste, or the astrological calculation of their birthdays is not favourable to the union, when it is broken off, and the intended husband receives back the jewels and presents he may have given the girl on the Magune.

[52.] Wywharee Josee (Brahmun), Goluk, Khutree, Koshtee, Gooruwu, Wys, Ahir, Lar, Dewagun, Kanure Sonar, Purdesee Sootar, Lohar, Kasar Bhande Wikunar, Jyn, Nhawe Kusbekur and Gungateerkur, Malee, Bhat Koonbee, Kan Kamate Surwude Josee, Gondhulee, Konk. Goulee, Hulwaee, Lodhee Purd, Chupperbund, Burbhoonje, Buldee, Sekwutee Rajwutee, Koombhar, Dhungur, Kootekur, Simpee, Jungum, Goolwee Wanee, Bungur Wanee, Kanure Goulee, Lingaet Wanee, Koombee Wanee, Marathe Telee, Rungaree, Ghisaree, Sungur, Purit, Booroor, Kolartee, Dohor, Mang, Hulalkhor, Brahmunjaee, Goolwee Wanee, Kachee, Lukheree, Dakote Josee.

2. As in answer (1). In the event of the intended hus-

* Reference to paragraphs in the Summary of Law and Custom.

band's defective caste, he is not entitled to receive back jewels from the girl's father.

[13.] Purdesee Lohar, Pahar Malee, Tylung Sarlee, Sarlee, Kamatee Tylung, Dhungur Kartik, Douree Gosawee, Ahir Simpee, Bhoee Marathe, Kolee, Wunjaree, Ramose, Chambhar.

3. In these castes it is not customary to give jewels, &c., previously to marriage. In other respects as in answer (1).

[13.] Konkune Sonar, Wywharee Josee, Punchal Sonar, Bhat Byragee, Ahir Goulee, Kachee Boondelee, Kachee Nurwure, Koombhar Purdesee, Kasar Bhande Kurunar, Jyshwur Telee, Batree Telee, Rathor Telee, Kirar, Purdesee Chambhar.

4. After the Magune the marriage must necessarily follow, nor can any jewels be returned by the girl's father.

[5.] Mewafurosh, Kahar Bhoee, Lonaree, Burhaee, Sultangur.

5. Should the breach of agreement be on the side of the intended husband, he does not receive back the jewels; if on the other hand, the girl is notwithstanding to be married as agreed upon, unless she have been given away to some one else by her father in the interval, when the marriage of the intended husband must be concluded with some other family, by the girl's father, in terms of the original agreement.

[3.] Sootar, Koombhar, Mhar.

Do. Wotaree. In the second case the girl's father gives the intended husband and his new bride ornaments of equal value to those presented to his own daughter.

6. It is not the custom to give jewels previously to marriage. Should money have been given by the intended husband's family, or the girl's father (Hoonda), it is returned on the breaking off the agreement in consequence of a death* in the family (Prutikool).

[1.] Purbhoo.

---

* This is not a universal cause of breaking off the contract, but it is considered right to do so in the Brahmun and higher castes. The practice of giving Hoonda, money and jewels, on either side, is pretty general, though reprobated by the *Sastrus*: the sums given vary according to the beauty of the girl, the age of the intended husband, and the fortune of the parties.

7. After the Oopadya Brahmun has received from the girl's parents a cocoa-nut, and has given over the intended husband to their charge, the marriage cannot be prevented by the caste; only by an order from the Suptusring goddess.

[1.] Kantaree.

8. After the Magune, or agreement to marry, the marriage must take place. If the parties break their agreement in any point by the intervention of the caste, exclusion from caste is the consequence of not attending to their recommendation.

[1.] Komtee.

9. If on the man's side there be a dislike to conclude the marriage, a dissolution of the engagement may be amicably procured by the mediation of the caste.

[20.] Konkune Sonar, A. P. Wys. Sonar, Sootar and P. Sootar, Ghisaree, Dhungur Kartik, Komtee, Rungaree, Koombhar, Simpee, Tilelee Wanee, Wunjaree, Hulwaee Purd, Kulwantin, and Patranykin, Chambhar, Bhat, Douree Gosawee.

10. If the girl be proved of lower caste, the intended husband may receive back his jewels, &c.; otherwise he cannot, there being no fault on her side: neither are the jewels returned if the intended husband prove of lower caste.

4 Koombee, Johure, 2 Patrawut.

11. The caste take a fine of 7½ rupees from a man causelessly breaking off an intended marriage. Marriage is annulled by his discovered impotence, or the girl may be married to another. If not annulled, presents are returned.

[3.] Dakote Josee, Kykaree, and (without specifying any amount of fine) Moolamgar.

12. On the agreement of both parties, the marriage may not take place.

Bruhmkshutriy.

1. Before the celebration of the marriage, should it be discovered that either of the parties has lost caste, or is of a lower caste, or that the stars are unfavourable, or that the

man is impotent, or that the parties are of the same Gotr, the marriage is broken off, and the parties married to others.

[87.] Castes of Poona.

Do. Ugurwale, not mentioning the unfavourable astronomical conjunction.

2. In the first, second, and fourth cases the marriage takes place.

[1.] Kolatee.

3. Should the husband become incurably blind or diseased, the marriage would be broken off, otherwise not.

[1.] Marwaree.

(4, 5.) On the Restrictions as to Age and Consanguinity of the Parties, and Consent of whom necessary.

1. Marriage must be contracted with a girl of the same caste, of a different Gotr (adnam of a Rishee's lineage), and whose age is less than that of the intended husband. Nor can any one marry his mother, sister, daughter; father's brother's* or sister's daughter; his mother's brother's or sister's daughter; or his own brother's or sister's daughter; though the Gotr is a different one in some of these cases (the wife by marriage taking the adnam of the husband). The Brahmuns cannot intermarry even with the lineage of the brothers of their Rishee, nor with any Sugotr or connection within three or four degrees. But cases occur among the Tylung Brahmuns of marriage with a sister's daughter, and here occasionally among the Desust with a mother's brother's daughter; but such marriages are irregular, and only tolerated from the poverty of the parties, and consequent difficulty of marrying the girls. The D. Josee, Kacharee, and Lukheree mention three prohibited relations—daughters

* Choolt buhin, At, Mama, Mousee, or Mous buhin; Bhachee, Pootranee.

of a mother's brother or sister, and Sugotry: also the Moolamgar mention those of the same adnam, and sister's daughters. The Brahmunjacc and R. Josee marry their mother's brother's daughter. The Kykaree marry the daughter of a mother's brother, not of a mother's sister. The Kast do not marry their mother's brother's daughter.

[53.] Gooruwu, Kantaree, Wys, A. Lar, D. P. Sonar, Sootar, P. Sootar, Lohar, Kasar (2), Jyn, Nhawee (2), P. Malee, Bhat, Byragee, Bhat Koonbee, Kamatee Tylung, Kanr. Kamatee, Surwude Josee, Gondhulee, Hulwaee, Johuree, 2 Patrawut, Lodhee Purd, Kirar, Koombhar, B. S. R. Koombhar, Dhungur Kartik, Simpee, Jungum, Til, B. Wanee, Ling Goulee, Koonbee Wanee, Bhoee, Rathor Jyshwur Telee, Rungaree, Sultungur, Lonaree, Koolee, Wunjaree, Purit, Booroor, Chambhar, P. Chambhar, Mhar, Hulalkhor.

2. Vide (1). Marriages are contracted in preference between families who have intermarried for several previous generations.

[21.] Khutree, P. Lohar, T. Sarlee, Wotaree, Konk. Goulee, Kachee B. and N., Burbhoonje, Mewafurosh, P. Koombhar, Dhungur Koot, Douree Gosawee, Holar, A. Simpee, Ling. Wanee, Marathee Boee, Ghisaree, G. Wanee, Ramosee, Dohor, Mang.

The age of the girl should be less than that of the intended husband; and the marriage should be concluded before the Shanee. The Burhaee caste stated that marriages may be concluded with a girl whose age is under twenty.

1. Marriage is occasionally deferred till after that period from poverty or temporary exclusion of the family from caste privileges, or inability to procure a husband answering all the requisites of caste, Gotr, astrological conformity, &c.

[61.] Koshtee, A. Sonar, Burhaee, P. Sootar, Lohar, P. Lohar, P. Malee, Bhat Byragee, and Koonbee, T. Sarlee, Sarlee, Kamatee Kanure, Surwude Josee, Wotaree, Gondhulee, Konk. Goulee, A. Goulee, Hulwaee, 2 Patrawut, Lodhee Purd, Kachee Boondele, Chupurbund, Kachee Nur, Burbhoonje, Kirar, Mewaf, Koombhar Mar, B. P. S. R. Koombhar, Dhungur (2) Douree Gosawee, Simpee, Johuree, Tilelee Wanee, Ling Goulee, Ling Wanee, Koonbee Wanee, M. Bhoee, K. Bhoee, M. Telee, B. R. J. Telee, Rungaree, Ghisaree, Sungur, Lonaree, Kolee, Wunjaree, Booroor Kolatee,

Ramosee, P. Chambhar, Sultungur, Dohor, Mhar, Mang, Hulalkhor.

2. As in (1). The girl married after maturity must first perform penance under the directions of a Brahmun, (Oopadya, Poorohit, or other qualified person of the first caste). The Lingaets occasionally perform penance by direction of their own Jungums.

[15.] Wywharee Josee, Goluk, Purbhoo, Kantaree, Wys Sonar, Dewagun Sonar, Kasar (2) Nhawee Kusb and Gung Malee, Jungum, B. Wanee Purd Chambhar, Brahmukshutree, G. Wanee, Brahmunjaee.

A case occurred at Poona in 1825, in which the Josee conducted the penance and marriage of a mature Brahminee after a consultation: other cases are said to occur, but the parties do not divulge them, as readmission is contrary to the *S*astrus.

3. A girl arriving at maturity before marriage is excluded from caste, and remains unmarried.

[10.] Khutree, Gooruwu, Konk. Sonar, Lar. Sonar, Punchal Sonar, Kan Sonar, Sootar, Jyn, Kamatee T., Ahir Simpee.

4. According to the *S*astrus this is a great crime on the part of the parents; it is otherwise considered by present custom.

[1.] Marwaree.

5. A girl may be married after maturity.

[7.] Ugurwale, Moolamgar, R. Josee, D. Josee, Lukheree, Kykaree, Holar.

6. No marriage is delayed beyond a girl's maturity.

[1.] Kast.

1. The parents of the girl, or her nearest relation present, or friend acting as guardian, have the right of giving her away in marriage, which is considered a duty to be performed before her maturity. In the latter cases the caste, or its chief authorities, are usually assembled to give their consent,

without which, or that of nearer relations, no marriage can take place.

[85.] Castes of Poona.

2. A marriage concluded without the consent of parents is not therefore annulled.

[5.] Kacharee, G. Wanee, Moolamgar, Lukheree, Holar.

3. Do. if the consent of the brother or uncle of the girl had been obtained.

[5.] Kast, Brahmunjaee, Rawul Josee, D. Josee, Kykaree.

4. Do. if concluded with the proper ceremonies, and between persons of unexceptionable caste.

[1.] Brahmukshutree.

5. The marriage is not annulled. If by the girl's consent, that is sufficient. If by compulsion, the Sirkar will fine the offending party.

[1.] Ugurwale.

(9.) On the Ceremonies at the Time of Marriage.

1. After the Magune, a Lugunputrika is usually written by the Brahmun Josee, containing the names of the parties, and the day and hour at which the marriage is to be celebrated, in the form of an order. At the appointed time oil and turmeric are put on the persons of the bride and bridegroom, religious ceremonies are performed, and the parties, with their relations and friends on both sides, go in procession to the house of the lady's father. The parties hold a veil suspended between them, and she is given away by her father to her new family. After two or three days' festivity (according to the astrological calculations of the Josee), during which time the father-in-law gives presents of clothes, &c., to his daughter and guests, whether Brahmuns or of the caste, she is conducted with the same public procession

to her father-in-law's house (Wurat), where she remains until the Shance: she afterwards lives occasionally at both houses. At that period some construct a Mukur; female relations give the wife fruits and grain, presents of clothes, &c. (Woteebhurun or Phulsogun), after her sitting apart for several days. Ceremonies are conducted by Brahmuns on the occasion.

[84.] Khutree, Koshtee, Gooruwu, A. Lar. D. P. Kan. Sonar, Purd, Sootar, Koonbee, Burhaee, Kasar bh. k., Jyn, Nhawee G. Malee, P. Malee, Bhat Byragee, Bhat Koonbee, Sarlee, Kan Kamatee, Surwude Josee, Gondhule, Konk. Goulee, A. Goulee, Hulwaee, Kachee Boondele, Chupperbund, Kachee N. Burbhoonje, Dhungur (2), A. Simpee, Mar. Bhoee, Kahar Bhoee, Mar Telee, Rungaree, Ghisaree, Sungur, Lonaree, Kolee, Wunjaree, Purit, Booroor, Kolartee, Ramosee, Chambhar, Dohor, Komtee, Konk. Sonar, Mewaf., Koombhar, Simpee, T. Wanee, Sultungur, Johuree, 2 Patruwut, Lodhee Purd, Kirar, Koombhar Purd, Buldee Koombhar, S. R. Koombhar, Chambhar P., Kataree, Wotaree, Wys Sonar, Lohar, Jungum, Bungur Wanee, Sotar, N. Kusbekur, Mhar, Ling. Wanee, Ling. Goulee, Brahmunjaee, Lukheree, R. Josee, Kast, Brahmukshutree, D. Josee, Moolangar, Kykaree, Holar (not mentioning the Lugunputrica).

The Lingaet castes have their marriages performed by, and give Huks to, both Brahmun Josees and their own Jungums. The Bhats also perform their own marriages.

All other castes pay Huks, two, ten, &c., rupees to the officiating Brahmun Josee.

2. At the time of marriage oil and turmeric are put on the parties, the caste are invited to eat at the bride's father's house, and the religious worship of the caste is performed. After which, the veil and other marriage ceremonies being concluded, in some castes the bridegroom gives money to the caste. When the girl has arrived at maturity, the Woteebhurun is performed, and the caste are feasted.

[11.] Purd. Lohar, Kasar bh. wikunar, T. Sarlee, Kamatee Tylung, Douree Gosawee, Koonbee Wanee, B. Telee, Rathor Telee, Jyshwur Telee, Mang, Hulalkhor.

3. As in 2. The Patell, Mhar, and Mehitra sometimes receive presents of clothes, and the Bullooteedars Pan and cocoanuts.

[5.] D. Sonar, Dhungur Kartik, Burbhoonje, Purit, Wunjaree.

4. Independently of the foregoing customary observances, the Suptapudee (Hom sacrifice, and walking seven steps over the consecrated floor) is an essential part of the marriage ceremony. The Gurbhad an Sunskar is performed at the maturity of the girl.

[3.] Wywharee Josee, Goluk, Purbhoo.

5. Religious ceremonies and application of the turmeric are similar to other castes. A dispute has occurred in Poona respecting the Pooja performed to the five Kulus (mango leaves placed on turmeric, cocoanuts, &c.) at the fifth day of the Nahun (period of maturity), or that on which the Moort (astrological observation) is taken: some construct the Mukur, others not. On the Phulsogun flowers are thrown by the Mutputtee and five married women.

[1.] Kacharee.

6. After the turmeric has been applied, and the Deokaree (religious ceremony) performed as in other castes, the Jungum and Bhut pronouncing the Mungulashtuk marry the parties, then follows Pooja of the five Kulus, &c.

[1.] Goolwee Wanee.

7. The Ugurwale caste have their marriages performed by a Gour Brahmun in preference to a Dekhunee. The husband has suspended over him a royal umbrella (Padshaee Chutr) for five days after the marriage.

REPLIES FROM DHARWAR.*

In marriages of Brahmuns, the male must have been previously invested with the Brahminical thread, and the Answer from Noulgoond.

* These are replies to queries prepared by Mr. J. Warden, from two Brah-

marriage ceremonies performed as ordained by the *Sastrus*; the god, fire, and a few Brahmuns being present as witnesses of the solemnization. On the fourth day the idol is removed from the elevated situation which it holds during these ceremonies, and the parties take their leave: this latter rite is called *nagolee*.

A marriage performed as above, agreeably to the *Sastrus*, cannot be annulled. Four days is the time usually required to go through the ceremonies, though, where a sufficient reason may exist to warrant a departure from this established rule, the whole of the ceremonies may be performed in one day; but in no case can any one of the rites be remitted, such a circumstance being sufficient to invalidate the marriage.

The Bunyans observe the same ceremonies as Brahmuns, though they sometimes take sixteen days to complete them.

The Jyn caste also observe the same ceremonies as the Rajpoots, which they perform according to the rules laid down in the sacred writings of the caste, called the Boodhmuth *Sastru*.

The Punchal, like the Brahmun caste, observe the Moonj ceremony; in other respects their rites are taken from the Kumlakur *Sastru*, or sacred ordinances of the Soodru caste.

The Koorumutrul caste observe the same rites on a marriage as the Punchal caste.

In many castes which do not tolerate the Nikka, the Brahminical ceremony of marriage is observed. Brahmuns are obliged to act up to the letter of the *Sastrus*, but in other castes the rules of the *Sastrus* are modified by local usages and the custom of the country.

---

muns at Noulgoond and Dummull, in the service of Government. "The former is known in the vicinity of Dharwar as a man of talent and general information, and the latter is a Bhut. This information may be therefore relied on as correct."

The lower castes, moreover, do not consult the *Sastrus* in performing the subsequent ceremony of the Phulsobun, but merely imitate as far as they can the Brahmuns, who are guided on that occasion, as well as at the Shadee, by the *Sastrus*.

The Nikka being permitted in the Soodru caste, its members do not at their marriages consult the stars; nor do they observe the ceremonies of the Moonj: difference of Gotru is not necessary, nor the presence of fire. Their marriage ceremonies are performed thus: the bride and bridegroom are shown to each other; the caste of both is ascertained to be the same, and the consent of the parents to the union duly obtained. The ceremony of betrothing is then performed as follows:—

A number of the caste assemble, in whose presence the parents mutually promise their children in marriage; sugar and betel are distributed to the assembly; the betrothed female is decked out with ornaments and new clothes presented to her by the parents of her betrothed husband; and, finally, a period is fixed for the solemnization of the marriage, which is performed accordingly; and on the fourth day the Nagolee, or ceremony of taking leave, is performed. It is not necessary in the Soodru caste to perform the Phulsobun, though, where either party can afford it, they often imitate the Brahmuns in this particular.

The Soodru caste does not consider a female impure during her courses.

If parties wish to give entertainments at weddings, there is no objection to their doing it. The bridegroom or his parents usually decorate the bride with new clothes and ornaments, and when her parents are opulent they on their part often present their son-in-law as a dowry with cash, clothes, household utensils, elephants, horses, cattle, enam lands, or even villages, according to their ability. A marriage once performed according to the rules laid down in the *Sastrus*, as before mentioned, cannot in any caste be annulled.

Answer from Dummull.

In the Brahmun caste, the following ceremonies are necessary to legalize a marriage, viz.:—

1. The female being selected.
2. Poonyawachun is performed.
3. The Muntupdeo is brought and deposited in the house.
4. The Nandeehu rite is performed.
5. The Gutukarstarpun.
6. The Muddoopurk.*
7. The Soomoorth achopun.
8. The Kunyadan.
9. The making a mutual vow to be true and faithful to each other through life.
10. Kunyapaneegram.
11. Kunkunbundun.
12. Ugniprutishtapun.
13. Tunth Bandhun.
14. Yeokotur Bandhun.
15. Vivahahom.
16. Kunya Bhooshunaprudhan.
17. Suptapudee.
18. Lajahom.
19. Dhoorvaaroondithee Duraun.
20. Sheshahom.
21. Nakballee.

The above are the ceremonies to be observed at a Shadee; those for the Phulsobun, or ceremony observed upon the female's attaining the age of puberty, are as follows:—

1. Poonyawachun.
2. Gurbadhan Sunkul.

* The ceremony of rice-throwing, described in a subsequent part of this answer.

3. Hom.
4. Attiring in new clothes.
5. Phul Dan,
   and
6. Ghurpurwurush.

Marriages are performed in the Kshutriy Vys, Punchal and Goojur after the same manner as in the Brahmun caste.

The Bunyan caste in their marriage ceremonies substitute for Lajahom, Sheshhom, and Suptapudee the following rites :—

1. Oongur Phulpooja.
2. Kunya Purmeswuree Pooja.
3. Naguswuree Pooja.
4. Lekh Pooja.
5. Balnagur Pooja.
6. Gunga ditto.
7. Gotur ditto.
8. Bhaskuracharee Pooja,
   and
9. Irunnee ditto.

To the ceremonies observed by Brahmuns, the Punchallee caste adds that of Kalleekapooja.

The Goozeratees follow the same forms as the Punchallees, with the exception that they substitute for Kalleekapooja the Phoordurrapooja and Krishna Deotapooja.

The Brahmuns and Kshutree caste make use of the Ved Muntrus, and the Vys Punchall Goojur of the Pooran Muntrus, in their marriage ceremonies.

The Lingaets solemnize their marriage thus :—

Turmeric and oil mixed together are rubbed over the bodies of the man and woman, who are then bathed, and covered with a blanket, which is not taken off till the close of the marriage ceremony, when a feast is given to the Jungums and the rest of the caste. Twenty-two twigs of the holy fig-tree being then procured, four new earthen vessels are placed in four sides of a square (east, west, north, and south,) and a cord passed round them, so as to form an enclosure, in which, the man and woman and their relatives being seated, they anoint themselves with oil, bathe, and eat their meal. The officiating priest is then seated on a stool with the persons to be married, and five small vessels being placed before him, he consecrates the "Mungul Soothur," or small silk thread (to which a small gold ornament is appended), worn light round the neck by married women as a token that they are married, and which on the death of the husband is taken off and broken: this the Gunacharee, Stawur Dya, Mutputtee, and the bridegroom's Gooroo, then touch with their hands, and deliver to the man, who fastens it on the woman's neck. The atchooturpun ceremony is then performed. A piece of thread being fastened to a Pan beeree, it is attached to the woman's wrist: she is then adorned with a chaplet of flowers, and with the bridegroom paraded through the streets, mounted on bullocks; the whole being concluded by the Nagole, or leave-taking ceremony. A matrimonial union thus formed is indissoluble.

The only ceremony observed by the Lingaet caste at the Shanee, or the period of the female's attaining a state of puberty, is to cause the man and woman to be bathed, their parents at the same time exchanging presents and giving a feast to the caste.

The marriage ceremonials observed by the Dhungur, Lohar, Koombhar, Hujjam, or Nhaweo, Dhobee, or Purit, Koorwur, and other inferior castes, are as follow:—

On the first day, the betrothed are anointed with turmeric and oil, and then bathed; on the second day, they worship their god, and in company with their assembled relations partake of a dinner; on the third day, the couple are carried about the house on a person's shoulders, and afterwards bathed;

the "*Bahasing,*" or chaplet, being then tied on, they, mounted on bullocks, proceed to the temple sacred to the tutelary god of their caste, whom they worship accordingly. The man, upon their return, is made to stand on a grinding-stone and the woman on a basket of rice, with a curtain between them, the other persons present scattering at the same time a quantity of coloured rice over their heads, and tying a bracelet on the right wrist of the man and the left of the woman: the man then fastens the Mungul Soothur round the female's neck, and both having tied a small quantity of sugar and spice in a corner of their clothes, a nose-ring is put into a zinc vessel containing rice, into which both dive their hands in search of it, and the one who finds it deposits it in the hand of the other. This ceremony having been gone through three several times, the whole concludes by the local astrologer immersing the nose-ring in a cup of water, which is sprinkled over the man and woman.

The same ceremonies are observed on the Shanee by these as by the Lingaets, as mentioned above; other inferior castes observe the above rites, with the following slight difference, viz:—

In the Dher caste, the Chulevadee scatters the rice over the heads of the couple. In the Chambhar caste, the Poojaree performs this task, and the man and woman parade on horseback, or, if a horse be not procurable, on foot; the bullock not being used by the Chambhar caste in marriage ceremonies.

(10.) Presents in Jewels, Money, and Personal Service.

1. It is not customary to offer a daughter in marriage on condition of service to the father: it may occasionally

happen that a marriage takes place by mutual agreement between a dependant resident orphan and his master's daughter.

[60.] Wywharee Josee, Goluk, Purbhoo, Koshtee, Gooruwu, Kantaree, Wys, Ahir, Lar, Dew, K. Sonar, P. Sootar, Lohar, Lohar P. Kasar bh. w., Patruwut, Jyn, Nhawee K. and G., Malee, P. Malee, Bhat Byragee, Bhat Koonbee, T. Sarlee, Kamatee T. and Kan, Wotaree, Gondulee, Johuree, K. A. Goulee, Hulwaee, Lodhee P., Kachee B. Chuppurbund, Kachee N., Burbhoonje, Mewaf., P. Koombhar, Dhungur Kartik, Douree Gosawee, Simpee, A. Simpee, T. Wanee, Ling. Goulee, P. and K. Wanee, M. K. Bhoee, Mar. Rat. and Jysh. Telee, Rungaree, Lonaree, Kolee, Booroor, Ramosee, P. Chambhar, Sultungur.

2. It is customary to give a daughter in marriage on condition of service to the father on the part of the Ghur-jowahee, either for a fixed or unlimited period.

[26.] Sootar, Patruwut Sulkur, Koonbee, Koombhar, Dhungur Kootekur, Jungum, Bungur Wanee, Sungur, Wunjaree, Purit, Chambhar, Dohor, Mhar, Mang, Hulalkhor, Brahmunjaee, Kacharee, R. Josee, G. Wanee, Bruhmukshutree (without mentioning agreement of service, merely as Ghur-jowahee), D. Josee, Moolamgar, Kykaree, Holar, Do. with the concurrence of the caste Lukheree, Ugurwale.

3. It is neither customary to give a daughter in marriage on condition of service nor as a Ghur-jowahee.

[8.] Komtee, Khutree, Kan. Sonar, Burhaee, Surwude Josee, Kirar, Bat. Telee, Ghisaree, and Kast.

4. Should a man have a daughter and no son, he may give her in marriage to a Ghur-jowahee, who is invested with the management of the house and property, but who becomes proprietor only of such property as his father-in-law gives him at his marriage, or with the consent of his other relations.

[4.] Punchal Sonar, Kasar, bh. kr. S. R. Koombhar, B. Koombhar.

5. It is customary with us to marry a daughter to a man

of the caste on his paying money to the father-in-law, and engaging to serve him for a certain period.

[1] Kolatee.

(11.) On the Period between the Solemnization of Marriage and the Maturity of the Wife.

1. While the girl remains at her father's in the period between marriage and Shanoo, whether her husband refuse to receive her, or her parents refuse to send her to him, the jewels given previously remain on her person; except in the event of her adultery or other crime, when they are given up to the husband. If the husband die, the jewels remain with the wife; if the wife die, with the husband.

[73.] Purbhoo, Khutree, Koshtee, Gooruwu, Wys. Ahir, Lar, Dew, P. Sonar, P. Sootar, P. Lohar, Kasar (2), Jyn, Nhawee K. and G. Malee, P. Malee, Bhat Byragee, Bhat Koonbee, T. Sarlee, Sarlee, Kamatee T. and Kan, Surwude Josee, Gondhulee, A. Goulee, Hulwaee, Lodhee P. Chuppurbund, Burbhoonje, Kirar, Mewaf., Koombhar, B. Purd, S. R. Koombhar, Dhungur Kart and Koot, Douree Gosawee, A. Simpee, B. Wanee, Kan. Goulee, Ling. and Koombee Wanee, Mar, Bhoee, and Telee, Bat. Rat. Jysh. Telee, Rungaree, Ghisaree, Lonaree, Kolee, Wunjaree, Purit, Booroor, Chambhar, Sultungur, Dohor, Hulalkhor, Kast, Bruhmukshutree, Brahmunjaee, D. Josee, G. Wanee, Kacharee, R. Josee, Lukheree, Kykaree, Holar, Moolamgar, Ugurwale.

2. As in answer (1). The girl's jewels may, however, be given up to the husband, on his being hard pressed by creditors, for the settlement of their claims.*

[3.] Lohar, K. Bhoee, P. Chambhar.

3. As in answer (1). The caste inquire into the cause of the refusal on either side, and arrange the cohabitation of the husband and wife.

[4.] Komtee, Kantaree, Wotaree, Konk. Goulee.

4. As in answer (1). And if the widow contract a second

---

* This is applicable to other castes.

marriage (Pat), she gives up her jewels to her late husband's heirs.*

[4.] Kachee B. and Nur. Jungum, Sungur.

5. If the husband refuse to receive her, the girl retains her jewels; if her parents refuse to send her, the husband takes them; if *either* die, the jewels are delivered over to the husband's parents or relations.

[4.] Sootar, Ramosee, Mhar, Mang.

6. In case of refusal, as in answer (5). In case of death, as in (1).

[7.] Konkunee Sonar, Kanure Sonar, Johuree, Burhaee, Koonbee, 2 Patrawut.

7. The husband has the right to the wife's jewels in all cases. He assigns her maintenance in the event of a disagreement.

[2.] Wywharee Josee, Goluk.

8. The husband's pleasure is consulted on giving up or taking the jewels. Should he die, the wife is entitled to them.

[2.] Simpee, Til. Wanee.

9. If the parents refuse to send her, &c., as in answer (1); the husband takes them in the event of her adultery.

[1.] Komtee.

10. If the husband refuse to receive his wife from apprehension of her bad temper or morals, the jewels remain with her; should the father refuse to send her, the husband will receive back the jewels, her father providing for her maintenance. The survivor is heir to the jewels.

[1.] Marwarree.

(12.) ON THE DISCOVERY OF AN IRREGULAR MARRIAGE.

1. After the Magune and before the marriage, should it

---

* This applies to cases of Pat in other castes.

be discovered that either is of a lower caste, or has lost caste, or that the stars are not favourable to the union, or that the man is impotent, or that the parties are of the same Gotr, the marriage is broken off; and should any money (Hoonda) have been given to the other party by the girl's father, it is returned: should the marriage have taken place before such discovery, the presents of clothes and utensils given at the time of marriage are not returned. An agreement to pay Hoonda money is sometimes carried into effect, sometimes not: should either the bride or bridegroom die in the interval between marriage and cohabitation, the Hoonda already paid is not repaid, and that remaining unpaid is generally not exacted. In this case the husband may marry again, the girl may form Pat (except in Brahmun and other higher castes). If impotence is discovered after marriage and before Shanee, the girl, with the consent of her caste, may form Pat. A discovery that the astrological conjunction is unfavourable, or that the parties are of the same Gotr, has no effect in dissolving a marriage already concluded.

[46.] Wywharee Josee, Goluk, Purbhoo, Kantaree, K. Dew Kan. Sonars, Sootar, Burhaee, and Purd Sonar, Lohar, Kasar b. k., S. Patruwut, Jyn, Koonbee, Malee, T. Kan. Kamatee, Wotaree, Johuree, Kan. Goulee, P. Hulwaee, Lodhee P., Mar. Koombhar, Dhungur (2), A. Simpee, Jungum, T. B. Wanee, Ling. Goulee, P. and K. Wanee, Bhoee M. and Kahar, Mar. Telee, Rungaree, Purit, Kolatee, Ramosee, Chambhar M., Mhar, Hulalkhor, Kast, Bruhmukshutree.

2. In the four cases first mentioned in (1), the marriage is broken off. In case of the death of either party between marriage and cohabitation, presents of clothes, &c., given at the marriage are not returned.

[28.] Koonbee, Khutree, A. Sonar, Lohar P., P. Malee, Bhat Byragee, Surwude Josee, A. Goulee, Kachee B. Chupperbund, Burbhoonje, Kirar, Mewaf., B. P. S. R. Koombhar, Bat. Rat. Jysh. Telee, Ghisaree, Sungur, Lonaree, Kolee, Wunjare, Purd. Chambhar, Sultungur, Dohor, Mang.

3. In the four cases first mentioned the marriage is broken off, and should Hoonda have been paid it is returned. On occasion of the death of either party, the Hoonda already paid is not returned; that remaining unpaid is not generally given, though occasionally a man will keep his promise.

[14.] **Koshtee, Gooruwu, Wys Lar P. Sonar, Kasar bh. w., K. G. Nhawe, Bhat Koonbee, T. Sarlee, Sarlee, Gondhulee, Kachee N., Douree Gosawe, Simpee.**

4. It is not customary with us to give Hoonda money, but presents are promised to be given at the Wurat, viz. the period when the bride is conducted to her husband's house. With this exception, as in (1).

[1.] **Booroor.**

5. If, contrary to custom from marrying in a foreign country, there should not have been full inquiry into caste and family, and the woman should be discovered to be of lower caste, she is excluded entirely; and the husband is readmitted only on performing a pilgrimage to some sacred place.

[1.] **Marwarree.**

6. As in (1), with the exception that a widow may form Pat.

[6.] **Brahmunjaee, R. Josee, Holar, G. Wanee, Lukheree, Kacharee.**

7. As in (6), but we do not regard the astrological conjunction.

[1.] **Moolamgar.**

8. As in (6). But we have not the custom of Hoonda. The boy's father gives to the girl's father from 30 to 50 rupees, and from six to nine asses after the marriage.

[1.] **Kykaree.**

9. As in (2). This caste has no Hoonda.

[1.] **Ugurwale.**

10. A marriage is annulled on discovery of either party being of lower caste.

[6.] Bruhmukshutree, Brahmunjaee, D. Josee, Moolamgar, L. Wanee, G. Wanee, Lukheree.

11. Marriage cannot be annulled.

[2.] Ugurwale, Rawul Josee.

12. On discovery after marriage that the parties are of lower caste, they are both excluded. A marriage is not dissolved by the man's impotence or unfavourable astrology. On the death of the husband the widow does not form Pat. On discovery after marriage of Sugotr, the husband must maintain his wife as a sister.

[2.] Kast, Bruhmukshutree.

1. In the event of the husband's impotence, or the married pair continually quarrelling, the husband gives his wife a Chhor-chittee, and she is at liberty to form Pat with another.

[67.] Khutree, A. D. Sonar, P. Sootar, Kasar bh. w., 2 Patrawut, Jyn, K. and G. Nhawee, Koonbee, P. Malee, Malee, Bhat Byragee, Koonbee, T. Sarlee, K. Kamatee, Surwude Josee, Wotaree, Kon. Goulee, A. Goulee, Johuree, Lodhee P., Kachee B., Kachee N., Purd. Koombhar, S. R. Koombhar, Dhungur Kartik, Jungum, Kahar Bhoee, K. Wanee, M. Telee, Lonaree, Kolartee, Dohor, Mhar, Mang, Hulalkhor, Lohar B., Mewaf., Burbhoonje, Simpee, B. Telee, Ghisaree, Booroor, Ramosee, Chambhar, Sultungur, Koshtee, Gooruwu, Kantaree, Lar Sonar, Lohar T., Kamatee T., Sarlee, Gondhulee, Kirar, Douree Gosavee, Brahmunjaee, D. Josee, G. Wanee, B. Josee, Moolamgar, Lukheree, Kacharee, Kykaree, Holar.

2. On the first event being proved, and on their constant disagreement, the husband gives his wife a Chhor-chittee, and she forms Pat with another. If the husband lose caste, or be discovered to be of lower caste, before cohabitation, the wife may form Pat.

[14.] Koombhar, A. Simpee, Dhungur Kartik, T. Wanee. B. Wanee, Ling. Goulee, P. Wanee, Hulwaee, M. Bhoee, Rungaree, Sungur, Kolee, Wunjaree, Purit.

3. In our castes, after a marriage has been celebrated it cannot be annulled.

[9.] Wywharee Josee, Goluk, Purbhoo, Kon. Sonar, Punchal Sonar, Kan. Sonar.

4. During the husband's life there can be no Pat in our caste.

[9.] Buldee Koombhar, Jysh. Telee, Bat. Telee, Purd. Chambhar, Komtee, Burhaee, Chuppurbund, Wys Sonar, Kasar bh. k.

5. The wife is at liberty to form Pat in the event of the husband proving impotent, or incurably diseased, or going abroad for residence.

[1.] Sootar.

(13.) On the Distinctions between a Woman's First and Second Marriages.

1. The following are the distinctions between Lugun (shadee) and Pat (nikah). 1. The Pat is less expensive. Parties to whom a marriage would cost 400 rupees could form Pat for 40 rupees. 2. At the Lugun, the parties have turmeric applied to the person, which ceremony is dispensed with at Pat. 3. At the Lugun, the parties sit facing each other; at the Pat, side by side. 4. The Lugun ceremonies occupy four days; those of the Pat are performed at night, on the Krishn puksh (between the full and new moon), and are despatched in a short time. 5. The advice given to the parties at marriage is dispensed with at Pat: a Chit from the Sirkar officer is shown to the Brahmun Josee.

[38.] Khutree, A. Dew. Sonar, Purd. Sootar, Kasar bh. W., 2 Patrawut, Jyn, K. G. Nhawee, Koonbee, P. Malee, Malee, Bhat Byragee, Bhat Koonbee, T. Sarlee, K. Kamatee, Surwude Josee, Wotaree, Kan. Goulee, A. Goulee, Johuree, Lodhe Purd., Kachee B., Kachee N., Purd. Koombhar, S. R. Koombhar, Dhungur Kartik, Jungum, Kahar Bhoee, K. Wanee, M. Telee, Lonaree, Kolatee, Dohor, Mhar, Mang, Hulalkhor.

2. 1. The expense of Pat is one-quarter that of Lugun, 2, 3, 4 (as in 1). 5. A water-pot is displayed at Pat, and the woman receives a Saree and Cholee.

[14.] Koombhar, A. Simpee, Dhungur Koot., T. Wanee, B. Wanee, Ling. Goulee, P. Wanee, Hulwaee, M. Bhoee, Rungaree, Sungur, Kolee, Wunjaree, Purit.

3. At the Lugun, the ceremonies are continued for four days; turmeric is applied, the Lugun-putrika is calculated by the Josee, the bride is conducted to her husband's house, and with her husband performs the Sat-bouree, all of which are omitted at Pat. The parties form a Pat by their own will and pleasure; the man conducts the woman to his house, performs the usual ceremonies, and gives an entertainment to his caste.

[10.] Lohar B., Mewaf., Burbhoonje, Simpee, B. Telee, Ghisaree, Booroor, Ramosee, Chambhar, Sultungur.

4. At Pat, the parties touch foreheads, &c., and the caste are feasted. Huks are due to the Patell, head man of caste, &c.

[10.] Koshtee, Gooruwu, Kantaree, Lar. Sonar, Lohar Kamatee T., Sarlee, Gondhulee, Kirar, Douree Gosawee.

1. In the event of a woman's forming the connection of Pat, her children by her first husband remain under his charge, if still living; otherwise under that of his next representative; infants, while at the breast, only remain in their mother's charge after her Pat.

[82.] Komtee, Khutree, Koshtee, Gooruwu, Kantaree Wys. A. Lar. Dew. Sonar, Sootar, Burhaee, Purd. Sootar, Lohar T., Lohar B., 2 Kasar, 2 Patruwut, Jyn, K. and G. Nhawee, Koombee, Malee, P. Malee, Bhat Byragee, Bhat Koonbee, T. Sarlee, T. and K. Kamatee, Surwude Josee, Wotaree, Gondulee, Johuree, Kon. Goulee, A. Goulee, Hulwaee Purd., Lodhee Purd., Kachee B., Chupperbund, Kachee N., Burbhoonje, Kirar, Mewaf., Koombhar, P. Koombhar, B. Koombhar, S. Koombhar, Dhungur(2), Douree Gosawee, Simpee, A. Simpee, Jungum, T. Wanee, B. Wanee, Ling. Goulee, Purd. Wanee, Koonbee Wanee, Mar. Bhoee, Kahar Bhoee, M. B. R. J.

Telee, Rungaree, Ghisaree, Sungur, Lonaree, Kolee, Wunjaree, Purit, Booroor, Kolatee, Ramosee, Chambhar Mar, Purd. Chambhar, Sultungur, Dohor, Mhar, Mang, Hulalkhor.

2. In our caste the custom of Pat does not exist.

[9.] Wywharee Josee, Goluk, Purbhoo, Konk. Sonar, Punchal Sonar, Kanure Sonar, Kast, Bruhmukshutree, Ugurwale.

(15.) On the Relations of Husband and Wife while Residing together.

1. The husband's pleasure must be consulted in gifts made by the wife, whether residing with him, with her father, or separate, all her property being his.

[78.] Purbhoo, Komtee, Khutree, Koshtee, Gooruwu, Wys. A. L. D. P. Sonar, Burhaee, P. Sootar, Lohar, P. Lohar, Kasar (2), Jyn, Nhawee (2), Malee, P. Malee, Bhat Byragee, Bhat Koonbee, T. Sarlee, Sarlee, Kamatee Tyl. Kan, Surwude Josee, Wotaree, Gondhulee, Konk. Goulee, A. Goulee, Hulwaee P., Lodhee P., Kachee B. and Nur, Chuppurbund, Burbhoonjee, Mewaf., Koombhar, B. and Purd. Koombhar, Dhungur (2), Douree Gosawee, A. Simpee, Jungum, B. Wanee, Kan. Goulee, Ling. Wanee, Koonbee Wanee, Mar. Bhoee, Kahar Bhoee, Mar. B. Telee, Rungaree, Ghisaree, Sungur, Lonaree, Kolee, Wunjaree, Purit, Booroor, Kolartee, Chambhar, Dohor, Mang, Hulalkhor, Kirar, S. R. Koombhar, Simpee, Til. Wanee, Rat. and Jysh. Telee, Ramosee, P. Chambhar, Sultungur.

2. A wife is entitled to make small presents for good and charitable purposes (Dhurm).

[4.] Wywharee Josee, Goluk, Sootar, Mhar.

3. The husband is proprietor of all the wife has during his life.

[3.] Kan. Sonar, Konk. Sonar, Kantaree.

4. The husband's pleasure must be consulted in gifts made by the wife in the first two cases in (1). If separated, she may, like a widow, give away some part of her property. Her husband is her heir.

[4.] Johuree, Koonbee, 2 Patrawut.

5. The wife has no right to give away property unless separated from her husband, receiving a certain sum from him. Her husband is her heir.

[7.] D. Josee, Brahmunjaee, G. Wanee, Kacharee, Lukheree, Moolamgar, Holar.

6. As in (5), in every case.

[1.] Kykaree.

7. As in (5), except as Dandhurm.

[1.] Bruhmukshutree.

8. The wife may give away her own jewels, and may confer Dandhurm from the property of her father-in-law: when separated, she may make presents to a certain extent.

[1.] Ugurwale.

(18.) On the Separation between the Husband and Wife.

1. If a husband and wife separate by mutual choice, the husband pays the debts his wife may incur for her maintenance: he is not bound to pay the debts of a repudiated wife, unless he afterwards retake her.

[56.] Khutree, Koshtee, Wys. A. Sonar, Burhaee, P. Sootar, P. Lohar, Kasar bh. w., Jyn, P. Malee, Bhat Koonbee, T. Sarlee, Sarlee, Kamatee (2), Surwude Josee, A. Goulee, Hulwaee, Kachee (2), Kirar, Mewaf., Koombhar, P. Koombhar, Dhungur (2), Douree Gosawee, Jungum, Ling. Goulee, Ling. Wanee, Koonbee Wanee, Mar. Bhoee, Kahar Bhoee, Mar. Telee, Rathor and Jyswur Telee, Rungaree, Ghisaree, Sungur, Lonaree, Kolee, Wunjaree, Purit, Booroor, P. Chambhar, Sultungur, Dohor, Hulalkhor, Kast, Bruhmukshutree, Brahmunjaee, D. Josee, Kacharee, G. Wanee, Lukheree, Moolamgar.

2. As in answer (1), as to mutual separation. The husband is also bound to pay debts incurred for a repudiated wife's maintenance, so long only as she conduct herself according to the rules of her caste.

[29.] Purbhoo, Gooruwu, Kataree, Lar. D. P. Sonar, Sootar, Lohar, Koonbee, Johuree, 2 Patrawut, Nhawee (2), Malee, Bhat

Byragee, Gondhulee, Konk. Goulee, Lodhee Purd., S. R. Koombhar, Simpee, A. Simpee, Til. Wanee, B. Wanee, Kolartee, Ramosee, Chambhar, Mhar, Mang.

3. The husband pays maintenance debts (Unnuwustr) in both cases.

[11.] **Wywharee Josee, Goluk, Konk. and Kan. Sonar, Kasar bh. Kr. Wotaree, Buldee Koombhar, Batree Telee, R. Josee, Kykaree, Holar.**

4. A wife living separate would be excluded from caste, and therefore her debts and maintenance would not be provided for.

[1.] **Komtee.**

5. In the first case, the husband would pay; in the second, the wife's conduct is investigated a few days after her husband has "turned her out," and she is excluded from caste if guilty of adultery or disgraceful crime.

[1.] **Burbhoonje.**

The Chuppurbund stated that neither case was known to have occurred in their caste.

6. A wife is sometimes obliged to live separate, owing to the enmity of another favourite wife. The husband is bound to provide for the debts and maintenance of a separated wife so long as she live a moral life.

[1.] **Marwarree.**

All the castes agree in stating that the husband is obliged to prove his accusations of crime against his wife before the assembled caste, who exercise their discretion in assigning Prayuschit, or excluding the woman from caste privileges. Those sects of the Brahmuns who acknowledge the authority of, or refer cases to, a Dhurmadhikaree, obey his orders; but a reference is now unusual.

7. A wife, if amicably separated from her husband, will have her subsistence debts paid by him, and may give away

some part of her property. A repudiated wife may receive as much also, but she can claim nothing if addicted to vicious courses.

[4.] Johuree, Koombee.
[2.] Patrawut.

8. A separated wife while living virtuously would receive maintenance, and have her debts paid by her husband and son.

[1.] Ugurwale.

A wife may be turned out of her husband's house on the following accounts: adultery, especially with a man of lower caste; homicide; procuring abortion; entertaining designs against her husband's or children's life by putting poison in their food, &c.; disobedience to her husband's commands; quarrelling with her relations in the house; or infraction of caste rules. Theft is not considered so great a moral offence. **Answers from 67 of the Poona castes.**

It is usual to allow the wife food and clothing if dismissed by her husband for a smaller offence. If she be turned out of caste (as on adultery with a man of low caste, or repetition of that offence), the husband is not bound to maintain her.

1. A virtuous wife will not quit her husband even on his losing caste; she is, however, allowed in this case to marry another man by Pat.

[29.] Khutree, Wunjaree, Kolartee, Paradosh, K. Nurwuree, P. Lohar, Dh. kootr., Ahir Goulee, Burbhoonje, P. Koombhar, Buldee Koombhar, Surwude Josee, Wotaree, Chupperbund, Kan. Sonar, Dewagun Sonar, Kachee Boondelee, L. Purdesee, Booroor, Patranykin, Wys Sonar, Koombhar, Batree Telee, Sarlee, S. R. Koombhar, Rathor Telee, Tambut, Dhungur Kartik, Burhaee.

2. A virtuous wife will not quit her husband on any account; she has, however, the liberty of repudiating him if impotent.

[20.] Goulee Wanee, Nhawee Gungatilkur, Tylung Sarlee, Kantaree, Gondhulee, Kulwantin, Bhat Byragee, Purit, Nhawee, Kolee, Ling. Wanee, Rungaree, Bungur and Tilelee Wanee, Mar Telee, Simpee, Malee, Chambhar, Mang, Mhar.

(19.) ON THE CONSEQUENCES OF ADULTERY BY THE WIFE.

1. A woman committing adultery with a man of her own caste, if not habitually, is purified on penance, and readmitted to caste privileges and her husband's society; if with a man of another caste, she is excluded from caste privileges; and the paramour is obliged to pay the husband his marriage expenses and a fine.

[31.] Khutree, Koshtee, Kantaree, Lohar Purd., Nhawee Kus., Bhat Koonbee, Ty. Sarlee, Sarlee, Kamatee Ty., A. Goulee, Kachee Nur., Dhungur Kartik and Koot., Douree Gosawee, A. Simpee, Jungum, Ling. Goulee, Ling. Wanee, Koonbee Wanee, Mar. Bhoee, Mar. Telee, Batree Telee, Lonaree, Kolee, Mang, Johuree (exclusive of expenses), 2 Patrawut, Koonbee, Moolamgar (in the first case only: the caste levy a fine on the paramour), Brahmunjaee (the punishment is not uniform to the woman, nor is the paramour always obliged to pay).

2. As in (1), with the exception that it is not customary to oblige the paramour to pay money to the husband.

[29.] Wywharee Josee, Goluk, Wys. A. P. Sonar, 2 Kasar, Jyn, Malee, Kamatee Kan., Surwude Josee, Koombhar, B. and S. R. Koombhar, Til. Bun. Wanee, Rat. J. Telee, Rungaree, Purit, P. Chambhar, Sultungur, Dohor, Hulwaee, Simpee, D. Josee, Holar, G. Wanee, Bruhmukshutree.

3. As in (2), the wife in the first case paying fine to the caste.

[7.] Lodhee Purd., Kachee Boondelee, Chuppurbund, Ghisaree, Booroor, Hulalkhor, P. Koombhar.

4. A wife committing adultery is punished by her husband and the caste. It is not the custom to levy money on the paramour.

[4.] Lohar, Konk. Goulee, Wunjaree, Ramosee, Lukheree. Do.

There is no rule as to the punishment in adultery with a low caste man; the woman loses caste.

5. As in (2), the wife in the first case providing a feast for the caste. The paramour is obliged to pay only after complaint to the Sirkar.

[4.] Nhawee Gung. P. Malee, Sungur, Chambhar.

6. A wife committing adultery is turned out of caste.

[6.] Purbhoo, Konk. Kan. Lar. Sonar, Burhaee, Burbhoonjee, Kast.

7. Both the wife and paramour are obliged to provide eatables for the caste in the first case; in the second, she is excluded. The paramour pays the husband nothing.

[4.] Dewagun Sonar, Sootar, Gondhulee, Mhar, R. Josee.

8. As in (3), but, in the first case, the fine is provided for by the husband and paramour.

[3.] Gooruwu, P. Sootar, Kirar.

9. The woman is excluded from caste in both cases, and the paramour pays marriage expenses and a fine to the husband.

[1.] Komtee.

10. In the first case, the woman is married by Pat to her paramour, he paying the husband's marriage expenses; in the second, she is excluded from caste.

[1.] Bhat Byragee.

11. If the husband is unwilling to receive his wife, she may be connected by Pat with her paramour.

[4.] Purd. Sootar, Hulwaee, Kachee (2), Koombhar.

12. In the first case, the woman is purified and retaken by her husband, should he be willing to do so; otherwise, and in the second case, the woman is excluded, and the paramour pays the husband's marriage expenses (and fine to the caste).

[2.] Wotaree and Johuree (omitting distinction as to caste).

13. In the first case, the woman preferring to remain with her paramour, he is obliged to pay the husband's marriage expenses: no fine is levied. In the second case, the woman is turned out of caste.

[1.] **Kahar Bhoee.**

14. In cases of adultery, the caste levy a fine of 60 rupees on the woman: if the husband, without the caste's knowledge, have taken this money from the paramour, he is obliged to give the caste a dinner.

[1.] **Kolartee.**

15. A woman committing adultery is turned out of caste; the husband does not receive his marriage expenses from the paramour, neither is he punished, except by fine imposed by the caste or Sirkar.

[1.] **Marwarree.**

16. In case of adultery with a man of her own caste, the woman is punished. If with another caste-man, the paramour is obliged to pay a fine and the husband's marriage expenses.

[1.] **Kacharee.**

17. After admonition from the caste once or twice repeated, the parties are excluded. This forms their punishment.

[1.] **Ugurwale.**

18. In case of adultery with a man of higher caste, the caste assemble and oblige the paramour to give to the husband three asses, and two to the caste, when the husband may retake his wife. If with another caste, the woman must perform penance and give alms; if with a lower caste-man, she is excluded. Nothing is in the last case levied from the paramour.

[1.] **Kykaree.**

(20.) Consequences to the Children.

1. The child of a woman living in adultery, she being excluded from caste, is admitted into her caste on the footing of a slave-woman's child. The mother provides maintenance, &c.

[23.] **Khutree, Koshtee, A. Sonar, Jyn, P. Malee, Bhat Koonbee, Sarlee, Kamatee Ty., Kamatee Kan., Surwude Josee, Douree Gosawee, A. Simpee, Mar Bhoee, Mar. Telee, Jysh. Telee, Rat. Telee, Rungaree, Ghisaree, Lonaree, Kolee, Purit, Booroor.**

2. Such child is maintained by the mother, but has no caste.

[36.] **Wys. Lar. Dew. P. Sonar, Wywharee Josee, Goluk, Komtee, Kachee Bondele, Kantaree, Sootar, Burhaee, Lohar, Gooruwu, Nhawee Kus. and Gung., Malee, Lodhee Purd., Kirar, Koombhar, Dhungur Kart., Simpee, Til. Wanee, Bun. Wanee, Ramosee, Sultungur, Mhar, Mang, Kasar, 2 Chuppurbund, Burbhoonje, B. S. R. Koombhar, Kolartee, Dohor.**

3. Such child is maintained by the father, but has no caste.

[14.] **Purbhoo, Konk. Sonar, Kan. Sonar, Lohar Purd., Tylung Sarlee, Konk. Goulee, A. Goulee, Dhungur Koot., Jungum, Ling. Goulee, Ling. Wanee, Koombee Wanee, Bat. Telee, Wunjaree.**

4. Such child is readmitted if the mother reobtain caste; otherwise it remains excluded, and is maintained by the mother or her paramour.

[13.] **Bhat Byragee, Wotaree, and Mewaf., Sungur, P. Chambhar, P. Sootar, Hulwaee, Kachee N., P. Koombhar, Kahar Bhoee, Gondhulee, Chambhar, Hulalkhor.**

(25.) Widowhood.*

1. After the husband's death, his widow has authority to give away property only in case he died after partition. 78 Castes.

* *Vide* relations of husband and wife as to property.

2. A widow is entitled to make small presents for good and charitable purposes (Dhurm).

[8.] Wywharee Josee, Goluk, Sootar, Mhar, Koonbee, Johuree, 2 Patruwut.

3. A widow is independent as to the property she may have.

[3.] Konk. and Kan. Sonar, Kantaree.

4. A widow is under the authority of her husband's brother, but during her life she is at liberty to give away part (not the whole) of her late husband's property. On her death, the remaining property goes to her brother-in-law and nephews (should she have no sons).

[1.] Marwarree.

(27.) On the Age of Majority and Relations of Parent and Child.

1. The age of majority is not limited: when a youth has sufficient judgment to conduct the affairs of his family, or to acquire his own livelihood (from about fifteen to twenty-five), he is qualified to sign documents, make oath, and give judicial depositions. An infant is entitled to receive a share of property.

[50.] Khutree, Koshtee, Gooruwu, A. Lar. D. P. Sonar, P. Sootar, Kasar bh. w., Nhawee Gung., Malee, P. Malee, Bhat By., Jyn, Bhat Koonbee, Sarlee, Kamatee Ty., Kamatee Kan., Surwude Josee, Hulwaee, Lodhee Purd., Kachee Nur., Koombhar, B. Koombhar, P. Koombhar, S. R. Koombhar, Dhungur Kartik and Koot., A. Simpee, Til. Wanee, B. Wanee, Mar. Bohee, K. Bhoee, Mar. Telee, Rungaree, Ghisaree, Lonaree, Kolee, Purit, Booroor, Chambhar, Dohor, Ugurwale, Gondhulee, P. Rathor, Kachee Boond, Kirar, Bat. Telee, Jysh. Telee, Wunjaree, Hulalkhor.

2. As in (1). The period mentioned by these castes is twenty years of age.

[29.] Purbhoo, Kantaree, Sootar, Burhaee, Lohar, P. Lohar, Nhawee Kus., Ty. Sarlee, Wotaree, Konk. Goulee, Chuppurbund,

Burbhoonjee, Mewaf., Douree Gosawee, Simpee, Jungum, Ling. Goulee, Ling. Wanee, Koonbee Wanee, Rathor Telee, Sungur, P. Chambhar, Sultungur, Mhar, Mang, Komtee, Konk. Sonar, Kan. Sonar (age eighteen), Johuree.

3. As in (1). The period for receiving property is any time after birth, and that of ability to make oath and sign documents sixteen years of age.

[4.] Wywharee Josee, Goluk, Wys. Sonar, Kasar bh. w.

4. As in (1). The period mentioned by these castes is twelve years of age.

[2.] Kolartee, Ramosee.

5. At eighteen or twenty years of age a boy is fit to transact business, and the guardianship of his uncle (father's brother) ceases.

[12.] Bruhmukshutree, Brahmunjaee, Holar, Kast, R. Josee, Ugurwale, D. Josee, Kacharee, G. Wanee, Lukheree, Kykaree, Moolamgar.

(31.) On Precedence among Sons.

1. The son of the elder wife (viz. the wife first married) is considered the eldest son, though born subsequently to a son by a younger wife, and as such entitled to the Burepuna.

[84.] Goluk, Purbhoo, Khutree, Koshtee, Gooruwu, Wys. Sonar, Konk. Sonar, Lar. Sonar, P. Sonar, Sootar, Purd. Sootar, Lohar, T. Lohar, Lohar B., Kasar, bh. k. (2), Patruwut, Jyn, Nhawee K. and G. Malee, P. Malee, Bhat Byragee, Bhat Koonbee, Ty. Sarlee, Kamatee Ty., Kamatee K., Surwude Josee, Wotaree, Johuree, Konk. Goulee, Ahir Goulee, Hulwaee, Lodhee Purd, Kachee B., Chuppurbund, Kachee N., Burbhoonje Kirar, Mewafurosh, Buldee Koombhar, Purd. Koombhar, S. R. Koombhar, Dhungur (2), Douree Gosawee, Simpee, A. Simpee, Jungum, Tilelee Wanee, Bungur Wanee, Ling. Goulee, P. Wanee, Koonbee Wanee, Mar. Bhoee, K. Bhoee, Mar. Telee, B. Telee, R. Telee, Jyshwur Telee, Rungaree, Sungur, Lonaree, Kolee, Wunjaree, Purit, Booroor, Kolatee, Purd. Chambhar, Sultungur, Dohor, Mhar, Mang, Hulalkhor, Kast, Bruhmukshutree, Brahmunjaee, D. Josee, R. Josee, G. Wanee, Kacharee, Moolamgar, Kykaree, Holar.

2. The son first born or first seen by his father, of whichsoever mother, is considered the eldest son.

[15.] Komtee, Kataree, Ahir Sonar, Kanare Sonar, Burhaee, Koonbee, Sarlee, Gondhulee, Koombhar, Ghisaree, Ramosee, Mar. Chambhar, Ugurwale, Lukheree.

3. There is a discrepancy on the point both in the *Sastrus* and custom. In some authorities and families the son of the elder wife, in others the first-born son, is the elder.

[1.] Wywharee Josee.

1. Of twin sons, the one *last* born is the elder.

[69.] Goluk, Purbhoo, Komtee, Khutree, Koshtee, Gooruwu, Kantaree, Konk. Lar. D. P. Sonar, Sootar, Burhaee, Purd. Sootar, Lohar, B. Kasar (2), Patruwut, Jyn, Nhawee K., Koonbee, P. Malee, Bhat Koonbee, Ty. Sarlee, Sarlee, Kan. Kamatee, Surwude Josee, Wotaree, Gondhulee, Konk. Goulee, Ahir Goulee, Lodhee P., Kachee B., Chuppurbund, Kachee N., Kirar, Mewafurosh, Koombhar, B. Koombhar, S. R. Koombhar, Dhungur Kootekur, Douree Gosawee, Simpee, A. Simpee, Jungum, T. Wanee, Ling. Goulee, K. Wanee, Mar. Bhoee, Mar. Telee, Rungaree, Lonaree, Wunjaree, Purit, Booroor, Ramosee, Chambhar, Mang. Brahmunjaee, Ugurwale, Kast, Bruhmukshutree, R. Josee, G. Wanee, Kacharee, Lukheree, Holar, Moolamgar, Dakotee Josee.

2. The first-born is the elder.

[26.] Wys Sonar, A. Sonar, Lohar T., Nhawee G., Malee, Bhat Byragee, Kamate Ty., Johuree, Burbhoonje, Purd. Koombhar, Dhungur Kartik, B. Wanee, Kahar Bhoee, B. Telee, R. Telee, J. Telee, Ghisaree, Sungur, Kolee, Kulatee, Purd. Chambhar, Sultungur, Dohor, Mhar, Hulalkhor, Kykaree.

3. The son whose face is first seen by the father is the elder.

[2.] Kanare Sonar, Lingaet Wanee.

4. Both customs are extant.

[1.] Wywharee Josee.

(32.) On the Distinctions of Legitimate and Illegitimate Children.

1. The child by a regular marriage (Lugun) and one by a widow's marriage (Pat) enjoy equal shares on inheritance,

but the former, though younger, is entitled to Burepuna and Manpan.

The child by a kept woman is not entitled to a share, nor to a seat with the family at meals, nor in general to caste privileges.

[38.] Khutree, Koshtee, Kantaree, P. Sootar, Lohar Boondele, Kasar (2), Jyn, Nhawee Kus. Malee, P. Malee, Bhat By., Bhat Koombee, Ty. Sarlee, Sarlee, Kamatee Ty., Kamatee Kan., Wotaree, Hulwaee, Burbhoonje, Dhungur (2), Douree Gosawee, A. Simpee, Jungum, Tilelee Wanee, Bungur Wanee, Kan. Goulee, Ling. Wanee, Koombee Wanee, Mar. Bhoee, Mar. Telee, Sungur, Lonaree, Kolee, Simpee, Johuree, R. Josee.

2. In the first two cases as in answer (1). It is not customary to keep women in these castes (persons secretly offending against this rule being amenable to caste punishment, as among the Gossains).

[24.] Komtee, Burhaee, Surwude Josee, A. Goulee, Lodhee Purd., Kachee Boondele, Chuppurbund, Kachee Nurwuree, Mewafurosh, Koombhar, Koombhar Purdesee, S. R. Koombhar, Kahar Bhoee, Bat. Rat. J. Telee, Chambhar, Purd. Chambhar, Sultungur, Dohor, Hulalkhor, Moolamgar, Helar, R. Josee.

3. As in (1). The child by a kept woman can only receive its parent's voluntary gifts.

[18.] Gooruwu, Wys Sonar, Ahir. Lar. Dew, Sonar, Sootar, Lohar, Nhawee Gung., Gondhulee, Konk. Goulee, Kirar, Rungaree, Ghisaree, Wunjaree, Purit, Booroor, Mhar, Kykaree (the illegitimate child is received into caste).

4. As in (1), with the exception that Pat does not exist in these castes.

[9.] Wywharee Josee, Goluk, Purbhoo, Konk. Sonar, Punchal Sonar, Kan. Sonar, Ugurwale, Bruhmukshutree, Kast.

5. There is no distinction between a child by Lugun or Pat; the offspring of a kept woman is considered as a slave.

[7.] Marwarree, Ramosee, Mhar, Brahmunjaee, Kacharee, G. Wanee, Lukheree (the illegitimate child is not received into caste).

6. There is no distinction between the three.

[1.] Kolartee.

7. The child by regular marriage receives 3 rupees more than the child by Pat.

[1.] Dakotee Josee.

1. The child of a kept woman is considered of the mother's and not of the father's caste.

[60.] Goluk Purbhoo, Khutree, Koshtee, Gooruwu, Kantaree, Wys. Sonar, Ahir Sonar, Konk. Lar. Dew. Pun. Kan. Sonar, Sootar, P. Sootar, Lohar, P. Lohar, Kasar (2), Jyn, Nhawee (2), Malee, P. Malee, Bhat By. and Koombee, Ty. Sarlee, Ty. Kamatee, Kan. Kamatee, Wotaree, Hulwaee, Burbhoonje, Kirar, Dhungur (2), Douree Gosawee, Simpee Ahir, Jungum, Til. Wanee, Bun. Wanee, Kan. Goulee, Ling. Wanee, Koom. Wanee, Mar. Bhoee, Mar. Telee, Rungaree, Ghisaree, Sungur, Lonaree, Kolee, Purit, Booroor, Johuree, Kast, Bruhmukshutree, Ugurwale, Brahmunjaee, Kacharee, G. Wanee, R. Josee, Lukheree.

2. Should the kept woman be of the father's caste, the child may be admitted to caste on assembling and feasting them; if of a lower caste, the child remains of the mother's caste.

[3.] Gondhulee, Ramosee, Mang.

3. The child of a kept woman is esteemed of low caste, equal to the child of a slave-woman.

[3.] Simpee, Konk. Goulee, Wunjaree.

4. The custom of keeping women is not recognized as correct; should any man do so, the girl and her child, if any, do not enter the Brahmun's house.

[1.] Wywharee Josee.

5. A boy would be of the father's, a girl of the mother's caste.

[1.] Kolartee.

6. A child by an adulterous connection is of the mother's caste, and if of a low caste, the child will be a Burunsunkur.

[1.] Marwarree.

7. The child by a kept woman is of the father's caste.

[1.] Kykaree.

Twenty-four castes state that it is against rule to keep women: *vide* (2) of preceding.

The offspring of the child of a slave-woman, if connected with a superior caste, becomes of higher caste, and in two or three generations the progeny may become connected with Koombees.

1. The father must provide for the maintenance, marriage, and other expenses of his children by a kept woman.

[55.] Purbhoo, Khutree, Koshtee, Gooruwu, Wys. A. Lar. Dew. Kon. Sonar, Sootar, P. Sootar, Lohar, P. Lohar, Kasar bh. Kr Nhawee (2), Malee, P. Malee, Bhat By. and Koonbee, Ty. Sarlee, Kamatee Ty. and Kan., Wotaree, Gondhulee, Konk. Goulee, Hulwaee, Kirar, Dhungur Kartik, Douree Gosawee, Ahir Simpee, Til. Bun. Wanee, Mar. Bhoee and Telee, Rungaree, Ghisaree, Sungur, Lonaree, Kolee, Wunjaree, Purit, Booroor, Kolartee, Goluk, Johuree, Marwaree, Kast, Brahmunjaee, G. Wanee, Kacharee, R. Josee, Lukheree, Bruhmukshutree, Kykaree. Twenty-four castes, as before.

2. Should the mother remain obedient, the father must provide for Sunsar expenses; not otherwise.

[14.] Kantaree, Konk. Sonar, Punch. Sonar, Kasar bh. W., Jyn, Burbhoonjee, Dhungur Kootekur, Simpee, Jungum, Ling. Goulee, Ling. Wanee, Koonbee Wanee, Ramosee, Mang.

3. As in (2). Fidelity on the woman's part is essential.

[1.] Wywharee Josee.

4. The father should maintain his child and provide for its marriage expenses, if capable; or the mother may do so.

[1.] Ugurwale.

1. The child by a kept woman is not entitled to inherit his father's property, except in default of all other heirs.

[57.] Khutree, Koshtee, Kantaree, Wys Sonar, Ahir. Lar. D. P. Sonar, Sootar, P. Sootar, Lohar, Kasar (2), Jyn, Nhawee (2), Malee, P. Malee, Bhat Koonbee, Ty. Sarlee, Sarlee, Kamatee, Ty. Wotaree, Gondhulee, Hulwaee, Burbhoonjee, Dhungur Kartik, Douree Gosawee, Simpee, A. Simpee, Jungum, Til. Wanee, Bun. Wanee,

Ling. Goulee, Ling. Wanee, Koonbee Wanee, Bhoee Marathe, Mar. Telee, Rungaree, Ghisaree, Sungur, Lonaree, Kolee, Wunjaree, Purit, Booroor, Kolartee, Ramosee, Mang, Johuree, Kast, Brahmunjaee, G. Wanee, Kacharee, R. Josee, Lukheree, Kykaree. Twenty-four, as before.

2. Such child will be entitled to succeed to the mother's,* but not to the father's property and debts.

[10.] Wywharee Josee, Goluk, Purbhoo, Gooruwu, Konk. Kan. Sonar, Bhat By., Kamatee Kan., Konk. Goulee, Kirar.

3. Such child will only be entitled to what remains after providing for—1. The Kreea of his deceased father; 2. His debts; 3. Feeding the caste assembled on the occasion, in the event of there being no relations.

[2]. P. Lohar, Dhungur Kootekur.

4. A child by a kept woman (slave-girl) is entitled to no right of property whatever.

[3.] Marwaree, Ugurwale, Bruhmukshutree.

(34.) On the Causes of Adoption.

1. Adoption of a son is allowed to prevent Wuttun or other property from becoming without heirs; to assist the father in his old age; and to secure the performance of funeral obsequies and Sraddh.

[92.] Wywharee Josee, Goluk, Purbhoo, Komtee, Khutree, Koshtee, Gooruwu, Marwaree, Kantaree, Wys. Sonar, Ahir Sonar. Konk. Sonar, Lar. Sonar, Dewagun Sonar, Koombhar, Johuree, 2 Patrawut, Punchal Sonar, Kanure Sonar, Sootar, Burhaee, Purd. Sootar, Lohar, Purd. Lohar, Kasar (2), Jyn, Nhawee (2), Malee, Pahar Malee, Bhat Byragee, Bhat Koombee, Tylung Sarlee, Sarlee, Kamatee Tylung, Kamatee Kanure, Wotaree, Gondhulee, Konk. Goulee, Ahir Goulee, Hulwaee, Kacheo Nurwuree, Burbhoonje,

---

* In all cases such child is heir to the mother's property. The child of a professional dancing girl is of the mother's caste, and succeeds to her property; she also provides for all the Sunsar expenses. Occasionally, her husband (if married) or her paramour may provide for the child.

Mewafurosh, Koombhar, Buldee Koombhar, S. R. Koombhar, Dhungur Kartik, Dhungur Kootekur, Douree Gosawee, Simpee Ahir, Simpee, Jungum, Tilelee Wanee, Bungur Wanee, Ling. Goulee, Ling. Wanee, Koonbee Wanee, Marathe Bhoee, Kahar Bhoee, Mar. Telee, Batree Telee, Rathor Telee, Jyshwur Telee, Rungaree, Ghisaree, Sungur, Lonaree, Kolee, Wunjaree, Purit, Booroor, Ramosee, Chamthar, Sultungur, Dohor, Mhar, Mang, Hulalkhor, Bruhmukshutree, Ugurwale, Kacharee, Moolamgar, Kast, Brahmunjaee, G. Wanee, R. Josee, Lukheree, Dakote Josee, Kykaree.

2. In these castes it is not the custom to adopt.

[9.] Surwude Josee, Lodhee Purdesee, Kachee Boondele, Chuppurbund, Kirar, Purd. Koombhar, Kolartee, Purd. Chambhar, Holar.

1. Adoption is allowed in case of a begotten son becoming unfit to conduct the family affairs (Oopuyogu), as insane, degraded from caste privileges, &c., but not if he is in possession of his senses and enjoys caste.

[25.] Lohar, Nhawee Kus, P. Malee, Bhat By., Sarlee, Tylung Kamatee, Kan. Kamatee, Konk. Goulee, Mewafurosh, Dhungur Kartik, Jungum, Ling. Goulee, Koonbee Wanee, Mar. Bhoee, K. Bhoee, Jyshwur Telee, Lonaree, Kolee, Wunjaree, Chambhar, Sultungur, Dohor, Mhar, Mang, Hulalkhor, Bruhmukshutree, Kast, G. Wanee, R. Josee, D. Josee, Brahmunjaee, Lukheree, Kykaree, Kacharee.

2. Adoption is allowed in case of a son becoming an out-caste, but not on account of insanity.

[2.] Wywharee Josee, Goluk.

3. In case of a son becoming Oopuyogu (as in answer 1), he is himself allowed to adopt a son.

[1.] Khutree.

4. In case of a son losing caste entirely, or becoming insane, without prospect of having a son, adoption is allowed.

[1.] Koonbee.

5. An out-caste man may be readmitted in some cases. A madman has in general no wife nor children; should he

have a wife, an adopted son, from among the relations, may be given her.

[2.] Ugurwale, Moolamgar.

(36.) On the Disability to Adopt from Insanity or Loss of Caste.

1. A man who is insane, or who has lost caste privileges, is not allowed to adopt: if his wife is free from such disability she may adopt, with consent of the caste (viz. with the head man, &c.—*See* Castes.)

[72.] Khutree, Koshtee, Gooruwu, Wys. A. D. Kan. Sonar, Sootar, Burhaee, Koonbee, Johuree, 2 Patruwnt, Purd. Sootar, Lohar, P. Lohar, Kasar (2), Jyn, Nhawee (2), Malee, P. Malee, Bhat B., Bhat K., T. Sarlee, Sarlee, Kamatee Ty., Kamate, Kan., Wotaree, Gondhulee, Konk. Goulee, A. Goulee, Hulwaee, Kachee N., Burbhoonjee, Mewaf., Koombhar, B. Koombhar, S. R. Koombhar, Dhungur (2), Douree Gosawee, Simpee, A. Simpee, Jungum, T. Wanee, B. Wanee, Ling. Goulee, Ling. Wanee, K. Wanee, Mar. Bhoee, K. Bhoee, Mar. Telee, B. Telee, R. Telee, Jyshwur Telee, Rungaree, Ghisaree, Sungur, Lonaree, Kolee, Wunjaree, Purit, Booroor, Ramosee, Chambhar, Sultungur, Dohor, Mhar, Mang, Hulalkhor.

2. A man who is insane can receive an adopted son with consent of his near relations. No man who has lost caste can adopt.

[6.] Wywharee Josee, Goluk, Kantaree, Konk. Sonar, Lar. Sonar, Punchal Sonar.

3. Neither an insane nor an out-caste man can adopt.

[2]. Purbhoo, Komtee.

4. Previous insanity is no bar to adopting, if reason afterwards return.

[1.] Marwaree.

5. As in (1): the wife must adopt from among the Bhowbund. No mention is made of the caste.

[10.] Bruhmukshutree, Rawul Jogee, Lukheree, Kacharee, Kykaree, Kast, Brahmunjaee, D. Josee, G. Wanee, Moolamgar.

6. The wife's consent, or the relations', is necessary in the first case. A permanently excluded person cannot adopt.

[1]. Ugurwale.

(37.) On the Restriction as to the Age of the Adoptee.

1. The age of the adopter is unlimited; that of the adoptee may be any period from one to twenty-five.

[45.] Khutree, Koshtee, Gooruwu, Wys. Ahir. Konk. Lar. Dew. Punch Sonar, P. Sootar, P. Lohar, Kasar (2), Nhawee G., Malee, Bhat K., Wotaree, Gondhulee, Hulwaee, Kachee Nurwure, Mewaf., Buldee Koombhar, Douree Gosawee, A. Simpee, Jungum, Bungur Wanee, Ling. Wanee, Koombee Wanee, Rathor Telee, Rungaree, Kolee, Purit, Sultungur, Hulalkhor, Bruhmukshutree, R. Josee, Lukheree, Kacharee, Kykaree, Kast, Brahmunjaee, D. Josee, G. Wanee, Moolamgar, Ugurwale.

2. Do. Twenty is the period mentioned as the limit.

[21.] Kantaree, Burhaee, Lohar, P. Malee, Sarlee, Bhat Byragee, Kamatee T. and Kan. Ahir Goulee, Burbhoonje, Dhungur K., S. R. Koombhar, Ling. Goulee, Mar. Bhoee, K. Bhoee, Ghisaree, Lonaree, Wunjaree, Booroor, Dohor, Mang.

3. Do. The age of the adoptee may be any period from five to twenty-five.

[5.] Sootar, Nhawee Kusbekur, Kon. Goulee, Ramosee, Mhar.

4. Do. do. to twelve.

[7.] Tylung Sarlee, Dhungur Kootekur, Mar. Telee, Batree Telee, Jyshwur Telee, Komtee, Koombhar.

5. There is no limit as to age.

[3.] Wywharee Josee, Goluk, Simpee.

6. As in (1). The limit mentioned for the adoptee's age is thirty.

[2.] Tilelee Wanee, Chambhar.

7. The adoptee should be taken before the Moonj ceremony has been performed.

[1.] Kanure Sonar.

8. The adoptee should be taken before the Moonj; or, if not, before marriage; but it is allowable to adopt a near relation's son after that period.

[1.] Purbhoo.

9. As in (1). The limit mentioned is fifty. The age in no case ought to exceed that of the adopter.

[1.] Sungur.

10. The adoptee should be taken while young.

[5.] Jyn, Johuree, Koonbee, 2 Patrawut.

11. The adopter should be about forty years of age; but, if a widow, the age is not limited. The adoptee should be under fourteen, as affection more readily arises between the parties.

[1.] Marwaree.

(39.) Who are not Adoptible.

1. An only son cannot be given in adoption; and, of three, the second is taken in preference to the eldest and youngest.

[60.] Purbhoo, Komtee, Khutree, Gooruwu, Kataree, Wys. A. Konk. Lar. Dew. P. Kan. Sonar, Sootar, Burhaee, Lohar, P. Lohar, Koonbee, Johuree, 2 Patrawut, Kasar bh. K., Jyn, Nhawee (2), Malee, T. Sarlee, Wotaree, Gondhulee, Konk. Goulee, A. Goulee, Kachee N., Burbhoonje, Mewaf., Koombhar, S. R. Koombhar, Dhungur Kootekur, Douree Gosawee, A. Simpee, Jungum, B. Wanee, Ling. Wanee, Koombee Wanee, Mar. B. R. J. Telee, Rungaree, Kolee, Wunjaree, Booroor, Ramosee, Chambhar, Saltungur, Mhar, Mang, Hulalkhor, G. Wanee, Kast, Dakote Josee, Kacharee.

2. An only son ought not to be given in adoption; but, in the event of his uncle's having acquired separate property, and having no children, he may be given to him in adoption.

[18.] P. Sootar, Kasar bh. w., P. Malee, Bhat Byragee, Bhat

Koombee, Kamatee L., Sarlee, Kamatee Kan., Hulwaee, Buldee Koombhar, Dhungur Kartik, Ling. Goulee, Mar. Bhoee, Kahar Bhoee, Ghisaree, Lonaree, Purit, Dohor.

3. An only son may be adopted if it is the wish of both parties.

[4.] **Simpee, Tilelee Wanee, Sungur, Koshtee.**

4. Do., and in order to preserve family property.

[6.] **R. Jogee, Brahmunjaee, Moolamgar, Bruhmukshutree, Lukheree, Kykaree.**

5. As in (2), the object being the succession to the uncle's Wuttun.

[2.] **Wywharee Josee, Goluk.**

6. An only son ought not to be adopted, unless in case of the parents being young, and consequent danger of the uncle's estate becoming heirless; in which case the parents may give their only son in adoption to his uncle.

[1.] **Marwaree.**

(40.) On the Consent and Forms necessary in Adoption.

1. In an adoption, it is necessary to have the free consent of the adoptee's parents,* of the adopter's brother and near relations, uncle, and cousins (suge sodre), or his son-in-law, wife's father or brother, and of his caste.

[24.] **Konkunee, Kanaree, Wys. Sonar, Gooruwu, Jungum, Bhat Byragee, Gondhulee, Marwaree, Dhungur (2), Ghisaree, Kulawantin, Kolatee, Koshtee, Ahir Goulee, Surwude Josee, Koombhar, P. Lohar, Kantaree, Simpee, Nhawee, Burbhoonjee, Chambhar, Mang.**

2. Of the adopter, adoptee, and their respective parents.

[10.] **Ahir Sonar, P. Scotar, Tambut, Nhawee Gung., Patra-**

---

* Most of the castes stated that the mother's consent was not absolutely necessary, though of course advisable. The Marwaree stated that the mother had no right during the father's life to give or refuse.

nykin, T. Sarlee, Rungaree, Bungur and Tilelee Wanee, Kachee Nurwuree.

3. Of the parents of both parties and the near relations of the adopter; and the Sirkar order.

[7.] Lingaet Wanee, Malee, Bhat, Mar. Telee, Khutree, Wotaree, Booroor.

4. Of the adopter and his wife, and of his brother, if before partition.

[5.] Dewagun Sonar, Buldee, S. R. Koombhar, Goulee, Sungur.

5. Of the Sirkar and Pergunnah Wuttundars, if a Wuttundar; of the caste, if an Oopuree.

[3.] Sootar, D. Gosawee, Wunjaree.

6. Of the near relations, and of the Patell, Koolkurnee, and Mehitra, in presence of the Pandree (assembled inhabitants of a village).

[5.] Sarlee, Kolee, Purit, Hulwaee, P. Mhar.

7. The adoptee's mother's disapproval will prevent an adoption taking place.

[1.] Batree Telee.

8. Should the person's consent necessary not be procurable, after the attempt on the part of the caste to persuade him, another boy may be adopted in order of relationship.

[11.] Bruhmukshutree, Brahmunjaee, R. Jogee, Lukheree, Kacharee, Kast, D. Josee, G. Wanee, Moolamgar, Ugurwale.

(44.) On the Consequences of a Begotten Son Appearing or Born subsequent to Adoption.

1. If, after an adoption, a son should be born by marriage, the latter (Ouruspootr) is entitled to the Burepuna and Man; both take equal shares of the father's property at his death.

[68.] Wywharee Josee, Goluk, Khutree, Koshtee, Goorawu,

Kantaree, Wys. Sonar, A. Konk. Lar. D. P. Kan. Sonar, Sootar, Lohar, P. Lohar, Kasar bh. k., Jyn, Nhawee (2), Malee, P. Malee, Bhat Byragee, T. Sarlee, Sarlee, Kamatee T., Kamatee Kan., Wotaree, Gondhulee, Konk. Goulee, Kachee N., Burbhoonjee, Mewaf., Koombhar, B. Koombhar, Dhungur (2), Douree Gosawee, Simpee, A. Simpee, Jungum, Tilelee Wanee, B. Wanee, Ling. Goulee, Koombee Wanee, Mar. Bhoee, Kahar Bhoee, Mar. Rat. Jysh. Telee, Rungaree, Ghisaree, Sungur, Lonaree, Kolee, Wunjaree, Purit, Booroor, Ramosee, Sultungur, Mhar, Mang, Hulalkhor, Burhaee, S. R. Koombhar, Batree Telee, Ahir Goulee, Dohor, G. Wanee, Lukheree, Kast, R. Josee, Moolamgar.

2. The Ouruspootr is entitled to a larger share than the Dutpootr, and to the Burepuna and Man.

[8.] **Purd. Sootar, Kasar bh. w., Bhat Koonbee, Hulwaee, Ling. Goulee, Johuree, Koonbee, 2 Patrawut.**

3. A doubt would be determined by the assembled caste.

[3.] Gooruwu, Tambut, Bhat.

4. As in (2). And so in case of reappearance.

[3.] **Wys. Sonar, Wunjaree, Purit.**

5. The Ouruspootr is considered superior to the Dutpootr.

[1.] Purbhoo.

6. As in (2). The Ouruspootr is entitled to two-thirds of the father's property at his death, the Dutpootr to one-third.

[1.] Komtee.

7. The Dutpootr is entitled to the Man-pan; shares are equal on partition.

[1.] Chambhar.

8. The Ouruspootr shares the father's good and bad fortune; the Dutpootr the former only.

[1.] Marwaree.

There are never two adopted, unless successively, on the death of the first. The Wys. Sonars stated that a man might adopt two sons, one to each wife: other castes stated they had never known of two adopted at once. Forty-five castes stated that if two were adopted, they would share equally.

[15.] Dewagun Sonar, Lingaet Wanee, P. Lohar, Dhungur (2), Ahir Goulee, Kachee Nurwuree, Khutree, Wotaree, Sungur, Ghisaree, 3 Koombhars, Paradosh.

1. Adoptions may be annulled if made contrary to caste custom. Several of the caste inquire into the irregularity complained of, and their decision is carried into effect (whether declaring the validity or annulment of the adoption).

[42.] Goluk, Burhaee, Purd. Sootar, Lohar B., Kasar (2), Patrawut, Jyn, Nhawee (2), Malee, P. Malee, Bhat Koonbee, Wotaree, Gondhulee, Konk. Goulee, Kachee N., Burbhoonje, Mewafurosh, Koombhar, B. Koombhar, Dhungur Kartik, B. Wanee, Lingaet Goulee, P. Wanee, Koombee Wanee, Kahar Bhoee, B. Telee, R. Telee, J. Telee, Ghisaree, Kolee, Wunjaree, Booroor, Ramosee, Chambhar, Sultungur, Dohor, Mhar, Mang, Hulalkhor.

2. As in (1). Any irregularity or defective performance in the adoption of customary rule, as the adoption of a father's brother or one elder than the adopter, is a cause of its annulment, on a decision of several of the caste sitting in judgment thereon.

[24.] Gooruwu, Kantaree, Wys. A. L. D. P. Sonar, Sootar, Lohar, Koombee, Tylung Sarlee, Sarlee, Tylung Kamatee, Kan. Kamatee, Johuree, S. R. Koombhar, Dhungur Kootekur, Douree Gosawee, Jungum, T. Wanee, Mar. Bhoee, Mar. Telee, Rungaree, Sungur, Purit.

3. As in (1). Examples of irregularities justifying annulment are: adoption of a father's brother or sister's son, or an elder than the adopter, or of a boy without the necessary consent, or of a boy who is a cripple, or disabled in senses or understanding.

[5.] Wywharee Josee, Khutree, Koshee, A. Goulee, Hulwaee.

4. Should an adopted son turn out of bad habits (Wraty), as dissolute and deceiving, or unfit for the management of

affairs, he may receive maintenance only. An adoption made contrary to established rule (Uwidhee) is void.

[1.] Purbhoo.

5. An adoption is annulled if made without the consent of relations, or without giving information thereof to the Raja, or without the performance of established ceremonies by the Oopadhy Brahmun.

[1.] Komtee.

6. An adoption cannot be annulled unless the adopted son is afterwards excluded from caste.

[1.] Konkune Sonar.

7. An adopted son who acts disobediently to his father may receive maintenance only, but the adoption is not annulled.

[2.] Kanare and Konkune Sonar.

8. As in (1). The causes of annulment may be the adoption of one who ought not to be adopted, or the omission of customary observances.

[1.] Bhat Byragee.

9. As in (1). An adoption is annulled by not having been concluded according to custom: several of the caste decide on the alleged omission.

[1.] Simpee Kapre wikunar.

10. An adoption, if from among relations or families of the same Gotr, and concluded with the concurrence of the caste, cannot be annulled.

[1.] Ahir Simpee.

11. An adoption, if concluded with the concurrence of the caste, cannot be annulled; if without consulting them, it may.

[1.] Lonaree.

12. In such case the separating adopted son might take a

small share ($\frac{1}{16}$) without being chargeable with the payment of his adoptive father's debts.

[1.] Lingaet Wanee.

13. In case of a man maintaining a relation's child, but writing a Khut to the effect that he should not be heir, and afterwards regularly adopting him, the subsequent adoption bars the effect of the Khut, and the adoptee would be heir, not the widow.

[1.] Ugurwale.

(45.) On Adoption by Wives and Widows.

1. A young widow whose Shanee has not yet arrived may adopt a son in the event of her not wishing to form Pat; such adoption to be celebrated subsequent to her Shanee.

[38.] Koshtee, Gooruwu, A. L. Sonar, Sootar, Lohar T., Koonbee, Sarlee, Kamatee Ty., Gondhulee, Burbhoonje, Douree Gosawee, Simpee, T. Wanee, B. Wanee, Ling. Goulee, Ling. Wanee, Mar. Bhoee, Kahar Bhoee, B. Telee, R. Telee, Rungaree, Ghisaree, Sungur, Lonaree, Kolee, Wunjaree, Sultungur, Dobor, D. Josee, R. Jogee, Moolamgar, G. Wanee, Lukheree (not mentioning the period), Kast, Brahmunjaee, Kykaree, Kacharee.

2. In the event of the husband's death before the wife's Shanee, should he have left property, and should the widow desire to adopt, she may do so with the consent of her relations and caste, the celebration to be subsequent to the Shanee.

[34.] Kantaree, Wys. D. Kan. Konk. P. Sonar, Purd. Sootar, 2 Patrawut, Kasar (2), Jyn, Nhawee, Malee, Bhat Byragee, Bhat Koonbee, Wotaree, Johuree, Konk. Goulee, A. Goulee, Kachee N., Koombhar, Dhungur (2), A. Simpee, Jungum, Koonbee Wanee, Purit, Booroor, Mhar, Mang, Chambhar, Bruhmukshutree.

3. Such widow may adopt with consent of the relations, but not by her own will and pleasure.

[5.] Purbhoo, Hulwaee, Mewafuroah, J. Telee, Hulalkhor.

4. As in (2), including Wuttun or immovable property.

[5.] Khutree, Lohar B., P. Malee, Ty. Sarlee, K. Kamatee.

5. In our caste, should there be in the family an heir to the late husband, the widow cannot adopt; otherwise she is at liberty to do so.

[2.] S. R. Koombhar, B. Koombhar.

6. The widow may adopt if she have her husband's order to do so.

[2.] Wywharee Josee, Ugurwale (or with the consent of the assembled caste).

7. A widow, before her Shanee, has no right to adopt a son, but in case of great necessity (viz. to preserve an heir to property and prevent the extinction of the family name) she may do so after her Shanee.

[1.] Goluk.

8. She may adopt, if she have her husband's order to do so, with the consent of the caste, and before several witnesses.

[1.] Komtee.

9. She may adopt after her Shanee, in the event of there being no heir to the property.

[1.] Burhaee.

10. She may adopt after her Shanee, with consent of the Mehitra or Naik, relations, and caste.

[2.] Marathe Telee, Ramosee.

1. A widow left by her husband's death alone, without any of her husband's relations near (partition having in general previously taken place), is allowed to adopt a son.

[49.] Purbhoo, Gooruwu, Kantaree, A. Kan. Sonar, Sootar, Purd. Sootar, Lohar, Kasar bh. w., Nhawee Kus., P. Malee, Bhat Byragee, Bhat K., Sarlee, Kamatee Ty., Kamatee Kan., Hulwaee, Kachee Nurwuree, Koombhar, B. Koombhar, S. R. Koombhar, Dhungur K., Simpee, Tilelee Wanee, Bungur Wanee, Lingaet Goulee, Lingaet Wanee, Koombee Wanee, Mar. Bhoee, Kahar Bhoee, Jyshwur Telee,

Ghisaree, Simpee, Lonaree, Wunjaree, Boorор, Dohor, Mang, Hulalkhor, Goluk, Kasar bh. K., Konk. Goulee, A. Goulee, Burbhoonjee, Mewaf., Rat. Telee, Dhungur Kootekur, Sultungur, Mhar.

2. A widow in such circumstances (Bewaris) may adopt, but the consent of the caste must be first obtained; so in case of the husband's continued absence.

[42.] Khutree, Koshtee, Wys. Konk. Lar. D. P. Sonar, Burhaee, Jyn, Nhawee G., Koombee, Johuree, 2 Patrawut, Malee, Tylung Sarlee, Wotaree, Johuree, Patrawut, Gondhulee, Douree Gosawee, Simpee Ahir, Jungum, Mar. Telee, Batree Telee, Rathor Telee, Rungaree, Kolee, Purit, Ramosee, Chambhar, Bruhmakshutree, Kast, Ugurwale, Dakote Josee, Brahmunjaee, G. Wanee, Kacharee, Lukheree, Kykaree, R. Jogee, Moolamgar (selecting a boy from the Bhowbund).

3. Such widow may adopt, if by her husband's order previously given, and after consulting his relations.

[1.] Wywharee Josee.

4. Such widow is not allowed to adopt.

[1.] Komtee.

5. The widow may adopt for the preservation of her husband's name; and in case of a husband's absence, when no further hope remains of the wife's bearing a son, she may send to her husband, and on his Chithee, or order, may adopt.

[1.] Marwaree.

If no news of such absent husband arrive for a long period, she may adopt.

[7.] Kast, R. Jogee, Ugurwale, Brahmunjaee, Lukheree, Kykaree, Moolamgar (with the husband's order).

In the castes which admit adoption, a man going to a distant country may adopt a boy by sending a written order to his wife, who conducts the ceremonial. After he has not been heard of for a long period (twelve to twenty-five years, *vide* Widowhood), the wife may adopt as his widow, subject to the foregoing rules.

[4.] Lingaet Wanee, Kacharee, G. Wanee, D. Josee, Bruhmukshutree (with the relations' consent, even without the husband's order).

1. Of two widows, the elder has the right to adopt. Should she not agree to do so, the relations and caste advise her: on her refusing to listen to such advice, the younger widow may, with the concurrence of the relations and caste, adopt a son according to the customary forms. There cannot be two adopted sons.

[72.] Goluk, Purbhoo, Khutree, Gooruwu, Kantaree, Wys. Ahir. Konk. Lar. Punchal, Kanaree, Sonar, Mar. Sootar, Burhaee, Purd. Sootar, Lohar, Tambut, Purd. Lohar, Kasar (2), Patrawut (2), Jyn, Nhawee (2), Koonbee, Malee, P. Malee, Bhat Byragee, Bhat Koonbee, Tylung Sarlee, Sarlee, Kamatee Tylung, Wotaree, Gondhulee, Johuree, Konk. Goulee, A. Goulee, Hulwaee, Kachee Nurwuree, Burbhoonjee, Mewafurosh, Koombhar, Buldee Koombhar, S. R. Koombhar, Dhungur (2), Douree Gosawee, Simpee w., Jungum, Tilelee Wanee, Bungur Wanee, Ling. Goulee, Punchum Wanee, Koonbee Wanee, Marathe Bhoee, Kahar Bhoee, Mar. Telee, Batree Telee, Rathor Telee, Jyshwur Telee, Rungaree, Sungur, Lonaree, Kolee, Wunjaree, Purit, Booroor, Ramosee, Mar. Chambhar, Sultungur, Mhar, Mang, Hulalkhor.

2. The elder widow has the right of adoption, the elder wife having the right of performing the Ugneehotr and other ceremonies. The younger widow in some places adopts.

[1.] Wywharee Josee.

3. The *S*astrus ought first to be consulted; but it is not the custom for two widows to adopt. One widow adopts; the elder has the right, but in the event of her living irregularly, the younger. Should the husband have ordered both widows previously to his death to adopt, they may do so, if not contrary to the *S*astrus.

[1.] Komtee.

4. Two widows may not adopt two sons: by mutual

agreement either of them may adopt. Should they not agree, one, viz. the elder; and in default, as in (1).

[1.] Koshtee.

5. Should there be even four widows, the elder, with the concurrence of the rest, is to adopt.

[1.] Dewagun Sonar.

6. Of two widows, the elder has the right to adopt during their joint lives: after the death of one, the right devolves on the survivor.

[1.] Kamatee Kanare.

7. The right to adopt is vested in the elder; but should the relations and the caste so determine, adoption by the younger will be valid.

[1.] Ahir Simpee.

8. Both widows must agree in the adoption. There can be no adoption by one of them without such agreement.

[1.] Ghisaree.

9. It is customary for each of two widows to adopt.

[1.] Dohor.

10. These castes have not the custom of adopting.

[8.] Surwude Josee, Lodhee Purdesee, Kachee Boondele, Chuppurbund, Kirar, Purd. Koombhar, Kolartee, Purd. Chambhar.

1. In adoptions by a woman, it is necessary to have, first, her husband's order; secondly, the concurrence of her relations or (several of) her caste: she cannot adopt simply by her own will and pleasure.

[62.] Goluk, Khutree, Koshtee, Wys. Sonar, Ahir Sonar, Kan. Sonar, Lar Sonar, Punchal Sonar, Kanare Sonar, Burhaee, Purd. Sootar, Lohar, Tambut, Purd. Lohar, Kasar (2), Jyn, Nhawee (2), Pahar Malee, Bhat Byragee, Bhat Koonbee, Tylung Sarlee, Sarlee, Kamatee Tylung, Wotaree, Gondhulee, Kon. Goulee, Ahir Goulee, Kachee Nurwuree, Burbhoonje, Mewafurosh, Koombhar, Buldee Koombhar, Sekwute Rajwute Koombhar, Dhungur (2), Douree

Gosawee, Simpee wikunar, Ahir Simpee, Jungum, Tilelee Wanee, Bungur Wanee, Lingaet Goulee, Punchum Wanee, Koonbee Wanee, Bhoee Mar., Kahar Bhoee, Maratte Telee, Batree Telee, Rathor Telee, Jyshwur Telee, Lonaree, Kolee, Wunjaree, Purit, Booroor, Ramosee, Chambhar, Sultungur, Mhar, Mang.

2. As in (1). In default of the husband's order, the consent of the relations is necessary; some add the concurrence of the caste.

[14.] Wywharee Josee, Purbhoo, Kantaree, Mar. Sootar, Patrawut (2), Koombee, Malee, Johuree, Hulwaee, Rungaree, Ghisaree, Sungur, Hulalkhor.

3. As in (1). In default of the husband's order, the consent of the son of a near relation is necessary; should there be none, with the consent of a distant relation. The widow should adopt a boy from among those of her own, or, in default, of another Gotr.

[2.] Komtee, Gooruwu.

4. A widow must not adopt a son during her husband's life; in the event of his death, or losing caste, the widow may adopt.

[1.] Dohor.

5. A widow must not adopt but with the concurrence of several of her relations or caste.

[1.] Dewagun Sonar.

6. A widow must adopt by the order of her husband.

[1.] Kamatee Kanure.

(46.) On Guardianship.

1. A child left without parents, or paternal relations, is placed under the guardianship of his maternal uncle, or more distant relation or trustworthy friend or servant, usually by verbal bequest previously to his parent's death,

before three or four witnesses of the same caste. The same person is guardian of person and property.

[59.] Khutree, Koshtee, Gooruwu, Kantaree, A. Lar. D. P. Sonar, P. Sootar, Lohar, Kasar bh. k., Jyn, Nhawee (2), Malee, P. Malee, Bhat By., Bhat Koonbee, Sarlee, Kamatee Ty. and Kan., Surwude Josee, Gondhulee, Konk. Goulee, Hulwaee, Kachee Boond., Koombhar, Bul. S. R. Koombhar, Dhungur Kart., A. Simpee, Jungum, Til. Wanee, B. Wanee, Ling. Goulee, Ling. Wanee, Koonbee Wanee, Mar. Bhoee, Kahar Bhoee, Mar. Telee, Jyshwur Telee, Rungaree, Ghisaree, Sungur, Lonaree, Kolee, Purit, Booroor, Ramosee, Chambhar, Dohor, Kast, Bruhmukshutree, Brahmunjaee, G. Wanee, Kacharee, Lukheree, R. Jogee, D. Josee.

2. As in (1), omitting the bequest in presence of the caste.

[29.] Wywharee Josee, Goluk, Purbhoo, Wys. Sonar, Konk. Kan. Sonar, Burhaee, P. Lohar, Kasar bh. w., A. Goulee, Ty. Sarlee, Wotaree, Lodhee P., Chuppurbund, Kachee, Nurwuree, Burbhoonje, Kirar, Mewafurosh, Purd. Koombhar, Dhungur Kootekur, Douree Gosawee, Simpee, Batree Telee, Rathor Telee, Wunjaree, Purd. Chambhar, Sultungur, Mang, Hulalkhor.

3. A child left without parents or paternal relations is placed with his property under his maternal relations or friend, &c., by direction of the Patell and Koolkurnee: should no other become guardian, the village officers will themselves fulfil those duties.

[2.] Sootar, Mhar.

4. The caste are guardians.

[1.] Komtee.

5. The caste place the child and his property under charge of a relation or friend competent from talent and probity to perform the trust.

[4.] D. Josee, Kykaree, Moolamgar, Holar.

6. Several of the caste place the child and property under charge of a trustworthy friend, &c., before witnesses. Two Yads are made out of the property; one is kept by the guardian, and one by a man of repute in the caste.

[1.] Ugurwale.

(56.) On the Choice of a Manager during Community of Property.

1. Should the elder of a family be unfit for the management of the property, &c., one of the others, of superior skill and knowledge in affairs, is chosen in his stead; he is not entitled as manager to any larger share on partition, but, on attending Durbar, he usually receives presents of greater value (as 2 to 4 rupees for cloth).

[64.] Khutree, Koshtee, Gooruwu, Wys. Sonar, A. Sonar, Konk. Sonar, Lar. Sonar, D. Sonar, P. Sonar, Koonbee, Johuree, 2 Patrawut, Sootar, Lohar, Purd. Lohar, Kasar bh. k., Jyn, Nhawee (2), Malee, Pahar Malee, Bhat Byragee, Sarlee, Kamatee Tylung, Kamatee Kan., A. Koulee, Lodhee Purd., Kachee Boondele, Chuppurbund, Kachee N., Kirar, B. Koombhar, Purd. Koombhar, S. R. Koombhar, D. Josee, G. Wanee, Lukheree, Dhungur Kartik, Douree Gosawee, A. Simpee, Jungum, Tilelee Wanee, Bungur Wanee, Ling. Goulee, Ling. Wanee, Koonbee Wanee, Mar. Bhoee, Kahar Bhoee, Mar. Telee, Rathor Telee, Jyshwur Telee, Ghisaree, Sungur, Lonaree, Kolee, Wunjaree, Booroor, Chambhar, Purd. Chambhar, Sultungur, Dohor, Mhar, Hulalkhor.

2. Should the elder be unfit to manage the property, a younger would transact the family affairs in his stead. All take equally on partition.

[1.] Marwaree.

3. In that case, the cleverest among several relations manages the family affairs: he is not therefore entitled to a larger share on partition.

[36.] Wywharee Josee, Goluk, Purbhoo, Komtee, Kataree, Kan. Sonar, Burhaee, Purd. Sootar, Kasar bh. w., Bhat Koonbee, T. Sarlee, D. Josee, Wotaree, Gondhulee, Konk. Goulee, Hulwaee, Bhurbhoonje, Mewafurosh, Koombhar, Dhunghur, Simpee, B. Telee, Rungaree, Purit, Kolatee, Ramosee, Mang, Bruhmukshutree, Kast, Brahmunjaee, Ugurwale, R. Josee, Kacharee, Kykaree, Moolamgar, Holar.

(56.) On the Right of the Manager to Alienate Family Property during Community.

1. The elder in the family, being manager, has the right of selling or mortgaging family property, whether immovable or movables, without the consent of the others.

[24.] Komtee, Khutree, Koshtee, Burhaee, Pahar Malee, Bhat Byragee, Tylung Sarlee, Kamatee Tylung, Wotaree, Ahir Goulee, Lodhee Purdesee, Kachee Boondelee, Chuppurbund, Burbhoonje, Buldee Koombhar, Purdesee Koombhar, Sekwutee Rajwutee Koombhar, Dhungur Kootekur, Ahir Simpee, Tilelee Wanee, Kabar Bhoee, Rungaree, Lonaree, Wunjaree.

2. The consent of the rest of the family is necessary.

[24.] Koonbee, Purbhoo, Khutree, Sonar Dewagun, Sonar Kanure, Sootar, Kasar Bhande wikunar, Bhat Koonbee, Sarlee, Surwude Josee, Koombhar, Simpee Kaprekuree, Jungum, Bungur Lingaet Wanee, Lingaet Goulee, Lingaet Wanee, Koombee Wanee, Bhoee Marathe, Patree Telee, Ghisaree, Kolee, Purit, Ramosee, Mhar.

3. The consent of the rest is necessary in general, but should they be absent, or incapable of understanding, from infancy or other cause, the elder, being manager, may himself sell or mortgage the family property.

[14.] Gooruwu, Punchal] Sonar, Purdesee Scotar, Purdesee Lohar, Jyn, Nhawee (2), Konkunee Goulee, Hulwace Purdesee, Marathe Telee, Sungur, Kolatee, Chambhar, Mang.

4. The consent of the rest is necessary to such contracts of sale or mortgage, if above the value of 100 to 200 rupees of movables, and for all immovable property.

[11.] Wys. Sonar, Kasar Bhande Kurunar, Kachee Nurwure, Kirar, Mewafurosh, Douree Gosawee, Rathor Telee, Jyshwur Telee, Purdesee Chambhar, Sultungur, Hulalkhor.

5. The consent of the rest is necessary for sale, but not for mortgage, the money being wanted for the Sunskars of the family.

[4.] Tambut, Malee, Gondhulee, Ramosee, Booroor.

6. The elder, being manager, has the right, strictly

speaking; but he ought to acquaint the most intelligent of the family before concluding the sale or mortgage.

[3.] Kamatee Kanure, Dhungur Kartik, Domre.

7. The consent of the rest is necessary as to immovable, but not as to movable property.

[6.] Ahir Sonar, Konkune Sonar, Lar. Sonar, Johure, Patrawut Salkur and Punkur.

8. The consent of the rest is necessary in all cases; but a latitude is given as to mortgage in a period of family distress, the elder informing the rest of what he does. The custom of selling a Wuttun is unknown.

[2.] Wywharee Josee (Brahmun), Goluk.

9. The right is vested in the manager, but he should make the contract witnessed by the rest. The juniors in a family are bound to respect and obey the elder.

[1.] Marwaree.

(56.) On the Right of One of a Family in Community to Alienate Family Property.

1. One of several relations has no right to give or sell any part of the family property without the consent of the rest.

[29.] Purbhoo, Komtee, Kataree, Dewagun Sonar, Kanure Sonar, Sotar, Lohar Tambut, Purd. Lohar, Jyn, Sarlee, Kamatee Kanure, Surwude Josee, Gondhulee, Koombhar, Dhungur Kartik, Douree Gosawee, Jungum, Ling. Goulee, Ling. Wanee, Koombee Wanee, Bhoee Mar., Mar. Telee, Ghisaree, Kolee, Purit, Ramosee, Dohor, Mhar, Goolwee Wanee, Rawul Jogee, Kacharee, Kykaree, Holar.

2. One of several relations has no right to give or sell any part of the family property without the consent of the manager (Karbaree).

[24.] Khutree, Koshtee, Burhaee, Kasar bh. w., Pahar Malee, Bhat Byragee, Bhat Koonbee, Tylung Sarlee, Kamatee Tylung,

Wotaree, Ahir Goulee, Lodhee Purdesee, Kachee Boondele, Chuppurbund, Burbhoonje, Buldee Koombhar, Purd. Koombhar, S. R. Koombhar, Dhungur Kartik, Ahir Simpee, Kahar Bhoee, Rungaree, Sungur, Lonaree.

3. The same as (2), except that in the event of want of funds, and the absence of the other relations, one may sell or mortgage a part of the family property for necessary Sunsar expenses.

[17.] Gooruwu, Punchal and 3 Sonar, Sootar Purd., Nhawe (2), Konk. Goulee, Hulwaee Purd., Simpee, Tilelee Wanee, Bungur Wanee, Wunjaree, Kolatee, Chambhar, Mang, Johuree, Patrawut (2).

4. One of several relations may, with the consent of the Karbaree, dispose of movables to the value of 100 or 200 rupees: immovable property can only be sold or mortgaged with the consent of all.

[19.] Wys. Sonar, Lar. Sonar, Ahir Sonar, Konk. Sonar, Kasar bh. k., Kachee N., Kirar, Mewafurosh, Rathor Telee, Jyshwur Telee, Sultungur, Purd. Chambhar, Hulalkhor (not mentioning the consent of the Karbaree), Bruhmukshutree, Kast, Ugurwale, Brahmunjaee, Dakote Josee, Moolamgar.

5. One of several relations may sell or pledge the family movables if distressed for funds, and may mortgage the Wuttun without the others' consent. The custom of selling a Wuttun is unknown.

[4.] Wywharee Josee, Goluk, Malee, Booroor.

6. One of several relations must obtain the Karbar's consent to such alienation; but in the event of his absence, in case of necessity, he is at liberty to a certain extent.

[1.] Koonbee.

7. One of several relations may alienate part of the common property with the attestation of the rest.

[1.] Marwaree.

8. It is not necessary to ask the consent of a young

brother; one grown up and residing near should be consulted in sale and mortgages.

[1.] Lukheree.

9. Any brother may alienate property on account of Sunsar or trades without the others' consent; but it is preferable to obtain it.

[1.] Ugurwale.

(57.) On the Enjoyment and Partition of Property Acquired by One of a Family during Community.

1. A Wuttun or other property acquired by one of a family, whether by his own exertions or by aid of his relations or the family property, is brought into the common stock, and at a subsequent partition all take equal shares, neither the acquirer nor the manager obtaining a larger portion.

[88.] Wywharee Josee, Goluk, Koonbee, Johuree, Patrawut (2), Komtee, Khutree, Koshtee, Gooruwu, Kataree, Wys. Sonar, Dewagun Sonar, Punchal Sonar, Burhaee, Purdesee Sootar, Lohar Boondelee, Kasar (2), Jyn, Nhawee Kusbekur and Gungatilkur, Malee, Pahar Malee, Bhat Byragee, Bhat Koonbee, Tylung Sarlee, Sarlee, Kamatee Tylung, Kamatee Kanure, Surwude Josee, Wotaree, Gondhulee, Konkune Goulee, Ahir Goulee, Hulwaee, Lodhee Purdesee, Kachee Boondelee, Chuppurbund, Kachee Nurwuree, Burbhoonje, Kirar, Mewafurosh, Koombhar, Buldee Koombhar, Purdesee Koombhar, Koombhar Sekwutee Rajwutee, Dhungur Kartik, Dhungur Kootekur, Douree Gosawee, Simpee, Kaprekuree. Ahir Simpee. Jungum, Tilelee Wanee, Bungur Wanee, Lingaet Goulee, Lingaet Wanee, Marathe Wanee, M. Bhoee, Kahar Bhoee. Marathe Telee, Batree Telee, Rathor Telee, Jyshwur Telee, Rungaree, Ghisaree, Sungur, Wunjaree, Booroor, Kolatee, Ramosee, Chambhar, Purdesee Chambhar, Sultungur, Dohor, Mang, Hulalkhor, Brumukshutree, Kast, Ugurwale, Brahmunjaee, Rawul Jogee, Lukheree, Kykaree, Kacharee, Moolamgar, G. Wanee, Holar.

2. Immovable property so acquired is brought into the common stock; but at a subsequent partition the acquirer

is entitled to a somewhat larger share, and the privileges of Burepuna. Movables are shared equally, nor does the Karbaree receive a larger share.

[6.] Sonar Lar, Sootar, Lohar, Kolee, Purit, Mhar.

3. All property so acquired is brought into common, and at a subsequent partition is shared equally, but the acquirer is entitled to Man-pan and Burepuna if gained by his own exertions.

[2.] Ahir and Konkune Sonar.

4. The acquirer is entitled to a larger share on partition of property so acquired by himself.

[2.] Purbhoo, Kanure Sonar.

5. The acquirer (if in a separate place) keeps the larger portion of his acquisitions. It is also customary to make an equal partition.

[1.] Marwaree.

6. The elder is entitled on partition to 3 rupees more than any other.

[1.] D. Josee Mankur.

(58.) On the Causes of Partition.

1. The causes of partition of property among a father and his sons, though not general, are quarrels of the parties, or the extravagance of one of the number. One son may receive his share from his father, the others remaining with property in common as before, and the sons take what the father freely gives them. Brothers usually separate on account of the quarrelling of their wives, the appropriation of an undue share of the proceeds by one, or the refusal of one to listen to the advice of the rest.

It is not a universal custom to draw up a Farikhut or

deed of partition; the property being divided before three or four witnesses, proof of the fact is easy.

[83.] Purbhoo, Khutree, Koshtee, Gooruwu, Kataree, Wys. Sonar, A. Sonar, Konk. Sonar, Lar. Sonar, D. Sonar, P. Sonar, Kan. Sonar, Sootar, Burhaee, Koonbee, Johuree, 2 Patrawut, Purd. Sootar, Lohar, Purd. Lohar, Kasar (2), Jyn, Nhawee (2), Malee, Pahar Malee, Bhat Byragee, Bhat Koonbee, T. Sarlee, Sarlee, Kamatee T., Kamatee Kanure, S. Josee, Wotaree, Gondhulee, Konk. Goulee, A. Goulee, Hulwaee, Lodhee Purd., Kachee Boondele, Chuppurbund, K. Nurwuree, Burbhoonje, Kirar, Koombhar, B. Koombhar, Purd. Koombhar, S. R. Koombhar, Dhungur (2), Douree Gosawee, Simpee, A. Simpee, Jungum, Tilelee Wanee, Bungur Wanee, Kanure Goulee, Koonbee Wanee, Ling. Wanee, Mar. Bhoee, Kahar Bhoee, Mar. Telee, Batree Telee, Rathor Telee, Jyshwur Telee, Rungaree, Ghisaree, Sungur, Lonaree, Kolee, Wunjaree, Purit, Booroor, Ramosee, Chambhar, Purd. Chambhar, Sultungur, Dohor, Mhar, Mang, Hulalkhor.

2. As in answer (1). A separation of property is proved by the parties cooking in separate places, and by the separate performance of Nywedy and Wys Deo (ceremonies of placing food before the household god and sacrificing with the Hom).

[2.] Wywharee Josee, Goluk.

3. As in answer (1); but the practice of Farikhuts on partition is universal in this caste.

[1.] Komtee.

4. As in answer (1); but the practice of Farikhuts on partition is unknown in these castes. In the former, a separation is proved by the fact of the distribution at the time of earthen pots to several of the caste.

[2.] Kolatee and Mewafurosh.

5. If several relations eat and carry on trade separately, they are held to be separate, though no Farikhut have passed. But unless a Farikhut exists between father and son, they are not held separate.

[1.] Marwaree.

6. The causes of partition are the quarrelling of the

women or the Karbarees. Partition is proved by a Farikhut, or by witnesses only.

[4.] Kacharee, G. Wanee, Brahmunjaee, Holar.

7. A father and son do not take shares (as in 6).

[6.] R. Jogee, Kykaree, Ugurwale, Kast, Brahmukshutree, Moolamgar.

(61.) On the Reservation of Property on a Partition.

1. On a partition, a deduction is first made for the parents, should they be alive, or their Kreea; for the marriage expenses of the unmarried boys and girls of the family; and for the expense of building a temple, or other charitable acts directed to be performed by the father.

[50.] Khutree, Koshtee, Purd. Lohar, Kasar bh. Kur., Jyn, P. Malee, Bhat Byragee, Sarlee, Kamatee Tylung, Kan. Kamatee, Surwude Josee, A. Goulee, Kachee Nur., Burbhoonje, Kirar, Mewafurosh, Purd. Koombhar, Dhungur Kartik, D. Gosawee, Simpee, A. Simpee, Tilelee Wanee, Ling. Goulee, Ling. Wanee, Koonbee Wanee, Bhoee Mar., Kahar Bhoee, Mar. Telee, B. Telee, Ghisaree, Sungur, Lonaree, Wunjaree, Purit, Booroor, Purd. Chambhar, Sultungur, Dohor, Hulalkhor, Bruhmukshutree, Kast, Ugurwale, R. Josee, Lukheree, Kacharee, Brahmunjaee, Kykaree, G. Wanee, Moolamgar, Holar.

2. On a partition between brothers, deduction is first made for the marriage of the unmarried brothers and sisters, and for the expense of building a temple, or gifts directed by the father at his death, or agreed upon by the survivors.

[8.] Kan. Sonar, T. Sarlee, Konk. Goulee, Dhungur Kootekur, Jyshwur Telee, Kolatee, Ramosee, Mang.

The father's Kreea is of course to be provided for.

[38.] Wywharee Josee, Goluk, Purbhoo, Komtee, Johuree, 2 Patrawut, Gooruwu, Wys. Sonar, A. Sonar, Konk. Sonar, Lar. Sonar, D. Sonar, P. Sonar, Sootar, Burhaee, Purd. Sootar, Lohar, Kasar bh. w., Nhawee (2), Malee, Bhat Koombee, Wotaree, Gondhulee, Hulwaee, Lodhee Purd., Kachee Boondele, Chuppurbund, Koombhar, B. Koombhar, S. R. Koombhar, Jungum, B. Wanee, Rungaree, Kolee, Chambhar, Mhar.

3. As in (1), including pious expenses directed by the deceased, or agreed upon by the survivors, and provision for the maintenance of a widowed sister residing with them.

[1.] Koonbee.

4. Provision should be made for building wells, Dhurmsalas, gardens, temples, feeding Brahmuns, or other pious expenses, in which consist virtue and good name.

[1.] Marwaree.

(62.) On a Partition between Father and Sons.

1. A father, being manager, has the power of dismissing a son for ill conduct, or on quarrelling with him, of property *ad libitum*. If the father is incapable of acting as manager, the son carries on the family affairs in his name and by his orders, giving his father subsistence, &c., and money sufficient for alms and religious duties. In general, the Wuttun is not divided until the father's death, when all the brothers receive equal shares, the elder being entitled to the Burepuna only. If the elder has been dismissed, the younger, having been manager, continues to enjoy the property of the family, including the movables, paying his father's debts.

[52.] Khutree, Koshtee, Gooruwu, Kantaree, A. Sonar, Konk. Sonar, Lar. Sonar, Dewagun Sonar, P. Sonar, Sootar, Burhaee, Purd. Sootar, Lohar, Kasar (2), Jyn, Nhawee (2), Malee, P. Malee, Bhat Byragee, Bhat Koombee, Sarlee, Kamatee Tylung, Kamatee Kanure, Hulwaee, Kachee Boondele, Kacheo N., Kirar, Purd. Koombhar, Dhungur Kartik, A. Simpee, Jungum, Bungur Wanee, Ling. Goulee, Ling. Wanee, Koombee Wanee, Bhoee Marathe, Kahar Bhoee, Mar. Telee, Batree Telee, Rathor Telee, Rungaree, Lonaree, Kolee, Wunjaree, Chambhar, Purd. Chambhar, Sultungur, Dohor, Mhar, Hulalkhor.

2. The shares of the father and sons on a partition are not equal. The son is to take what the father is pleased to give: another son remaining with the father, or born sub-

sequently to the dismissal of the former, will take what remains on the father's death, paying the father's debts. There are few Wuttundars among these castes.

[17.] Purd. Lohar, Tylung Sarlee, Surwude Josee, Wotaree, Konk. Goulee, A. Goulee, Lodhee Purd., Chuppurbund, Burbhoonje, Buldee Koombhar, S. R. Koombhar, Dhungur Kootekur, Douree Gosawee, Simpee, Tilelee Wanee, Purit, Ramosee.

3. The son has no right to take a share from his father. The father gives at pleasure to his son; and should another son be afterwards born, the debts and inheritance will be divided equally between them on the father's death.

[16.] Wywharee Josee, Goluk, Komtee, Kan. Sonar, Mewafurosh, Koombhar, Jyshwur Telee, Ghisaree, Sungur, Booroor, Kolartee, Mang, Kast, Kykaree, R. Jogee, Bruhmukshutree.

4. The father and son's shares on a partition are equal; a son born afterwards, or a second son remaining with the father, will on his death take the remaining property, being chargeable with the debts.

[2.] Purbhoo, Gondhulee.

5. The son takes what the father is pleased to give him. (*Vide* Partition between Brothers).

[5.] Wys. Sonar, Johuree, Koonbee, 2 Patrawut.

6. The father is absolute in disposing of property acquired by himself, and receives a larger share of that acquired by his sons.

[1.] Marwaree.

7. The father and son do not divide property in general. In such case, a son born after partition would take the father's remaining property, and pay his debts, without connection with the separated son.

[8.] G. Wanee, Brahmunjaee, Kacharee, Ugurwale, Lukheree, D. Josee, Moolamgar, Holar.

8. On the birth of another son as in (4). But should

two sons be afterwards born, the Wuttun should be equally divided between the three.

[1.] Johuree.

By the answers of seventy-five castes, it appears that the adopted son is on the same footing as one begotten, viz. he has no share *de jure* on quarrelling and separating from his father, but must take what the father is pleased to give him.

1. A son has no right to demand a partition from his father, so long as the latter conduct himself according to good custom (being sane in mind and not a spendthrift), whether as to immovable or movables, hereditary or acquired property. What the father freely gives, the son may take. But should at any time the father begin to act improperly, the son must make arrangements for preserving the family property, and giving his father maintenance with filial obedience.

[78.] Wywharee Josee, Khutree, Kantaree, Wys. A. Konk. Lar. P. Kan. Sonar, Sootar, Burhaee, Purd. Sootar, Lohar, Purd. Lohar, Kasar bh. K., 2 Patrawut, Jyn, Nhawee (2), Koonbee, Malee, P. Malee, Bhat Byragee, Bhat Koonbee, Ty. Sarlee, Sarlee, Ty. Kamatee, Surwude Josee, Wotaree, Gondulee, Johuree, Konk. Goulee, A. Goulee, Hulwaee, Lodhee Purd., Kachee B., Chuppurbund, Kachee N., Burbhoonje, Kirar, Mewafurosh, Koombhar, B. Koombhar, Purd. Koombhar, S. R. Koombhar, Dhungur (2), Douree Gosawee, Simpee, Jungum, T. Wanee, B. Wanee, Ling. Goulee, Punchum Wanee, Koonbee Wanee, Mar. and Kahar Bhoee, Mar. B. R. and J. Telee, Rungaree, Ghisaree, Sungur, Lonaree, Kolee, Wunjaree, Purit, Booroor, Kolartee, Ramosee, Chambhar, Purd. Chambhar, Sultungur. Dohor, Mhar, Hulalkhor.

2. While the father lives, the son has no right to have a partition; after the father's death, the son is proprietor of all.

[2.] Dewagun Sonar, Ahir Simpee.

3. On a partition between father and son, the Wuttun and hereditary property are divided equally; of property acquired by the father he takes the larger share.

[1.] Purbhoo.

4. Partition must be made at the father's pleasure.

[1.] Goluk.

5. While the father conducts himself well, the son should remain in obedience to him, and the father should treat the son with kindness; should the father conduct himself ill, the son or sons, and the father, are all to take equal shares of the property.

[1.] Komtee.

6. The father and son should divide equally property inherited from the grandfather.

[1.] Koshtee.

7. There is no partition between father and son. The father may put his son in charge of his Wuttun or other property, for the purpose of supplying the latter with food and clothing, but the son, during the father's life, has no power to sell or give it in pledge. The father conducting himself well, the son is to take what he gives with good will. One of several sons has no right to a partition.

[1.] Gooruwu.

8. The son is to receive partition at the father's pleasure, and is to give and receive what is due to, or required by, the father.

[1.] Kamatee Kanare.

9. The son is to take what the father gives with good will; but should the father attempt to give away the whole of the property to another, not the son, the son may prevent his doing so, and there must be a partition.

[1.] Kasar b. Wikunar.

10. As in (1). The son, in the event of the father's bad management of the property, or other ill conduct, is, with the concurrence of the caste, to provide for his father and secure the family property.

[1.] Mang.

(63.) ON A PARTITION BETWEEN BROTHERS.

1. In a partition among brothers, all take equal shares.

[95.] Wywharee Josee, Goluk, Komtee, Khutree, Koshtee, Gooruwu, Kantaree, Wys. Sonar, A. Sonar and other Sonars, Sootar, Burhaee, Purd. Sootar, Marwaree, Lohar, Purd. Lohar, Kasar (2), Jyn, Nhawe (2), Malee, Pahar Malee, Bhat Byr., Bhat K., T. Sarlee, Sarlee, Kamatee T. and Kan., Surwude Josee, Wotaree, Gondhulee, Konk. Goulee, A. Goulee, Hulwaee, Lodhee Purd., Kachee B., Chuppurbund, Kachee N., Burbhoonjee, Kirar, Mewafurosh, Koombhar, Buldee Koombhar, Purd. Koombhar, S. Raj. Koombhar, Dhungur (2), Douree Gosawee, Simpee, A. Simpee, Jungum, Tilelee Wanee, B. Wanee, Ling. Goulee, Koonbee Wanee, Ling. Wanee, Mar. and K. Bhoee, Mar. Telee, Batree Telee, Rathor Telee, Jyshwur Telee, Rungaree, Ghisaree, Sungur, Lonaree, Kolee, Wunjaree, Purit, Booroor, Kolatee, Ramosee, Chambhar, Purd. Chambhar, Sultungur, Dohor, Mhar, Mang, Hulalkhor, Bruhmukshutree, Kast, Ugurwale, R. Jogee, Kykaree, Lukyaree, G. Wanee, Kacharee, Brahmunjaee, Moolamgar, Holar.

2. The brothers take equal shares of the father's property; but should one of them have acquired property, he takes a larger share of such acquisitions. (*Vide* Community of Property.)

[1.] Purbhoo.

3. As in (1). It is not customary for the elder son to take the property, and provide for the subsistence of the rest.

[3.] Johuree, 2 Patrawut.

4. The elder receives 3 rupees in addition to his share.

[1.] Dakotee Josee.

(63.) ON THE LIABILITY OF HEIRS TO PAY THE DECEASED'S DEBTS.

1. A son is bound to repay all his father's debts. If one of several brothers, copartners, die, the creditors demand payment of the manager. On a partition, the debts are distributed in proportion to the shares of the property.

[74.] Wywharee Josee, Goluk, Komtee, Koshtee, Gooruwu,

Kataree, Wyr. A. Konk. Lar. D. P. Sonar, Kan. Sonar, Sootar, Burhaee, Purd. Sootar, Lohar, P. Lohar, Kasar bh. K., Jyn, Nhawee Kus. and G., Malee, P. Malee, Bhat By., T. Sarlee, Sarlee, Kamatee T. and Kan., Surwude Josee, Gondhulee, Koombhar, Purd. Koombhar, Dhungur Kartik and Koot., Douree Gosawee, Simpee, A. Simpee, A. Goulee, Hulwaee, Chuppurbund, Kachee Nurwuree, Burbhoonjee, Kirar, Mewafurosh, Jungum, T. B. Wanee, Ling. Wanee, Koonbee Wanee, Bhoee (2), Mar. B. Telee, R. G. Telee, Rungaree, Ghisaree, Sungur, Lonaree, Kolee, Wunjaree, Purit, Booroor, Kolartee, Ramosee, Chambhar, P. Chambhar, Sultungur, Dohor, Mhar, Mang, Hulalkhor.

2. The heirs are to pay the debts of the deceased in proportion to their shares; or, if the debt is large and the assets small, a dividend is paid to the creditors, as in cases of bankruptcy. In the case of coparcenary, *vide* answer (1).

[9.] Khutree, Kasar bh. w., Bhat Koonbee, Koonbee, Lodhee Purd., Kachee B., B. Koombhar, S. R. Koombhar, Johuree.

3. The son is bound to repay the father's debts according to his ability; several brothers sharing debts equally, but not those incurred after the separation. Several brothers living in common, the debts of one will be defrayed by the family, and after a partition by the members of it equally.

[1.] Marwaree,

4. The son or other relations receive the property and pay the debts of the deceased. The Karbaree pays debts during community, and they are partitioned on a separation.

[12.] Bruhmukshutree, Kast, Ugurwale, R. Jogee, D. Josee, Lukyaree, G. Wanee, Kacharee, Brahmunjaee, Kykaree, Moolamgar, Holar.

(67.) On Exclusion from Inheritance.

1. The causes of exclusion of persons from sharing in an inheritance are insanity and blindness, provided their marriage has not been concluded; otherwise they take as usual. A man who has committed an offence against caste rules is

not debarred from his share, and is readmitted on paying a fine; but if he have lost caste, he is not entitled to inherit. A man who is impotent is not debarred from taking his share.

[37.] Gooruwu, Wys. Sonar, Burhaee, Purd. Sootar, Kasar bh. w., Jyn, Nhawee K. and G., P. Malee, Bhat Byr., Bhat Koonbee, T. Sarlee, Sarlee, Kamatee T. and Kan., Surwude Josee, Hulwaee, Lodhee Purd., Chuppurbund, Burbhoonje, Mewafurosh, Dhungur Kootekur, Douree Gosawee, Ling. Goulee, Koonbee Wanee, Mar. Bhoee, Kahar Bhoee, Mar. Telee, B. Telee, Jyshwur Telee, Rungaree, Ghisaree, Lonaree, Wunjaree, Purit, Booroor, Dohor.

2. As in answer (1). An impotent man sometimes receives food and clothing, sometimes a share. Occasionally, a man's family, on his losing caste, will not be excluded with him, in which case they will receive his share.

[35.] Khutree, Koshtee, Kantaree, A. Sonar, Konk. Lar. D. and P. Sonar, Sootar, Lohar, Lohar Boondele, Kasar bh. k., Malee, Wotaree, Gondhulee, A. Goulee, Kachee B. and N., Kirar, Koombhar, B. Purd. S. R. Koombhar, Dhungur K., A. Simpee, Jungum, B. Ling. Wanee, R. Telee, Kolee, Chambhar and P. Chambhar, Sultungur, Mhar, Hulalkhor.

3. None are excluded from inheritance on these accounts.

[2.] Komtee, Sungur.

4. Insane and blind persons, &c., if possessing understanding, may receive their share of the proceeds of a Wuttun, their relations being managers. Should they, however, be without any family, they will be entitled to maintenance only.

[2.] Wywharee Josee, Goluk.

5. Such persons are not excluded from inheritance, but the other relations will undertake the management of their shares, or preserve the property for their families.

[3.] Simpee, Tilelee Wanee, Kolartee.

6. The wives of insane and blind persons will appoint a

Goomashta to their Wuttun, and receive the share. As to loss of caste, *vide* answer (1).

[1.] Sonar Kanure.

7. Insane, imbecile, or ex-caste persons are excluded from inheritance. Their shares are, however, given to their wives and children, if any.

[1.] Purbhoo.

8. Such persons are to be maintained by the rest of the family.

[1.] Konk. Goulee.

9. Blind and ex-caste persons take no share; lame or deformed persons are not excluded.

[1.] Ramosee.

10. A blind man is alone excluded; an ex-caste man receives his share on readmittance.

[1.] Mang.

11. Insane, blind, out-caste, and imbecile persons are entitled to their share if the wife is living; otherwise, to maintenance. Impotent men to free gifts only.

[4.] Johuree, Koonbee, 2 Patrawut.

12. No cause of exclusion is recognized.

[1.] Marwaree.

13. Ex-caste persons receive no share, if permanently excluded: of the others, some receive a share of paternal property, others not. In case of marriage, they receive a share.

[12.] Bruhmukshutree, Ugurwale, D. Josee, G. Wanee, Brahmunjaee, Moolamgar, Kast, R. Jogee, Lukyaree, Kacharee, Kykaree, Holar.

1. A father has not the power of excluding his son from the possession of his property.

[64.] Wywharee Josee, Goluk, Komtee, Khutree, Koshtee, A.

Konk. Kan. Sonar, Burhaee, Lohar, P. Lohar, Kasar (2), Jyn, P. Malee, Bhat By., Bhat Koonbee, Ty. Sarlee, Sarlee, Kamatee Ty. and Kan., Surwude Josee, Wotaree, Gondhulee, Konk. Goulee, A. Goulee, Chuppurbund, Burbhoonje, Kirar, Mewafurosh, Koombhar, Dhungur (2), Simpee, A. Simpee, Bhoee Mar., Kahar Bhoee, Mar. B. Rat. Jy. Telee, Rungaree, Ghisaree, Sungur, Lonaree, Kolee, Purit, Booroor, Kolartee, Ramosee, P. Chambhar, Sultungur, Mang, Hulalkhor, Johuree, Kast, Brahmunjaee, Kacharee, R. Josee, G. Wanee, Moolamgar, Lukheree, Kykaree, Holar.

2. A father has the power to prevent his son's enjoying his property during his life. After his death the son will inherit.

[16.] **Purbhoo, Lar Sonar, Dew. Pun. Sonar, Nhawee Kusb., Rungaree, Malee, Lodhee Purd., Kachee Boond., Buldee and S. R. Koombhar, Tilelee Wanee, Bungur Wanee, Wunjaree, Chambhar, Dohor.**

3. A father has no such power.

[13.] **Gooruwu, Wys. Sonar, Sootar, P. Sootar, Hulwaee, Kachee Nurwuree, P. Koombhar, Douree Gosawee, Jungum, Ling. Goulee, Ling. Wanee, Koonbee Wanee, Mhar.**

4. The son is heir after the father's death, and it rests with him to provide for the family affairs, should his father become a prodigal, or insane, or otherwise conduct himself improperly.

[1.] **Kataree.**

5. The father has power to prevent a son's possessing his property.

[2.] **Bruhmukshutree, D. Josee.**

(68.) On the Performance of the Deceased's Kreea.

1. If one of several relations die, his Kreea is performed by his eldest or youngest son; should he have none, by his brother or brother's son; if none, by any Sugotr heir (as a sister's son). If the individual whose duty it is refuse to perform Kreea, he is put out of caste, and is only readmitted

on begging pardon and paying a fine to the caste, when he is allowed to receive his share of the inheritance. A distant Purgotr connection is not entitled to any share on account of performing Kreea.

[45.] Khutree, Koshtee, Purd. Lohar, Kasar bh. k., Jyn, P. Malee, Bhat Byragee, Bhat Koonbee, T. Sarlee, Sarlee, Kamatee T., Kamatee Kan., S. Josee, Gondhulee, Konk. Goulee, A. Goulee, Lodhee Purd., Kachee B., Chuppurbund, Kachee N., Bhurboonje, Kirar, Mewafurosh, Koombhar, Purd. Koombhar, Dhungur (2), Douree Gosawee, A. Simpee, Ling. Wanee, Mar. Bhoee, Kahar Bhoee, Mar. Telee, Batree Telee, Rathor Telee, Jyshwur Telee, Ghisaree, Sungur, Wunjaree, Booroor, Chambhar, Sultungur, Domre, Mang, Hulalkhor.

2. As in answer (1). The individual refusing is, however, entitled to his share, but is put out of caste, and only readmitted on begging pardon and performing the Kreea. If the proper person should be absent, any of the Dushantil Bhow may perform it.

[38.] Purbhoo, Gooruwu, Sonar Wys, A. Sonar, Konk. Sonar, Lar Sonar, D. Sonar, P. Sonar, Kanure Sonar, Sootar, Koonbee, Johnree, 2 Patrawut, Burhaee, Purd. Sootar, Lohar, Kasar bh. w., Nhawee (2), Malee, Wotaree, Hulwaee, B. Koombhar, S. R. Koombhar, Simpee, Jungum, Tilelee Wanee, Bungur Wanee, Ling. Goulee, Koonbee Wanee, Rungaree, Lonaree, Kolee, Purit, Ramosee, Chambhar, Mhar, Ugurwale, Brahmunjaee, Kast, D. Josee, Bruhmukshutree, R. Jogee, Kacharee, G. Wanee, Lukyaree, Moolamgar, Holar.

3. As in answer (1). The individual refusing is put out of caste, and his share of the inheritance is given to his son. He is readmitted on performing Prayuschit to the caste, and the Kreea is performed by some other person at his charges.

[2.] Wywharee Josee, Goluk.

4. No instance is known of such refusal.

[2.] Komtee, Kolatee.

5. The individual refusing must defray the charges of the performance of Kreea by another, or must send money to Supteesring (a sacred place near Nasik), or must feed the

caste, by way of Prayuschit, out of the proceeds of his share. The actual performer of the Kreea receives no share.

[1.] Kataree.

6. As in (1). The individual refusing is not debarred his share, but it is considered an unusual act.

[1.] Marwaree.

7. A man before his death (having only distant relations) may, on the refusal of one of them to perform his Kreea, give his property to another on condition of his doing so. The survivors cannot then dispossess such person.

[3.] Bhat Byragee, Gondhulee, Bungur Wanee.

8. A Wuttun service is often given to a stranger if the holder die without near relations, and his distant relations then perform Kreea for their own purification only.

[1.] Punchal Sonar.

9. If an heir refuse to perform Kreea, the Sirkar may have it performed out of the attached proceeds of the deceased's estate.

[1.] Doure Gosawee.

10. Should a man die without near relations, the caste meet and appoint a Dhurm-pootr to perform the deceased's Kreea; and in such case what remains of the deceased's property, after paying his funeral expenses and an entertainment to the caste, is given away in charity. An heiress is subject to the same rules; but she appoints a Dhurm-pootr or some relation of the deceased as the actual performer of the funeral ceremony.

[3.] Wys Sonar, Kasar, Sarlee.

11. A relation performing the Kreea of a man dying without property does not thereby render himself liable to pay his debts.

[2.] Wys Sonar, Sarlee.

The non-performance of the Kreea, Sraddh, and Sootuk does not affect the inheritance, but merely the purity of the party refusing to perform what is considered a religious duty. Nor does the actual performer, whether by order of the heir or the caste, become thereby entitled to a share in the inheritance; he only receives a turban or other present as heir.

All the Castes.

The deceased obtains Gutee (happiness after death) by the performance of Kreea by his heir.

[1.] Jungum.

Should a near relation be disabled from sickness, he should appoint the deceased's sister's or daughter's son to perform his Kreea in his stead.

[1.] Punchal Sonar.

The Kreea is usually performed according to the orders of the Josee; the expense varies according to the property of the deceased and the ability of the heir, it being usual, if he can afford it, to give alms and an entertainment to the caste.

55 Castes.

Among the Jyns, it is not customary to perform Kreea in the Oswal and Surawugee castes. Among the Ugurwale, Wanees, &c., the son performs the ceremonies; if none, the caste or daughter, or her son, or any one of the family.

[1.] Marwarree.

(69.) On the Custom regarding Absentees.

1. Should one of several brothers go to a distant country, and be unheard of for twelve years, his widow and children, or relations, are entitled to share his property and perform his Kreea.

[33.] Komtee, Koshtee, Kantaree, Sonar Wys., Kan. Sonar, P.

Malee, Koonbee, Johurse, 2 Patrawut, Bhat Byragee, T. Sarlee, Sarlee, Kam. Tylung, Surwude Josee, Wotaree, A. Goulee, Hulwaee, Lodhee Purd., Chuppurbund, Dhungur (2), Douree Gosawee, Ling. Goulee, Ling. Wanee, Koonbee Wanee, Bhoee Mar, Ghisaree, Lonaree, Wunjaree, Booroor, Ramosee, Dohor.

2. A man's Kreea cannot be performed nor his property shared until certain intelligence of his death have arrived.

[19.] Wywharee Josee, Goluk, Burhaee, Purd. Lohar, Kan. Kamatee, Konk. Goulee, K. Boondele, K. Nurwuree, Kirar, Mewafurosh, Simpee, T. Wanee, K. Bhoee, B. Telee, R. Telee, Sungur, Purd. Chambhar, Sultungur, Hulalkhor.

3. As in (1), but the limit is fifteen years.

[20.] Gooruwu, P. Sonar, Sootar, P. Sootar, Lohar, Kasar bh. w., Nhawee (2), Malee, Bhat K., Gondhulee, Buldee Koombhar, S. R. Koombhar, Jungum, Jyshwur Telee, Rungaree, Kolee, Purit, Chambhar, Mhar.

4. The limit is twenty years: *see* (1).

[8] A. Sonar, Konk. Sonar, Lar. Sonar, D. Sonar, Burbhoonje, Koombhar, Bungur Wanee, Mang.

5. The limit is twenty-five years: *see* (1).

[8.] Purbhoo, Khutree, Kasar bh. k., Jyn, Purd. Koombhar, A. Simpee, Mar. Telee, Kolartee.

6. In the castes of Oswal and Surawugee, it is not customary to perform Kreea. It is performed by the Ugurwale, Wanees, &c. After a long absence, the wife or brother will be entitled to the property.

[1.] Marwarree.

The precise limit is not to be considered absolutely fixed to the year named by the castes; it would vary according to the probability of return in different cases.

(71.) On the Privileges attached to Primogeniture or Seniority in a Family.

1. The Wureelpuna consists of the Deo Dewhara (the right of placing, and on partition of taking, the family idols),

the right side of the house, and precedence on all occasions of ceremony and receiving Pan.

[24.] Wys Sonar, Kanure Sonar, Purdesee Sootar, Jyn, Gondhule, Ahir Goulee, Hulwaee, Dhungur (2), Doure Gosawee, Simpee, Jungum, Tilelee Wanee, Bungur Wanee, Lingaet Goulee, Koonbee Wanee, Marathe Bhoee, M. Telee, Rathor Telee, Jyshwur Telee, Ramosee, Purd. Chambhar, Sultungur, Dohor, Bruhmukshutree, Kast, R. Josee, Ugurwale, Brahmunjaee, G. Wanee, Kacharee, Lukheree, Kykaree, Moolamgar, Holar.

2. The Wureelpuna consists in the Deo Dewhara, and the right side of the house. All are entitled to Manpan.

[18.] Khutree, Koshtee, Gooruwu, Punchal Sonar, Purd. Lohar, Pahar Malee, Bhat Byragee, Tylung Sarlee, Sarlee, Kamatee Tylung, Wotaree, Konkunee Goulee, Purdesee Koombhar, Batree Telee, Rungaree, Sungur, Wunjaree, Booroor.

3. The Wureelpuna is the same as in answer (1); the elder is also entitled to put his name on the Khut on occasion of the sale of a field belonging to the family, and to take the turban, Pan, &c., usual on such occasions.

[12.] Ahir Sonar, Konkunee Sonar, Lar Sonar, Dewagun Sonar, Sootar, Lohar, Malee, Koombhar, Kolee, Purit, Chambhar, Mhar.

4. The elder is entitled to Deo Dewhara only.

[9.] Kataree, Lodhee Purdesee, Kachee Boondele, Chuppurbund, Kachee Nurwuree, Burbhoonje, Ahir Simpee, Lingaet Wanee, Kolatee.

5. To the Deo Dewhara and Manpan only.

[4.] Kanure Kamatee, Surwude Josee, Kahar Bhoee, Lonaree.

6. To the Deo Dewhara and right side of the house, and on marriage, at the time of giving and receiving presents of clothes, to the privilege of first putting on the turban.

[4.] Kasar bh. w., Bhat Koonbee, Buldee Koombhar, S. R. Koombhar.

7. To the right side of the house and Manpan only.

[3.] Kirar, Ghisaree, Mang.

8. To the Manpan and Kool Dhurm (the privilege of

fasting and worshipping the god on occasion of religious ceremonies of the caste).

[3.] Purbhoo, Komtee, Hulalkhor.

9. To the Deo Dewhara, Manpan, Gundh (rubbing sandal-dust on the forehead), Sowasur (privilege of having his wife invested at ceremonies and festivals of marriage, Shanee, Gurbhadhan, building a house), the privilege of witnessing deeds of sale, &c., and receiving Manpan on such occasions.

[2.] Nhawee Kusbekur and N. Gungatilkur.

10. To the Deo Dewhara, Manpan, Gundh, Saksh (witnessing deeds), Sirpao (receiving a turban at the Dussora and other festivals), and the Pruthum-bhag or right of first choice in partition.

[2.] Wywharee Josee, Goluk.

11. To the Deo Dewhara, and to the privilege of taking on partition the one of several houses or bullocks on which the payment of Teerwa to the Sirkar has been customarily excused.

[1.] Kasar Bhande kurunar.

12. To the Deo Dewhara, right side of the house, and to the Manpan, if a Wuttundar.

[4.] Koonbee, Johuree, 2 Patrawut.

13. The elder has no extraordinary privileges whatever.

[2.] Burhaee, Mewafurosh.

14. The elder is entitled to 3 rupees, independent of the Deo Dewhara, right side of the house, Manpan, &c.

[1.] Dakote Josee Maukur.

(71.) On Succession of Sons by Different Wives.

1. A man dies, leaving three sons by his elder wife, and two sons by his younger. The sons are entitled to equal shares; they do not succeed through their mothers.

[93.] Wywharee Josee, Goluk, Purbhoo, Komtee, Khutree,

Koshtee, Gooruwu, Kantaree, Wys. Sonar, A. Sonar, Konk. Sonar, Lar Sonar, Punchal Sonar, Kan. Sonar, Sootar, Burhaee, Lohar T., Lohar B., Kasar bh. K, 2 Patrawut, Jyn, Nhawee (2), Koonbee, Malee, Pahar Malee, Bhat Koonbee, Bhat Byragee, T. Sarlee, Kamatee Ty., Kamatee Kan., Surwude Josee, Wotaree, Gondhulee, Johuree, Konk. Goulee, A. Goulee, Hulwaee, Lodhee Purd., Kachee B., Chuppurbund, Kachee N., Burbhoonje, Kirar, Mewafurosh, Koombhar, B. Koombhar, Purd. Koombhar, Dhungur (2), Douree Gosawee, Simpee, A. Simpee. Jungum, T. Wanee, B. Wanee, Ling. Goulee, Ling. Wanee, Koonbee Wanee, Mar. Bhoee, Kahar Bhoee, Mar. Telee, B. Telee, R. Telee, J. Telee, Ghisaree, Lonaree, Kolee, Wunjaree, Purit, Booroor, Ramosee, Chambhar, Purd. Chambhar, Sultungur, Dohor, Mhar, Mang, Hulalkhor, Bruhmukshutree, Brahmunjaee, Kacharee, Kykaree, Lukheree, Ugurwale, D. Josee, R. Jogee, Kast, G. Wanee, Moolamgar, Holar.

2. In such case it is customary for the sons to inherit through their mothers, the first three sharing one-half of the property among them, and the remaining two the remaining half in the same manner.

[6.] Dewagun Sonar, Purd. Sootar, Kasar (2), S. R. Koombhar, Sungur, Kolatee.

3. Should both wives be living at the time of the husband's death, their sons will succeed to their mother's respective half-shares; should one or both have previously died, the sons take equal shares.

[1.] Rungaree.

(72.) On the Succession of Widows.

1. If one of several relations die without sons, the widow is entitled to an equal share with the brothers, and she is permitted to adopt and to give away in Dhurm, &c., any part of that share. But she is not entitled to anything in the event of her taking to vicious courses, or living separately from her husband's relations.

[31.] Koshtee, Burhaee, Purdesee Sootar, Purd. and wikunar Lohar, Kasar (2), Jyn, Johuree, Patrawut (2), Pahar Malee,

B. Byragee, Bhat Koonbee, Sarlee, Kamatee Tylung, Kamatee Kanuree, A. Simpee, A. Goulee, Hulwaee, Kachee Nurware, Purd. Koombhar, Dhungur Kartik, Lingaet Goulee, L. Wanee, Koonbee Wanee, Mar. Bhoee, Mar. Telee, Batree Telee, Rungaree, Wunjaree, Dohor.

2. The same as (1). But a widow cannot give away part of immovable property so coming to her share without the consent of her husband's relations.

[24.] Purbhoo, Gooruwu, Wys. Sonar, A. Sonar, Konkune Sonar, Lar. Sonar, D. Sonar, Punchal Sonar, Kanure Sonar, Sootar, Maleo, Tylung Sarlee, Gondhulee, Konk. Goulee, Koombhar, Douree Gosawee, Jungum, Jyshwur Telee, Lonaree, Kolee, Purit, Ramosee, Chambhar, Mhar.

3. The widow is not entitled to a share, but if she adopt a son from the family of a near relation, she receives food and clothing, and is allowed to give alms, &c., while residing with her husband's relations. If she lives separately, she receives an allowance for food only, and is deprived of this in the event of living disorderly.

[10.] Komtee, Kataree, Lohar Purd., Wotaree, Burbhoonje, Mewafurosh, Rathor Telee, Sungur, Sultungur, Hulalkhor.

4. The same as (3), with the exception that it is not customary for a widow to adopt a son.

[8.] Khutree, Kirar, Buldee Koombhar, Sek. Raj. Koombhar, Simpee, Ghisaree, Booroor, Purd. Chambhar.

5. The same as (1), with the same exception, that a widow does not adopt.

[6.] Surwude Josee, Lodhee Purd., Kachee Boondele, Chuppurbund, Kahar Bhoee, Kolatee.

6. The same as (1). The widow is not allowed to dispose of her whole share.

[5.] Nhawee Kusbekur and Gung., Dhungur K., Mang, Marwaree.

7. Do. The widow can give a small part only.

[2.] Tilelee and Bungur Wanee.

8. A widow is only entitled to food and clothing. She may adopt, if ordered by her husband to do so before his death: she may in that case give alms, &c., out of the proceeds of the Wuttun, or movables; but may not give away the share of the Wuttun to which she then succeeds in right of her son; she is not entitled to the management of the Wuttun; she receives food and clothing, though living separately and addicted to vicious courses.

[2.] Wywharee Josee, Goluk.

In the castes which allow of a widow's marrying again (Pat), should she have before been entitled to a share, she gives it up to her husband's relations, from whom she receives nothing after such marriage. They give her a Bewaris chit on the occasion. After an adoption, no widow can marry.

9. A widow is only entitled to movables; she should live with the relations on equal terms with them, &c. (as in 1).

[1.] Koonbee.

(I.) On the death of one of a family, after having received his partitioned share, without sons, but leaving a widow or daughter, if a Wuttundar:—

1. The younger brother should perform the Kreea, or, should there be none, the elder; the brothers should take shares of the Wuttun, giving from the proceeds maintenance and clothes to the widow and daughters, and paying the marriage expenses of the latter, according to their ability, and performing the duties of the Wuttun.

[2.] Wywharee Josee, Goluk.

2. The marriage expenses of the daughters are to be first provided for; the deceased's share of the Wuttun with that deduction is to be given to the widow, who may perform her husband's Kreea by a Goomashta

(Dhurm-pootr);* or her adopted son may perform it, otherwise the brother.

[2.] Kan. Sonar, Mang.

3. The widow may direct any one of the brothers to perform the service of the Wuttun; she is at liberty to give the Wuttun to one of them. Should there be no widow, the brother shall perform the Kreea, and all of them, after paying the daughter's marriage expenses, share the remaining property equally.

[1.] Lohar.

4. The widow is heir to the husband's Wuttun: should there be no widow, the brothers take equal shares after paying the daughter's marriage expenses out of the estate, and perform the duties of the Wuttun.

[18.] Gooruwu, Wys. Sonar, A. Sonar, Konk. Sonar, Lar. Sonar, D. Sonar, P. Sonar, Sootar, Nhawee (2), Malee, Gondhulee, Koombhar, Jungum, Kolee, Purit, Chambhar.

5. In case of a Wuttun or Enam, the widow will receive a fixed sum for maintenance only, not a share of the property: she will be entitled to the jewels usually worn by her. The widow receives a share, if the deceased was not possessed of extensive property: she may adopt: she forfeits all by assuming vicious courses.

[1.] Ugurwale.

6. The widow receives food and clothing whilst living virtuously; she may adopt to preserve the succession to a Vritee or Wuttun.

[1.] Bruhmukshutree.

(II.) If not a Wuttundar, or if of a caste not usually Wuttundars.

* The term Dhurm-pootr is also applied to the person appointed by a widow becoming a Suttee without natural heirs to assist in her funeral rites.

1. The widow is heir to the husband's property. Should there be no widow, or should she have formed Pat with another, the brothers in equal shares, after paying the daughter's marriage expenses, take the property.

[58.] Khutree, Koshtee, Burhaee, Purd. Sootar, Lohar Boondelee, Kasar (2), Jyn. P. Malee, Bhat Koonbee, Bhat Byragee, T. Sarlee, Sarlee, Kamatee T. and Kan., Surwude Josee, Wotaree, A. Goulee, Hulwaee, Kachee Boondele and Nurwuree, Burbhoonje, Kirar, Mewafurosh, B. Koombhar, Purd. Koombhar, S. R. Koombhar, Dhungur (2), Douree Gosawee, Simpee, A. Simpee, Tilelee Wanee, Bungur Wanee, Ling. Goulee, Ling. Wanee, Koombee Wanee, Mar. Bhoee, Kahar Bhoee, Mar. Telee, B. Telee, R. Telee, Jy. Telee, Rungaree, Ghisaree, Suugur, Lonaree, Wunjaree, Booroor, Kolartee, Ramosee, Purd. Chambhar, Sultungur, Dohor, Hulalkhor, Johuree, 2 Patrawut.

2. As in (5). The brothers are to pay the daughter's marriage expenses, even if the deceased have left no property.

[2.] Lodhee Purdesee, Chuppurbund.

3. The widow is allowed maintenance of food and clothing, and if there be a daughter, she is permitted to make a provision out of the deceased's property for the daughter's marriage expenses and presents (Andul) to them.

[3.] Komtee, Kataree, Konk. Goulee.

4. The widow is heir to the husband's share if he die without a son; the daughter is entitled to nothing during her life.

[1.] Marwaree.

(73.) On the Succession of Daughters.

1. Before or after partition, should one of several brothers die, leaving no son or widow, but a daughter, the daughter has no right to succeed to his property, except to such part as may have been given to her in Dhurm by her father or

paternal uncle. The brother of the deceased is entitled to the property, providing for marriage expenses.

[45.] Wywharee Josee, Khutree, Kantaree, Wys. Lar. Dew. Sonar, Burhaee, Lohar B., Kasar (2), Jyn, Nhawee, Malee, P. Malee, Bhat Koonbee, Ty. Sarlee, Kan. Kamatee, Surwude Josee, Wotaree, Konk. Goulee, A. Goulee, Hulwaee, Kachee B., Kachee N., Burbhoonje, Mewafurosh, B. Koombhar, S. R. Koombhar, Dhungur (2), T. Wanee, Koonbee Wanee, R. J. Telee, Rungaree, Sungur, Lonaree, Wunjaree, Ramosee, Chambhar, Purd. Chambhar, Sultungur, Mhar, Mang.

2. After partition between two brothers, the daughter has a right to such movables only as may have been given to her by her parents previously to their death. It is not the custom for such daughter to enjoy immovable property without the consent of the father's brother, &c., who are heirs to it on the death of the parents.

[22.] Goluk, Purbhoo, Komtee, Koshtee, Gooruwu, Kanure Sonar, Sootar, Lohar, Bhat Byragee, Sarlee, Kamatee T., Gondhulee, Lodhee Purd., Chuppurbund, Kirar, Douree Gosawee, A. Simpee, B. Wanee, Kahar Bhoee, Mar. Telee, Booroor, Kolartee.

3. The right appertains to the Bhow-bund, not to the daughter.

[9.] A. Sonar, 2 Patrawut, Koombhar, Purd. Koombhar, Jungum, B. Telee, Ghisaree, Hulalkhor.

4. On the death of one of two brothers, either before or after partition, leaving a daughter, her father's brother will perform her parent's funeral rites, and solemnize her marriage, but will himself succeed to the property. The brothers may give a grown-up girl gifts of movables only.

[17.] Punchal Sonar, Purd. Sootar, Ling. Goulee, Ling. Wanee, Kolee, Bruhmukshutree, Kast, Ugurwale, R. Jogee, D. Josee, Lukyaree, G. Wanee, Kacharee, Brahmunjaee, Kykaree, Moolamgar, Holar.

5. In the above case, the daughter has a right to what may have been given to her as a free gift; the father's brother succeeds to the whole property.

[2.] Mar. Bhoee, Simpee.

6. As in (5), the father's brother providing for his orphan niece's marriage.

[3.] Konk. Sonar, Koonbee, Purit.

7. In the above case the father's brother* is heir; the daughter is entitled to what may have been given on a partition to her by her father.

[4.] Johuree, Koonbee, 2 Patrawut.

8. The widow is heir to the husband's property; his Kreea is to be performed by the brother's son (Pootrunya), or, if there be no relation of the husband's alive, by a Dhurmpootr: the widow may give what she pleases to the daughters, even a house.

[1.] Purbhoo.

(74.) ON THE SUCCESSION OF FATHERS AND BROTHERS.

1. A man dying after partition, without widow or sons, his brothers will succeed to his property in preference to his father.

[50.] Gooruwu, Kantaree, D. Sonar, Sootar, Purd. Lohar Lohar, Kasar bh. k., Jyn, Nhawee (2), Malee, P. Malee, Bhat Byragee, Sarlee, Kamatee Ty. and Kan., Surwude Josee, Wotaree, Hulwaee, Kirar, Mewafurosh, Koombhar, Purd. Koombhar, A. Simpee, Jungum, Ling. Goulee, Koonbee Wanee, Bhoee Marathe, Kahar Bhoee, Telee Mar., B. Telee, R. Telee, Jyshwur Telee, Lonaree, Kolee, Wunjaree, Chambhar, Sultungur, Dohor, Mhar, Hulalkhor, Kast, Ugurwale, G. Wanee, Kacharee, Moolamgar, Bruhmukshutree, D. Josee, Brahmunjaee, Kykaree..

2. The father will succeed in preference to the brothers.

[44.] Wywharee Josee, Goluk, Koonbee, Johuree, 2 Patrawut, Marwaree, Komtee, Khutree, Koshtee, Wys. Sonar, A. Sonar, Konk. Sonar, Lar. Sonar, P. Sonar, Kan. Sonar, Burhaee, Lohar Purd., Kasar bh. w., Bhat Koonbee, Ty. Sarlee, Gondhulee, Konk.

---

* In the term "father's brother" are included his representatives, or in default of them, other male relations of the deceased father of the girl.

Goulee, Lodhee Purd., Kachee B., Chuppurbund, Kachee N., Burbhoonje, A. Goulee, Buldee Koombhar, S. R. Koombhar, Dhungur Kootekur, Douree Gosawee, Simpee, Tilelee Wanee, B. Wanee, Ling. Wanee, Rungaree, Purit, Purd. Chambhar, Booroor, Kolartee, Rawul Jogee.

3. The father and brothers will divide the deceased's property.

[3.] Dhungur Kartik, Ghisaree, Sungur.

4. As in answer (3); the father receiving the larger share.

[2.] Ramosee, Mang.

5. The father and brother will take equal shares.

[1.] Purbhoo.

6. The brother, and in some cases the father, will take the property.

[2.] Lukheree, Holar.

(74.) On the Death of a Man without Heirs.

1. A man dying without heirs, his caste will take charge of his property, and, after performing his Kreea and charitable gifts in his name, will provide an entertainment for the caste with the remainder. On a man's becoming liable under the Maratha Government to confiscation for any great crime, it was usual to commute it to a fine on the representation of the relations.

[39.] Purbhoo, Burhaee, Purd. Lohar, Kasar bh. w., Bhat Byragee, Bhat Koonbee, Kamatee Ty., Kamatee Kan., Surwude Josee, A. Goulee, Kirar, 2 Patrawut, Johuree, Mewafurosh, Buldee Koombhar, Purd. Koombhar, S. R. Koombhar, Dhungur Kartik, Dhungur Koontekur, Douree Gosawee, Ling. Goulee, Koonbee Wanee, Kahar Bhoee, Rathor Telee, Jysawur Telee, Rungaree, Ghisaree, Booroor, Purd. Chambhar, Sultungur, Hulalkhor, Bruhmukshutree, Kykaree, Brahmunjaee, Moolamgar, D. Josee, R. Jogee, Lukyaree.

2. The Sirkar will succeed to the property of a man dying without heirs. In regard to forfeiture, as in answer (1).

[33.] Khutree, Koshtee, Gooruwu, Wys. Sonar, A. Sonar, Konk. Sonar, Lar. Sonar, D. Sonar, P. Sonar, Kan. Sonar, Marwaree, Sootar, Lohar, Kasar bh. K., Malee, Sarlee, Wotaree, Gondhulee, Kachee B., Kachee N., Burbhoonje, Koombhar, Simpee Ahir, Ling. Wanee, Bhoee Mar., Mar. Telee, Batree Telee, Lonaree, Kolee, Wunjaree, Purit, Dohor, Mhar, Mang.

3. The Sirkar cannot succeed to private property while any relations are to be found. A man should be punished by the Sirkar for his crimes, but not by confiscation.

[2.] Wywharee Josee, Goluk.

4. The Sirkar will succeed, after the deceased's debts are paid. As to forfeiture, as in answer (1).

[2.] Simpee, Te Wanee.

5. The Sirkar will succeed, after the deceased's Kreea and debts are provided for. As to forfeiture, as in answer (3).

[3.] Sungur, Goolwee Wanee, Holar.

6. The caste will succeed, after the deceased's Kreea and debts are provided for. As to forfeiture, as in answer (1).

[4.] Purd. Sootar, Hulwaee Purd., Lodhee Purd., Chuppurbund.

7. A man dying without heirs, the Mehitra of his caste, or Naik (if a Ramosee), or Jungum, in the Pergunnah, will have authority to appoint a successor to perform the duties of his village Wuttun, and to procure the Sirkar's approbation to the appointment. The same heads of caste will cause the payment of a fine from an offender for a general crime committed against the Sirkar, whose pleasure must be obeyed should it be unpaid.

[5.] Nhawee Kus. and Gungatilkur, Jungum, Ramosee, Chambhar.

8. The Sirkar will succeed, should there be property

remaining after Kreea and Jat bhojun have been provided for. As to forfeiture, as in answer (1).

[3.] P. Malee, Konk. Goulee, Mar. Telee.

9. The Gooroo, Muttaputee, &c., will succeed after the deceased's Kreea has been provided for. *Vide* answer (1).

[4.] Komtee, Jyn, Lingaet Wanee, Lingaet Kacharee.

10. After the deceased's Kreea has been performed, the remaining property is sent to the goddess Sreesuptusring (a name of Parwutee, the Koolswamee of this caste). Her temple is about eighteen coss from Nasik.

[1.] Kantaree.

11. The Sirkar's pleasure is to be obeyed both in such escheats and forfeitures.

[2.] Tylung Sarlee, Kolartee.

12. Should there be no relations nor persons connected by Gotr with the deceased, the Sirkar is heir. Confiscation by Government is not customary, except for great offences; in small matters the caste is supreme.

[1.] Koonbee.

13. The Sirkar has a right to extensive heirless property. The caste provides for Kreea and other expenses out of a small amount of property.

[1.] Kast.

(77.) On the Limitation of Gifts and Bequests.

1. A man directing a gift to be paid to any one after his death must ask the consent of his sons, or brothers, or other heirs: after his death, should any one claim a bequest unknown by the heirs to have been made by the deceased, they are not to comply with it, except (Koshtee) as to bequests of movables of small value.

[74.] Khutree, Koshtee, Gooruwu, Kantaree, Wys. Sonar, Ahir.

Konkune, Lar. D. and P. Sonar, Sootar, Burhaee, P. Sootar, Lohar, P. Lohar, Kasar bh. k., Jyn, Nhawee K. and G., Malee, P. Malee, Bhat Byragee, T. Sarlee, Sarlee, Kamatee T. and K., Surwude Josee, Wotaree, Gondhulee. A. Goulee, Hulwaee, Lodhee Purd., Chuppurbund, Kachee N., Burbhoonjee, Kirar, Mewafurosh, Koombhar, Purd. Koombhar, Dhungur Kootekur, Douree Gosawee, Ahir Simpee, Jungum, Bungur Wanee, Ling. Wanee, Mar. Bhoee, Kahar Bhoee, Mar. Telee, Batree Telee, R. Telee, G. Telee, Ghisaree, Sungur, Lonaree, Kolee, Wunjaree, Purit, Chambhar, Purd. Chambhar, Sultungur, Dohor, Mhar, Hulalkhor, Bruhmukshutree, Kast, Ugurwale, R. Josee, Moolumgar, Dakote Josee, Brahmunjaee, Lukheree, G. Wanee, Holar, Kacharee.

2. A Wuttun cannot be either sold or given away. Should there be no son, the other relations will not consent to alienate a Wuttun. But an Enam field or house acquired by the party may be given with consent of the relations.*

[2.] Wywharee Josee, Ugurwale.

3. A man is entitled to make gifts according to his circumstances by an attested Khut.

[3.] Komtee, Konk. Goulee, Kolatee.

4. A son must perform the commands of his father in gifts of movables; should he fail, the caste will reprimand him; and should he refuse to hear reason, he will be put out of caste.

[6.] Kasar bhande wikunar, Bhat Koombee, Kachee Boondele, B. Koombhar, S. R. Koombhar, Rungaree, Mang.

5. A father making such bequests in his son's absence, but before several creditable witnesses, the son must fulfil them (*vide* answer 1).

[5.] Dhungur Kartik, Ling. Wanee, Koombee Wanee, Booroor, Ramosee.

6. The son is not bound to pay a claimant to such gift unless he produce the father's Danputr.

[1.] Sonar Kanure.

* And gifts may be made of a field, or any small portion of property, either by attested Khut, or before sons and relations who comply with the bequest after the death of the party.

7. The father's Danputr will of course be fulfilled: there are no compulsive measures adopted to compel the son's performance of his father's verbal bequests, though it is his duty to attend to them.

[2.] Simpee, Tileleo Wanee.

8. The father's Danputr is essential for gifts of land and immovable property. Generally, bequests of houses, &c., may be made verbally before the heirs; or, should they not be present, before creditable witnesses, and the heirs will fulfil them. They have no right to object to gifts of movables.

[1.] Purbhoo.

9. Without an attested Danputr, the grant will only hold good during the grantor's life (except by consent of the heirs, *vide* 1).

[2.] Nhawee Kusbekur and Gungatilkur.

10. The heirs and relations' consent is necessary to such grant of a Wuttun, and in gifts of money: should there be a grown-up son, his consent should be asked by the father; otherwise he may, on his father's death, decline compliance.

[4.] Johuree, Koonbee, 2 Patrawut.

11. The son is bound to perform his father's bequests, but not to the extent of the whole property. Whatever grant has been attested by the heirs, the heirs must carry into effect.

[1.] Marwaree.

12. It is not the custom in this caste to give away houses or other property.

[1.] Kykaree.

On the Limitations to Mortgage or Pledge.

1. In pledging property, if all the relations are in common, and after partition, in pledging houses or immovable property, it is customary for them to attest the Gahan Khut, containing a specification of the contract and the rate of interest; otherwise the Koolkurnee, &c., write the Khut in the event of the party's inability to do so.

[47.] Wywharee Josee, Goluk, Komtee, Khutree, Kantaree, Burhace, P. Sootar, Lohar B., Kasar, Jyn, P. Malee, Bhat Byragee, Bhat Koonbee, Sarlee, Kamatee T., Kamatee K., Wotaree, A. Goulee, Hulwaee, Lodhee Purd., Kachee B., Kachee N., Burbhoonje, Kirar, Buldee Koombhar, Purd. Koombhar, S. R. Koombhar, Dhungur Kartik, A. Simpee, B. Wanee, Ling. Goulee, Ling. Wanee, Koonbee Wanee, Mar. Bhoee, Kabar Bhoee, Batree Telee, R. Telee, Rungaree, Ghisaree, Wunjaree, Sungur, Lonaree, Booroor, Purd. Chambhar, Sultungur, Dohor, Hulalkhor.

2. Even after partition, a Wuttundar cannot pledge his share without the attestation of the other relations to the Gahan-putr, which should be written by the Koolkurnee, and also attested by the Desmookh, Despandhy, Patell, Chougole, and Bullootee.

[20.] Gooruwu, Wys. Sonar, A. Sonar, Konk. Sonar, Lar Sonar, D. Sonar, P. Sonar, Kan. Sonar, Sootar, Lohar, Nhawee, Malee, Gondhulee, Jungum, Kolee, Purit. Chambhar, Mhar, Mang.

3. If the borrower be a man of credit (Put), no writing is passed between the parties; each makes a private entry of the transaction in his account-book.

[2.] Simpee, Tilelee Wanee.

The other answers contain nothing materially different from the above.

4. The attestation of the relations is necessary to a mortgage-deed of a Wuttun; that of strangers is sufficient for a pledge of movables.

[4.] Johuree, Koonbee, 2 Patrawut.

APPENDIX B.

ON THE CUSTOMS OF GOSAWEES OR GOSAEENS.

On the Customs of Gosawees or Gosaeens.

A Gosawee, as may be discovered from the appellation, which is a compound of the Sunskrit word गो (Go) passion, and स्वामी (Swamee) master, was originally a person who, in honour of God and for the benefit of his own soul, had so completely mastered his passions as to be able to devote his whole life to the exercise of the strictest devotion and most rigid austerities. Their origin.

2. The founder of the sect, according to the traditions of the Gosawees themselves, was Sunkur Achary, whose principal disciples are the Brahmuns of the Siw order. The Gosawees accordingly worship that deity in the shape of the Lingum; as the Byragees, the other kind of Indian devotees, do Vishnoo, in his incarnation of Ram. Sunkur Achary, in his Gosawee character, nominated four Chelas or disciples, named, 1st, Neera Troteeka Achary; 2nd, Shringee Rushee Pritvee Oodha Achary; 3rd, Dhurmbootee Swuroop Achary; 4th, Pudum Achary.

3. Neera Troteeka then chose three disciples immediately subordinate to himself, viz. Geeree, Sagur, and Purwut. Shringee Rushee Pritvee Oodha Achary had also three followers, named Pooree, Suruswuttee, and Bharuttee. Dhurmbootee Swuroop and Pudum had only two followers each: the names of those of the former were Teert and Asrun, and of the latter Bun and Urrun.

4. The four disciples of Sunkur Achary provided for the performance of the discipline they had imposed upon themselves by the establishment of four muths, or temples, in four different quarters. The first was situated in the north, the second in the south, the third in the west, and the fourth —viz. that of Pudum Achary—in the east.

5. These establishments are said to have been afterwards subdivided, and the fraternity then consisted, as it does at the present time, of ten different sects, composed of the followers of the above-mentioned ten persons, appointed to be disciples to the four Gosawees who established their muths in the four different quarters. Each sect bears the name of the person of whose followers it professes to be composed: thus, there is the Sagur sect, the Purwut sect, the Pooree sect, and so on. The whole are equal in rank, one having no objection to eat with the other. In the early periods of the institution of the order, Gosawees supported themselves by the alms they received from good men.

6. In process of time the fraternity became less distinguished for their devotion than their ancestors, and some of the disciples commenced trading, or followed the profession of arms; while others, wandering still farther from the road they professed to follow, formed matrimonial connections, and became in every respect as worldly as their neighbours. The latter, in consequence, are not acknowledged as brethren at all, except in the Dukhun.*

* To compensate the good Gosawee for the fallen state of these apostates,

7. Those Gosawees who still adhere to the ancient landmarks of their order are called Dundee or pilgrims (literally mendicants who carry a staff); the traders are distinguished by the name of Dunglee; and the married Gosawees are called Ghurbaree Gosawees. As the latter no longer profess to be guided by the original laws of their order, they will be spoken of separately.

8. All Gosawees live in buildings called muths or temples; those especially devoted to purposes of worship are called Purrumpuragut muths, or ancient temples descending from generation to generation; the others are simple dwellings. Dwellings.

9. The written laws by which Gosawees are professedly guided are the Dhurm and Munoo Shastrus: all questions, however, relating to the internal administration and discipline of the order are decided by an assembly called the Dusname, which should consist of the disciples of the ten founders from whom they take their names; but as in some places members of each sect are not to be found, as many as there may happen to be are authorized to meet, their decisions being as irrevocable as those of a perfect assembly. From the Dusname there is no appeal. In the event of a difference of opinion occurring among the members of the assembly, it is usual to convene a grand meeting of the residents in the surrounding country, whose opinion decides the point at issue, provided it has not in the meantime been settled, as it is very desirable in all cases that it should be, by the original referees. Laws.

10. The laws of the fraternity are said to be most correctly expounded at Benares, Jhansee, and Hyderabad, and least so at Poona, the maladministration for several years under the

---

some are still found to be sufficiently devout to deserve the name of Purrumhonsh, or "the most devout of all devotees." The hearts of these men are said to be as unspotted as the feathers of the sacred Honsh, whose name they bear, and their minds so unceasingly abstracted in the contemplation of the Deity as to be able to raise their bodies from the earth into the air.

Mahratta Government of the empire, of which this was the capital, having it is said induced a relaxation of principle on the part of the Gosawees, and occasionally actuated the Dusname to give opinions at variance with those of the same assembly at other places, although the customs and privileges of the order are avowedly similar in all parts of India where the members of it are to be found.

Muhunt. 11. If any member of a muth be particularly distinguished by his acts of hospitality, veneration for his ancestors, and a life of morality, he receives from the Dusname the honorary title of Muhunt. This distinction is not to be purchased at any other price, neither riches nor length of years giving any claim to it, if unaccompanied by the qualities mentioned. There can only be one muhunt in a muth, and his authority does not extend beyond the limits of his own establishment. The Dusname, being absolute, may at any time deprive the muhunt of his honorary degree, if he shall appear to the assembly to have ceased to deserve it. It is generally conferred upon the Gooroos of muths who are the abbots of the Purrumpuragut muths, or the monasteries, and supreme members of the muths used as dwellings.

Gooroo. 12. Every Gosawee calls the person who chose him for his disciple his Gooroo,* or spiritual master. Of these Gooroos there may be many in one muth, whose respective Chelas or disciples are subordinate to them, while they as well as their disciples are subject to the authority of the head of the establishment, who is called the Gooroo of the muth. This person has considerable power over his disciples, having the whole internal administration of the establishment. He can expel any disciple who may be found guilty of misappropriating the common property, of gambling, of drunkenness, of

* It may here be observed, that whatever is said of the powers of the Gooroo of a muth applies also to the authority of any Gosawee who has pupils or disciples of his own, in so far as under such circumstances he can exercise it.

fornication, or contempt of his authority. If his orders be disobeyed, they are enforced by the assembly of the Dusname, which has appellate jurisdiction in all such cases.

13. If, on the other hand, the Gooroo establish any bylaws for his muth subversive of the fundamental principles of the order, he may be dismissed by the authority of the Dusname, which will nominate his successor from among his disciples, or leave it to their discretion to select the fittest member for the situation.

14. The Gooroo is empowered to advance the public money of the establishment to the most intelligent of his disciples for purposes of trade. During their absence on such expeditions they are independent of the Gooroo, but the moment they return they again become subordinate to him, and must deliver over their profits to him to dispose of for the public benefit in such manner as he may deem most proper.

15. The Gooroo is bound to support any of his disciples who, after separating their interests from those of the establishment, come to want; upon the same principle, every Gosawee is bound to support the disciple of his choice, whether alienated from him or not, whenever he may stand in need of assistance.

16. When a Gooroo is too old to continue his duties, or from other causes becomes unfit for his situation, the most intelligent of his disciples is selected in his stead; should any discussion arise as to his successor, the point is decided by the Dusname.

17. The establishment of a muth may consist of any number; the most devout, intelligent, and conciliatory member is generally appointed Gooroo, and each may introduce as many of his own peculiar disciples as the capital of the muth can support.

18. When the Gooroo finds his death approaching, he names the disciple whom he wishes to succeed him, and who

must be appointed accordingly. The nomination on the part of the Gooroo may be either by word or in writing; though, in the former case, the fact should be witnessed by some of the members of a foreign muth.

19. If the Gooroo die suddenly, without having appointed a successor, his disciples select one of their own body to preside over them: should they differ as to the most proper person to be nominated, the question is adjusted by a decree of the Dusname, which is final. During the consideration of the question by this assembly, the muth and all the property of its establishment are taken possession of by the Dusnames, who provide for the due administration of its affairs until the successor to the chiefship is nominated.

Chelas or disciples.

20. The duty of a Chela or disciple may be said to be a passive submission to the will and caprice of his Gooroo, who is in the place of his father, and to whom he is, in respect to support, protection, and inheritance, as a son. So much, indeed, does this principle appear to prevail among Gosawees, that, in speaking of the Gooroo of the person to whom they are disciples, they call him grandfather Gooroo; in the same manner, they speak of a grandson and great-grandson disciple. The disciple may be alienated by his Gooroo and deprived of his inheritance: this is done by the Gooroo giving him such portion of his property as he pleases, taking a deed of separation from him, and appointing, by a witnessed writing or by word, in the presence of three or four respectable brethren, another person his heir.

Gosawunee, or female Gosawees.

21. Gosawees, being professedly unmindful of distinction of sex, admit females into their community, the form of initiation being the same as that for the males. Female children, however, are never selected or purchased as disciples, it being necessary to their admission that they should have arrived at years of discretion.

22. Those Gosawee devotees whose desire it is to be considered free from every natural feeling or prejudice prevailing in this world, appear publicly in a state of perfect nakedness; their bodies, which are defiled by filth and ashes, are, they say, to them as statues, no longer susceptible of any excitement that is not created by the contemplation and adoration of the deity, which engrosses their whole mind, and leaves not a thought for this world. The less devout, but less ostentatious and indecent, class bind a cloth round the waist, and the generality of Gosawees wear as much clothing as other men: the texture of their apparel is coarse, and the colour a dingy red. They sometimes allow their hair to be sufficiently long and matted to be twisted round their heads, something in the shape of a turban. Costume.

23. The Gosawunees unite in their persons, in token* of the perfect oblivion of sex, the costume of both male and female; they wear the turban, the Ungar, or long robe, reaching from the neck to the knees, and the Dhotee.

24. In Hindoostan proper, persons of the Brahmun, Kshutree, and Wysh castes can alone be introduced among Gosawees, and initiated into their orders. In the more southern countries of India, the members of the Soodru caste are also admitted.

25. Candidates may be of any age; some are admitted gratuitously, others in consideration of the payment of money; and, during periods of famine, many sell themselves to Gosawees for personal support.

* In illustration of this, it may be observed that the *lusus naturæ*, best known by the designation of hermaphrodite, wears the female Saree and the male Ungreka. These persons, whether born of the highest or the lowest caste, are outcastes from their birth, and considered the vilest and most polluted of beings: they live upon alms, which they exact from the Brahmun at whose door they press their request, and who is willing to purchase their absence at any price. Their condition is supposed to be induced by the debauchery committed by them on earth before the transmigration of their souls.

26. The candidate is received with the consent of the Gooroo and Chelas of the establishment to which he is to be attached on the one side, and that of his own parents or nearest relatives on the other.

27. His head is first shaved, when he immediately becomes a Gosawee in a state of probation; after remaining so a year or two, and making himself familiar with the usages of the order, the ceremony of Beeja Hom (a sacrifice to fire) is celebrated, when he becomes a perfect Gosawee. If a person of too inferior caste to have been admitted into the fraternity has through inadvertence been regularly initiated and eaten with the brethren, he is branded with a hot coin, deprived of the clothes that may have been given to him, and ejected from the muth. The Gooroo who admitted him will then go before the Dusname in the attitude of submission, and pray for mercy and pardon at its hands; which, if granted, restores the Gooroo and his establishment to their former rank, and, if denied, leaves them equally outcastes with the person who deceived them.

28. During the noviciate of the candidate, his parents are at liberty to withdraw their child, and any contribution they may have given; but after the solemnization of Beeja Hom, he is irrevocably attached to the Gosawee sect, and as much alienated from his family by birth as if he had never belonged to it; not even performing Sootuk or mourning upon the death of its members.

29. The natural child of a Gosawee, if born of a Brahmun, Wysh, or Soodru woman, has rank and rights equal to those of a Chela or disciple, after he shall have been initiated in the usual way; the only peculiarity being that the ceremony cannot be performed by the father: the uncle or next nearest relative should officiate.

Discipline.

30. The discipline of the order is either severe or relaxed, as the Gooroo of a muth or the majority of the Dusname

are of harsh or mild dispositions. The crimes, however, for which a member should be ejected from the fraternity are specified: they are—taking away the life of a cow, a Brahmun, a woman, a Gooroo, or a child; and for having had sexual intercourse with other than a Hindoo woman. The punishment is ordered by the Gooroo, or the Dusname. If such criminals throw themselves on the mercy of their brethren, their punishment is occasionally commuted to fine and penance: such indulgence is never allowed to Gosawunees, who are always expelled for serious offences.

Sale and mortgage of Muths.

31. The Purrumpuragut muths, which appear to be as much consecrated and devoted to worship as any other Hindoo temples, cannot be sold or mortgaged for any purpose whatever. If any are so surreptitiously, the offender is ejected from the muth, and the sum for which it was sold or mortgaged paid to the buyer or mortgagees by the Gooroo and his disciples. The same plan is adopted in cases of illegal mortgages or sales of the other kind of muths. Such sanctity is avowedly not considered to attach to the muths which are the dwellings of the Dunglee or merchant sect of Gosawees; the right, however, even in respect to them is limited to the Gooroo: he may sell or mortgage the muth in which he presides, and his act is confirmed by the disciples, who generally redeem it. It is not usual to divide the property in a muth and sell the building after having once made common stock. If from any cause such arrangement be made, the Gooroo takes to himself what portion he pleases, and decides the amount to be allotted to each of his subordinates. If any disciple wish to separate his interests from those of the rest, he receives such share of the whole property as the Gooroo may please to give him, and a deed of partition is taken from him.

32. The right of Government to distrain muths used as

dwelling-houses for the payment of the debts of the Gooroo, after having referred the subject without effect to the Dusname, is admitted. This assembly, however, generally manages to adjust the matter without requiring a recourse to such an extreme measure. A muth, not being supposed to consist of shares, the distraint of it for the payment of debts due by other members of the establishment than the Gooroo is considered as unjust as the sale or mortgage of it by one of the disciples in liquidation of his own debts. Such sales or mortgages are always recognized, in so far that the purchaser or mortgagee is not allowed to lose by the fraud of the seller or mortgager, who is punished for such acts by his Gooroo or the Dusname.

Of land attached to Muths.

33. Land is bought from Enamdars when it is found necessary to build a muth: by this arrangement the Government has no right in the land. If it be charged with a Joree, or quit-rent, a permanent remission of it is solicited from, and in general granted by, Government, or the amount of the right of Government is paid as part of the price, and the annual charge defrayed by the Enamdar himself; should land, however, after the completion of the muth, be saddled with a tax, the establishment pays it.

34. It is usual to allow the public to partake of the water of a river, well, or tank within the limits of a muth, for bathing, cooking, and drinking, but they are not permitted to erect a mote (the usual machinery for drawing water from wells), or to apply the water to purposes of agriculture.

35. Treasure found in the land of a muth is considered the property of the finder, no inquiry as to the owner being made.

Division of property.

36. A division of property and interest sometimes takes place between Chela and Gooroo; the only tie which in that case remains between them is, that each supports the other when in distress. The riches acquired by them under such

circumstances belong in virtue of the partition exclusively to him who earns them, the Chela having only a very remote interest in the wealth of his Gooroo, depending upon the contingency of his dying without other disciples, or not having named an heir in the prescribed form.

37. The alienated Chela is not responsible for the debts of his late Gooroo, whether incurred before or after the alienation.

If an alienated disciple die, leaving no disciples of his own, his Gooroo takes his property, pays the expenses of his funeral, and settles debts, in communication with the Dusname. If the deceased leave no property, the Gooroo is not responsible for his debts, but must pay the expenses of his funeral: if the Gooroo of the alienated Chela who may die in these reduced circumstances be also dead, the Gooroo's heirs are bound to do what would have been his duty.

39. If a Gooroo proceed upon his travels, and no one hear of him for ten or fifteen years, the person who would succeed in the event of his death (that is, one of his disciples) performs the ceremonies observed on the death of a relation, which consist of assuming the appearance and performing the ceremonies of mourning, and entertaining the fraternity in the name of the deceased. The Gosawees differ from most other Hindoos in burying their dead instead of burning them. This probably originated in the Brahmun custom of burying their Sunyasees, or devotees.

40. If a Gosawee die very poor, leaving one or more rich disciples in a state of alienation, the Dusname obliges him or them to bear the expenses induced by that event. If a Gosawee die in indigent circumstances, and have no disciples of any kind, the Dusname performs the last ceremonies due to him on earth.

41. One-fourth of a Gosawee's fortune is devoted to ceremonies consequent to his death, and another quarter to the erection of a suitable tomb over his remains.

Ghurbaree Gosawees.

42. Upon perusing the information that I have collected regarding this class of dissenters from the fraternity of Gosawees, I find that it relates only to the peculiarities of the institution of marriage, the existence of which among them forms the grand distinction between their fundamental laws and those of the rest of their brethren; and that the greater portion of what is said upon this subject even has been anticipated in the replies to queries relating to marriage among Hindoos in general, which were furnished to me in the southern Mahratta country, and have been already embodied in the report upon Hindoo law by Mr. Steele.

43. The following are the points in which the institution, as it exists among Gosawees, differs from the laws of marriage among other Hindoos.

44. A Gosawee is not permitted to marry other than a Gosawunee; if he do so, his marriage is not annulled, but his wife is not acknowledged as a Gosawunee. The Gosawunees must marry before they reach their fifteenth year. Failing to do so (unless they can give a satisfactory reason for the omission), they are obliged to pass their lives in continency; loss of caste being held out as the punishment inflicted upon her who may be found to have lost command over her passions. These maidens have not the privilege of becoming disciples, as females of other Hindoo castes may, but must pass their lives with their parents or nearest relations.

45. A female of any Hindoo caste who is initiated as a disciple is not allowed to marry.

46. A man of the Geeree sect (one of the ten sects of Gosawees already enumerated) cannot marry a woman of his own sect, but may select a wife from any of the remaining nine. Should a person inadvertently commit this irregularity,

his wife must eat separately from her husband and his family.

47. A Brahmun Bhut performs the marriage ceremonies.

48. A marriage can be annulled on account of impotency alone. If a woman arrive at the age of puberty and hear no tidings of the approach of an absent husband, she enters into a left-handed connection (Pat) with another man, who, however, is obliged to give her up if required by the husband, and is reimbursed in the amount of his expenses. If, on the other hand, the husband decline taking his wife, he is reimbursed, and she is no longer his wife. The husband, though he may take his wife, is not obliged to support her illegitimate offspring. The Pat is not allowed to widows.

49. If a man separate from his wife, and give her a Chhor Chittee, or deed of divorce, they can never reunite. If no such paper be given at the time of separation, he may take her back. Adultery on the part of a Gosawunee is followed by expulsion from the order, if committed with other than one of the brethren. The wife who has received a deed of divorce may form a Pat connection; she who has not is not at liberty to make such contract without her husband's permission.

50. The assembly of the Dusname exists upon exactly the same principles among the Ghurbaree as among other Gosawees; as, however, the former are divided into families consisting of man and wife with their offspring and collateral relatives, there is of course no such person as the Gooroo of the muth.

51. The above information, as far as it goes, may, I think, be considered correct. It was obtained by referring queries to the pilgrims who in 1825 visited the source of the Godaveree at Trimbuk, near Nasik. They at first received the proposal to disclose the laws of their order to the public authorities with the greatest hauteur; when, however, it was explained to

them that the measure was only adopted to enable Government to decide upon civil suits in which their brethren were parties, they relented, and cheerfully imparted what was solicited. As, therefore, the motive for giving the information at all was to benefit themselves, it is not likely that they have practised deceit to the prejudice of their own rights. Several thousand Gosawees of the first rank, from all parts of India, attended the Yatra, and each had access to, and ascertained the accuracy of the information given by another. The same question was frequently put in two or three different shapes, and an air of consistency pervades the whole, which could not perhaps have been effected by falsehood, even if it had been an object to have kept us in ignorance.

(*Signed*) JOHN WARDEN.

INDEX.

A.

B.

30 *

C.

D.

E.

F.

M.

N.

O.

P.